STUDIES IN MODERN BRITISH RELIGIOUS HISTORY

Volume 15

Martyrs and Martyrdom in England
*c.*1400–1700

Concepts of Christian martyrdom changed greatly in England from the late middle ages through the early modern era. The variety of paradigms of Christian martyrdom (with, for example, virginity or asceticism perceived as alternative forms of martyrdom) that existed in the late medieval period, came to be replaced during the English Reformation with a single dominant idea of martyrdom: that of violent death endured for orthodox religion. Yet during the seventeenth century another transformation in conceptions of martyrdom took place, as those who died on behalf of overtly political causes came to be regarded as martyrs, indistinguishable from those who died for Christ.

The articles in this book explore these seminal changes across the period from 1400–1700, analyzing the political, social and religious backgrounds to these developments. While much that has been written on martyrs, martyrdom and martyrologies has tended to focus on those who died for a particular confession or cause, this book shows how the concepts of martyrdom were shaped, altered and reshaped through the interactions between competing religious and political groups.

THOMAS S. FREEMAN is Research Officer at the British Academy John Foxe Project and he is affiliated with the University of Sheffield.
THOMAS F. MAYER is Professor of History at Augustana College.

STUDIES IN MODERN BRITISH RELIGIOUS HISTORY

ISSN 1464–6625

General editors

Stephen Taylor
Arthur Burns
Kenneth Fincham

This series aims to differentiate 'religious history' from the narrow confines of church history, investigating not only the social and cultural history of religion, but also theological, political and institutional themes, while remaining sensitive to the wider historical context; it thus advances an understanding of the importance of religion for the history of modern Britain, covering all periods of British history since the Reformation.

Previously published titles in this series are listed at the back of this volume.

Martyrs and Martyrdom in England
*c.*1400–1700

Edited by
THOMAS S. FREEMAN and THOMAS F. MAYER

THE BOYDELL PRESS

First published 2007
The Boydell Press, Woodbridge

ISBN 978–1 84383–290–4

The Boydell Press is an imprint of Boydell & Brewer Ltd
PO Box 9, Woodbridge, Suffolk IP12 3DF, UK
and of Boydell & Brewer Inc.
Mt Hope Avenue, Rochester, NY 14620, USA
website: www.boydellandbrewer.com

A CIP catalogue record for this book is available
from the British Library

This publication is printed on acid-free paper

Typeset by Pru Harrison, Hacheston, Suffolk
Printed in Great Britain by
Biddles Ltd, King's Lynn

CONTENTS

ABBREVIATIONS

A&M [1563]	John Foxe, *Actes and monuments of these latter and perillous dayes . . .* (1563), RSTC 11222
A&M [1570]	John Foxe. *The Ecclesiasticall history contayning the Actes and monuments . . .* (1570), RSTC 11223
A&M [1576]	John Foxe, *The Ecclesiasticall history contayning the Actes and monumentes. Newly inlarged* (1576), RSTC 11224
A&M [1583]	John Foxe, *Actes and monuments of matters most speciall in the church.* (1583), RSTC 11225
BL	British Library
CSPD	*Calendar of State Papers. Domestic Series of the Reigns of Edward VI, Mary, Elizabeth and James I*, ed. R. Lemon and M. A. E. Green (12 vols, 1856–72)
CWTM	*The Complete Works of St. Thomas More* (15 vols, New Haven, CT, 1963–97)
EETS	Early English Text Society
L&P	*Letters and Papers, Foreign and Domestic, of the Reign of Henry VIII*, ed. J. S. Brewer, J. Gairdner and R. S. Brodie (21 vols, 1862–1932)
ODNB	*Oxford Dictionary of National Biography* (60 vols, Oxford, 2004)
RSTC	W. A. Pollard and G. R. Redgrave, *A Short-Title Catalogue of Books Printed in England, Scotland, and Ireland and of English Books Printed Abroad, 1475–1640*, 2nd edition, revised and enlarged by W. A. Jackson, K. J. Ferguson and K. F. Pantzer (3 vols, 1976–91)
STC [Wing]	D. Wing, *Short-Title Catalogue of Books Printed in England, Scotland, Ireland, Wales and British America and of English Books Printed in Other Countries 1641–1700*, 2nd edition, revised and enlarged by the Index Committee of the Modern Language Association of America, 3 vols (New York, 1972–88)
TNA	The National Archive, London

CONTRIBUTORS

John Coffey is Reader in Early Modern History at the University of Leicester. He is the author of *Persecution and Toleration in Protestant England, 1558–1689* (Harlow, 2000), and *John Goodwin and the Puritan Revolution; Religion and Intellectual Change in Seventeenth-Century England* (Woodbridge, 2006).

Thomas S. Freeman is Research Officer for the British Academy John Foxe Project and is affiliated with the University of Sheffield. He is the co-editor (with Susan Doran) of *The Myth of Elizabeth* (Basingstoke, 2003) and the co-author (with Elizabeth Evenden) of *Religion and the Book in Early Modern England: The Making of Foxe's Book of Martyrs* (Cambridge, forthcoming).

Brad S. Gregory is the Dorothy G. Griffin Associate Professor of Early Modern European History at the University of Notre Dame. He is the author of *Salvation at Stake: Christian Martyrdom in Early Modern Europe* (Cambridge, MA, 1999) and the editor of *The Forgotten Writings of the Mennonite Martyrs* (Leiden, 2002).

Victor Houliston teaches English at the University of Witwatersrand, Johannes-burg. He is the author of *Robert Persons's Jesuit Polemic, 1580–1610* (Aldershot, forthcoming).

Dr Andrew Lacey is a Tutor for the Institute of Continuing Education at the University of Cambridge and a Librarian in the Faculty of Architecture and the History of Art. He is the author of *The Cult of King Charles the Martyr* (Wood-bridge, 2003).

Thomas F. Mayer is Professor of History at Augustana College and the author of *Reginald Pole: Prince and Prophet* (Cambridge, 2000). He is the editor of the series 'Catholic Christendom, 1300–1700' for Ashgate.

Dr Danna Piroyansky completed her doctorate at the University of London, under the supervision of Prof. Miri Rubin. She teaches medieval history at the Hebrew University of Jerusalem, and is working on her first book, *Martyrs in the Making: Political Martyrdom in Late Medieval England* (Basingstoke, forth-coming).

Richard Rex is Reader in Reformation History at the Faculty of Divinity in the University of Cambridge, and a Fellow of Queens' College, Cambridge. His publications include *The Lollards* (Basingstoke, 2002) and *Henry VIII and the English Reformation* (2nd edn, Basingstoke, 2006).

Alec Ryrie is Reader in Church History at Durham University. His recent books include *The Origins of the Scottish Reformation* (Manchester, 2006) and (as editor) *The European Reformations* (Basingstoke, 2005).

Dr William Wizeman, SJ, is Assistant Pastor of Corpus Christi Church, New York and he is the author of *The Theology and Spirituality of Mary Tudor's Church* (Aldershot, 2006).

EDITORIAL NOTE

All translations have been done by the individual authors in this work unless otherwise credited. Unless otherwise indicated, the place of publication of all works is London. All dates are new style; that is the year is reckoned to have begun on 1 January.

Introduction

Over their Dead Bodies: Concepts of Martyrdom in Late Medieval and Early Modern England*

THOMAS S. FREEMAN

In early-modern England, martyrs mattered. This, of course, was true throughout Western Europe, but the situation in England was unique. For one thing, in England members of the national Church, as well as Catholic and Protestant dissenters from it, all venerated different, competing, sets of martyrs from their own ranks, many of whom had been executed within living memory. Competing martyrological traditions flourished because the recurring shifts in English royal policy, which had created both Catholic and Protestant martyrs, meant that the danger of persecution always seemed present and that the subject of martyrdom always appeared relevant. And because these traditions, and the different confessions which fostered them, were in competition, with no certain victory before the end of days, martyrology and martyrological writing flowered in a hothouse climate of fear and hatred.

The greatest martyrology of the Reformation in both size and influence, John Foxe's *Acts and Monuments*, incorporated some of these martyrological traditions, and in turn it also stimulated, in some cases provoked, others. For English Protestants, whether dissenting or conforming, the work provided a bridge, connecting themselves, via the Lollards, the Henrician martyrs and the Marian martyrs, with the apostles and the martyrs of the early Church.[1] Despite the

---

* I would like to thank Kenneth Fincham, Victor Houliston, Thomas McCoog, Richard Rex, Alec Ryrie and Ethan Shagan for reading this introduction and for their helpful comments, which saved me from numerous errors. In this chapter, quotations from medieval and early-modern sources retain their original spelling, except that *i/j*, *u/v* and long *s* are modernised; while *y* used as a thorn has been replaced with *th* and superscriptions are aligned. Also standard abbreviations in quotations have been expanded and punctuation, particularly capitalisation, has been modernised.

[1]   Admittedly there was not complete agreement among all English Protestants as to the status of particular martyrs. Some radical Protestants denounced episcopal martyrs such as Cranmer, Ridley and Latimer as 'pseudo-martyrs' (e.g. *The Writings of Henry Barrow, 1587–1590*, ed. Leland H. Carlson (1962), p. 284) while certain Laudian writers rejected some of Foxe's martyrs, such as John Oldcastle, as rebels and traitors (e.g. John Pocklington, *Altare Christianum* (1637), STC 20075, p. 92). But all of these Protestants accepted

enormous cost of printing it, Foxe's *magnum opus* went through nine editions between 1563 and 1684 and, additionally, it spawned numerous abridgements and imitations.[2] And while there was no single English Catholic martyrology to rival it, the sufferings of the English Catholic martyrs inspired wave after wave of works extolling them.[3]

The enduring popularity of martyrologies is a reflection of the power that martyrs had to inspire their contemporaries. The most striking evidence of this power was the ability of martyrs to incite others to lay down their lives in the same causes. Germain Gardiner and John Larke (the former parish priest of Thomas More), both declared at their executions in 1544 that they had been inspired to die for the catholic faith by the examples of Thomas More, John Fisher and the Carthusians executed by Henry VIII.[4] Reports of Laurence Saunders's martyrdom moved Joyce Lewes to publicly, and fatally, renounce Catholicism during Mary Tudor's reign.[5] Julins Palmer, a fellow at Magdalen College, paid for one of the students at the college to journey to Gloucester to watch the burning of John Hooper and report the details of it to him. He also personally witnessed the executions of Nicholas Ridley and Hugh Latimer, and their examples led him to embrace Protestantism and embark on a path that would that would lead him to the stake.[6] And John Mush, the confessor and hagiographer of Margaret Clitherow, claimed that one of the two 'motives' which inspired her was the patience and constancy of Catholic martyrs.[7] It may not be true that Henry Walpole, who would himself earn the crown of martyrdom, was converted when drops of Edmund Campion's blood spattered on him, but he certainly was present at Campion's execution and was moved by it to write a poem of thirty stanzas in the martyr's honour.[8] According to a letter attached to a manuscript account of the martyrdom of John Almond, a Protestant spectator was so impressed by Almond's 'undaunted courage and bold spirit', that he went from the execution to prison where he spoke with an incarcerated priest, who converted him to Catholicism.[9]

It might be objected that these examples stem from martyrological accounts

the vast majority of Foxe's martyrs as genuine and they also accepted the validity of his chain of martyrs of the True Church leading from the Reformation through the Lollards and back to the apostles.

[2] See Damian Nussbaum, 'Whitgift's "Book of Martyrs": Archbishop Whitgift, Timothy Bright and the Elizabethan Struggle over John Foxe's Legacy', in *John Foxe: An Historical Perspective*, ed. David Loades (Aldershot, 1999), pp. 135–53, and David Scott Kastan, 'Little Foxes', in *John Foxe and his World*, ed. Christopher Highley and John N. King (Aldershot, 2002), pp. 117–29.

[3] Brad Gregory, *Salvation at Stake: Christian Martyrdom in Early Modern Europe* (Cambridge, MA, 1999), p. 289.

[4] Thomas Stapleton, *Tres Thomae* (Douai, 1588), pp. 349–50.

[5] *A&M [1563]*, p. 1619.

[6] *A&M [1570]*, p. 2118.

[7] John Mush, *An abstracte of the life and martirdome of Mistres Margaret Clitherowe* (Mechelin, 1619), RSTC 18316.7, sig. A3v.

[8] Scott Pilarz, ' "Campion dead bites with his friends' teeth" ': Representations of an Early Modern Catholic Martyr', in *John Foxe and his World*, pp. 222–3.

[9] J. H. Pollen, *Acts of English Martyrs* (1891), p. 193.

and may therefore be greatly exaggerated, if not wholly untrue. Yet examples of conversions inspired by the martyrs exist outside the pages of martyrologies. Elated by the martyrdom of Edmund Campion, one Thomas Busbridge travelled to Rome and there, in 1582, converted to Catholicism.[10] Hearing of the martyrdom of Henry Walpole, a Spanish noblewoman, Donna Luisa de Carvajal, decided to imitate Campion, Walpole and the other mission priests and journey to England to preach the gospel. Like her models she was prepared to suffer martyrdom and she was, in fact, imprisoned twice. She died in London while awaiting repatriation to Spain.[11] And sometimes rather surprising individuals were moved by the example of the martyrs. In his youth, the Catholic controversialist Florimond de Raemond had been so impressed with the courage of the Huguenot martyr Anne du Bourg that he temporarily embraced Calvinism.[12]

Yet martyrologists also hoped, and expected, that their works would inspire readers to quotidian imitation of the martyrs, not in dying a Christ-like death but in living a Christ-like life. Foxe wrote his martyrology in the conviction that knowledge of 'the actes of Christes martyrs' would 'minister to the readers thereof wholesome admonitions of lyfe, with experience and wisdome bothe to know God in his workes, and to worke the thyng that is godly'.[13] Throughout the *Acts and Monuments*, Foxe presented martyrs as models to be followed in marital relations, conduct towards magistrates and superiors, devotion to God, cultivation of the soul and even proper behavior in business and trade.[14] Identical assumptions were made by Foxe's confessional adversaries. Indeed, it is is striking how similar were the underlying conceptions and assumptions of both Protestant and Catholic about martyrdom. During the Roman jubilee of 1575, Carlo Borromeo advised the pilgrims flooding into Rome of the spiritual benefits that they would gain from visiting the sites where the early Christian martyrs suffered and died: 'That fiery flame of Christian religion which burned in the heart of St. Lawrence shall inflame your souls to the fervent love of God, when you shall contemplate the manifold memories of his martyrdom, in the place where he roasted upon the gridiron.'[15] The great Counter-Reformation saint cannot have realised that he was echoing words that Foxe had written five years

---

[10] John Tedeschi, 'The Dispersed Archives of the Roman Inquisition', in *The Prosecution of Heresy: Collected Studies on the Inquisition in Early Modern Italy* (Binghamton, NY, 1991), p. 31.
[11] Michael E. Williams, 'Campion and the English Continental Seminaries', in *The Reckoned Expense: Edmund Campion and the Early English Jesuits*, ed. Thomas M. McCoog (Woodbridge, 1996), p. 296.
[12] Barbara Sher Tinsley, *History and Polemics in the French Reformation: Florimond de Raemond, Defender of the Church* (Susquehanna, PA, 1992), p. 22. For other examples of French Catholics converted to Protestantism by the deaths of Huguenot martyrs see David el Kenz, *Les bûchers du roi* (Seyssel, 1997), pp. 63–4.
[13] *A&M [1583]*, sig. *1r. For other comments by Foxe on the value of martyrs as models for godly behaviour in daily life see *A&M [1583]*, sigs. *3r and *6r; also see *A&M [1563]*, sig. B6r.
[14] For detailed discussion of this point see Thomas S. Freeman, ' "Great searching out of bookes and autors": John Foxe as an Ecclesiastical Historian' (Rutgers University, Ph.D. thesis, 1995), pp. 294–356.
[15] Quoted in Gregory, *Salvation at Stake*, p. 312. For other Catholic writers emphasising the importance of the martyrs as models of virtue see pp. 311–13.

earlier, when he was recounting the story of St Laurence: 'Now let us draw near to the fire of martyred Laurence, that our cold hearts may be warmed thereby.'[16]

The homiletic and didactic power of martyrological writings demonstrates the central role martyrs and ideas of martyrdom played in Reformation Europe. The martyrs were certainly not representative Christians but they were objects of admiration, and extolled as objects of imitation, by Catholic and Protestant alike. In England, where repeated fierce gusts of persecution, blowing from continually changing points in the religious compass, produced windfalls of martyrs in both confessions, the veneration of the martyrs had a lasting influence on the development of the different religious denominations. It moulded their ideas of their past and their ideas of how they related to the world around them, in short, their whole sense of identity. The influence of martyrological writings, moreover, seeped out from English religious culture into English culture as a whole, powerfully shaping English literature and even flowing over the bounds of literacy to impact visual and popular culture.[17]

I

Yet if martyrdom is at the heart of early modern English religion and religious culture, for the past few decades it has been consigned to the margins of scholarship. Only lately has this begun to change, first with Brad Gregory's seminal comparative study of Christian martyrdom in Reformation Europe and then with Anne Dillon's discussion of English Catholic martyrs and martyrologies and, most recently, with Susannah Monta's analysis of discourses of martyrdom in early-modern England.[18] Yet these works arose, like so many Venuses, out of an ocean of neglect. Furthermore, there are major areas that remain unexplored. There is still no history of religious persecution in early-modern England and some of the major episodes of religious persecution, such as the prosecution of Protestants in the reign of Mary Tudor, have gone virtually unexamined.[19] Nor has there been a study of the development of the ideas of martyrdom in Reformation England.

---

[16] *A&M [1570]*, p. 102.
[17] For the influence of martyrological writing on English literature see Susannah Brietz Monta, *Martyrdom and Literature in Early Modern England* (Cambridge, 2005) and Alison Shell, *Catholicism, Controversy and the English Literary Imagination, 1588–1600* (Cambridge, 1999). For a superficial, but broad, overview of the impact of the influence of Foxe's martyrology on English drama see Marsha S. Robinson, *Writing the Reformation: Actes and Monuments and the Jacobean History Play* (Aldershot, 2002). For the influence of martyrological works on visual culture see Anne Dillon, *The Construction of Martyrdom in the English Catholic Community, 1535–1603* (Aldershot, 2002), pp. 114–276 and Tessa Watt, *Cheap Print and Popular Culture, 1550–1640* (Cambridge, 1991), pp. 158–9. For Protestant martyrologies impinging on popular culture see Watt, *Cheap Print*, pp. 90–6 and 100–1.
[18] See nn. 3 and 17 above.
[19] There have been studies of concepts of persecution and toleration in early modern England, most notably Alexandra Walsham, *Charitable Hatred: Tolerance and Intolerance in England 1500–1700* (Manchester, 2006) and John Coffey, *Persecution and Toleration in Protestant England, 1558–1689*

There are several reasons for this neglect of crucially important topics. The first is that these fields have lain fallow in the past few decades because they had been overtilled in preceeding centuries. This earlier work, however, consisted largely of narrative and anecdote, and contained little analysis. It was also extremely partisan and dominated by confessional prejudice. The relatively neglected fields of martyrdom and persecution now need further cultivation and promise bountiful harvests when this done.

Another basic reason for the long lack of serious study of martyrdom in the English Reformation is the distaste which scholars feel for martyrs and the religious 'fanaticism' which they epitomise. The author of a recent book on popular religion in early modern England has boasted that: 'My focus will be upon the majority of England's inhabitants, with the result that martyrs, "puritans" and spiritual misfits may not enjoy quite the level of attention to which they have become accustomed.'[20] It might be objected that martyrdom cannot be divorced from a study of the religious life of England's inhabitants, since they venerated martyrs, read about martyrs, pored over illustrations of martyrs, attended dramas about martyrs and, as Tessa Watt has shown, placed pictures of the martyrs upon the walls of their houses. Catholic and Protestant martyrs were even the subjects of ballads sung by their co-religionists.[21] Yet what is particularly revealing, and somewhat unsettling, about this passage is the author's dismissive grouping of the martyrs together with 'spiritual misfits' (whoever they may be). At least one scholar has even attempted to explain away the willingness of early modern martyrs to die for religion as a form of mental disorder.[22] Barbara Diefendorf is more thoughtful in expressing her unease about martyrdom, when discussing the execution of the Huguenot martyr Pierre de la Place: 'The contemporary reader, however, is likely to find the story vaguely disturbing. The qualities of faith that steeled a man for martyrdom are not qualities we readily understand, and we find it hard to empathise with La Place's quiet submission to an unjust fate.'[23] But whether or not we find it easy to empathise with the martyrs, their contemporaries

(2000), but they are not studies of how persecutions were implemented or managed. Sarah Covington, *The Trail of Martyrdom: Persecution and Resistance in Sixteenth-Century England* (Notre Dame, IN, 2003) is a collection of anecdotes centred around the stages of persecution (arrest, trial and execution) but it is not a narrative history of persecution in early modern England. John Foxe as an author and historian has been the object of intense scholarly scrutiny, but the persecution that half of his martyrology is devoted to describing has yet to find its historian.

[20] Christopher Marsh, *Popular Religion in Sixteenth-Century England: Holding their Peace* (Basingstoke, 1998), p. 7.

[21] For ballads about evangelical and Protestant martyrs see Watt, *Cheap Print*, pp. 90–6; for ballads about Catholic martyrs see Arthur F. Marotti, *Religious Ideology and Cultural Fantasy: Catholic and Anti-Catholic Discourses in Early Modern England* (Notre Dame, IN, 2005), pp. 67–8. At the time of Edmund Campion's trial, the Privy Council ordered copies seized of a popular ballad which began 'Campion is a champion' (*CSPD, 1581–90*, p. 31).

[22] Seymour Byman, 'Ritualistic Acts and Compulsive Behaviour: The Pattern of Tudor Martyrdom', *American Historical Review*, 83 (1978), pp. 625–43.

[23] Barbara B. Diefendorf, *Beneath the Cross: Catholics and Huguenots in Sixteenth-Century Paris* (New York and Oxford, 1991), p. 107.

and co-religionists did, and they did so to such extent that we can not fully comprehend their religious beliefs, without studying their martyrs and their conceptions of martyrdom.

Of course, there were innumerable instances of coexistence and cooperation between the members of different religious groups in Reformation England. Firm political control, economic self-interest, local loyalties, ties of friendship and kinship, all often permitted the members of rival confessions to coexist without open conflict. But the absence of open conflict is not concord. The village of Hadleigh, for example, may have seemed a peaceful, prosperous community until Mary's accession brought largely submerged conflicts to the surface and triggered denunciations, banishments and even burnings that left a legacy of ill-will for decades.[24] The existence of everyday cooperation was often precariously erected on a thin crust covering the magma of sectarian hatred and fear.

The study of martyrs and conceptions of martyrdom in England has also been impeded by one of the major aspects that makes martyrdom so central to English religious life: the fact that each confession has its own deeply rooted martyrological tradition. The great works of martyrology, which supplied the source material for generations of scholars, ignored – or at best disparaged as briefly as possible – the martyrs and martyrologies of their opponents. The effects of this have proved to be remarkably enduring. With a few important exceptions (notably the monographs of Brad Gregory and Susannah Monta), the studies of English martyrs, martyrologies and conceptions of martyrdom have been divided along confessional lines. Yet the martyrologies took their shape, and the conceptions of martyrdom their definition, from a process of fierce inter-confessional controversy. If England produced the greatest martyrology of the Reformation, the *Acts and Monuments*, it also produced a seminal anti-martyrology, Nicholas Harpsfield's sixth dialogue, in his *Dialogi sex*, which in turn powerfully influenced both subsequent editions of Foxe's book and later Catholic attacks on it. These works were only the most prominent among a series of martyrological and anti-martyrological works written by Catholics and Protestants in early-modern England, which became the fortified strongpoints of confessional Maginot lines. But contemporaries read, and responded to, the martyrological, and anti-martyrological works of religious adversaries, and it was the cross-confessional polemic that created, crystalised and defined what became commonly held conventions and conceptions about martyrs.

[24] On Hadleigh, see John Craig, *Reformation, Politics and Polemics: The Growth of Protestantism in East Anglian Market Towns, 1500–1610* (Aldershot, 2001), pp. 152–75.

II

In her chapter in this volume, Danna Piroyansky demonstrates the ubiquity and importance of concepts of martyrdom in late medieval English religion. She also shows that there were several routes to martyrdom in the late Middle Ages, apart from enduring persecution for a set of theological beliefs. People who died unmerited deaths were popularly venerated as martyrs as were those 'warriors of God' who died fighting for God. There was also great popular veneration of virgin martyrs, such as St Catherine, St Lucy or St Barbara, who were honoured as much (or more) for having died to preserve their chastity as for having died for the gospel. Those individuals who underwent experiences that fostered spiritual identification with Christ through non-violent imitation of the pain and humiliation he endured, for example, by means of extreme asceticism, were also regarded as martyrs.

After Becket, contemporary or near-contemporary English people who died for the faith were rare and fell into three groups. Perhaps paradoxically, the first group of these 'modern' martyrs was entirely spurious: children supposed to have been ritually murdered by Jews. Although the authenticity of these stories was virtually unquestioned, the persecution, if not the very existence of such martyrs was fictitious, while their attributes and characters were stereotypical and entirely interchangeable. The key to their popular veneration was their innocence. It was believed that they died for neither doctrine nor cause; in fact, apart from their supposed deaths, there was nothing noteworthy about them at all.[25]

Numerous English medieval political leaders who met violent ends resisting authority were popularly venerated as martyrs.[26] Some of the cults of these figures, such as those of Archbishop Richard Scrope and of Henry VI, proved to be exceptionally popular, and enduring.[27] Yet most of these political cults proved ephemeral. Following his execution in 1397, there was some veneration of Richard, earl of Arundel, but it died out quickly, with the last miracle credited to him occurring around 1404.[28] A cult of Simon de Montfort rose suddenly and spectacularly after the death of the baronial leader at the battle of Evesham in

---

[25] See André Vauchez, *Sainthood in the Later Middle Ages*, trans. Jean Birrell (Cambridge, 1997), pp. 147–56, and Miri Rubin, 'Choosing Death? Experiences of Martyrdom in Late Medieval Europe', in *Martyrs and Martyrologies*, ed. Diana Wood, Studies in Church History 30 (Oxford, 1993), pp. 164–7; see also Danna Piroyansky's chapter in this volume. Both Vauchez and Rubin treat these martyrs as part of a larger category of innocent victims of violence who were venerated as martyrs.

[26] See Simon Walker, 'Political Saints in Later Medieval England', in *The McFarlane Legacy: Studies in Late Medieval Politics and Society*, ed. R. H. Britnell and A. J. Pollard (Basingstoke, 1995), pp. 77–106.

[27] For Scrope's cult see Walker, 'Political Saints', pp. 84–5 and 90–1, as well as John W. McKenna, 'Popular Canonization as Political Propaganda: The Cult of Archbishop Scrope', *Speculum*, 45 (1970), pp. 608–23. On the cult of Henry VI see Leigh Ann Craig, 'Royalty, Virtue, and Adversity: The Cult of Henry VI', *Albion*, 35 (2003), pp. 187–209, and Thomas S. Freeman, ' *"Ut verus Christi sequestor"*: John Blacman and the Cult of Henry VI', *The Fifteenth Century*, 5 (2005), pp. 127–42.

[28] Walker, 'Political Saints', p. 81.

1265. A collection of 196 posthumous miracles credited to the earl was compiled in Evesham Abbey and it reveals a cult that ranged from Kent through London, and across the southern Midlands. But once again the cult was transient; the last datable miracle attributed to de Montfort took place in 1279 and his cult had disappeared by the early fourteenth century.[29] After a generation or two, the most fervent political passions cooled and most political saints were forgotten. The others continued to be honoured because their cults had developed characteristics that led to their being venerated for reasons that were entirely apolitical. Henry VI, for example, was widely revered as a thaumaturge who healed or aided those in mortal peril and Richard Scrope became an unofficial, but immensely popular, patron saint of the city of York.[30]

The final group of contemporary martyrs, at least to those who shared their religious convictions, were the Lollards. Yet although the Lollards did not lack candidates for martyrdom, their unyielding resistance to the cults of saints appears to have throttled the development of a strong martyrological tradition. There were only three Lollard martyr-narratives in over a century of executions for heresy: the examinations of John Oldcastle, William Thorpe and Richard Wyche. Upon closer inspection, however, this handful of works appears even more meagre. The first of these, an account of Sir John Oldcastle's trial, was circulated, not by his followers, but by the authorities in order to discredit him. The third work, Wyche's narrative, survived in a single copy in Prague, and was unknown in England. Only Thorpe's account of his own examinations qualifies as a popular Lollard martyrological work.[31]

Moreover, while there is scattered evidence of individual Lollards regarding executed co-religionists as martyrs, there is virtually no evidence of any cultic veneration of them.[32] As Richard Rex shows in his chapter in this volume, the oft-cited case of Richard Wyche is misleading; Wyche was venerated as a saint and a martyr, but he was not – at least at the time of his execution – a Lollard. He was really a type of the political martyr: the innocent victim of those in authority.[33] A powerful martyrological tradition would develop around those

---

[29] Walker, 'Political Saints', p. 82.

[30] On the metamorphosis of Henry VI's cult, see Craig, 'Royalty, Virtue and Adversity', pp. 200–9; on changes in Scrope's cult see Danna Piroyansky, ' "Martyrio pulchro finites": Archbishop Scrope's Martyrdom and the Creation of Cult', in *Richard Scrope: Archbishop, Rebel, Martyr*, ed. Jeremy Gregory (Stamford, Lincolnshire, forthcoming). I am grateful to Dr Piroyansky for permitting me to read her article in advance of its publication.

[31] Wyche's narrative is Prague University Library MS III. G., fos. 89v–94v; for an analysis of this account see C. Nolcken, 'Richard Wyche, a Certain Knight, and the Beginning of the End', in *Lollardy and the Gentry in the Later Middle Ages*, ed. M. Aston and C. Richmond (New York, 1997), pp. 127–54. On Wyche, also see Richard Rex's chapter in this volume. On the textual history of William Thorpe's examinations see *Two Wycliffite Texts*, ed. Anne Hudson, EETS, o.s. 301 (Oxford, 1993), pp. liii–lix. Also see Anne Hudson, *The Premature Reformation: Wycliffite Texts and Lollard History* (Oxford, 1980), pp. 220–2, on Thorpe's and Wyche's examinations.

[32] For individual Lollards honouring those put to death for heresy as martyrs see Gregory, *Salvation at Stake*, p. 70.

[33] According to the *Great Chronicle of London*, after Joan Boughton's execution in 1494, her ashes were

Lollards executed for heresy but this was the creation of later English Protestants, not of the Lollards themselves.

Thus while pre-Reformation England venerated martyrs and provided a climate in which martyrological sensibilities blossomed, it had no real tradition, at least since Becket, of venerating contemporaries who died for religious causes as martyrs. The situation was slow to change in the early English Reformation. Henry VIII, with regal generosity, supplied a number of martyrs, both evangelical and Catholic. Brad Gregory's meticulous analysis of the theology of two of the most prominent of these martyrs, William Tyndale and Thomas More (and as Gregory observes, both men were martyrologists as well as martyrs), shows that from the early days of the English Reformation both Catholics and evangelicals had developed remarkably similar, Christocentric concepts and models of martyrdom. Yet paradoxically, while both sides had clear ideas of what martyrdom was, and both sides had candidates for martyrdom, both confessions were slow in developing a martyrological tradition during Henry's reign. Reformers had much to hope for from a king who had dissolved the monastaries, who had overthrown shrines and whose archbishop of Canterbury was the reliably evangelical Thomas Cranmer; they were thus reluctant to burn their bridges by depicting Henry as a persecutor of God's saints.[34] (As Alec Ryrie demonstrates, this was a major reason for the evangelical creation of the myth of Stephen Gardiner as a bloodthirsty persecutor and the man truly responsible for the burning of the godly during Henry's reign.)[35] Similar hopes, based on Henry's religious conservatism, most notably on the theology of the Eucharist, impeded the development of a Catholic martyrological tradition. Despite the fame and international reputations of both Thomas More and John Fisher, the first work devoted solely to Henrician Catholic martyrs, Maurice Chauncy's account of the Carthusians executed by Henry, was not printed until 1550.[36]

The fact that More, Fisher and the Carthusians were executed as traitors also made many English people, otherwise sympathetic, reluctant to praise, much less venerate them. Furthermore, Henry's government also acted ruthlessly and effectively to suppress potential cults of Catholic martyrs. Fisher's tomb and chantry chapel at St John's College, Cambridge, were eradicated and his heraldic arms defaced; even the college statutes were redrafted to remove the name of the

---

gathered and carried away in an earthen pot, as a 'precious relic' (*The Great Chronicle of London*, ed. A. H. Thomas and I. D. Thornley (1938), p. 252). However, this theft may have been motivated as much by a desire to see the remains of Boughton, who had considerable status and family connections (her daughter was the widow of a lord mayor of London), properly treated, as by a desire to revere her ashes as the relics of a martyr.

34 Alec Ryrie, 'The Unsteady Beginnings of English Protestant Martyrology', in *John Foxe: An Historical Perspective*, ed. David Loades (Aldershot, 1999), pp. 52–66, and Alec Ryrie, *The Gospel and Henry VIII: Evangelicals in the Early English Reformation* (Cambridge, 2003).

35 See Alec Ryrie's chapter in this volume; also see Michael Riordan and Alec Ryrie, 'Stephen Gardiner and the Making of a Protestant Villain', *Sixteenth Century Journal*, 34 (2003), pp. 1039–63.

36 Gregory, *Salvation at Stake*, pp. 259–69.

martyr who, in all but name, was the founder of the college.[37] In his discussion of the destruction of the most famous martyr's shrine in England, the tomb of St Thomas Becket, Thomas Mayer reminds us of the tremondous impact the eradication of these monuments had on contemporaries and the atrocity stories which they stimulated among Catholics throughout Europe. Yet Clark Hulse demonstrates the benefit the Henrician government reaped from this destruction, by insightfully describing how the burial of Thomas More's headless body within the Tower precincts inhibited, although it did not entirely prevent, veneration of More:

> With no tomb, or shrine, there could be no pilgrimages, no public ceremonies. The cult of Thomas More developed instead in the interior and exile spaces of Tudor culture. It flourished in the secret underground of a now illegal English Roman Catholicism, and above all in the privacy of the recusant family. Deprived of a body, a public site, a shrine, and driven into hiding, the cult of Thomas More centered instead around substitute bodies, namely the portraits and written accounts of More that already existed or were soon produced.[38]

When More's head, which had been impaled on London Bridge, was to be taken down and thrown into the Thames, Margaret Roper procured it by bribing the executioner. It is indicative of the depth of the Henrician government's concern to prevent cultic veneration of its victims that Margaret Roper was summoned before the Privy Council, and accused of keeping 'her father's head as if it was a relic' ('caput patris quasi reliquiae').[39] And, of course, the dissolution of monastic houses and the dispersal of their communities also eliminated groups who would have spearheaded martyr cults as well as removing potential shrines for these martyrs.[40]

Nevertheless, some significant seeds were sown in Henry's reign. English evangelicals, while reluctant to tilt directly at the king, were more ready to celebrate Lollards (executed by his predecessors) as martyrs – and to begin forging the historiographical chain that would link Lollardy to English Protestantism for centuries to come. The examinations of Thorpe and Oldcastle were printed in one volume, in 1530, by William Tyndale or George Constantine, or, very possibly, the two of them in collaboration.[41] During the following decade, John Bale began

---

[37] R. F. Scott, *Records of St. John's College, Cambridge* (Cambridge, 1934), p. 281, and Richard Rex, 'John Fisher', in *ODNB*.

[38] Clark Hulse, 'Dead Man's Treasure: The Cult of Thomas More', in *The Production of English Renaissance Culture*, ed. David Lee Miller, Sharon O'Dair and Harold Weber (Ithaca, NY, 1994), p. 208.

[39] Stapleton, *Tres Thomae*, pp. 346–7. Roper defended herself by stating that she was simply concerned that her father's head should not be thrown in the river and that she intended to bury it. She was released through the good offices of her friends (ibid., pp. 347–8).

[40] This is a point made by Richard Rex in his paper, 'Why were there No Catholic Martyrs in Henrician England?', delivered at the Sixteenth-Century Studies Conference, St Louis, 1999.

[41] *The examinacion of master William Thorpe preste accused of heresy . . .*, ed., George Constantine? or William Tyndale? (Antwerp, 1530), RSTC 24045.

his researches into the Lollard past which would bear their first, but far from last, fruits in a new, and expanded, account of the trial and martyrdom of Oldcastle.[42] And meanwhile, More's family and friends quietly stirred the embers of his reputation, while Maurice Chauncy nursed the memory of his slaughtered comrades. The memories of the Catholic martyrs were hardy seedlings which survived the winter of Henry VIII's reign and the reign of his son, to blossom in the late spring of Mary's accession to the throne.[43]

III

With the accession of Edward VI, and the increasingly open championship of advanced Protestantism by his government, it was natural for there to have been some memorialisation of the evangelical martyrs of the previous reign. Endurance of persecution was, after all, one of the marks of the True Church, and English evangelicals were quick to identify themselves as victims of persecution, even in the halcyon days of Edward VI.[44] Yet there were problems inherent in the glorification of the executed evangelicals. For one thing, a number of them had held theological opinions that were embarrassingly at odds with current official religious positions; worse still, Archbishop Cranmer had been prominently involved in the proceedings against some of them, such as John Frith and John Lambert. And the godly clergy of Edward VI's reign were too concerned with the problem of dissidents from their own religious policies to be entirely comfortable with praising those who had defied religious authority in the previous reign.[45]

Similar considerations should have militated against the glorification of Henrician Catholic martyrs during Mary's reign. Again, the memory of these figures must have been an uncomfortable one for such leaders of the Marian Church as Stephen Gardiner, Edmund Bonner and Cuthbert Tunstall, all of whom had – as Protestants frequently reminded them – supported the policies which

---

[42] John Bale, *A brefe chronycle concerninge the examinacyon and death of the martyr syr J. Oldecastell* (Antwerp, 1544), RSTC 1276.

[43] On the early memorialisation of More, see Dillon, *Construction of Martyrdom*, pp. 36–45. (It should be noted, however, that Dillon may be incorrect in dating the composition of Harpsfield's biography of More to Mary's reign. Harpsfield's movements and activities in the reigns of Edward VI and Mary indicate that much of the work was written while Harpsfield was in exile at Louvain; see the article on Nicholas Harpsfield in the *ODNB*.) On the composition of the different editions of Chauncey's martyrology, see *Cause of the Canonization of Blessed Martyrs . . . Put to Death in England in Defence of the Catholic Faith (1535–1582): Official Presentation of Documents in Martyrdom and Cult* (Vatican City, 1968), pp. 11–13, and E. Margaret Thompson, *The Carthusian Order in England* (1930), pp. 345–52.

[44] Catherine Davies, ' "Poor Persecuted Little Flock" or "Commonwealth of Christians": Edwardian Protestant Concepts of the Church', in *Protestantism and the National Church in Sixteenth-Century England*, ed. Peter Lake and Maria Dowling (Beckenham, Kent, 1987), pp. 78–102.

[45] See Diarmaid MacCulloch, *Thomas Cranmer: A Life* (New Haven, CT, 1996), pp. 371 and 530–1; also see Catherine Davies, *A Religion of the Word: The Defence of the Reformation in the Reign of Edward VI* (Manchester, 2002), pp. 67–86, and Thomas S. Freeman, 'Dissenters from a Dissenting Church: The Challenge of the Freewillers 1550–1558', in *The Beginnings of English Protestantism*, ed. Peter Marshall and Alec Ryrie (Cambridge, 2002), pp. 129–34.

these martyrs had died opposing. And Mary's government had its own reasons for finding it difficult to glorify those who opposed royal religious policy for conscience's sake.

That both confessions in England developed potent martyrological traditions by the middle of the sixteenth century, despite these considerations, is partly due to two remarkable individuals. One of these was John Bale, a former Carmelite turned evangelical preacher, who brought the antiquarian researches he had begun while still a friar to the service of the reformed religion.[46] Throughout the 1540s Bale composed, or edited, a series of works saturated with martyrological themes and tropes.[47] These efforts culminated in Bale's edition of Anne Askew's account of her examinations, 'the first piece of popular English martyr writing to stand four-square within the emerging Protestant martyrological tradition'.[48] Why was Bale's appreciation of the potential of martyrological writing so well developed especially when compared to other English evangelicals?[49] Part of it may have been due to his work on Carmelite hagiography before he left the order. However, much of it was undoubtedly due to Bale's intense interest in the book of Revelation, together with his conviction that it contained prophecies of events which had already occurred in the history of the Church. When these historical events were identified, and equated with passages in the final book of the Bible, the identies of the True and False Churches, and the unfolding of God's plan in human history would be made manifest.[50] And since St John's vision emphasised the role of martyrs, it was hardly surprising that Bale's writings would do so as well.

Whatever Bale's motivations in writing them, his martyrological works were exceptionally important. He virtually created English Protestant martyrology.[51]

[46] Peter Happé, *John Bale* (New York, 1996) provides a useful overview of Bale's life and career. Richard Copsey, *Carmel in Britain*, 3 vols (Faversham, 1992–2004), III, pp. 51–73 and 283–325, is indispensible on Bale's research in his early years. On Bale's antiquarian researches see May McKisack, *Medieval History in the Tudor Age* (Oxford, 1971), pp. 11–25, and *The Recovery of the Past in Early Elizabethan England: Documents by John Bale and John Joscelyn from the Circle of Matthew Parker*, ed. Timothy Graham and Andrew G. Watson, Cambridge Bibliographical Society 13 (Cambridge, 1998). On Bale's importance as a martyrologist see Leslie P. Fairfield, 'John Bale and the Development of Protestant Hagiography in England', *Journal of Ecclesiastical History*, 24 (1973), pp. 145–60, and Leslie P. Fairfield, *John Bale: Mythmaker for the English Reformation* (West Lafayette, IN, 1976).
[47] Bale, *Brefe chronycle*; also see John Bale, *A dysclosing or openynge of the Manne of synne* (Antwerp, 1543), RSTC 1309, fos. 41r–v, 66r and 93r; John Bale, *The epistle exhortatorye of an Englyshe Christiane* (Antwerp, 1544), RSTC 1291, fos. 6r and 12v–15r; John Bale, *A mysterye of inyquyte contayned within the heretycall Genealogye of Ponce Pontolabus* (Antwerp, 1545), RSTC 1303, fos. 31v, 39r and 61v–62r and John Lambert, *A treatyse made by Iohan Lambert . . .*, ed. John Bale (Wesel, 1548), RSTC 15180, fos. 4r–5r.
[48] Ryrie, 'Unsteady Beginnings', p. 53. There is a useful modern edition of Askew's examinations: *The Examinations of Anne Askew*, ed. Elaine V. Beilin (Oxford and New York, 1996).
[49] For other evangelical writers who cultivated martyrological themes in their writings see Ryrie, 'Unsteady Beginnings', pp. 55–6 and 63–4.
[50] See Fairfield, *John Bale*, pp. 22–7, 50–5 and 157–64, as well as Copsey, *Carmel in Britain*, pp. 287–325 and 351–3. For Bale's apocalyptic thought see Katherine R. Firth, *The Apocalyptic Tradition in Reformation Britain 1530–1645* (Oxford, 1979), pp. 32–68.
[51] See Fairfield, *John Bale*, pp. 145–60, and Ryrie, 'Unsteady Beginnings', pp. 64–5.

But Bale not only extolled Lollard, evangelical and Protestant martyrs, he denigrated Catholic martyrs. In addition to his more strictly martyrological writings, Bale's *Acts of the English Votaries* is a significant contribution to the development of ideas of martyrdom in sixteenth-century England. Although the *Acts*, a *chronique scandaleuse* of the English clergy, was largely devoted to an assault on clerical celibacy and on papal usurpation of royal power, it contained passages of caustic anti-martyrology, particularly in undermining traditionally popular martyrs such as William of York and Thomas Becket.[52] This was one of the great strengths of Bale's polemical writing, its mixture of martyrology and anti-martyrology in potent cocktails. In his words, 'A great dyfference is there of the martyrs whom they [the Catholics] make, from the martyrs whom they canonyse' and Bale worked ceaselessly to emphasise the contrast.[53] This polemical tactic may not have been invented by Bale, but he perfected it, and his comparisons between the 'false' saints and martyrs traditionally venerated in England with the 'true' saints and martyrs, persecuted for the Gospel, did a great deal to help establish a new paradigm for martyrdom.[54] This was particularly true because Bale's contrast of true and false martyrs greatly influenced his protégé John Foxe.[55]

What Bale did for English Protestant martyrology, Reginald Pole did for English Catholic martyrology. Even after Henry VIII had ascended or descended to his eternal reward, English Catholics were generally reluctant to mention, at least in print, the martyrs he had executed, and declined to cite More or Fisher even when drawing on their writings.[56] The conspicuous exception to this self-imposed restraint was Cardinal Pole. Indeed, it may have been the executions of More and Fisher that goaded Pole, who had hitherto been quietly pursuing his studies at the university of Padua, into outspoken opposition to Henry VIII.[57] Certainly, *De unitate*, Pole's blistering attack on Henry, written in 1535–6,

---

[52] John Bale, *The first two partes of the Actes, or unchast examples of the the English votaryes* (1551), RSTC 1273.5, II, fos. 85v–86r and 91v–97r. Particularly significant is Bale's contrast between the 'false' martyr Becket and two 'true' martyrs, who were branded in 1154 and then banished from England, for denying Purgatory and other offences (fos. 94v–95r).

[53] *Examinations of Anne Askew*, p. 79. For further examples of Bale's contrasting 'true' and 'false' saints and martyrs see pp. 6–13 and 75–86. Also see Bale, *Brefe chronycle*, sigs. A2v–A3r, G4r–v and G7r–v.

[54] Rainer Pineas, 'William Tyndale's Influence on John Bale's Polemical Use of History', *Archiv für Reformationsgeschichte*, 53 (1962), pp. 79–86, credits Tyndale with making desultory essays into martyrology and anti-martyrology. Nevertheless Pineas concedes that Bale expanded and developed these themes tremendously (see pp. 83–5 and 90–6).

[55] Cf. Bale, *Brefe chronycle*, sigs. A2r–A3r with *A&M [1563]*, sigs. B4r and B6r. For good examples of Foxe using this tactic see *A&M [1563]*, p. 1250. and *A&M [1570]*, pp. 693–4.

[56] Diarmaid MacCulloch, *Tudor Church Militant: Edward VI and the Protestant Reformation* (1999), p. 119, and *Sermons Very Fruitful, Godly and Learned by Roger Edgeworth Preaching in the Reformation c.1535–1553*, ed. J. Wilson (Woodbridge, 1993), pp. 35 and 61.

[57] Thomas Starkey, who had been in Pole's household from 1532 to 1534, claimed that the executions of More and Fisher convinced Pole of the righteousness of their cause (TNA, SP 1/105, fo. 46r). Pole had met More some time before 1518 and they remained correspondents (Thomas F. Mayer, *Reginald Pole: Prince and Prophet* (Cambridge, 2000), p. 47). In his writings, Pole emphasised his personal friendship with both More and Fisher (Thomas F. Mayer, 'Nursery of Resistance: Reginald Pole and his Friends', in *Political Thought and the Tudor Commonwealth*, ed. P. A. Fideler and T. F. Mayer [1992], p. 60).

lauded More and Fisher as divinely appointed witnesses to England, whose martyrdoms had pointed the English to the truth amid the chaos of heretical teachings. In murdering them, Henry had shown himself to be a greater persecutor than Nero or Domitian and a worse enemy to Christianity than the Turk.[58] Pole's veneration for More and Fisher, and his ardent appreciation of the sanctity of martyrdom, stayed with him when he returned to England, after decades in exile, as papal legate and archbishop of Canterbury. In a seminal sermon he preached at Whitehall on St Andrew's day, 1557, to mark the third anniversary of England's reconciliation with Rome, Pole extolled More and Fisher, in terms which echoed *De unitate*, as divine witnesses, to the laity and clergy respectively, to England, and to London.[59] Pole also appears to have been the keystone in a triumphal arch of works erected to the memories of the two great Henrician martyrs. He attempted to commission a life of Fisher and may well have supported, or even facilitated, the 1557 edition of More's works.[60] Ellis Heywood, who may have been one of Pole's secretaries, dedicated his *Il Moro*, a dialogue in which More is depicted as a Socratic sage, to the cardinal, while Pole's close associate Pedro de Soto saved the holograph of More's *De tristitia Christi*.[61]

In the St Andrew's day sermon, Pole also used the occasion to undermine the claims to sanctity made on behalf of the Protestant 'pseudo-martyrs' recently executed in London.[62] As was the case with Bale, trail-blazing martyrology was accompanied by path-breaking anti-martyrology. There is little doubt that Pole masterminded the effective campaign to disseminate, in both print and manuscript, the recantation the duke of Northumberland made at his execution.[63] There is even less doubt that Pole sponsored Nicholas Harpsfield's systematic subversion of the sanctity of Archbishop Cranmer's martyrdom, now known as 'Bishop Cranmer's Recantacyons'.[64] William Wizeman has declared that 'the two-sided

---

[58] Reginald Pole, *Pro ecclesiasticae unitatis defensione, libri quatuor* (Rome, 1538?), fos. 4v, 89r and 106v. Also see the discussion of this work in Mayer, *Reginald Pole*, pp. 13–61, particularly 27–8 and 31, and Gregory, *Salvation at Stake*, pp. 265–7.

[59] Eamon Duffy, 'Cardinal Pole's Preaching: St. Andrew's Day 1557', in *The Church of Mary Tudor*, ed. Eamon Duffy and David Loades (Aldershot, 2006), pp. 190–6. This is not the only time that Pole held up the example of the martyrs as models to be followed (see Mayer, *Pole*, p. 205). It is yet another reminder of the value of martyrs in providing homiletic examples.

[60] Mayer, *Reginald Pole*, p. 66, and Duffy, 'Pole's Preaching', p. 199 n. 65. In addition to his personal relations with More, Pole had interesting ties to More's family. Antonio Bonvisi, who had been one of Thomas More's closest friends (and the godfather to his son John) acted as a liaison between Pole and the newly crowned Queen Mary. In the previous reign, members of More's family, as well as Nicholas Harpsfield, a protégé of William Roper, More's son-in-law, resided in Bonvisi's house in Louvain (see Archivo Segreto Vaticano Bolognetti 94, fos. 29r–v, 63v–70r and 73v–77r; I owe this reference to Thomas Mayer); also see the articles on Antonio Bonvisi and Nicholas Harpsfield in the *ODNB*.

[61] Mayer, 'Nursery of Resistance', p. 71 n. 37.

[62] Duffy, 'Pole's Preaching', pp. 196–9.

[63] See Thomas Mayer's chapter in this volume. William Dalby, a London merchant with evangelical sympathies, wrote that after Northumberland's recantation: 'There were a great number turned with his words' (BL, Harley MS 416, fo. 141v).

[64] Bibliothèque Nationale, MS Latin 6506; printed as *Bishop Cranmer's Recantacyons*, ed. Lord Houghton with an introduction by James Gairdner, Philobiblon Society Miscellanies 15 (1877–84). Also

effort of defending English Catholic martyrs and vilifying Protestant ones was a creation of the Marian Church'.[65] This is an important observation, but it might be more precisely qualified by stating that it was largely a creation of Pole and those under his patronage. And just as Bale's influence persisted through his protégé John Foxe, Pole's persisted through his protégé Nicholas Harpsfield.[66]

IV

Scholars have described the printing of a number of large and important Protestant martyrologies – those composed or compiled by Ludwig Rabus, Adriaen van Haemstede, Jean Crespin and John Foxe – as responses to an unprecedently severe period of persecution for 'mainstream' Protestants.[67] (The Anabaptists had already endured even more intense persecution, but lacking printing centres of their own, they initially developed oral, rather than printed, martyrological traditions.)[68] It is a logical conclusion but martyrologies were neither automatic nor inevitable responses to intense persecution. (Foxe's first martyrology, the *Commentarii rerum in ecclesia gestarum*, was completed during Edward VI's reign – before English Protestants knew that they would be facing renewed persecution – even though it was not printed until 1554.)[69]

It might be more precise to say that intensified persecution of Protestants catalysed important transformations in Protestant attitudes towards martyrdom and these attitudes fostered the creation of martyrs. Throughout the 1540s, Jean Calvin, Heinrich Bullinger, Guillaume Farel, Peter Martyr Vermigli and Pierre Viret vehemently, and repeatedly, assailed 'Nicodemites' as they termed those

see MacCulloch, *Cranmer*, pp. 584–607, and the *ODNB* article on Nicholas Harpsfield. Pole's client George Lily had a copy of the *Recantacyons*, which would further suggest Pole's sponsorship of the work; it was probably sent to Lily for stylistic revision (BL, Additional MS 48029, fos. 58r–59v and the *ODNB* article on Lily).

[65] William Wizeman, *The Theology and Spirituality of Mary Tudor's Church* (Aldershot, 2006), p. 234.

[66] One indication of Pole's influence on Harpsfield's thought occurs in Harpsfield's praise of Fisher and More, which strikingly echoes Pole's St Andrew's day sermon: 'Iam Rossensis et Morus fuere duo tam Angliae, quam totius Europae lumina; alter Christi, alter laicorum, dignitate, doctrina ac virtute facile princeps' ('Now Rochester and More were two lights not only of England, but of all Europe; the one easily the chief of clergy, the other of laypeople, in honour, orthodoxy and virtue') (Nicholas Harpsfield, *Dialogi sex contra summi pontificatus, monasticae vitae, sanctorum sacrarum imaginum oppugnatores, et pseudomartyres* (Antwerp, 1566), sig. Qq5v).

[67] See William Monter, 'Heresy Executions in Reformation Europe, 1520–1565', in *Tolerance and Intolerance in the English Reformation*, ed. Ole Peter Grell and Bob Scribner (Cambridge, 1996), pp. 56–8, and Andrew Pettegree, 'European Calvinism: History, Providence, and Martyrdom', in *The Church Retrospective*, ed. R. N. Swanson, Studies in Church History 33 (Woodbridge, 1997), pp. 228–9 and 231–44. Robert Kolb has reinforced this correlation between persecution and the production of martyrologies by maintaining that a lack of intense persecution inhibited the development of a Lutheran martyrological tradition (Robert Kolb, *For All the Saints: Changing Perceptions of Martyrdom and Sainthood in the Lutheran Reformation* (Macon, GA, 1987), pp. 88–94).

[68] Gregory, *Salvation at Stake*, pp. 212–31.

[69] For the dating of the *Commentarii* see Elizabeth Evenden and Thomas S. Freeman, *Religion and the Book in Early Modern England: The Making of Foxe's 'Book of Martyrs'* (Cambridge, forthcoming), ch. 2.

who maintained that it was permissible to dissimulate one's true religious beliefs and outwardly conform to the religious practices prescribed by authority.[70] Their hostility to Nicodemism led these Reformers, and their like-minded colleagues, to place a premium on martyrdom. As David Nicholls has observed, 'in his original *Institution* of 1536 Calvin devoted only one short paragraph to martyrs, as one kind of witness among many others to God's working in history, whereas by 1552 he was urging the faithful to be prepared for persecution and martyrdom and, if it comes, to accept it joyfully, because faith should always be confessed and never denied, and witnessing the truth is more precious than life itself'.[71]

The onslaught on Nicodemism on the Continent coincided with increasing resistance to religious persecution in England. The double set of executions in July 1540, of the evangelicals Robert Barnes, Thomas Garrett and William Jerome, and of the Catholic priests Richard Featherstone, Edward Powell and Thomas Abell, ushered in a period of conspicuous persecution in what might be termed the ferocious forties. (The enduring consequences of Robert Barnes's execution, and the circumstances surrounding it, are examined in detail in Alec Ryrie's contribution to this volume.) The last seven years of Henry VIII's reign were characterised by high-profile martyrs suffering in highly publicised executions. Recently scholars, notably Alec Ryrie, have persuasively challenged the traditional view that there was a severe persecution of evangelicals following the Act of Six Articles.[72] Nevertheless, within three years, three evangelicals on the fringes of the royal court were executed at Windsor. Three years after this, a gentlewoman, Anne Askew, was burned with two men at Smithfield. These executions do not seem to have stemmed from the enforcement of a coherent religious policy but were, instead, the first stages in wider attempts to incriminate evangelical sympathisers around the king as sacramentarian heretics. They were part of a whole series of attacks and counter-attacks, including the Prebendaries Plot, the execution of Germain Gardiner, the disgrace of John London, and the efforts to dislodge Katherine Parr, all of which originated in attempts to determine the religious policies of the next reign, by removing or, at the least, compromising leading evangelicals and evangelical sympathisers at court.[73] That these heresy executions did not lead to large-scale purges is partly due to the surprising steadfastness of those who, like Anne Askew, chose to die rather than accuse others.

[70] The pejorative term is derived from Nicodemus, a pharisee sympathetic to Christ, who visited him secretly at night (John 3: 1–10). The standard work on Nicodemism is Carlo Ginzburg, *Il nicodemismo: simulazione et dissimulazione religiosa nell'Europa del '500* (Turin, 1970). For the attacks of Calvin and other leading Protestants on Nicodemism see Carlos M. N. Eire, 'Calvin and Nicodemism: A Reappraisal', *Sixteenth Century Journal*, 10 (1979), pp. 45–69; Carlos M. N. Eire, 'Calvin's Attack on Nicodemism and Religious Compromise', *Archiv für Reformationsgeschichte*, 76 (1985), pp. 45–69; Peter Matheson, 'Martyrdom or Mission? A Protestant Debate', *Archiv für Reformationsgeschichte*, 80 (1989), pp. 154–72, and Andrew Pettegree, *Marian Protestantism: Six Studies* (Aldershot, 1996), pp. 86–117.
[71] David Nicholls, 'The Theatre of Martyrdom in the French Reformation', *Past and Present*, 121 (1988), pp. 49–73 at p. 66.
[72] Ryrie, *The Gospel and Henry VIII*, pp. 13–57, esp. pp. 23–39.
[73] Ibid., pp. 48–9 and 53–7.

(Admittedly, Henry himself brought investigations of heresy to an abrupt halt once they came too close to his inner circle. Yet if a number of the king's courtiers or personal servants had been denounced by condemned heretics, Henry might have been induced to purge his court and council of heretics.)

This increasing resistance is the most interesting feature of the persecutions of the 1540s. Admittedly many prominent evangelicals, among them Thomas Becon, Robert Wisdom, Robert Singleton, Edward Crome, William Tolwin and Nicholas Shaxton, publicly recanted during this period.[74] But, now, for the first time, such behaviour was criticised by other evangelicals. Robert Crowley bitterly attacked Nicholas Shaxton for recanting in 1546.[75] And when William Tolwin, the rector of St Antholin, submitted and did public penance in 1541, John Bale responded with a detailed refutation of Tolwin's recantation and an injunction to gospellers to stand firm against Bishop Bonner. And while John Bale was not without sympathy for Tolwin, he declared that, by recanting, Tolwin had forfeited his good name for ever.[76] One Londoner, writing to his brother on 2 July 1546, described the trial and torture of Anne Askew, and referred, with apparent contempt, to 'Dr Crome's canting, recanting, decanting or double decanting'.[77] And one of the major reasons why Anne Askew wrote her remarkable account of her ordeals was to justify her earlier recantation to her co-religionists and to reassure them of her constancy.[78]

It is doubtful that the constancy of these individuals was inspired by Calvin, Bullinger or other anti-Nicodemite writers; instead, it is much more likely that it stemmed from an awareness of how high the stakes had become and the crucial importance of ensuring that those of the correct religious sympathies were in power.[79] When Edward VI succeeded Henry, with Edward Seymour and an evangelical faction firmly in power, the situation changed dramatically. As the Edwardian regime initiated radical religious reforms, it was now time for Catholic attitudes to harden. Just as evangelicals only grudgingly and gradually lost faith in Henry VIII, conservatives were initially unwilling to acknowledge the radicalism of Edwardian religious reforms. As they witnessed the damage that

---

[74] Susan Brigden, *London and the Reformation* (Oxford, 1989), pp. 336, 348–52 and 363–70; also see Susan Wabuda, 'Equivocation and Recantation during the English Reformation: The "Subtle Shadows" of Dr Edward Crome', *Journal of Ecclesiastical History*, 44 (1993), pp. 224–42. Ryrie, in particular, emphasises the 'culture of recantation' among evangelicals in this period (Ryrie, *Gospel and Henry VIII*, pp. 85–9). Ryrie is entirely correct, especially as he is contrasting the often ambivalent reality with the mythology of stark martyrdom and persecution created by Foxe. However, this was a transitional period and I believe that I am also correct in emphasising the new and increasing intolerance of compromise in the face of persecution that began to appear in this period.

[75] Robert Crowley, *The confutation of the xiii articles whereunto Nicholas Shaxton subscribed* (1548), RSTC 6083.

[76] John Bale, *Yet a course at the Romyshe foxe* (Antwerp, 1543), RSTC 1309, fo. 39r–v.

[77] *L&P*, XXI: 2, p. 586.

[78] See *Examinations of Anne Askew*, pp. 58–63, for Anne's detailed and somewhat defensive account of the signing of her recantation.

[79] See Ryrie, *Gospel and Henry VIII*, pp. 84–5, for the limited impact Continental debates on Nicodemism had in England during this period.

had been done, however, leading conservatives such as Stephen Gardiner and Edmund Bonner reluctantly came to resist the new religious order and eventually they went to prison rather than accept the new royal religious policies.

During Mary's reign, the lines were drawn even more starkly. English Protestant leaders, many of whom had close personal and ideological ties to the anti-Nicodemite Swiss Reformers, declared that Protestants could not, at the risk of imperiling their souls, attend Mass. This message was zealously, if not endlessly, broadcast to the Protestant laity.[80] Surprisingly, the message took hold, despite the obvious risks it carried for Marian Protestants; consistent failure to attend Mass could not fail to attract attention and was frequently the high road to the stake. Even so, hundreds of people refused to compromise their consciences and paid the ultimate price.[81]

This defiance marks a sea change in the history of English religious dissent. Generally, individual Lollards and Henrician evangelicals had not hesitated to recant their beliefs in order to survive and their co-religionists did not think the worse of them for doing so.[82] As late as 1546, no less a figure than John Hooper, who would become the second Marian martyr to be burned, was sceptical of Calvin's anti-Nicodemism and felt that it might be permissible to attend Mass; a position that he would vehemently reject less than a decade later.[83] A number of Marian Protestants did recant, but in this changed climate such actions were regarded as shameful aberrations to be passed over in silence or explained away.[84]

---

[80] See Thomas Freeman, ' "The Good Ministrye of Godlye and Vertuouse Women": The Elizabethan Martyrologists and the Female Supporters of the Marian Martyrs', *Journal of British Studies*, 39 (2000), pp. 12–13.
[81] The experiences of Gertrude Crockhay are indicative of both the pressures that the refusal to attend Catholic services placed on evangelicals and their increasing reluctance to compromise. In 1557, she had to flee overseas after she stood godmother to a child who was baptised in a clandestine service conducted according to the Edwardian rite. Returning to London, while Mary was still on the throne, she was finally persuaded to attend evensong. Afterwards, she was conscience-stricken and convinced that she was damned. The leader of the chief London underground Protestant congregation, John Rough, comforted her and persuaded her to confess her fault to the congregation. She did so, but soon fell mortally ill afterwards. She refused the last rites and contemptuously dismissed the threat that she would be denied a Christian burial, declaring that she was happy that she would not rise with those buried according to the rites of the Church, but would instead rise against them. She was indeed denied burial in consecrated ground, but her husband finally persuaded the authorities to allow him to bury her in his garden rather than to have her interred alongside a highway (*A&M [1583]*, pp. 2145–6).
[82] See Hudson, *Premature Reformation*, p. 158, and Wabuda, 'Equivocation and Recantation', pp. 224–42.
[83] *Original Letters*, ed. Hastings Robinson, Parker Society, 2 vols (Cambridge, 1846–7), I, pp. 38–40. However, by the beginning of Mary's reign, Hooper's views had altered. He wrote to a group of Protestants, sharply admonishing them not to 'pollute' themselves 'with any rites, ceremonies, or usages not instituted by God'. He concluded: 'I know there be many evasions made by men and [they] judge a man may with suregard of conscience be at the masse. But forasmuch as M. Calvine, M. Bullynger, and others have thoroughly answered them, such as be in doubte, may reade theyr bookes' (*Certain most godly, fruitful and comfortable letters of such true saintes and holy martyres . . .*, ed. Henry Bull (1564), RSTC 5886, pp. 143–5).
[84] When Robert Watson, a prominent Norwich Protestant and a former protégé of Archbishop Cranmer, secured his release from prison in 1555 by signing a qualified statement of belief in the Eucharist, he wrote and printed a defensive account of his arrest and release within months (see Robert Watson, *Aetiologia*

But why did this sudden repudiation of Nicodemism occur and why did it gain such wide acceptance?

Leading Protestants in Mary's reign may have been clear-sighted enough to realise that the continued existence of Protestantism, in the face of sustained persecution, depended on a widespread refusal to compromise with the Catholic authorities.[85] (And this in turn underscores one crucial difference between the Marian Protestants and earlier religious dissidents in England, such as the Lollards or the Henrician evangelicals: to a startling degree the old Edwardian clerical elite succeeded in maintaining their leadership over the committed Protestant laity.)[86] This, however, does not explain why so many ordinary Protestants refused to save themselves through outward conformity. Perhaps the shock of having the high expectations of complete godly reform, which flourished in Edward VI's reign, suddenly blasted in Mary's reign, convinced many Protestants that these were desperate times, if not the end times, which necessitated intransigent resistance to evil. The sudden, apparently unquestioning, rejection of Nicodemism by many rank and file Protestants is one of the unexplained mysteries of the English Reformation, but it ensured that the persecution of Protestants in Mary's reign had seminal importance.

For one thing, the refusal on this scale of religious dissidents to save themselves by denying, or even concealing, their beliefs was unprecedented and it meant the Marian persecution would have a remarkable immediate impact. That this impact was perpetuated across centuries, ensuring that the fires of Smithfield always smouldered, was the achievement of John Foxe. It was all but inevitable that there would be a martyrological response to the Marian persecution; it was by no means inevitable that this response would be a massive history of the Church, from the apostolic era to Elizabeth. A group of Marian exiles planned two martyrologies, one in English, one in Latin; the Latin martyrology was duly composed by Foxe, the English martyrology – apparently planned as a collection of the writings of the Marian martyrs – was never written, although Foxe would

---

Roberti Watsoni Angli, in qua explicatur, quare deprehensus annum unum & menses pene quatuor, propter Evangelium incarceratus fuit . . . (Emden, 1556), RSTC 25111, as well as the *ODNB* article on Watson). When rumours circulated that he had recanted, Hooper immediately sent a letter from prison, angrily denying the rumours. Numerous manuscript copies of this letter survive, indicating its wide dissemination (Emmanuel College Library MS 260, fos. 225v–226r and 251r; BL, Lansdowne MS 389, fos. 4v–5r and BL, Additional MS 19400, fo. 28r).

[85] It is worth noting that, in the next reign, when Catholics were faced with sanctions for refusing to attend church, leading Catholic clergy began to insist on a policy of forbidding outward conformity to a heretical regime; on this topic, see Alexandra Walsham, *Church Papists: Catholicism, Conformity and Confessional Polemic in Early Modern England* (Woodbridge, 1999). It is suggestive that Catholic writers, arguing that attendance at Church of England services was sinful, repeated – and even cited – the anti-Nicodemite writings of Continental Reformers and Marian martyrs (Walsham, *Church Papists*, pp. 36–7).

[86] This is a point that has not been sufficiently emphasised or explored. See, however, Thomas S. Freeman, 'Publish and Perish: The Scribal Culture of the Marian Martyrs', in *The Uses of Script and Print, 1300–1700*, ed. Julia Crick and Alexandra Walsham (Cambridge, 2004), pp. 235–54, and Thomas S. Freeman, 'Dissenters from a Dissenting Church'.

eventually make use of the material collected for it.[87] Several lists of the Marian martyrs (one, by Thomas Brice, in verse) and numerous printings or reprintings of the works of individual martyrs appeared between the death of Mary Tudor and the first edition of Foxe's *Acts and Monuments* in 1563.[88] Essentially Foxe treated all of his smaller competitors in the same way that US Steel treated its rivals; he swallowed them up and incorporated them into one giant monopoly.[89] In doing so, Foxe made the persecutions of Lollards, evangelicals and early English Protestants – at least for English Protestant readers – an integral part of the history of the Church. He also immortalised the Marian persecution by including a graphic and detailed account of it in a work which, in its unabridged form, remained in print until 1684, and which, in innumerable abridgements, never went out of print.[90]

Foxe not only enshrined the Marian martyrs, he also enshrined a Christ-like type of martyrdom, which these martyrs personified: stoical, calm and passive.[91] Foxe did not create this new model of martyrdom; in applying this standard to his martyrs, he was following in the footsteps of his mentor, John Bale. But Foxe's work established this model as the one to which all English Protestant martyrological writers sought to conform. Moreover, Foxe was driven to embrace this Christocentric model even more fervently by the strictures of his most severe and relentless critic, Nicholas Harpsfield. In the most substantial and important contemporary criticism of the *Acts and Monuments*, the sixth dialogue of his *Dialogi sex*, Harpsfield castigated Foxe over and over again for glorifying 'pseudo-

---

[87] See BL, Harley MS 417, fo. 119r; printed in *The Remains of Edmund Grindal*, ed. William Nicholson (Cambridge, 1843), pp. 226–7.
[88] Lists of the Marian martyrs are in: Thomas Brice, *A compendious regester in metre* . . . (1559), RSTC 3726; Robert Crowley, *An epitome of cronicles . . . continued to the reigne of Quene Elizabeth* (1559), RSTC 15217.5, and John Knox, *The copie of an epistle sent unto the inhabitants of Newcastle and Berwicke* (Geneva, 1559), RSTC 15064. Writings of the Marian martyrs printed during this brief period include: John Bradford, *A godlye meditacyon compared by J. B. latelye burnte in Smithfielde* (1559), RSTC 3483; John Bradford, *Godlie meditacions* . . . (1559), RSTC 3483; John Bradford, *The complaynt of veritie, made by J. Bradford* . . . (1559), RSTC 3479 (this also contains writings by Ralph Allerton, John Hooper and Robert Smith); John Bradford, *All the examinacions of the martir J. Bradforde* . . . (1561), RSTC 3477; John Bradford, *The hurte of hearing masse* (1561?), RSTC 3494; John Hooper, *An apologye made by the reverende father J. Hooper* . . ., ed. Henry Bull (1562), RSTC 13742; Hugh Latimer, *27 sermons preached by the ryght reverende . . . maister Hugh Latimer*, ed. Augustine Bernher (1562), RSTC 15726 and Nicholas Ridley, *A frendly farewel, which maister doctor Ridley, did write* . . ., ed. John Foxe (1559). A set of John Hooper's sermons, *An oversight, and deliberation upon the prophete Jonas* (RSTC 13764), was reprinted, after a gap of ten years since the last edition, in 1560.
[89] The most important and most striking example of Foxe incorporating a rival martyrological work into his own *Acts and Monuments* is his competition, then colloboration, with Henry Bull, the editor of an important collection of letters written by the Marian martyrs. See Susan Wabuda, 'Henry Bull, Miles Coverdale, and the Making of Foxe's "Book of Martyrs" ', in *Martyrs and Martyrologies*, ed. Diana Wood, Studies in Church History 30 (Oxford, 1993), pp. 245–58, and Freeman, ' "Good Ministrye" ', pp. 8–33.
[90] See the references in n. 2 above.
[91] See Patrick Collinson, ' "A Magazine of Religious Patterns": An Erasmian Topic Transposed in English Protestantism', in *Godly People: Essays on English Protestantism and Puritanism* (1983), pp. 499–525; Thomas S. Freeman, 'The Importance of Dying Earnestly: The Metamorphosis of the Account of James Bainham in Foxe's Book of Martyrs', in *The Church Retrospective*, ed. R. N. Swanson, Studies in Church History 33 (1997), pp. 267–88, and the next chapter in this volume.

martyrs' as martyrs. Harpsfield disparaged Foxe's heroes and heroines as true martyrs for a number of reasons: some were criminals and rebels, most unlearned, some demon-possessed and a few were insane.[92] But one fundamental reason disqualified them all: they died for heresy, not the true faith of Christ. As Harpsfield put it: 'We oppose Foxe, not with the number of martyrs, but rather with their weight, not with their deaths, but with the causes of their deaths.'[93]

In applying this patristic criterion (so alien to the popular medieval concepts of martyrs as innocent victims, ascetics or virgins), which made suffering for true religion the essence of martyrdom, Harpsfield forced Foxe to revise the later editions of the *Acts and Monuments*. At times (when Harpsfield's objections were too cogent for comfort) Foxe did this by silent excision of controversial material.[94] At other times, where he thought he could make a case, Foxe launched elaborate and lengthy counter-attacks.[95] But whether he was accentuating the positive or eliminating the negative, Foxe was always refining, revising and reshaping his work so that it presented his 'athletes of Christ' with the attributes that he and Harpsfield agreed constituted a true martyr: the willingness to die for true doctrine and zeal in imitating Christ's passion as closely as possible. What Foxe and Harpsfield contested were not the characteristics of a true martyr, but merely whether Catholic or Protestant victims of persecution possessed those characteristics. Neither Foxe nor Harpsfield was original in defining these characteristics. Leaving aside their indebtedness to biblical, patristic and classical authors, they also drew heavily on the writings of earlier co-religionists; in the case of Foxe, on Bale, in the case of Harpsfield, on the writings of Thomas More and Miles Hogarde.[96] What differentiated the martyrological and anti-martyrological writings of Foxe

---

[92] Harpsfield, *Dialogi sex*, pp. 745–50, 767–8, 826–61, 894–5 and 959–61.

[93] 'Nos non tamen numero, quam pondere, nec tam morte, quam causa mortis contra Foxum pugnamus' (Harpsfield, *Dialogi sex*, p. 992).

[94] For example, Harpsfield's attack on Foxe's account, in his first edition, of a miracle that allegedly took place at the execution of martyrs in Brentford, resulted in Foxe omitting this story from subsequent editions (cf. *A&M [1563]*, p. 1670, with Nicholas Harpsfield, *Dialogi sex*, p. 962). Similarly, Harpsfield's arguments that John Randall, whom Foxe claimed was murdered by Catholics, actually committed suicide, were persuasive enough to induce Foxe to omit all mention of Randall in subsequent editions of his martyrology (cf. *A&M [1563]*, p. 490, with Harpsfield, *Dialogi sex*, pp. 747–8) And Harpsfield's objections that an oration Foxe addressed to Henry VIII, criticising the king for executing God's saints, 'proved' that Henry was not legitimately the supreme head of the English Church, led Foxe to drop the oration from his work (cf. *A&M [1563]*, pp. 533–4, and Harpsfield, *Dialogi sex*, pp. 989–91).

[95] Harpsfield's attack on Foxe's detailed criticisms of Oldcastle and his followers (*Dialogi sex*, pp. 747, 832–6 and 953–4) met with a massive rebuttal (*A&M [1570]*, pp. 633–700); Harpsfield's all too accurate description of the errors in Foxe's account of Eleanor Cobham and Roger Bolingbroke (or as Foxe referred to him, Roger Onley) was met with an elaborate (albeit tendentious) response (cf. *Dialogi sex*, pp. 826–31 with *A&M [1570]*, pp. 830–2); Harpsfield's claim that Thomas Bilney had recanted and thus was not a martyr (*Dialogi sex*, pp. 822–3) led to Foxe's detailed account of Bilney's death and martyrdom (*A&M [1570]*, pp. 1146–52), and Harpsfield's denial that Richard Hunne was murdered (*Dialogi sex*, pp. 847–9) inspired a rejoinder from Foxe (*A&M [1570]*, pp. 936–9).

[96] For More's influence on Harpsfield's anti-martyrology see Dillon, *Construction of Martyrdom*, pp. 64–6 and 342, although, in my opinion, Dillon overstates More's admittedly considerable influence. On Hogarde see Wizeman's chapter in this volume. For an example of an instance where Harpsfield appears to be echoing Hogarde compare the latter's rebutting claims that there were no English Catholic martyrs by

and Harpsfield from the writings of their predecessors was not a difference in conceptions of martyrdom, but the systematic way in which both presented these concepts. It was their thoroughness and the scale of their respective works, not their originality, that gave Foxe and Harpsfield their very considerable influence. Between them, Foxe and Harpsfield, the hammer and the anvil, forged the concept of martyrdom accepted by English Catholics and Protestants alike.

V

The struggle between intertwined martyrologies and anti-martyrologies lasted long after the lifetimes of Foxe and Harpsfield. Harpsfield's criticisms of Foxe seeped deeply into Recusant culture; for example, the Catholic convert William Alabaster composed a sonnet drawing on Harpsfield's attacks on Foxe's calendar of saints.[97] And Thomas Pounde, the Jesuit, sent another poem, casting Harpsfield's criticisms of Foxe (indeed some of the specific passages in *Dialogi sex*) into English verse, to an imprisoned Catholic.[98] Furthermore, just as Foxe had numerous imitators, so did Harpsfield. Nearly thirty years after Harpsfield's death, his criticisms of Foxe in the *Dialogi sex* formed the core of Robert Persons's *Treatise of Three Conversions*, a massive three-volume assault on the *Acts and Monuments* and the martyrs celebrated in it.[99] Thanks, in large part, to their repetition by Persons, many of Harpsfield's charges proved remarkably enduring.[100] These accusations not only damaged Foxe's reputation for accuracy, they perpetuated the concepts of true and false martyrdom held by both Foxe and Harpsfield. Victor Houliston's contribution to this volume has been to analyse Persons's seminal anti-martyrology in depth, placing it within the escalating, and

citing the examples of Alban, Thomas Becket and others (Miles Hogarde, *The displaying of the protestantes* (1556), RSTC 13558, fos. 66v–67v) with Harpsfield's rebutting the same argument by citing the same examples (Harpsfield, *Dialogi sex*, pp. 973–5). Also note the virtually identical lists of Henrician martyrs presented by Hogarde (*Displaying*, fos. 68v–69v) and Harpsfield (*Dialogi sex*, pp. 993–4).

[97] William Alabaster, *The Sonnets of William Alabaster*, ed. G. M. Story and Helen Gardner (Oxford, 1959), p. 3. This sonnet was written around 1597 or 1598 (see p. xxxvii), so it was not based on Persons's similar criticisms.

[98] TNA, SP 12/157, fos. 105r–110v. I am grateful to Alison Shell for directing me to this poem.

[99] Persons is, in general, not good about citing his sources, but he acknowledged his debt to the *Dialogi sex* numerous times (see Robert Persons, *A treatise of three Conversions of England* (3 vols, St Omer, 1604), RSTC 19416, II, pp. 77, 199, 269–70, 272–8 and III, pp. 279–84). And Persons's attack on the martyrs listed in the calendar of martyrs at the beginning of the *Acts and Monuments*, which takes up the second and third volumes of the *Three Conversions*, is a systematic development of the themes in Harpsfield's earlier attack on the martyrs in Foxe's calendar (Harpsfield, *Dialogi sex*, pp. 820–62).

[100] For example, Foxe, in the first edition of his martyrology, confused Henry Filmer, a martyr who was burned in 1543, with John Marbeck, a fellow evangelical who was convicted, but pardoned, for the same offence (*A&M [1563]*, pp. 625–6). Harpsfield spotted the error and suggested that this demonstrated Foxe's inaccuracy (*Dialogi sex*, pp. 962–3). Robert Persons repeated Harpsfield's charge in his *Treatise of Three Conversions*, III, pp. 62–3; Thomas Fuller denied it in his *The history of the Worthies of England* (1662), STC [Wing] F2440, pp. 91–2. The story of Foxe's error was, however, repeated for centuries; see, for example, John Milner, *The History Civil and Ecclesiastical . . . of Winchester* (2 vols, 1798), I, pp. 357–8.

intertwining, English Catholic and Protestant martyrological and anti-martyrological traditions.

Despite the importance of Harpsfield's anti-martyrology, and despite the effloresence of Catholic martyrological writing in Mary's reign, English Catholics did not develop a sustained martyrological tradition in print until the closing decades of the sixteenth century.[101] The Northern Rising of 1569, and Pius V's ill-judged excommunication of Elizabeth, triggered new persecution of Catholics. Yet once again, persecution did not instantly inspire martyrology. Three priests and eight Catholic laymen were executed in the decade following the excommunication of Elizabeth, yet only two works printed in this decade, neither of them martyrologies, extolled these victims as martyrs.[102]

This situation changed permanently and dramatically with the arrival of the Jesuits in England. William Allen, the future cardinal and, at this time, the head of the English Seminary at Douai, believed that martyrdom was the most efficacious means of restoring Catholicism in England.[103] For years he had lobbied for a mission to England and for years Everard Mercurian, the superior general of the Jesuits, had refused to approve it, partly from fears that such a mission would provoke the Elizabethan authorities to increased persecution of English Catholics.[104] When Mercurian finally agreed to authorise the mission, he ordered that it be conducted with discretion. There were be no direct dealings with heretics and Mercurian specifically forbade disputations with Protestants except in cases of absolute necessity.[105] In the event, these orders were not followed and instead Campion issued his famous 'Brag', a defiant challenge to the Elizabethan authorities to a formal debate. It has been traditionally maintained that the release of the 'Brag' was due to an innocent error, but Thomas McCoog has recently suggested

[101] Accounts of Catholic martyrs, particularly Thomas More, continued to circulate in manuscript (see Dillon, *Construction of Martyrdom*, pp. 46–7, Gregory, *Salvation at Stake*, p. 270, and Michael Questier, 'Catholicism, Kinship and the Public Memory of Sir Thomas More', *Journal of Ecclesiastical History*, 53 (2002), pp. 476–509). However, Thomas Stapleton's hagiography of More was not printed until 1612, William Roper's biography of his father-in-law was not printed until 1626, and Cresacre More's biography was only printed around 1631. The biographies by 'Ro. Ba.' and Nicholas Harpsfield were not published until the nineteenth century.

[102] The priests were John Storey, Cuthbert Mayne and Everard Haunse. I am counting Thomas Sherwood, a Douai student who was not yet ordained, as a layman. The two works hailing the condemned as martyrs are Nicholas Sander's *De visibili monarchia* (1571) and Richard Bristow's *A briefe treatise of divers plain and sure ways* (1574). See Thomas M. McCoog, 'Construing Martyrdom in the English Catholic Community, 1582–1602', in *Catholics and the 'Protestant Nation': Religious Politics and Identity in Early Modern England*, ed. Ethan Shagan (Manchester, 2005), p. 96, and Dillon, *Construction of Martyrdom*, p. 13.

[103] Eamon Duffy, 'William, Cardinal Allen, 1532–1594', *Recusant History*, 22 (1995), pp. 278–9.

[104] Thomas M. McCoog, ' "Striking Fear in Heretical Hearts": Mercurian and British Religious Exiles', in *The Mercurian Project: Forming Jesuit Culture, 1573–1580*. ed. Thomas M. McCoog (Rome and St Louis, 2004), pp. 645–73, and Thomas M. McCoog, 'The English Jesuit Mission and the French Match, 1579–81', *Catholic Historical Review*, 87 (2001), pp. 185–213.

[105] Thomas M. McCoog, ' "Playing the Champion": The Role of Disputation in the Jesuit Mission', in *The Reckoned Expense: Edmund Campion and the Early English Jesuits*, ed. Thomas M. McCoog (Woodbridge, 1996), pp. 119–39, esp. p. 125, and McCoog, 'French Match', p. 211.

that Campion, who advocated a more confrontational strategy than Mercurian did, deliberately issued the 'Brag' to force a disputation both upon Elizabeth's government and upon Mercurian.[106]

If Campion wished to provoke the Elizabethan authorities, he was spectacularly successful. The 'Brag', along with Campion's subsequent arrest, resulted in the public disputation that Campion had wished for.[107] And Campion's execution on 1 December 1581 opened the floodgates for a torrent of martyrological works, of which the most important were Robert Persons's *De persecutione Anglicana* and William Allen's *Glorious Martyrdom of XII Reverend Priests*.[108] The glorification of these martyrs now committed the English Catholics to printing martyrologies on a scale which exceeded any previous efforts to extol More, Fisher or the Carthusians and it likewise committed the English Protestants to extensive anti-martyrological attacks. The martyrological wars had intensified, but they were still being fought according to the standards deployed by Foxe and Harpsfield, and before them More and Bale.[109]

There were obvious benefits for English Catholics in commemorating the martyrdoms of Campion and the mission priests. Undoubtedly they helped to raise the morale of English Catholics and to provide a sense of cohesion for a persecuted minority. For the mission priests themselves an additional benefit may well have been their usefulness as examples in combating church papistry (that is, the belief that it was morally legitimate to attend Church of England services while inwardly remaining Catholic). Martyrs, who died in agony rather than renounce their faith, were a potent reproach to those who concealed their faith in order to avoid fines. It is probably not coincidental that systematic Catholic printed polemic against conformity and attendance at Church of England services dates from 1578, on the eve of the mission to England, with Gregory Martin's *Treatise of Schism*. In 1580, as the evangelising campaign he was conducting with Edmund Campion reached its zenith, Robert Persons rushed his *Brief Discourse Containing Certain Reasons why Catholics Refuse to Go to Church* into print.[110] Moreover, Thomas Worthington's account of the Jesuit martyr John Rigby, a former Catholic layman and repentent church papist, was specifically designed, *inter alia*, to warn Catholics of the spiritual dangers of outward confor-

[106] McCoog, ' "Playing the Champion" ', pp. 127–9 and 137–8, as well as McCoog, 'French Match', pp. 211–12.
[107] Peter Lake and Michael Questier, 'Puritans, Papists and the "Public Sphere" in Early Modern England: The Edmund Campion Affair in Context', *Journal of Modern History*, 72 (2000), pp. 587–627.
[108] See Thomas M. McCoog, ' "The Flower of Oxford": The Role of Edmund Campion in Early Recusant Polemics', *Sixteenth Century Journal*, 24 (1993), pp. 899–913, esp. 907–10.
[109] See in particular Dillon, *Construction of Martyrdom*, pp. 1–113. Peter Lake and Michael Questier brilliantly describe the strenuous efforts of Catholic martyrs to conform to these standards, and the equally strenuous efforts of the Protestant authorities to subvert these attempts, although they do not relate these behaviours to earlier martyrological and anti-martyrological traditions (*Antichrist's Lewd Hat: Protestants, Papists and Players in Post-Reformation England* (New Haven, CT, 2002), pp. 243–9.
[110] Walsham, *Church Papists*, pp. 24–5.

mity to the Church of England.[111] Martyrologies were also useful in winning sympathy for English Catholics from Catholics overseas, sympathy which could be transformed into financial aid, diplomatic pressure on the English government for toleration, and possibly even military intervention on their behalf.[112]

Yet there were also severe disadvantages for Catholics in producing martyrologies. These may have inflamed Catholics, in England and abroad, against the Elizabethan government, but they also provoked the outraged English authorities into a more intense persecution of Catholics. While William Allen and Robert Persons felt that Campion's death strengthened the faith of English Catholics, Claudio Acquaviva, Mercurian's successor, disagreed and considered not renewing the English mission. He only reluctantly changed his mind upon Persons's inaccurate assurance that the persecution would abate.[113] However, Acquaviva also apparently urged that the Jesuits concentrate on devotional, rather than martyrological, writing. (It is significant that in this period, Persons abandoned a projected biography of Edmund Campion and instead produced his classic *Book of Resolution*.)[114] Jasper Heywood, the deputy superior of the English mission, also opposed the production of martyrological works as counterproductive and needlessly confrontational; it has even been suggested that Heywood refused to authorise the printing of William Allen's *Glorious Martyrdom of XII Reverend Priests*.[115] As a result, while martyrological works devoted to English Catholics were printed throughout Europe in Latin, French, Spanish, German, Italian and Flemish, there was a dearth of Catholic martyrologies printed in English after 1582.[116]

English Catholic martyrology revived early in the seventeenth century because of its potency as a polemical weapon – albeit this time against an enemy within the same confessional fold. As the Appellant controversy intensified, both the Jesuits and the secular clergy began to claim the English Catholic martyrs for their own. Just as true martyrs were considered an indisputable sign of the sanctity of one side or another in inter-confessional conflicts, so they were held to validate the rectitude of one side or another in intra-confessional conflicts. (There was nothing novel in this tactic; in Mary's reign when the persecuted Protestants split into predestinarian and 'freewiller' factions, the predestinarians eagerly appropriated the Marian martyrs to gain a polemical advantage over the

---

[111] Dillon, *Construction of Martyrdom*, pp. 111–12. For other manuscript accounts of lay Cathololic martyrs which emphasise the desired virtues of refusal to attend Church of England services, refusal to deny the Catholic faith and lay subordination to clerical authority see Marotti, *Religious Ideology*, pp. 74–6.

[112] McCoog, ' "Playing the Champion" ', pp. 100–6; also see Williams, 'Campion and the English Continental Seminaries', pp. 295–6.

[113] Thomas M. McCoog, *The Society of Jesus in Ireland, Scotland and England, 1541–88: "Our Way of Proceeding?"* (Leiden, 1996), pp. 174–7.

[114] McCoog, 'Construing Martyrdom', pp. 100–3.

[115] Ibid., pp. 102–3.

[116] Ibid., pp. 100–6. The operative word here is 'printed': manuscript accounts of English martyrs and manuscript copies of their writings circulated among English Catholics throughout this period.

freewillers.)[117] In 1601, Thomas Worthington, the president of the English College at Douai, penned the first Catholic martyrology written in English since 1582.[118] This martyrology not only glorified Jesuit martyrs, it also used their executions, particularly the recent execution of John Rigby, to discredit Appellant arguments that Elizabeth's government was inclined to leniency in its dealings with Catholics.[119] This was the first salvo in the barrages of new martyrologies, and counter barrages of new anti-martyrologies, as the Jesuits and seculars each tried to appropriate as many martyrs for their causes as possible and also to denigrate the martyrs appropriated by their rivals. Even after the initial issues that kindled the Appellant controversy were settled, a new issue (the possibility of Catholic bishops being reinstated in England) hurled additional fuel into the fire.[120] These controversies generated further martyrological writing – including competing lists of genuine martyrs drawn up by the different factions – and laid the enduring foundations for English Catholic martyrological traditions.

Throughout the sixteenth century, the martyrological battles between the different confessions temporarily eased, only to be later renewed with increased vigour. After a faltering start, Protestant martyrology blossomed with the writings of Bale and then Foxe. In Mary's reign, the Henrician Catholic martyrs were memorialised and subsequently Pole's protégé challenged Foxe's martyrology with the first systematic anti-martyrology of the English Reformation. In 1581, Catholics initiated a series of martyrologies devoted to Campion and the mission priests. On each of these occasions, there were other, less confrontational strategies, that could have been employed. Instead, like rival bridge players, each side bid martyrs and then doubled and redoubled their bids. By the end of the century, Catholic and Protestant had established competing martyrological traditions and each confession carefully cultivated the memory of their own martyrs.

VI

Yet although these traditions were in competition, they were based on the same conceptions of martyrdom. These conceptions were interchangeable between the different confessions, and because they were interchangeable, the martyrological traditions built on each other, sharing not the same martyrs, but the same ideals of martyrdom. 'William Prynne's spectacularly public testing of boundaries and subsequent mutilation owed a great deal to the model of Edward Campion, while Campion's script can itself be read as an inverted chapter out of John Foxe.'[121] As

---

[117] Freeman, 'Dissenters', pp. 152–5.
[118] Thomas Worthington, *A relation of sixtene martyrs* (Douai, 1601), RSTC 26000.9.
[119] McCoog, 'Construing Martyrdom', pp. 106–18.
[120] Ibid., pp. 118–20; also see Lake and Questier, *Antichrist's Lewd Hat*, pp. 299–307.
[121] Shagan, 'Introduction', *Catholics and the "Protestant Nation"*, pp. 16–17. For a narrative account of the martyrdom of Prynne, see David Cressy, 'The Portraiture of Prynne's Picture's: Performance in the Public Stage', in *Travesties and Transgressions in Stuart England* (Oxford, 2000), pp. 213–33. For Prynne,

a result, the competing martyrological traditions acted as flying buttresses, coming from different directions to support the same ideas of martyrdom. By the seventeenth century, the varied conceptions of martyrdom prevalent in late-medieval England had largely been replaced by a single dominant conception of the martyr as someone who suffered, as Christ had suffered, meekly, passively and stoically.[122]

Moreover, as attempts to establish a national Protestant Church in England succeeded only in creating increasing numbers of Protestant dissenters, each dissident group established its own martyrological tradition. As Alexandra Walsham has observed, 'Among sixteenth- and seventeenth-century religious minorities, only the Family of Love failed to generate its own literature of perse-cution.'[123] (The reason for this is basic; the Family of Love was also alone in unequivocably encouraging conformity and Nicodemism. This is a compelling indication of the importance of anti-Nicodemism in fostering both resistance and martyrologies.)[124] But radical Protestants in England, unlike their Continental counterparts, used the standards and methodologies of their magisterial Protestant opponents, as epitomised in Foxe's *Acts and Monuments*, to create their own martyrological traditions.[125] John Field, the great propagandist of nascent presbyterianism, who had, at an early stage of his career, assisted Foxe by collecting information, initiated the traditions of dissenting martyrology by amassing a 'register' of documents recording the persecution of the godly from the years 1565–89.[126]

Foxean martyr narratives formed a continuous tradition within the English dissenting tradition from Field through the martyrologies and biographies of Samuel Clarke to Edmund Calamy's compendium of ejected ministers. But it was the Quakers who raised the imitation of John Foxe to its apogee. George Fox urged his followers to compile records of their sufferings (including any relevant documents). These accounts were to be sent to London, where Ellis Hookes, the first recording clerk of the Society of Friends, compiled a 'Book of Sufferings' that eventually swelled to forty-four folios in manuscript.[127] In the middle of the next century, Joseph Besse would use this material as the basis for a Quaker

and his fellow sufferers, deploying martyrological tropes to describe their ordeals, see the next chapter in this volume.

[122] See the next chapter in this volume for detailed discussion of this point.

[123] Walsham, *Charitable Hatred*, p. 173.

[124] On the the Familists see Christopher Marsh, *The Family of Love in English Society, 1550–1630* (Cambridge, 1993).

[125] Gregory, *Salvation at Stake*, pp. 219–31.

[126] Some of these documents were printed around 1593 (*A parte of a regester, contayning sundrie memo-rable matters . . .* (Middleburg, 1593), RSTC 10400); the remainder are MSS Morrice A and B at Dr Williams's Library and are calendered as *A seconde parte of a Regester*, ed. Albert Peele (2 vols, Cambridge, 1915). On Field and the compilation of his register see Patrick Collinson, 'John Field and Eliz-abethan Puritanism', in *Godly People*, pp. 335–70.

[127] George Fox, *A collection of many select and Christian epistles, letters and testimonies* (1698), STC [Wing] F1764, pp. 108–9. Also see John R. Knott, *Discourses of Martyrdom in English Literature, 1563–1694* (Cambridge, 1993), p. 217.

martyrology, which was modelled on the *Acts and Monuments*, in its documentation, methodology and thematic emphases.[128]

The Quaker accounts of their persecution epitomised a further important shift in the model provided by Foxe, as the Quaker martyrs differed from their Marian precursors in one crucial respect: although they suffered, sometimes grievously, for their cause (apart from a handful of Quakers executed in New England) none were put to death for it.[129] On one level, this observation unduly minimises the ordeals Quakers endured; hundreds died in prison and some died as a result of mob violence. Yet the manner of these deaths was difficult to fit within the Foxean paradigm of official, state-sponsored executions. Furthermore, since many persecuted Quakers were punished with the loss of goods, money or liberty, martyrdom in Quaker martyrological writings consisted of fines, imprisonment and the destruction of property (the latter described in great detail in Besse's work). Similarly, none of the subjects of what was arguably the greatest Nonconformist martyrology, Edmund Calamy's *Account*, were executed. They were the ministers ejected from their livings when the Act of Uniformity came into force on St Bartholomew's day, 24 August 1662.

Although the penalty was the loss of livings rather than the loss of lives, dissenters regarded, and described, these expulsions as martyrdoms, as when the ejected minister John Quick later referred to 'that unrighteous act, which *slew* in one day two thousand able and faithfull ministers of the gospell'.[130] Quick was implicitly making a comparison that other dissenters made explicitly, between the ejections of St Bartholomew's day 1662 and the notorious massacre of Protestants that took place on the same day in Paris in 1572. The Nonconformist minister, Philip Henry, who was expelled from his living, wrote on the first anniversary of the Act of Uniformity: 'this day twelve month I dyed, that fatal day to the godly faithful members of England, amongst whom I am not worthy to be numbered'.[131] Henry's bitterness is expressed more firmly, although less overtly, in passages in his diary, noting the fourth and eighth anniversaries of the Act. He ended these passages with the phrases 'how long Lord, holy and true?' and 'how

[128] Joseph Besse, *A collection of the sufferings of the people called Quakers*, 2 vols (1753). Also see Knott, *Discourses of Martyrdom*, pp. 218–19; John R. Knott, 'Joseph Besse and the Quaker Culture of Suffering', in *The Emergence of Quaker Writing: Dissenting Literature in Seventeenth-Century England*, ed. Thomas N. Corns and David Loewenstein (1995), pp. 126–41, esp. 126, and Richard Vann, 'Friends Sufferings – Collected and Recollected', *Quaker History*, 61 (1972), pp. 24–35.
[129] On the Quaker martyrdoms in Massachusetts see David S. Lovejoy, *Religious Enthusiasm in the New World* (Cambridge, MA, 1985), pp. 127–9; Carla Pestana, *Quakers and Baptists in Colonial Massachusetts* (Cambridge, 1991), pp. 33–6, and David D. Hall, *Worlds of Wonder, Days of Judgement* (Cambridge, MA, 1989), pp. 188–9. Also note Hall's interesting description of how the Quaker martyrs in New England modelled themselves on Foxe's martyrs (pp. 187–8).
[130] Dr Williams's Library, MS 38.34/5, p. 528; this is my emphasis. I am grateful to Peter Marshall for informing me about Quick's comment.
[131] Quoted in Geoffrey L. Nuttall, 'The Nurture of Nonconformity: Philip Henry's Diaries', *Transactions of the Honourable Society of Cymrodorion*, n.s., 4 (1998), p. 10. I am grateful to Grant Tapsell for bringing this article to my attention.

long Lord?'.[132] Henry was invoking the verse in Revelation where the martyrs cry out from under the alter: 'How long, O Lord, holy and true, dost thou not judge and avenge our blood on them that dwell on the earth?' and, in doing so, he was hailing himself and the other ejected ministers as martyrs slain by Antichrist.[133] In commemorating these ejected ministers, Calamy also equated them with earlier Protestant martyrs. Calamy, in fact, closely followed the model of Foxe's martyrology for his own work, particularly in his reliance on documents.[134]

Calamy's martyrology predictably provoked angry criticism from Anglican clerics when it was printed in 1702 and twelve years later John Walker produced a massive response: *An attempt towards recovering an account of the numbers and sufferings of the clergy of the church of England . . . in the late times of the grand rebellion.* Walker's work was divided into two parts, the first an anti-martyrology and the second a martyrology. The first part was a history of the Church of England, from 1640 to 1660, intended to show that the ejection of nonconforming ministers by the Act of Uniformity was a just reprisal for their unworthy behaviour in their livings and for the persecution of Anglican clergy during the Interregnum. The second part was a catalogue of the persecuted Anglican divines.[135] Just as Calamy had aleady used Foxe, and Besse would later use Foxe, as a model for their martyrologies, so Walker consciously imitated Foxe in his work.[136] Nor was this lost on Anglican contemporaries, who persistently hailed Walker as a successor to Foxe, calling his work 'a book of martyrology' and (with the *Acts*

---

[132] Nuttall, 'Nurture of Nonconformity', p. 10.

[133] Revelation 6: 10 (Authorised Version).

[134] David L. Wykes, ' "To let the Memory of these Men Dye is injurious to Posterity": Edmund Calamay's *Account* of the Ejected Ministers', in *The Church Retrospective*, pp. 385 and 389, as well as Burke W. Griggs, 'Remembering the Puritan Past: John Walker and Anglican Memories of the English Civil War', in *Protestant Identities: Religion, Sanctity and Self-fashioning in Post-Reformation England*, ed. Muriel C. McClendon, Joseph P. Ward and Michael MacDonald (Stanford, CA, 1999), pp. 164–70.

[135] *Calamy Revised: Being a Revision of Edmund Calamy's Account of the Ministers and Others, Ejected and Silenced, 1660–62*, ed. A. G. Matthews (Oxford, 1934), pp. xx–xxvi.

[136] Burke Griggs maintains that Walker worked deliberately to separate his martyrological collection from the martyrologies of both Foxe and Calamy by following a different methodology. Walker, Griggs argues, 'aspired to Sir Francis Bacon . . . following Baconian rules for determining the reliability of observations' (Griggs, 'Remembering the Puritan Past', p. 167). Walker never refers to Bacon (something Griggs neglects to mention) and Griggs apparently bases his claim on Walker's diligent efforts to provide accurate documentation for his work, most notably in sending out questionnaires to clergy of the Church of England (ibid., pp. 166–7). Yet, while Foxe did not send out questionaires, at least to our knowledge, he certainly had letters sent to his informants, cross-checking the accuracy of their accounts. In one case, an informant wrote to John Field, who was assisting Foxe, informing Field that he could not send him an account of the supposed providential death of a Marian persecutor 'because I am not able to get any that will or are able perfectly to reporte it' (BL, Harley MS 416, fo. 188r). In another case, where facts were in dispute, Foxe had a friend reinterrogate a witness that Foxe had already interviewed, and had the friend send him written confirmation of the disputed story (see BL, Harley MS 416, fo. 174r). This case is discussed in Thomas S. Freeman, 'Fate, Faction and Fiction in Foxe's *Book of Martyrs*', *Historical Journal*, 43 (2000), pp. 601–23. The so-called 'Baconian rules' for documentation are in fact ubiquitous features of martyrologies and, in relying on them, Walker was adhering to, rather than breaking, the conventions of martyrological writing.

and Monuments clearly in mind) insisted that it 'ought to be kept in every sanctuary'.[137]

All of these writers – Besse, Calamy and Walker – and their colleagues consciously worked within a Foxean paradigm because it was polemically effective. The Quakers tried to justify their *outré* behaviour and their defiance of authority. The dissenters sought to justify their nonconformity and also to alleviate the suspicions of their loyalty that resulted from the Civil War. And the Anglicans wished to highlight the sufferings of their clergy during the two decades before the Restoration. All of the martyrological writers within these different traditions could achieve these aims by identifying the victims they extolled with Foxe's martyrs. And the imitation of Foxe's method further strengthened this identification. A Quaker writer, John Whiting, responded to the charge that Quaker victims of persecution did not show the stoicism of true martyrs, by challenging readers to examine the writings of Quakers 'in relation to their sufferings, especially their epistles, etc. . . . and compare them with the speeches and letters of the martyrs in the *Book of Martyrs*'.[138]

By following the Foxean model so closely, and yet applying it routinely to those who had suffered lesser punishments than death, English Protestants had broadened the concept of martyrdom so that it could be used not only by dissenters, but even by the established Church. In the late Middle Ages, there had been several competing definitions of what entailed true martyrdom; it could be achieved through asceticism, virginity or simply suffering unmerited death. The confessional conflicts of the Reformation undermined many of these conceptions and in the later half of the sixteenth century Foxe and Harpsfield between them defined and crystallised an idea of martyrdom, largely dormant through the later Middle Ages, which established death for doctrinal truth as the only legitimate form of martyrdom.[139] This revived standard of martyrdom also insisted that the martyr not only suffer death, but suffer it in the appropriate manner: constant but passive, stoical, in as exact an imitation of the sufferings and death of Christ as possible.[140] By the beginning of the eighteenth century, in response to the successive waves of different persecutions, carried out by different groups of persecutors against different victims, during the Civil War, Interregnum and Restoration, the definition of martyrdom had been widened. The attributes of martyrdom remained unchanged, except that lesser penalties than death now won a martyr's

---

[137] See the article on John Walker in the *ODNB* and Griggs, 'Remembering the Puritan Past', p. 190.

[138] John Whiting, *Truth and innocency defended against falshood and envy* (1702), p. 74.

[139] Harpsfield insisted that only death was sufficient to create a martyr (*Dialogi sex*, pp. 821–2; there is an additional statement to this effect added in the second edition of the *Dialogi sex*, printed in Antwerp in 1573, p. 706). Foxe, partly in response to Harpsfield, maintained in places that martyrdom could be achieved without death (e.g. *A&M [1570]*, pp. 677 and 691–2), but almost invariably the *Acts and Monuments* associated martyrdom with death.

[140] See the next chapter in this volume for a more detailed discussion of this imitation of Christ.

crown, allowing almost every sect and denomination in England to lay claim to its own martyrological tradition.

Yet the boundaries of martyrdom expanded even further than this. In the Middle Ages, as we have seen, political figures were occasionally venerated as martyrs. During the Reformation, however, the definition of martyrdom became restricted to those who suffered, not only for a religious cause, but for the *true* religion, By the latter half of the seventeenth century, however, unambigously political figures were honoured, without hesitation, as martyrs. The development of this process, and the underlying reasons which made this politicisation of martyrdom particularly potent in England, are discussed in my chapter in this volume. Here, it will suffice to say that the persecution of religious deviance on the grounds of treason and other secular chages (discussed more fully below) and the ease with which the Christocentric model of martyrdom could be applied to all victims of the trial process, whether their offences were secular or religious, all played a part. (It is significant that, in contrast to most of countries in Reformation Europe, where sustained religious persecution occurred, religious persecution in England was largely state-sponsored and did not involve massacre, riot or even – for the most part – mob violence.)

The cult which grew up around the martyred Charles I (discussed in Andrew Lacey's chapter and, to a lesser extent, in mine) was a breakthrough in the development of political martyrdom. Andrew Lacey describes how Charles, although the leader of a losing political cause, was acclaimed by his followers, in extravagantly sacral terms, as another Christ, martyred for the sins of his people. And while the fact that Charles was both king and martyr contributed powerfully to the sacralisation of this failed political figure, monarchs, and indeed royalists, did not have a monopoly on political martyrdom. Indeed, John Coffey's chapter on Henry Vane the Younger's construction of himself, not merely as a martyr, but as one of the two witnesses whose martyrdom is prophesied in Revelation, shows the secularisation of religious (indeed radically religious and apocalyptic) conceptions of martyrdom. Vane also provides a striking example of the increasingly porous divisions seperating religious and political martyrdom.

VII

The number and strength of the competing martyrological traditions were unique to England and had crucially important consequences for English religion and politics. On the most obvious level, they powerfully influenced the writing of English religious history. Each English confession and denomination viewed its past through a martyrological lens that magnified persecution, suffering and heroism. Beginning in the sixteenth century with the works of Pole, Harpsfield, Persons and Allen, and continuing in later centuries through the martyrological collections of Richard Challoner, John Morris and John H. Pollen, Catholic historiography focused almost entirely on Catholic martyrs and confessors. The influence of martyrological writings on the historiography and self-perception of Quakers and Nonconformists has been frequently observed by scholars.[141] These martyrologically based interpretations past were unchallenged until recent decades and even now their influence is still felt. Much of the emphasis (or over-emphasis) on harmony and coexistence in the English Reformation is a reaction against the over-emphasis on persecution and martyrdom of earlier historical writing. And the oppressive and potent influence of martyrolgies has not been confined to religious history; Whig martyrologies dominated the historiography of the late Stuart era for centuries.[142]

Paradoxically the power of the martyrological traditions banked the fires of religious persecution. From the accession of Elizabeth onwards, England had one of the few official churches which had a heavy emotional investment in its own contemporary martyrs. While Foxe's great martyrology was, at least initially, championed by the principal figures of both the Elizabethan Church and state, nevertheless, in one respect, it effectively limited their power to punish religious dissent. Foxe's *Acts and Monuments* presented an influential interpretation of the past in which the execution of people for their religious beliefs was a distinguishing characteristic of the anti-Christian Church and, as Peter Lake and Michael Questier have observed, the perception that it was the defender of Christian liberty against such anti-Christian tyranny, 'had become central to the self-image of the English protestant state'.[143]

Having maintained that persecution was a particulary 'Catholic' vice, the English authorities were very concerned that they should not appear to be guilty of the same anti-Christian cruelty. This scrupulousness (or squeamishness) was most notoriously evident in the insistence of English Protestant apologists, throughout the sixteenth and seventeenth centuries, that English Catholics were not executed for their religious beliefs but as traitors.[144] It is easy to dismiss this as a cynical manipulation of semantics and legal technicalities, and it was probably meagre comfort to a condemned Catholic to know that he would avoid the stake by being disembowelled and castrated instead. However, there were two important restrictions on religious persecution inherent in this postion. The first is that it limited the Catholic victims of persecution to priests or, in extreme cases, those who sheltered them. The Protestant who refused to attend church under Mary ran a real risk of execution, the Catholic who refused to attend church under Elizabeth risked financial loss, but not his or her life. The second restriction was that it was

---

[141] For example, Craig W. Horle, *The Quakers and the English Legal System, 1660–1688* (Philadelphia, 1988), pp. ix–xi; Wykes, 'To Let the Memory', p. 380 and *Calamy Revised*, p. xvi.

[142] Melinda Zook, ' "The Bloody Assizes": Whig Martyrdom and Memory after the Glorious Revolution', *Albion*, 27 (1995), pp. 373–96, esp. 391–6.

[143] Lake and Questier, *Antichrist's Lewd Hat*, p. 233.

[144] The classic statement of this position was William Cecil, *The execution of justice in England . . . without any persecution for questions of religion* (1583), RSTC 4902. For later repetitions of this theme see Anthony Milton, *Catholic and Reformed: The Roman and Protestant Churches in English Protestant Thought, 1600–1640* (Cambridge, 1995), p. 40 and John Miller, *Popery and Politics in England 1660–1688* (Cambridge, 1973), p. 78.

much more difficult to execute dissident Protestants for treason since they were not committed to the papal deposition of Elizabeth or to a denial of the Royal Supremacy.[145] The determination not to execute people for heresy may not have spared the lives of Catholic priests, but it spared the lives of Catholic laypeople and radical Protestants.

Not all radical Protestants were spared, however. A handful of people were burned for heresy between the accession of Elizabeth and 1612, when Edward Wightman, the last person burned for heresy in England, was executed. Ian Atherton and David Como argue that elite opinion supported the execution of Wightman and further claim that 'After Wightman a number of religious radicals nearly met the same fate.'[146] In their discussion, however, it appears that only two individuals, at most, were in any danger of being burned for heresy between 1612 and the abolition of the High Commission in 1640–2.[147] It may be that the reluctance to execute people for heresy stemmed from propagandistic purposes, and a desire not to surrender the moral high ground to their Catholic adversaries, but whatever the motives behind it, it seems to have been real enough. In 1581, a bill which would have made membership in the Family of Love subject to capital punishment upon conviction for the third offence ignited a protracted debate among MPs as to 'whether process of death might be inflicted to an heretique'.[148] This reluctance did not prevent religious dissidents from being executed when they could be convicted of suitable secular offences nor did it spare people from mutilation, banishment, imprisonment, confiscation of property or fines for religious nonconformity. Yet, limited and attenuated as this forbearance was, it was a step, if only a faltering step, closer to religious tolerance than most European states of the time achieved.

If martyrologies and the memorialisation of martyrs limited religious persecution, they also stimulated religious divisions within England. Any dreams of a truly national, as opposed to an official or established, Church, vanished in the course of the seventeenth century, as recusant and dissenting groups became entrenched in their own doctrinal and ecclesiological positions. Martyrologies contributed mightily to this process. In the first place, they gave these religious minorities a sense of cohesion and also legitimacy, allowing them, through their martyrs, to identify themselves with the True Church. At the same time, the martyrologies, by keeping old wounds fresh and bleeding, exacerbated confessional and denominational hatred, turning faultlines between the different religious groups into yawning chasms.

---

[145] The notorious executions of John Greenwood, John Penry and Henry Barrow were not for treason but for seditious writings against the Church, in the case of Greenwood, and seditious writings against the queen, in the cases of Penry and Barrow. I would like to thank Ethan Shagan for reminding me of this point.

[146] Ian Atherton and David Como, 'The Burning of Edward Wightman: Puritanism, Prelacy and the Politics of Heresy in Early Modern England', *English Historical Review*, 120 (2005), pp. 1247–8.

[147] Ibid., p. 1248.

[148] *Proceedings in the Parliaments of Elizabeth I*, ed. T. E. Hartley, 3 vols (Leicester, 1981–95), I, pp. 536 and 539.

Yet paradoxically, by fostering religious disunity in England, the competing martyrological traditions helped to create a united Britain. Linda Colley has famously maintained that it was only a shared Protestantism that allowed the peoples of England, Wales and Scotland to overcome regional, linguistic and sectarian differences and unite to form a British nation.[149] It might be more accurately said that anti-Catholicism allowed the peoples of Britain to join together. Protestantism divided Britain into Anglican, Presbyterian, Baptist, Independent, Quaker and Methodist; it was only shared hatred and fear of Catholicism that allowed these disparate, rival Protestants to band together in an initially uneasy, but ultimately effective, union. And it was the memory of martyrs and persecution, perpetuated graphically in the pages of Foxe's book and other martyrologies that fanned the flames of anti-Catholicism for centuries.

A complete history of the development of ideas of martyrdom, and their cultural, social and political influence in Reformation England, is badly needed. This book does not fulfil that need, but it does take one or two steps in the right direction. The chapters in this volume do not provide a continuous narrative of the evolution of conceptions of martyrdom. But they do provide a series of snapshots of some of the key moments in that process. And it is a strength of this volume that it covers a wide chronological range, traversing several different periods, from the late Middle Ages through to the beginning of the eighteenth century, with some attention to events thereafter in the chapters by John Coffey and myself. This chronological scope is possible because the chapters of this volume are written by a variety of scholars with different specialisations. This approach allows the reader to see the subject of English martyrdom over the centuries which completely encompass one of the two great revolutions in English history, the Reformation, and to perceive how conceptions of martyrdom were affected by, and affected, that revolution and the Civil War, Restoration and 'Glorious Revolution' that all flowed from it. The different perspectives and methodologies employed by the different authors in this volume also allow the reader to see the subject from a number of different angles. Hopefully this volume will convey something of the way that concepts of martyrdom evolved in late medieval and early modern England. If it does so it will help illuminate a legacy of the English Reformation that was not only of considerable political and cultural, as well as religious, importance, but which also speaks directly to us today.

[149] Linda Colley, *Britons: Forging the Nation 1707–1837* (New Haven, CT, 1992).

1

'*Imitatio Christi* with a Vengeance': The Politicisation of Martyrdom in Early Modern England*

THOMAS S. FREEMAN

'Must then a Christ perish in torment in every age to save those that have no imagination?'   George Bernard Shaw, *Saint Joan*

One of the small woodcuts in Foxe's 'Book of Martyrs' depicts the Marian martyr Cicely Ormes being burned at the stake. In it she stands impassively, bound to the stake, with her hands held in prayer, as the flames roar around her. Yet the very same woodcut was also used as the title page of a pamphlet describing the murder of one John Brewen by his wife and her lover.[1] Now the woman standing in the flames was not the heroic Cicely Ormes, but the guilty Anne Brewen. This dual use of the same woodcut illustrates one of the major challeges faced by all early-modern martyrologists. Almost invariably the martyrs whom they wished to glorify had been executed in the same ways in which the most heinous criminals were executed. Martyr of God or common criminal? How could one tell the difference?

Faced with people willing to die for what they considered to be heretical beliefs, patristic writers such as Cyprian, Tertullian and Augustine made doctrinal orthodoxy the touchstone of martyrdom.[2] The drawback to this argu-

* Earlier versions of this chapter were read at the 'Religion in the British Isles, 1500–1800' seminar at the Institute of Historical Research in London and the 'Early Modern History' seminar at the University of Cambridge. An early version of this chapter was also given as a lecture sponsored by the History Department at the University of the South, Sewanee, Tennessee. I would like to thank those attending these sessions for their valuable comments and observations, especially Mark Goldie and Grant Tapsell. I would also like to thank Margaret Aston, Peter Marshall and Susannah Monta for reading an earlier version of this chapter and providing helpful criticisms and corrections of it.

[1]   Cf. *The trueth of the most wicked murdering of J. Brewen* (1592), RSTC 15095 with *A&M [1583]*, p. 2023.
[2]   Augustine made this point repeatedly; see, for example, *Contra epistolam Parmeniani* I.9.15; *Epistola*, 185.5.19 and 204; *Ennarationes in Psalmos*, 145.16; *In Ioannis Evangelium Tractatus*, 6.25 and 11.15, as

ment was that, during the Reformation, it was inevitably a circular one. An exchange between Elizabeth Young, arrested in 1558 for smuggling heretical books into London, and Thomas Darbyshire, the chancellor of the diocese, illustrates the problem. When Young taunted Darbyshire by claiming the Catholic Church had no one willing to die for God's word, he replied 'No? Did ye never heare that the Bishop of Rochester lost his head for the supremacie of the Pope?' And she answered 'Then he dyed not for Gods word.'[3] The claim that a person who died for his or her beliefs was demonstrably a martyr because those beliefs were true had no efficacy with those who believed they were false; some external verification of martyrdom was needed.

Traditionally miracles had supplied this verification. And indeed during the Reformation both Catholic and Protestant martyrologists continued to relate stories of the supernatural wonders performed by, or on behalf of, their martyrs. Yet miracles had a limited utility in authenticating the sanctity of a martyr. In the late Middle Ages, there had been increasingly critical scrutiny of claims that various saints and holy people, living and dead, had performed miracles.[4] During the early fifteenth century, Jean Gerson, the chancellor of the University of Paris, laid down guidelines for determining true from spurious miracles: miracles and divine revelations had to have religious significance and to support doctrinal truths; if they did not, they were fraudulent or diabolical marvels, but not divine miracles.[5] Gerson's teachings remained influential through the Counter-Reformation and, stimulated by humanist writers such as Erasmus, they helped to create an increasing sensitivity to the possibility of fraudulent miracles.[6] This in turn fostered a reaction in the sixteenth century, shared by Catholic and Protestant alike, against the prodigious marvels related in the *Legenda aurea* and other medieval hagiographies.[7]

well as *De sermone Domini in monte*, 9. For a survey of the writing of patristic authors on this theme see Henri Meylan, 'Martyrs du Diable', *Revue de théologie et de philosophie*, 9 (1959), pp. 114–19.

[3] *A&M [1570]*, p. 2272. Apart from following modern usage for the letters i, j, u and v, the original spelling has been retained in all quotations. Punctuation, particularly capitalisation, has, however, been modernised.

[4] See Klaus Schreiner, ' "Discrimen veri et falsi": Ansätze und Formen der Kritik in der Heiligen und Reliquienverschauung des Mittelalters', *Archiv für Kultergeschichte*, 48 (1966), pp. 1–53.

[5] Paschal Boland, *The Concept of Discretio Spirituum in John Gerson's De Probatione Spirituum and De Distictione Verarum Visionum a Falsis* (Washington, DC, 1959), pp. 31, 35 and 91.

[6] For Gerson's continuing influence see Cynthia J. Cupples, 'Âmes d'élite: Visionaries and Politics in France from the Holy Catholic League to the Reign of Louis XIV' (Princeton University, Ph.D. thesis, 1999), pp. 275–6. A number of Erasmus's colloquies – notably 'The Shipwreck', 'The Exorcism or the Spectre' and 'A Pilgrimage for Religion's Sake' – contained scathing, and very influential, attacks on 'superstition' and forged miracles (Desiderious Erasmus, *Colloquies*, trans. and annotated by Craig R. Thompson, *Collected Works of Erasmus*, XXXIX and XL (Toronto, 1997), I, pp. 351–67 and 531–44 and II, pp. 620–74). Also see Peter Marshall, 'Forgery and Miracles in the Reign of Henry VIII', *Past and Present*, 178 (2003), pp. 39–73, esp. 43–9 and Sherry L. Reames, *The Legenda Aurea: A Reexamination of its Paradoxical History* (Madison, Wisconsin, 1985), pp. 50–6 and 67.

[7] See Anne Dillon, *The Construction of Martyrdom in the English Catholic Community, 1553–1603* (Aldershot, 2002), pp. 85–8 and 321–2, as well as Susannah Brietz Monta, *Martyrdom and Literature in Early Modern England* (Cambridge, 2005), pp. 53–75. On the other hand, it is important to note that miracles still continued to be a feature of both Protestant and Catholic hagiographies and martyrologies; see the

In any case, the perception of miracles was subjective and the miracles themselves capable of being otherwise interpreted. Some enthusiastic Protestants claimed that the Holy Spirit, in the form of a dove, descended on the Marian martyr John Rogers as he was burning. The Catholic polemicist Miles Hogarde claimed instead that a flock of pigeons flew overhead and hysterical spectators saw what they wished to see.[8] And even if a miracle could not be attributed to natural causes, supernatural activity could be attributed to the devil as well as to God. Several verses in the New Testament, frequently cited in the Reformation, predicted that miracles would be performed by false prophets and false Christs.[9]

The behaviour of the martyr was also essential corroboration of his or her status as a servant of God. It was expected that the true martyr, fortified by the Holy Spirit, would be able to withstand the pains of execution, no matter how agonising, with supernaturally conferred constancy. When the martyrs succeeded in displaying the required stoicism they created potent propaganda for their own cause. In 1555, one of the chief Habsburg officials in the Low Countries observed this phenomenon when reporting to Charles V on the execution of Protestants in Tournai: 'the basis of these heretics' strength . . . [is] merely that simple people, seeing the public execution of such heretics with firm constancy and hearing their resolution and the prayers which they address to God before dying, fall into vacillations and doubt of their faith.'[10] Even at the height of anti-Catholic hysteria in 1679, five Jesuits executed for their putative participation in the 'Popish Plot', impressed and confused the hostile London crowds with the courage and calm they displayed.[11] And the constant, even cheerful, demeanour of Obadiah

---

nuanced discussions in Simon Ditchfield, *Liturgy, Sanctity and History in Tridentine Italy: Pietro Maria Campi and the Preservation of the Particular* (Cambridge, 1995), pp. 117–34, and Alexandra Walsham, 'Miracles in Post-Reformation England', in *Visions, Signs and Wonders: Representations of Divine Power in the Life of the Church*, ed. Kate Cooper and Jeremy Gregory, Studies in Church History 41 (Woodbridge, 2005), pp. 273–306. The continuities and changes in the use of the miraculous are perhaps epitomised by the fact that the great Roberto Bellarmine could at once insist that miracles were a perpetual mark of the True Church and also warily caution that the hagiographic collection which would become the *Acta sanctorum* might do more harm than good as the publication of old legends could provoke scepticism and even ridicule (Walsham, 'Miracles', p. 280 and Reames, *Legenda Aurea*, pp. 58–9).

8   Miles Hogarde, *The displaying of the Protestantes* (1556), RSTC 13558, fo. 64v. Interestingly, a dove was also supposed to have appeared over the head of the French Protestant martyr Geoffrey Vargle (Jean Crespin, *Histoire des vrays tesmoins de la verité de l'Evangile* (Geneva, 1570), p. 528). These are examples of a powerful tendency, discussed more extensively later in this chapter, in the Reformation, to conceptualise miracles which identified the martyr with Christ.

9   See, for example, Matthew 24: 23–4 and Mark 13: 21–2. Thomas More, while maintaining that miracles were a sign by which true martyrs were known, also cautioned that the devil would perform miracles on behalf of false martyrs (Thomas More, *A Dialogue Concerning Heresies*, ed. Thomas M. C. Lawler, Germain Marc'hadour and Richard C. Marius (*CWTM*, VI, 1, pp. 421–2 and 435). The evangelical polemicist John Bale caustically claimed that the devil's martyrs worked more miracles than God's martyrs did, just as Christ had predicted (John Bale, *The first examinacyon of Anne Askewe* [Wesel, 1546], RSTC 848, fo. 4v).

10   Quoted in Phyllis Mack Crew, *Calvinist Preaching and Iconoclasm in the Netherlands* (Cambridge, 1978), p. 76.

11   Andrea McKenzie, 'Martyrs in Low Life? Dying "Game" in Augustan England', *Journal of British Studies*, 42 (2003), pp. 172–3.

Holmes, a Baptist condemned to a public whipping in Massachusetts in 1651, moved many of the spectators to rush up and shake his hand after the punishment had been inflicted.[12]

As a result, the executions of martyrs were scanned keenly by their confessional opponents for any indication, no matter how slight, of inconstancy or weakness. The Catholic polemicist Nicholas Harpsfield ridiculed Thomas Cranmer's celebrated exhibition of fortitude in holding his hand in the fire, sarcastically pointing out that the hand would have burned no matter what the Archbishop did.[13] When the Catholic priest John Shert clutched at the rope at the moment of his hanging, Protestants interpreted it as a desperate attempt to save his life and thus a sure sign that Shert was not a true martyr, while Catholic apologists were quick to claim that it was nothing more than a natural reflex.[14]

However, even when the courage and constancy of a martyr was beyond dispute, this was not necessarily sufficient proof of sanctity, as can be seen from the puritan minister Robert Bolton's disparaging description of the behaviour of Catholic priests condemned to death:

> At last, they came to Tyburne, or some other place of just execution, and then they will needes beare the world in hand, that they are going towards heaven, to receive a crowne of martyrdome. They seeme there already to triumphe extraordinarily, and to contemne tortures. With an affected bravery, they trample upon the tribunals of justice, kisse the instruments of death, in signe of happinesse at hand, and throw many resolute, and reioycing, speeches amongst the people, as tho they had one foote in heaven already.[15]

Bolton's insinuation that the priests pretended to be brave out of a desperate love of glory and a desire to impress the spectators at their executions was a common charge levelled at the martyrs of all confessions.[16] Another common, albeit less subtle, explanation of the inconvenient stoicism of condemned heretics was that they were drunk.[17] Moreover, if the Holy Spirit could confer fortitude on martyrs,

[12] John Clarke, *Ill News from New-England* (1652), STC [Wing] C4477B, p. 26.
[13] Nicholas Harpsfield, *Dialogi sex contra summi pontificatus, monasticae vitae, sanctorum, sacrarum imaginum oppugnatores et pseudomartyres* (Antwerp, 1566), pp. 743–4. Also see Victor Houliston's chapter in this volume for Robert Persons's dismissal of the constancy of Protestant martyrs.
[14] William Allen, *A briefe historie of the glorious martyrdom of XII. priests* (Rheims, 1582), RSTC 369.5, sig. A7r.
[15] Robert Bolton, *Instructions for a right comforting of afflicted consciences* (1631), RSTC 3238, p. 75.
[16] A classic statement of this argument, used against English Protestant martyrs, is in Harpsfield, *Dialogi sex*, pp. 959–62, also see pp. 738–44 and 756–8. But Alexander Nowell, the dean of St Paul's, used the same argument to subvert the sanctity of Catholics martyred in Henry VIII's reign (*The reproufe of M. Dorman his proufe* [1566], RSTC 18742, fo. 123r). And both Catholics and magisterial Protestants denounced the 'false' constancy of Anabaptist martyrs: e.g. Hugh Latimer, *The seconde sermon of Maister Hugh Latemer* (1549), RSTC 15274, sigs., L8v–M1r. Miles Hogarde not only agreed that the courage of radical Protestant martyrs did not make them genuine martyrs, he also dexterously quoted Latimer's attack on the Anabaptists and applied it to all Protestant martyrs (Hogarde, *Displaying of the Protestantes*, fos. 43v and 45r–47v).
[17] See *A&M [1570]*, pp. 1398 and 1991, as well as Harpsfield, *Dialogi sex*, p. 894. Similarly the courage

it was believed that the devil could confer insensibility on heretics. According to John Foxe, the constancy of one Marian martyr led 'some superstitious old women' to 'blasphemously say that the devill was so stronge with him, and all such hereticks as he was, that they coulde not feele any payne almost, nor yet be sorry for their sinnes'.[18] And John Mush, the confessor of the Catholic martyr, Margaret Clitherow, declared that observers of her calm demeanour after she was condemned were divided in their opinions, 'malice makinge some to say, she was possessed of a merry devill, others of a more indifferent disposition, attributed it unto the comforte of the Holy Ghoste'.[19] Both martyrologists were unsubtle in conveying which of the contested interpretations of the martyr's stoicism they believed was correct, but they were both compelled to acknowledge that other interpretations existed. As with miracles, the constancy of the martyrs could be disconcertingly inconclusive proof of their status as God's agents.

Corroboration of sanctity could also be obtained from the conformity of a martyr's life and death to that of the passion of Christ. This mimesis is the essence of Christian martyrdom; as Donald Kelley cogently observed, martyrdom is 'imitatio Christi with a vengeance'.[20] The closer the similarity between the details of the death of Christ and the details of the death of the martyr, the more difficult it was to dismiss the martyr as a criminal or a heretic. Consequently, martyrologists, Catholic and Protestant, sought to emphasise the parallels – and if necessary create some – between the sufferings of their martyrs and those of Christ.

I

There is a profound paradox at work here. Michel Foucault has famously described how the regimes of early-modern Europe used executions, and the ritual degradations of the condemned which accompanied them, to demonstrate their power by imposing their will on their enemies.[21] Yet the vast majority of early-modern Europeans worshipped a god who was a condemned criminal and they commemorated the tortures and humiliations inflicted on him during his execution in all of their churches. Indeed the holiest days of the Christian year were celebrated by re-enacting those very tortures and humiliations. Monarchs and magistrates were seen as agents of God, but they were agents of a god who had been unjustly executed by magistrates.

This meant that with any execution in early-modern Europe, there was always

which the regicide John Barkstead displayed at his execution was attributed by his enemies as being alcohol induced (*A Complete Collection of State Trials*, ed. T. B. Howell, 33 vols [1816–26], V, p. 1306).

[18] *A&M [1583]*, p. 1691.

[19] John Mush, *An abstracte of the life and martirdome of Mistress Margaret Clitherowe* (Mechelin, 1619), RSTC 18316, sig. B8v.

[20] Donald R. Kelley, 'Martyrs, Myths and the Massacre: The Background of St. Bartholomew', *American Historical Review*, 77 (1972), p. 1328.

[21] Michel Foucault, *Discipline and Punish*, trans. A. Sheridan (New York, 1977).

the possibility that any criminal could subvert the symbolism of his or her punish-ment by invoking, consciously or unconsciously, the similarity of their fate to the passion of Christ. In the words of David el Kenz, 'The image of the suffering Christ imposes itself on the execution. It [the execution] perpetuated the horror of the original sacrifice.'[22] The regicide Thomas Scot recognised the ambiguous and multivalent nature of death on the scaffold when he prayed at his execution, declaring to God that he had been called forth 'as a publick spectacle, to some in a condition of shame and reproach, to others of comfort, and to thy blessed self, as one that is a witness for thee, that hath served thee with all faithfulness'.[23]

The power of the parallel between Christ and the martyrs was increased by the centrality of Christ's passion in late-medieval popular devotion. The rood, perched atop its screen, dominated every church in western Europe, the cross stood on every altar and the crucifixion was depicted in sculpture, stained glass and paintings. 'To be Christian was to be marked with the sign of the cross from baptism to grave and, as Julian of Norwich tells us, the image of the saviour on the cross was the final comfort set before the eyes of the dying.'[24] The crucifixion and passion were at the centre of private devotions as well as public worship. Devo-tional works unceasingly encouraged their readers to meditate on the passion and to identify with the agonies endured by God's son. Cults focusing on the physical suffering of Christ, such as the Devotion to the Wounds of Christ and the Devo-tion of the Words of Christ, flourished in the late Middle Ages.[25] When martyrs and martyrologists compared the victims of early-modern religious persecution to Christ, they were tapping into the basic religious experiences of generations of Christians.

The comparison of the martyr to Christ created a dilemma for Protestants. Most of the traditional means of expressing devotion to the martyred Christ were denounced by the Protestants, particularly the Calvinists: the roods, the stained glass, the sculptures, the cults, the stations of the cross and the passion plays. In time, even the crucifix itself had become, in many Protestant countries, including England, an object of suspicion. Yet Protestant martyrs sought to associate them-selves with the crucifix while also rejecting it. Geoffrey Guerin refused to hold a wooden cross at his execution but added that it was unnecessary because the cross was imprinted on his heart.[26] A particularly striking example of this veneration

[22] David el Kenz, *Les bûchers du roi* (Seyssel, 1997), p. 162. All translations in this chapter are mine unless otherwise acknowledged.
[23] *The Speeches and prayers of Major General Harrison* (1660), STC [Wing], S4874A, p. 62.
[24] Margaret Aston, 'Lollards and the Cross', in *Lollards and their Influence in Late Medieval England*, ed. Fiona Somerset, Jill C. Havens and Derrick G. Pitard (Woodbridge, 2003), pp. 99–100. Also see Eamon Duffy, *The Stripping of the Altars: Traditional Religion in England c.1400–c.1580* (New Haven, CT, 1992), p. 157.
[25] Duffy, *Stripping*, pp. 234–56 and Brad Gregory, *Salvation at Stake: Christian Martyrdom in Early Modern Europe* (Cambridge, MA, 1999), pp. 55–60.
[26] Antoine de la Roche-Chandieu, *Histoire des persecutions et martyrs de l'Eglise de Paris* (Lyons, 1563), p. 202. As is so often the case, martyr and martyrologist were invoking tropes of traditional hagiography. A number of different legends recount early Christian martyrs declaring, as they went to their deaths, that the

for the cross came in John Foxe's description of a miracle which he claimed occurred at the execution of six martyrs in Brentford, Essex. One of the martyrs 'desired of God some token to be given whereby the people might know that they died in the right'. While this martyr was praying 'a marvellous white cross' appeared on his breast. Significantly Foxe only printed this story in his first edition; fierce and pointed criticisms by the Catholic controversialist Nicholas Harpsfield about the authenticity of this tale subsequently forced Foxe to discard it.[27] If Foxe was avid to have one of his martyrs bear the sign of the cross, his confessional adversaries were equally determined to prevent it.

It is possible that the desire to associate martyrdom with Christ's passion may have been particularly intense among English Protestants because the image of the cross was both particularly important and particularly controversial within the English Reformation. In the Lutheran countries crosses and crucifixes were largely untouched and in Switzerland and Scotland they were abolished quickly, if ruthlessly, in England, however, they had become the objects of gradually mounting iconoclasm. Eventually the roods would be removed from the churches and burned. Even the crosses in public locations, such as those in marketplaces and by roadsides, were destroyed, although this took generations.[28] Moreover, in Mary's reign the process was temporarily reversed and, her younger sister, to the disgust of her godlier subjects, retained the cross in her royal chapel.[29] Frustration with the slow and uncertain eradication of this potent relic of traditional Catholicism only made zealous Protestants more insistent and outspoken in their denunciations of images of the cross. Even traditional gestures, such as making the sign of the cross or kneeling before a cross, were looked upon as superstition, if not idolatry. John Donne at once described and deplored the persistant antipathy towards physical representations of the cross in Protestant England:

> Since Christ embrac'd the Crosse it selfe, dare I
> His image, th'image of his Crosse deny . . .
> it bore all other sinnes, but is it fit
> That it should beare the sinne of scorning it?[30]

---

sign of the cross was in their hearts. In these stories the persecutors have the martyrs cut open and find crosses imprinted on the martyrs' hearts (Frederic C. Tubach, *Index Exemplorum: A Handbook of Medieval Religious Tales* [Helsinki, 1969], no. 1338). The most striking, and best-known, version of this story concerned St Clare of Montefalco, who declared that she felt the cross in her heart. According to reports submitted during the process of her canonisation, her body was dissected immediately following her death and the instruments of Christ's passion were found in her heart (André Vauchez, *Sainthood in the Later Middle Ages*, trans. Jean Birrell [Cambridge, 1997], pp. 441–2).

27 *A&M [1563]*, RSTC 11222, p. 1670 and Harpsfield, *Dialogi sex*, p. 962.

28 Margaret Aston, 'Cross and Crucifix in the English Reformation', in *Macht und Ohnmacht der Bilder: Reformatorischer Bildersturm im Kontext der Europäischen Geschichte*, ed. Peter Bickle, André Holenstein, Heinrich Richard Schmidt and Franz-Josef Sladeczek (Munich, 2000), pp. 253–72.

29 Aston, 'Cross and Crucifix', p. 259 and Patrick Collinson, *Archbishop Grindal* (Berkeley and Los Angeles, 1979), p. 97.

30 John Donne, 'The Crosse', in *John Donne: The Complete English Poetry*, ed. C. A. Patrides and Robin Hamiliton (London, 1994), pp. 351–2. I am grateful to Susannah Monta for bringing this poem to my attention.

And this rejection of the physical cross, in turn, led English Catholics to venerate it with even greater fervour.

This fervent veneration, and the intense suspicion it engendered among English Protestants, is revealed by the reactions to a prodigy which occurred on the estate of Sir Thomas Stradling in Glamorganshire in 1561. A tree blew over in a heavy storm, but standing in the trunk of the shattered tree was an erect cross. Stradling had pictures drawn of the cross and they circulated widely among Catholics. The Privy Council had Stradling sent to the Tower and interrogated other Catholics suspected of circulating copies of the picture.[31] Nicholas Harpsfield's *Dialogi sex*, a scathing and effective denunciation of such essential Protestant writers as Foxe and Jewel, contained only one illustration: an engraving of one of the pictures of the Stradling cross, smuggled out of England to the Plantin press in Antwerp.[32] Similarly, the only illustration in Thomas Stapleton's translation of Bede's *Ecclesiastical History* consists of three panels depicting the Northumbrian king Oswald erecting a cross, kneeling before it and then conquering his enemies under a banner displaying a crucifix.[33]

The opposing attitudes towards the cross seeped over from propaganda, polemic and history into martyrology. English Catholic martyrs missed few opportunities to demonstrate their veneration for their cross and English Catholic martyrologists missed few opportunities to contrast this reverence with the impiety of English Protestants. According to William Allen, when Edmund Campion was escorted to the Tower, he made the sign of the cross as he passed the Cheapside cross. In a marginal note, Allen added 'He doth reverence to the crosse which in these daies there [in England] is odious'.[34] When Alexander Briant carried at his sentence a wooden cross he had made, Allen drew the moral: 'He was not ashamed of his Master's Badge.'[35] And when Robert Johnson was reproved by the sheriff of London for making the sign of the cross at his execution, Allen pointedly noted: 'Crosses trouble them.'[36] At the same time, English Protestant martyrologists were careful to avoid any sign of reverence for the image of the cross, in any context. Even after describing Constantine's vision of the cross before his victory at the Milvian Bridge, Foxe hastened to caution the unwary against reading too much into the miracle:

> Wherein is to be noted (good Reader) that this signe of the Crosse, and those letters added withal, 'In hoc vince', was geven to him of God, not to

[31] TNA, SP 12/17, fos. 35r–39v.
[32] The picture appears in Harpsfield, *Dialogi sex*, between pp. 504 and 505. In the *Dialogi sex*, Harpsfield strenuously championed the sanctity and efficacy of images of the Cross against Protestant attacks (pp. 458–516).
[33] Bede, *The history of the church of Englande*, trans. Thomas Stapleton (Antwerp, 1565), RSTC 1778, fo. 77r (Bede describes the erection of the cross, and ascribes Oswald's victory to it, but he says nothing about Oswald's troops carrying a banner with the image of a cross on it).
[34] Allen, *Briefe historie*, sig. d6r.
[35] Ibid., sig. f5v.
[36] Ibid., sig. A7r.

induce any superstitious worship or opinion of the crosse, as though the crosse it self, had any such power or strength in it to obtayne victorie, but onely to beare the meanynge of an other thyng, that is to be an admonition for him to seeke and to aspire to the knowledge and fayth of Him, which was crucified upon the crosse, for the salvation of hym, and of all the world, and to set forth the glory of His name.[37]

Yet while English Protestants eradicated the physical images of the cross, and discouraged even the mildest forms of veneration to it, it would have been difficult to suppress entirely devotion which had been central to worship within living memory and which was linked to the most sacred mysteries of the Christian religion. By observing and emphasising the parallels between the martyrs and Christ, the traditional and deeply rooted veneration of the instrument of Christ's martyrdom was free to emerge, and indeed, to re-emerge with increased force since this was one of the few approved ways to express it. Instead of the rood or the crucifix the new signifiers of Christ's passion had become the bodies of the martyrs themselves.

II

Above and beyond instances of miraculous crosses, Foxe devoted considerable ingenuity to underscoring, if not actually creating, parallels between sixteenth-century martyrdoms and Christ's arrest, trial and execution. One case, that of George Eagles, will have to stand for many. George Eagles was a tailor who, during the reign of Edward VI, began a career as an unlicensed preacher in the area around Colchester. His itinerant zeal won him considerable local celebrity and the alias of 'Trudgeover the World'. During Mary's reign he continued his activities and for two years the authorities tried to apprehend him.[38] On 22 July 1556, his luck ran out. He was spotted and ran into a cornfield, temporarily eluding his pursuers. But one of them, Ralph Larden, climbed a tree and directed the others to where Eagles was hiding. Eagles was taken to Chelmsford and tried and convicted of sedition rather than heresy (he was charged with having prayed that God would either turn the queen's heart or take her away).[39] Instead of being burned as a heretic, he was hung, drawn and quartered as a traitor. This method of execution meant that he was dragged on a sled to the place of execution, hung, cut down just before death, castrated, disembowelled and finally beheaded. After death, the traitor's body was cut into four quarters and sent to different towns to be displayed as a grisly warning to others.

---

[37] *A&M [1570]*, p. 119.
[38] *A&M [1563]*, p. 1614; *Narratives of the Days of Reformation*, ed. J. G. Nichols, Camden Society, o.s. 77 (1859), pp. 210–11 and *Acts of the Privy Council*, ed. J. R. Dasent, 9 vols (1890–1907), V, pp. 310 and 312.
[39] *A&M [1563]*, pp. 1614–15.

In his initial account of Eagle's martyrdom, in the first edition of his martyrology, Foxe already attempted to link Eagle's fate with that of Christ. For example, Foxe called the £20 reward issued for Eagles's capture 'a worthy hire to entice any Jew to treachery' and he characterised Ralph Larden as a 'Judas knave'.[40] Most important was an incident which Foxe claimed 'did much set forth and declare the innocence and godliness of this man'.[41] According to Foxe, Eagles was executed between two thieves. One of the thieves mocked Eagles, but the other thief was reverent towards him and died penitent.[42] This unsubtle piece of typology, paralleling the account of the crucifixion in Luke 23: 39–43, made the desired identification of Eagles with Christ clear to all but the most obtuse reader.

Yet Foxe worked to increase further the association between Christ and Eagles in subsequent editions of his martyrology. Foxe's chief additions to the account of Eagles's martyrdom were graphic details of the mutilation of the martyr's body. For example, the second edition was enriched with descriptions of Eagles's head being cut off with a cleaver 'which sometimes hit his neck and sometimes his chin and did foully mangle him', of his bowels being cut out and burned and of his body being laid on fishstalls before it was cut into pieces. Foxe also took care to report that Eagles's head was placed on a pole at Chelmsford market cross but that the wind blew it off the pole and it tumbled about in the street for days.[43] Significantly, Thomas Brice carefully highlighted the same details in his 1559 poem commemorating the Marian martyrs:

> When George Eagles at Chelmsford towne
> was hanged drawn and quartered,
> his quarters carried up and doune
> And on a pole thei set his head . . .[44]

At first glance, the zeal of Foxe and Brice in recounting these details is very surprising. For one thing, these gruesome facts only served to remind his readers that Eagles was a convicted traitor. Foxe had been vehement in his insistence that Eagles had been 'condemned for a traytor, although the meanyng [i.e., the cause] was for religion'; in fact, Foxe tersely anticipated the objections of Catholics later in the sixteenth century when he observed that, in Eagles's case, the authorities had 'turned religion into a civell offense or crime'.[45] This insistence was understandable. Catholic polemicists had long sought to associate Protestantism with

[40] *A&M [1563]*, p. 1614.
[41] *A&M [1563]*, p. 1615.
[42] *A&M [1563]*, p. 1615.
[43] Cf. *A&M [1570]*, p. 2204, with *A&M [1563]*, p. 1615.
[44] Thomas Brice, *A compendious regester in metre, conteining the names and suffeynges of the membres of Jesus Christ* (1559), RSTC 3726, sig. D2r. On Brice's zealous Protestantism and active resistance to the Marian regime see the article on him in the *ODNB*.
[45] *A&M [1570]*, p. 2203, and *A&M [1563]*, p. 1614.

treason and sedition.[46] In fact, Nicholas Harpsfield had accused Foxe of acclaiming traitors as martyrs and cited George Eagles as an example of this. Harpsfield also acerbically contrasted Eagles's praying for the queen's death with martyrs of the early Church who prayed for the emperors who persecuted them.[47]

Moreover, the mutilation of the traitor's bodies and the displaying of its pieces were important components of the punishment for treason.[48] The mutilation of the traitor's body was the supreme expression of his powerlessness and it was also regarded as particularly shaming.[49] Perhaps even more dishonourable was the placing of the victim's remains on public display. For one thing, it exposed them to further abuse. In one case, the heads of two priests were placed on Oxford castle and townspeople slashed their faces with knives. And after Hugh Green, another priest, was executed at Dorchester in 1642, the crowd seized his head and used it as a football.[50]

The denial, moreover, of a proper burial entailed by the scattering of the remains was regarded as a terrible sanction.[51] The exhumations, in England, of the bodies of William Tracy, Catherine Martyr, Martin Bucer and Paul Fagius were exemplary punishments designed to underscore dramatically the heinousness of the 'criminals' on whom this punishment was inflicted and to shame and discredit them.[52] The royalist newspaper *Mercurius publicus* drew particular satisfaction from the dismemberment inflicted on the regicides and exultantly declared that the body parts of one of them, Thomas Scot, were 'disposed so far asunder that they will scarce ever meet together in one tomb'.[53] The same attitudes motivated the reinternment of the royalist hero the marquis of Montrose, who had been executed and dismembered in 1650. Immediately after his death pieces of his body were carefully gathered together by his adherents and buried. In 1660, his remains were exhumed, his bones washed several times in alcohol, dried and then annointed with perfumes and balsams. The coffin was filled with incense and aromatic spices and, only then, with the degradation of his remains finally purged, was he reburied.[54]

---

46 For example, Thomas More, *The Debellation of Salem and Bizance*, ed., John Guy, Ralph Keen, Clarence H. Miller and Ruth McGugan in *CWTM*, X, pp. 104–5; Thomas Stapleton, *A fortresse of the faith* (Antwerp, 1565), RSTC 23232, fo. 154r and Harpsfield, *Dialogi sex*, pp. 898–900. Also see Alec Ryrie's chapter in this volume.

47 Harpsfield, *Dialogi sex*, p. 847.

48 See David Nicholls, 'The Theatre of Martyrdom in the French Reformation', *Past and Present*, 121 (1988), pp. 59–60 and Kenz, *Les bûchers du roi*, p. 51, for discussion of this.

49 Nicholls, 'The Theatre of Martyrdom,' pp. 58–60.

50 Richard Challoner, *Memoirs of Missionary Priests*, ed. J. H. Pollen (1924), pp. 158 and 427–8.

51 On the early modern English concern that the departed receive suitable funerals and a proper burial see Clare Gittings, *Death, Burial and the Individual in Early Modern England* (1984), *passim*, but especially pp. 60–85.

52 Peter Marshall, *Beliefs and the Dead in Reformation England* (Oxford, 2002), pp. 122–3. For a similar attitudes in early modern France see Penny Roberts, 'Contesting Sacred Space: Burial Disputes in Sixteenth-Century France', in *The Place of the Dead: Death and Remembrance in Early Modern Europe*, ed. Bruce Gordon and Peter Marshall (Cambridge, 2000), pp. 131–48.

53 *Mercurius Publicus*, Thursday 11 October to Thursday 18 October, 1660, p. 672.

54 Gittings, *Death, Burial and the Individual*, p. 71.

At first sight, the brutal punishments inflicted on heretics and traitors in early-modern England appear to be nearly perfect expressions of the power of the early-modern state. John Bossy, writing from this Foucauldian perspective, has eloquently suggested that the hanging and drawing of Catholic priests, 'attended as they were by a ritual cuisine requiring dissection of the victim, boiling of entrails, and placing of heads in public situations, might well be considered sacrificial rites in the temple of monarchy, a deity fancying the boiled where older gods preferred the roast'.[55] And, following the Foucauldian paradigm, the hagiographers and martyrologists of both confessions should have scurried past these degrading details, passing over in silence the humiliations inflicted by the vengeful state on those who had transgressed its rules.

Instead they revelled in the shame, bathed in the blood and wallowed in the gore. We have already noted Foxe's care to record every detail of the degradation of Eagles's body. Peter Lake and Michael Questier have similarly observed the seemingly paradoxical fact that Catholic authorities emphasised the physical indignities visited upon martyred priests, while the Protestant authorities were 'reticent, even squeamish, about such matters'.[56] Certainly there was nothing reticent about the detailed Catholic accounts of the barbarous executions of Hugh Green and John Rigby (this last execution was so fearsomely botched that even the crowd protested).[57] The most humiliating aspects of the executions were related with apparent relish: the hagiographer of Stephen Rowsom made a point of noting that the priest had faeces flung at him as he was led to his doom.[58] John Gennings, in a hagiography of his brother, the martyred priest Edmund Gennings, not only described the disembowelling of his brother, he also detailed the executioner's contemptuous handling of Edmund's remains. John's hagiography also contains a woodcut which depicts Edmund being hung and dismembered, and subsequently, his limbs being boiled and carried in a basket to be displayed.[59] And, in fact, works such as Richard Verstegan's martyrologies contained pictures that left no detail of the tortures and excutions of Catholic martyrs undepicted.[60]

---

[55] John Bossy, *Christianity in the West, 1400–1700* (Oxford, 1985), p. 158.

[56] Peter Lake and Michael Questier, *The Antichrist's Lewd Hat: Protestants, Papists and Players in Post-Reformation England* (New Haven, CT, 2002), pp. 237–8. In his introduction to this book, Peter Lake incisively draws attention to the ways in which Catholic emphasis on the mutilation of Catholic martyrs, and Protestant reticence about these details, is contrary to Foucault's paradigm of the way executions worked (pp. xvii–xviii). I would add that this difference in approach does not seem to me to be confessionally based, as Lake seems to imply, but rather to stem simply from the fact it was in the interest of those sympathetic to the martyrs to emphasise these details. When, as in the case of George Eagles, such graphic details worked to the benefit of the Protestants, Foxe would then recount the details of a martyr's pain in painful detail.

[57] Challoner, *Memoirs*, pp. 244–5 and 426–7. For other examples of the readiness of English Catholic martyrologists to record the goriest details of the deaths of contemporary Catholic martyrs see *Acts of the English Martyrs*, ed. J. H. Pollen (1891), pp. 141, 352 and 356.

[58] *Acts*, ed. Pollen, p. 332.

[59] John Gennings, *The life and death of Mr Edmund Gennings priest* (St Omer, 1614), RSTC 11728, pp. 85–6 and 92. The woodcut is on p. 88.

[60] Dillon, *Construction of Martyrdom*, pp. 131–3 and 152–3.

Whatever the differences were between Catholic and Protestant, they agreed, in adherence to the model supplied by the King of Kings, that the outward humiliations were in reality the ineluctable signs of their glory. As Robert Southwell exclaimed:

> What argueth more impotencye, then to be bounde, condemned, whipped, tormented and killed and to lay the heade on the blocke at the hangemans pleasure? This sighte, sometime stirreth mercye, even in the moste cruell tyrantes. But which at the martyrs tombes diseases are cured, the divels rore, the monarches tremble, miracles are wrought, idols fall downe; then appeareth how forcible the blood of martyrs is.[61]

If pain and death suffered in Christ's cause were part of the glories of martyrdom, so was ridicule and humiliation suffered in the cause. This explains another paradoxical feature of Foxe's work: his determination to scrupulously record the ceremonies degrading Protestant martyrs who had been clerics from the priesthood. These elaborate ceremonies were carefully designed to humiliate their victims and to obliterate the sacred authority these victims had formerly enjoyed.[62] Nevertheless, Foxe took great pains to describe every detail of these shaming rituals.[63] The words of Nicholas Ridley, at his degradation from the priesthood, make the martyrologist's strategy clear. Forced to put on his clerical vestments as part of the ceremony, Ridley declared 'Dooe therein as it shall please you. I am well contented with that, and more than that. The servaunt is not above his master.'[64] And, in case his biblical quotation did not make his point sufficently clear, Ridley elaborated on how his humiliation identified him more closely with the Lamb of God. 'If they dost so cruelly with our Saviour Christe, as the Scripture maketh mention, and he suffered the same patiently, how much more doth it become his servauntes?'[65]

Moreover, Foxe's Catholic adversaries displayed an equal dexterity in invoking Christ's passion to turn judicial humiliation into signifiers of martyrdom. When Edmund Gennings was forced to wear a jester's coat at his trial, his hagiographer pointedly compared this treatment to similar humiliations that Herod Antipas and Pontius Pilate had inflicted on Christ.[66] William Allen invoked the same parallel when relating that Edmund Campion was paraded through the streets of London with the label 'Campion the seditious Jesuit' pinned

---

[61] Robert Southwell, *An epistle of comfort* (1587?), RSTC 22946, fo. 150v.

[62] Nicholls, 'Theatre of Martyrdom', pp. 55–7.

[63] For example, *A&M [1563]*, pp. 485, 1057–8, 1071 and 1100. Foxe's description of the degradation of Thomas Cranmer is particularly detailed (pp. 1492–6).

[64] *A&M [1563]*, p. 1374. Ridley was quoting Matthew 10: 24.

[65] *A&M [1563]*, p. 1374.

[66] Gennings, *Life and death of Mr Edmund Gennings*, p. 73. Heretics in France were occasionally forced to wear fool's clothes (Nicholls, 'Theatre of Martyrdom', pp. 56–7) but the use of this means of shaming an offender was very rare in England.

to his hat, while Richard Verstegan's picture of the incident prominently displays Campion wearing the shameful headgear.[67]

This apologetic strategy proved to be an enduring one and, in a harbinger of larger developments, it came to be deployed by political as well as religious offenders. For a striking example of this, consider the case of the puritan polemicist William Prynne. As part of his punishment for writing seditious books he was branded on the cheek with the letters 'SL' (for 'seditious libeller'). Prynne responded by writing verses declaring that the letters stood for 'stigmata Laudis', that is the stigmata of Archbishop William Laud, who was responsible for Prynne's prosecution.[68] By equating his wounds with the stigmata of Christ, Prynne was transforming what were supposed to be marks of shame into signs of holiness. This is precisely what Foxe and other martyrologists had done. By detailing the physical mutilations inflicted on their martyrs, they were linking the torn and rent bodies of Christ's martyrs with the wounded body of Christ himself. The servants, indeed, were not greater than their master and the more intense their agony, the more abject their humiliation and the more extreme their physical injury, then the closer they were to imitating perfectly the sacrifice of the son of God. Through this imitation the scars of criminality became marks of sanctity and the bodies of criminals objects of veneration.

III

The chief agents in comparing the martyrs to Christ were often the martyrs themselves. Convinced of the righteousness of their cause, they naturally were quick to see, and quick to seize, the parallels between their own circumstances and the passion narrative. The Marian martyr Richard Woodman, for example, consoled himself during the legal processes against him with the thought that Jesus had been charged with similar offenses. And later Woodman applied a well-known biblical trope of Christ's martyrdom, that of a lamb destined to be slain, to himself.[69] Furthermore, the martyrs went to great and deliberate lengths to make these associations clear to others. Foxe relates that Joyce Lewes, awaiting execution for heresy in Mary Tudor's reign, 'consulted how shee might behave herself that her death might be more glorious to the name of God, comfortable to his people and also more discomfortable unto the enemies of God'.[70] At her execution, Lewes drank from a single cup with sympathisers and pledged with them,

---

[67] Allen, *Brief historie*, sig. d5v. For Verstegan's picture see Dillon, *Construction of Martyrdom*, pp. 128 and 135. Robert Persons, describing Campion being paraded through London, also invokes the paralell to Christ (Robert Persons, *An epistle of the persecution of Catholikes in Englande* (Rouen, 1582?), RSTC 19046, pp. 82–3).

[68] William Prynne, *A new discovery of the prelates tyranny* (1641), STC [Wing], P4018, p. 65.

[69] Foxe. *A&M [1563]*, pp. 1588 and 1596. On the lamb led to the slaughter as a trope for Christ's martyrdom see Isaiah 53: 7, Acts 8: 32–6 and Romans 8: 36.

[70] *A&M [1563]*, p. 1620.

thus invoking both the Last Supper and Christ's ordeal in Gethsemene.[71] Other martyrs were even more determined and more systematic in comparing themselves to Christ. The French Protestant martyr Aymon de la Voye quoted Christ directly at his execution, crying 'Lord, Lord, why have you forsaken me?' When one of his judges replied 'Miserable Lutheran, it is you have abandoned God,' de la Voye sought refuge in another biblical quotation: 'Lord forgive them for they know not what they do.'[72]

But few of the confessional martyrs came close to rivalling Henry Burton (who was sentenced in 1637, along with William Prynne and John Bastwick, to have his ears cut off, confinement in the pillory, payment of a massive fine and incarceration for life, for the crime of publishing 'libellous' books) in the systematic thoroughness with which he compared his ordeals to Christ's passion. To cite only a few examples, when he saw the three pillories where he, Prynne and Bastwick were to be placed, Burton exlaimed 'Methinks I see Mount Calvary where the three crosses were pitched.' Offered a drink of water while in the pillory, Burton declared that 'his master Christ was not so well used, for they gave him gall and vinegar, but you gave me water to refresh me, blessed be God'.[73]

The relentless comparisons martyrs made between themselves and Christ built up to the extent that, in making such comparisons, a condemned criminal not only associated him or herself with Christ, he or she also established an association with other martyrs. John Lilburne, who was sentenced to be whipped while tied to the back of a cart and dragged two miles from the Fleet prison to Westminister, provides an example of this. As he was tied to the cart, he declared 'Welcome be the cross of Christ.'[74] Lilburne was not only invoking the example of Christ, he was also invoking Laurence Saunders, a Marian martyr, who kissed the stake and exclaimed 'Welcome the cross of Christ, welcome everlasting life'.[75]

Where the martyrs led, the martyrologists followed. Foxe's painstaking attempts to parallel George Eagles's martyrdom with the passion of Christ have already been described. But here, as in so many areas, Foxe was walking in the footsteps of his mentor John Bale. In his edition of the examinations of the Lollard martyr Sir John Oldcastle, Bale first invoked Christ's trial:

> A most fyt membre for Chrystes mysticall body is he that suffreth with the head therof. As this good Sir Johan Oldecastell did when he was with Christ examined of the proude bishops, scorned of the priests, disdayned of the worlde, ill reported, mocked, hated, reviled, accused and

---

[71] *A&M [1563]*, pp. 1620–1, cf. BL, MS 421, fos. 69r–71v and 73r–74r. This gesture was made by other English Protestant martyrs, see *A&M [1563]*, p. 1618 and *A&M [1570]*, p. 1398.

[72] Jean Crespin, *Histoire des martyrs*, p. 349.

[73] Prynne, *New discovery*, pp. 46–7 and 59.

[74] John Lilburne, *A worke of the Beast* (Amsterdam, 1638), RSTC 15599, p. 5.

[75] *A&M [1563]*, p. 1048.

commytted unto the laye judgement to be condempned by them unto moost shamefull and cruell death.[76]

Bale then compared Oldcastle's execution with the crucifixion, in order to obliterate the shame of the Lollard's ignominious death: 'More vyle was not his under the gallowes in an yron chayne, than was the hanging of his Lord Jesus Chryst upon the crosse in the time of his death.'[77]

Just as the zealous hunt for parallelisms between individual martyrs and Christ preceded Foxe, it also continued after him. Thomas Alfield, a hagiographer of Edmund Campion, invoked the legend of St Veronica wiping the face of Christ on his way to Calvary by describing a spectator wiping the dust from Campion's face as the Jesuit was led to execution.[78] John Mush's narrative of the last hours of Margaret Clitherow carefully evokes incidents in the life of Christ, particularly his vigil in the garden of Gethsemane and the crucifixion.[79] The Catholic martyrologist Laurentius Surius expresses the identification of the martyrs with Christ in the strongest possible terms, declaring that 'the totality of the holy martyrs makes up the totality of Christ, from whom the nature of sacred martyrdom flows'.[80]

These pervasive comparisons of Christ to contemporary martyrs had obvious potential drawbacks. There was the danger that such comparisons might seem blasphemous and discredit the martyr and his cause. William Hacket's public declaration in London in 1591, that he was Jesus Christ returned to judge the world, severely embarrassed the puritans with whom he was associated.[81] James Nayler's notorious entry into Bristol in what was perceived to be a blatant imitation of Christ's entry in Jerusalem on Palm Sunday not only resulted in severe punishment for Nayler, it did serious damage to the Quaker movement.[82]

Admittedly, there is, at least in theory, a considerable difference between emulation of Christ, which is enjoined on all Christians, and claiming to be Christ. Nevertheless, excessive praise of a martyr's identification with Christ (already more thorough and intense than that of most Christians) ran the risk of crossing the boundary separating the commendable from the condemnable. Even Foxe seems to have been concerned with at least one of his analogies between a

[76] John Bale, *A brefe Chronicle concerning the Examynation and death of the blessed martir of Christ sir Iohan Oldcastel* (1548?), RSTC 1278, sig. G6r.
[77] Bale, *Brefe Chronicle*, sig. G6v. For Bale comparing Anne Askew to Christ see *The Examinations of Anne Askew*, ed. Elaine Beilin (Oxford and New York, 1996), p. 51.
[78] Thomas Alfield, *A true reporte of the deathe and martyrdome of M. Campion . . .* (1582), RSTC 4537, sig. B4r.
[79] See Dillon, *Construction of Martyrdom*, pp. 319–20. For other examples of both English Catholic martyrs and martyrologists creating parallelisms, in both words and pictures, with Christ's life and passion see Dillon, *Construction of Martyrdom*, pp. 52–62, 95–6 and 135–6.
[80] Quoted in Gregory, *Salvation at Stake*, p. 277.
[81] Alexandra Walsham, ' "Frantick Hacket": Prophecy, Sorcery, Insanity and the Elizabethan Puritan Movement', *Historical Journal*, 41 (1998), pp. 27–66.
[82] Leo Damrosch, *The Sorrows of the Quaker Jesus: James Nayler and the Puritan Crackdown on the Free Spirit* (Cambridge, MA, 1996).

martyrdom and the events of Christ's passion. In the first edition of the *Acts and Monuments*, Foxe stated that a panic fell among the spectators at the beheading of Edward Seymour, the duke of Somerset. Foxe went on to declare that 'The like unto thys seemeth to have happened unto Christ, as the Evangelists wryte, when as the bishop's gard came to take him . . . they all fell down'.[83] In the second edition, however, Foxe printed the following disclaimer: 'touchyng the sayd duke of Somerset, that albeit at hys death relation is made of a sodeine fallyng of the people, as was at the takyng of Christ, this is not to be expounded as though I compared in any part the duke of Somerset with Christ'.[84] (It is significant that Somerset is a political offender whom Foxe not only venerated as a religious martyr, but whom Foxe also, at least implicitly, compared to Christ.)

Nevertheless, despite the dangers of appearing to blaspheme, even the most iconoclastic and radical Protestants sought, with considerable ingenuity and effort, to imitate, and to emphasise the imitations by their co-religionists, of Christ's passion and death. No matter how great the differences were between English Protestants and English Catholics in other areas, there was almost complete concord between them on the nature of martyrdom. Although they could not agree on who the true martyrs were, they agreed on what a true martyr was. Paradoxically, this harmony was largely forged in the fires of confessional controversy and the hotter those fires blazed, the more adamantine the concept of martyrdom became.

IV

By the end of the sixteenth century, the Christocentric model of martyrdom became dominant in early modern England, pushing other models of martyrdom into disuse. Yet during the Middle Ages there had been a number of different models of martyrdom, several of which enjoyed greater popularity than the Christocentric model.[85] One of these models was that of *miles Christi*, the knight of God, who attained martyrdom through his piety, chivalrous conduct and death. A notable example of this was Louis IX, who was hailed by Joinville in his hagiography as a martyr (a verdict confirmed in Louis's canonisation) because he died crusading in Tunis.[86] A particular example of this category of saint was the bishop who died defending the Church against those who threatened its liberties or possessions; Thomas Becket is by far the best-known example of this type of

[83] *A&M [1563]*, p. 881. Foxe is referring to Mark 14: 51–2 and John 18: 6.
[84] *A&M [1570]*, p. 1550.
[85] For a more detailed discussion of models of martyrdom in late-medieval England, see Danna Piroyansky's chapter in this volume.
[86] Robert Folz, 'La sainteté de Louis IX d'après les textes liturgiques de sa fête', *Revue d'histoire de l'Eglise de France*, 57 (1971), pp. 31–45. For Louis IX's own belief that death on a crusade was a form of martyrdom see Jacques le Goff, *Saint Louis* (Paris, 1996), pp. 883–6.

martyr.[87] Other models were those of ascetics who attained martyrdom through discipline of the body and of contemplatives who shared in the martyrdom of Christ through meditation on his passion.[88]

A particularly significant type of martyr was that of the innocent victim of lethal violence. The most striking example of this is St Guinefort, who was the centre of a popular cult. Guinefort was a dog who had been left alone with his master's infant son and had killed a snake who had threatened the boy. On their return, the parents found the baby covered with blood and saw blood dripping from the dog's jaws. Thinking that Guinefort had attacked their child, they threw the dog into a well where he drowned. But the canine's innocence was revealed when the body of the snake was discovered and a cult grew up around the well where he died. It became a popular pilgrimage site where a number of successful miracles were performed. St Guinefort was still venerated in the nineteenth century.[89]

The innocent victim was a type of martyr diametrically opposed to the type of martyr that came to dominance during the confessional battles of the Reformation: that of the martyr who died for Christ and the 'true' Church. The victim-martyrs did not die for a cause; they were honoured merely because they died suddenly, violently and, apparently, undeservedly. Their numbers included individuals murdered while on pilgimage, which at least was a holy activity, but also people struck by lightning or civilians slain in war.[90] In contrast, as Bale, Foxe, Harpsfield and Persons all agreed, it was the cause for which martyrs died, not fortitude or any other virtues that they may have possessed, nor the manner in which they died, which made them martyrs.[91] Yet the innocent victim was a type of martyr who, at least in popular sentiment, endured through the Reformation

---

[87] See Vauchez, *Sainthood*, pp. 292–5.

[88] See Clare Stancliffe, 'Red, White and Blue Martyrdom', in *Ireland in Early Medieval Europe*, ed. Dorothy Whitelock, Rosamund McKitterick and David Dumville (Cambridge, 1982), pp. 21–46, especially pp. 29–31; Vauchez, *Sainthood*, pp. 300–3, 313–15, 329–36, 350–4, 376–85 and 439–43, and Danna Piroyansky's chapter in this volume.

[89] Jean-Claude Schmitt, *The Holy Greyhound: Guinefort, Healer of Children since the Thirteenth Century*, trans. Martin Thom (Cambridge, 1983). For other examples of veneration of those who suffered an unjust death as martyrs see Vauchez, *Sainthood*, pp. 151–4 and Miri Rubin, 'Choosing Death? Experiences of Martyrdom in Late Medieval Europe', in *Martyrs and Martyrologies*, ed. Diana Wood, Studies in Church History 30 (Oxford, 1993), pp. 162–4. For another example of this tendency see Richard Rex's chapter in this volume.

[90] Vauchez, *Sainthood*, pp. 89, 149–50 and 153 n. 35. Thomas de la Hale, a Benedictine of Dover, was killed by French soldiers during a raid in 1295. He was not only venerated locally as a martyr but, unlike many victim-martyrs, his cult attracted considerable support from high ecclesiastics (see P. Grosjean, 'Thomas de la Hale, moine et martyr à Douvres en 1295', *Analecta Bollandiana*, 72 (1954), pp. 167–91).

[91] For an excellent summary of the pervasiveness of this concept, and its patristic origins, see Gregory, *Salvation at Stake*, pp. 329–39. The great evangelical Hugh Latimer went to the lengths of visiting the Henrician martyr James Bainham on the eve of his execution and interrogating him in order to ensure that he was dying for doctrinally correct – at least in Latimer's eyes – beliefs (see Thomas S. Freeman, 'The Importance of Dying Earnestly: The Metamorphosis of the Account of James Bainham in "Foxe's Book of Martyrs" ', in *The Church Retrospective*, ed. Robert N. Swanson, Studies in Church History 33 (Woodbridge, 1997), pp. 283–4).

and whose continuing existence would later help to blur the lines between religious and political martyrdom.

A particularly popular, although sinister, example of this type of martyr was the child, falsely held to have been murdered by Jews, who was venerated as a martyr.[92] Such children were not only examples of innocents dying an undeserved death as children, but were also linked with one of the most popular types of medieval martyr: the virgin martyr.[93] Although these martyrs died for the faith, in polar opposition to the martyrs of the Reformation that was a secondary feature of their martyrdom; the primary feature was the struggle to preserve their chastity from predatory persecutors who tried to compel them to renounce Christ and their virginity, not necessarily in that order.[94] The emphasis in hagiographies was on their invulnerability as well as their inviolability; invariably these martyrs would effortlessly withstand fearsome tortures and emerge unscathed from elaborate, if ineffectual, executions until finally dispatched in a swift and relatively painless manner.[95]

St Apollonia is an interesting example of this type. In Eusebius's ecclesiastical history, the original source for this story, Apollonia was an old woman of Alexandria. She refused to sacrifice to pagan idols despite enduring a rather unusual torture: her teeth were all pulled out. Finally she cast herself into a fire rather than renounce Christ. In the most popular medieval hagiography, the *Golden Legend*, Apollonia is a young and beautiful maiden. The authorities try to force her to marry and she casts herself into a fire rather than being compelled to surrender her chastity. The pulling of her teeth is barely mentioned and her self-immolation is treated in such a way that it becomes almost an assertion of invulnerability: 'Oh great and wondrous struggle of this virgin, who by the grace of a compassionate God went to the fire so as not to be burned, so as not to be consumed, as if neither fire nor torture could touch her!'[96]

The emphasis on the invulnerability of the martyr was typical of a great deal of medieval martyrological writing and it influenced perceptions of martyrdom in

---

[92] See Rubin, 'Choosing Death?', pp. 164–9, and Danna Piroyansky's chapter in this volume.

[93] See Duffy, *Stripping of the Altars*, pp. 171–7, and Karen A. Winstead, *Virgin Martyrs: Legends of Sainthood in Late Medieval England* (Ithaca, NY, 1997). Also see Danna Piroyansky's chapter in this volume.

[94] In the great medieval hagiography, the *Legenda aurea*, St Daria was consigned to a brothel but a lion providentially escaped from an ampitheatre and guarded the entrance to her room (Jacobus de Voragine, *The Golden Legend*, trans, William G. Ryan, 2 vols (Princeton, NJ, 1993), II, p. 255). In Voragine's tale of of the virgin martyr St Justina, her martyrdom is only mentioned in the final paragraph. Most of her legend is devoted to the unsuccessful efforts of Cyprian, a pagan magician, to seduce her by means of black magic (ibid., II, pp. 192–5).

[95] This is an aspect of the *Legenda aurea* and other popular late-medieval hagiographies which has been frequently discussed; see Gregory, *Salvation at Stake*, pp. 41–5, Rubin, 'Choosing Death?', pp. 169–70, and Winstead, *Virgin Martyrs*, pp. 28–9, 40–1 and 64–78. In the *Legenda aurea*, St Sophia is cast in a fiery furnace; she emerges unscathed although the flames leap sixty yards and incinerate six thousand spectators. Christina, similarly consigned to a furnace, walks around in it for five days, conversing with angels (Voragine, *Golden Legend*, I, pp. 185 and 387; for other examples, see I, pp. 29, 161 and 370, and II, pp. 181–3, 323 and 338–9). On the popularity of the *Legenda aurea* and similar martyrologies and their influence in shaping popular ideals of martyrdom, see Winstead, *Virgin Martyrs*, pp. 70–1 and 73–4.

[96] Cf. Eusebius, *Historia ecclesiastica*, VI.41.7, with Voragine, *Golden Legend*, I, pp. 268–9.

general. In a striking demonstration of this, Joan Boughton, who would be executed for heresy in 1494, declared that 'she was soo beloved with God and his angelys that all the ffyre in London would not hurt her'.[97] Such conceptions of martyrdom worked against the identification of a martyr with Christ. In fact, it is a paradoxical feature of late-medieval religion that while martyrs tended to be depicted as unaffected by the pains of torture and death, there was an almost sadistic emphasis on the agonies Christ suffered during his passion.[98]

The martyr modelled on Christ is rather rare in medieval hagiography. The only example of such a martyr in the *Legenda aurea* is Peter Martyr, indeed, Jacob de Voragine calls Peter's death his 'venerable passion'. Voragine went on to list the parallels between Christ and Peter Martyr: both were murdered for the truth, both were killed by unbelievers, both died in Passover season, both said the same prayer at death – 'Into thy hands, O Lord, I commend my spirit' – and both were betrayed for money.[99] And from outside the boundaries of Catholic orthodoxy, the Hussites associated Jan Hus with Christ and linked the martyrdoms of both.[100]

Probably the reason why Peter Martyr, an Inquisitor killed by heretics in northern Italy in 1252, was uniquely compared to Christ, was that he was the only martyr in the *Legenda aurea* to have died at the hands of contemporary unbelievers. (Similar considerations, in reverse, would also explain the association of Hus with Christ by the Bohemian reformer's followers.) Certainly, as we have seen earlier in this chapter, it was the exigencies of confessional conflict that led to the identification of the martyr with Christ during the Reformation. It was also the pressures of confessional struggle during the Reformation which led to an absolute insistence on the defence of orthodox doctrine as being the sole legitimate standard of martyrdom, making other models of martyrdom obsolete. Moreover, this trend in perceptions of martyrdom conformed to broad trends within both the Protestant and Catholic Reformations. The Christocentric nature of Protestant theology needs no emphasis here, but scholars have recently been drawing attention to the increasing Christocentric emphasis in Catholic theology, rooted in late medieval piety, which flowered during the Counter Reformation.[101] It was partly due to this Christocentric theological emphasis that one model of martyrdom, that based on the identification of the martyr with Christ, eventually dominated the concept of martyrdom to the exclusion of all other models.[102]

[97] *The Great Chronicle of London*, ed. A. H. Thomas and I. D. Thornley (1938), p. 252.
[98] On this, see Winstead, *Virgin Martyrs*, pp. 87–8, and Caroline Walker Bynum, *The Resurrection of the Body in Western Christianity, 200–1336* (New York, 1995), p. 314 n. 129.
[99] Voragine, *Golden Legend*, I, p. 259.
[100] Thomas A. Fudge, *The Magnificent Ride: The First Reformation in Hussite Bohemia* (Aldershot, 1998), pp. 126–8.
[101] Duffy, *Stripping of the Altars*, pp. 535–6, and Michael A. Mullett, *The Catholic Reformation* (1999), pp. 21–2.
[102] This did not mean that older models did not persist for some time. The veneration of martyrs who conformed to traditional models persisted among Catholic writers. Nicholas Harpsfield, who did as much

V

What is the significance of this association of early modern martyrdom with the sufferings and death of Christ? For one thing, it casts a stark light on Foucault's famous analysis of the meaning and significance of execution and lesser corporal punishments in early modern Europe.[103] Foucault was certainly correct in seeing the scaffold as a site of power but he failed to do justice to the multivalent nature of this power. Foucault recognised that the spectacle of execution could fail to achieve its purpose as a demonstration of state power for a number of reasons: the volatile emotions of the spectators, circumstances which created sympathy for the condemned, and more fundamentally, the potential for the process of penitence, pain and punishment to glorify the criminal by transforming him or her into either a sinner sanctified by repentance or a champion capable of heroic fortitude and resistance. Yet Foucault saw these alternative discourses as aberrations which only occurred when through incompetence or bad luck, the rituals of execution 'inadequately channelled' the power relations between the state and the condemned.[104]

The potential for martyrs to subvert the ceremonies of execution has been described by a number of scholars, notably David Nicholls, Peter Lake and Michael Questier.[105] Yet the possibility of inspiring parallels between Christ and the condemned extended beyond the ranks of those who died for purely religious causes. Any criminal paying the supreme penalty was following, in the most

as anyone to ensure the predominance of a Christocentric model of martyrdom, nevertheless praised as martyrs, because of their asceticism, the Carthusians whom Henry VIII persecuted: 'Tota enim illorum vita, tanta severitate transacta nihil aliud erat quam quotidianum martyrium' ('For their entire life, lived with such strictness, was nothing other than a daily martyrdom') (*Dialogi sex*, sig. Qq5v). Robert Persons boasted of the virgin martyrs in the Catholic calendar of saints and contrasted this with the lack of virgin martyrs in Foxe (*A treatise of three conversions* (3 vols, St Omer, 1604), RSTC 19416, III, sig. 8*1v). More subtly, numerous Catholic martyrologists emphasised the chastity and virginity of martyred priests (Lake and Questier, *Antichrist's Lewd Hat*, pp. 282–3). Interestingly, Protestant writers not infrequently tended to demonstrate a certain reverence for virgin martyrs (see Susannah Brietz Monta, *Martyrdom and Literature in Early Modern England* (Cambridge, 2005), p. 206). Foxe even declared that the virgin martyr St Agnes 'for her unspotted and undefiled virginitie, deserveth no greater prayse and commendation, then for her wylling death and martyrdome' (*A&M [1570]*, p. 131). Nevertheless, there was a gradual but perceptible devaluation of virginity in comparison to martyrdom and concurrently a devaluation of virgin martyrs in comparison to Christocentric martyrs. Robert Southwell wrote that 'as the combat of martyrdome is more violent, harde and victorious than that of virgins against the rebellions of the fleshe . . . So hath the crowne of martyrs a preeminence before them' (*Epistle of comfort*, fo. 195v).

103 See n. 21 above.

104 Foucault, *Discipline and Punish*, pp. 57–69, especially p. 68.

105 Nicholls, 'Theatre of Martyrdom', pp. 65–73; Lake and Questier, *Antichrist's Lewd Hat*, pp. 229–54. Thomas W. Laqueur has described the ability of those condemned even for non-political and non-religious offences to undermine the rituals of execution ('Crowds, Carnivals and the State in English Executions, 1604–1868', in *The First Modern Society: Essays in History in Honour of Lawrence Stone*, ed. A. L. Beier, David Cannadine and James M. Rosenheim [Cambridge, 1989], pp. 309–10 and 319–23). For an egregious example of the subversion of an execution see Alec Ryrie's discussion of Robert Barnes's execution in this volume.

literal sense, in the footsteps of his Saviour. The greater the torment and the greater the rituals of degradation which the condemned was forced to undergo, the greater was the potential for perceived resemblance to the sufferings of Christ. With this analogy the authoritarian rituals of punishment indicted the authorities as unjust, degradation extolled the criminal by associating him with Christ and the pain inflicted was not a source of humiliation but of enhanced spiritual power.

It is this potential which lay behind the supreme importance attached to the final speeches of the condemned in early modern Europe and to the use, brilliantly analysed by Peter Lake, of the final utterances of convicted murderers as religious propaganda.[106] This does not mean that every condemned criminal in early-modern Europe was regarded as a Christ-figure, far from it. And on many occasions executions were undoubtedly the highly effective displays of state power which Foucault envisioned.[107] But they were never unambiguous displays of state power; however nebulously, the aura of the crucified Christ always surrounded the condemned. Recently Paul Strohm, discussing the ways in which the humiliations inflicted on Jan Hus and Richard, duke of York, in the course of their executions, led to their being compared to Christ, marvels at the ineptitude of those who staged these executions:

> One would suppose that a persecutor with any sense would act urgently to foreclose any possibility of comparing his victim's sufferings to those of the crucified Christ, since any sharing-out of Christ's sufferings implies an ultimate possibility of sharing in Christ's final glory.[108]

This observation underscores the dilemma facing princes and magistrates in medieval and early modern Europe. To eliminate the possibility of comparisons between a condemned criminal and Christ, the authorities would have had to purge criminal punishments of the ceremonies of degradation and of expiation. Yet these ceremonies not only provided crucial political and judicial propaganda, they were also religious theatre, which would lead (hopefully) to the repentance of the offenders and the edification of the spectators.

Of course the aura of Christ-like sanctity shone much more brightly when the condemned was regarded as a martyr. Martyrdom was – because the martyr was, unlike the ordinary criminal, morally unambiguous – the purest and most potent

---

[106] Peter Lake, 'Puritanism, Arminianism and a Shropshire Axe Murder', *Midlands History*, 15 (1990), pp. 37–64, Peter Lake, ' "Deeds against Nature": Cheap Print, Protestantism and Murder in Early Seventeenth-Century England', in *Culture and Politics in Early Stuart England*, ed. Kevin Sharpe and Peter Lake (Stanford, CA, 1993), pp. 257–84 and Peter Lake, 'Popular Form, Puritan Content? Two Puritan Appropriations of the Murder Pamphlet from Mid-Seventeenth-Century London', in *Religion, Culture and Society in Early Stuart England: Essays in Honour of Patrick Collinson*, ed. Anthony Fletcher and Peter Roberts (Cambridge, 1994), pp. 313–34.
[107] However, Laqueur has also argued that a carnivalesque atmosphere occurring at executions further inhibited their effectiveness as displays of state power (Laqueur, 'Crowds, Carnivals and the State', pp. 305–55). I am grateful to Peter Marshall for bringing this article to my attention.
[108] Paul Strohm, *Politique: Languages of Statecraft between Chaucer and Shakespeare* (Notre Dame, IN, 2005), p. 213.

form of this identification of the condemned criminal with Christ. And the identification of Christ certainly facilitated and intensified, perhaps even made possible, the most important shift in early-modern martyrdom, and its most important legacy: the politicisation of the martyr. By this, I mean the transference of the veneration and reverence given to those who suffered for religious causes to those suffered for political causes.

VI

The Christ-like political martyr was not unknown in the later Middle Ages. We have already noted the examples of Peter Martyr and Jan Hus. Occasional examples arise with some of the cults of what have been termed the 'political saints'.[109] Implicit (but not, it should be noted, explicit) comparisons to Christ's passion were made in contemporary, or near-contemporary, accounts of Archbishop Richard Scrope, whose execution at the behest of Henry IV inspired one of the most successful of these cults.[110] A more thorough set of parallelisms to Christ's passion occurred in John Whethamstede's account of the execution of Richard, duke of York, a figure who, while undoubtedly political, has never been regarded as a saint. According to Whethamstede, York, who claimed the English throne, was crowned with a chaplet of grass and mockingly hailed as king by his enemies. Whether or not the incident actually took place, Whetehamstede certainly laboured to compare York's ordeal to Christ's passion, even writing that the duke's adversaries 'bent their knees before him like the Jews before the Lord'.[111]

However, such examples are rare. Reading through late medieval materials, one is struck by the rarity with which even the political saints were compared to Christ. For example the *Brut* chronicle, which was sympathetic to Thomas, earl of Lancaster (who would be popularly venerated as a saint), described how Thomas was betrayed by those he trusted and delivered to his enemies. It also describes how he was led to execution with a paper crown on his head (this in reference to his allegedly calling himself 'King Arthur' in treasonable negotiations with the Scots). The potential for pointing out parallels between the duke's tribulations and the passion of Christ is obvious but the *Brut*, despite its partisanship for

---

[109] For a discussion of these, see Simon Walker, 'Political Saints in Later Medieval England', in *The McFarlane Legacy: Studies in Late Medieval Politics and Society*, ed. R. H. Britnell and A. J. Pollard (Stroud, 1995), pp. 77–106.

[110] Danna Piroyansky, ' "Martyrio pulchro finites": Archbishop Scrope's Martyrdom and the Creation of a Cult', in *Richard Scrope: Archbishop, Rebel, Martyr*, ed. Jeremy Goldberg (Stamford, Lincolnshire, forthcoming). I am grateful to Dr Piroyansky for sending me a copy of this article before publication. Hagiographers of the archbishop noted in their accounts that he was led to execution on an inexpensive horse, without saddle (paralleling the entry of Christ into Jerusalem) and that he paraphrased Isaiah 53: 7 (considered to be a prophecy of Christ's passion), but none of them explicitly compared Scrope to Christ.

[111] Strohm, *Politique*, pp. 213–18; the quotation is on p. 215.

Thomas, and in marked contrast to Whetehamstede's account of the duke of York, never makes these comparisons.[112]

The difference between these political saints and the Christ-like political martyrs perhaps becomes clearer when we compare two royal figures, one, Henry VI, the centre of the most successful of the political cults and the other, Charles I, one of the most important of the Christ-like political martyrs. Henry, the opponent and victim of Edward IV, was the great success among later medieval English saints. Eventually his cult would gain official status under Henry VII, but for fifteen years before this, the cult enjoyed sudden, widespread and spontaneous popularity, attracting devotees throughout England. Moreover, the spark which animated this cult was the ubiquitous perception that, because his death was undeserved, Henry was a martyr.[113]

Yet although Henry was honoured as a martyr, one model which was never invoked for him was that of Christ's passion. Nowhere in the hymns to Henry is he compared with Christ nor do symbols suggesting such a comparison appear in the pictures or images of the king which appeared in books and churches after his death. None of Henry's recorded miracles do anything to make this connection. It is true that John Blacman, Henry's hagiographer, compares Henry and Christ in a few places. In extolling Henry's mercy, Blacman declares that, in this respect, the king was an 'imitator' of Christ.[114] Furthermore, people to whom Henry showed mercy and who turned on him, were compared by Blacman to the Jews turning on Christ.[115] Also one or two of the miracles Blacman attributes to Henry echo those of Christ in the gospels. Henry allegedly multiplied a small quantity of wheat into enough to feed his hungry soldiers.[116] And before he was captured, divine voices audibly warned him that he would be delivered to his enemies by treachery.[117] But these comparisons were not developed or made explicit. Right at the moment of Henry's capture, which would have made the perfect platform for launching into a comparison of Henry's martyrdom to Christ's passion, Blacman instead broke off and merely observed that Henry endured hardship and abuse 'like a true follower of Christ'.[118]

The contrast with the cult of Charles I could not be more pronounced.[119] The identification of Charles with Christ was made explicitly, even stridently, in

---

[112] *The Brut or The Chronicles of England*, ed. F. W. D. Brie, EETS, o.s. 131 and 136, 2 vols (1906 and 1908), I, pp. 216 and 219.
[113] On the popularity of the cult of Henry VI, and its origins, see Thomas S. Freeman, ' *"Ut verus Christi sequestor"*: John Blacman and the Cult of Henry VI', *The Fifteenth Century*, 5 (2005), pp. 127–9.
[114] John Blacman, *Henry the Sixth: A Reprint of John Blacman's Memoir*, ed. and trans. M. R. James (Cambridge, 1919), p. 40.
[115] Ibid., p. 41.
[116] Ibid., p. 43.
[117] Ibid., p. 41.
[118] For Blacman's motives in not glorifying Henry VI as a martyr, see Freeman, '*Ut verus Christi sequestor*', pp. 132–42.
[119] On the overall history of the cult of Charles I, see Andrew Lacey, *The Cult of King Charles the Martyr* (Woodbridge, 2003); also see Andrew Lacey's chapter in this volume. Although Lacey's observations on the thoroughness of the comparison of Christ with Charles I are well taken, I do think that his claim that 'the

works printed after his execution, such as Richard Watson's *Regicidium Judaicum: or a discourse about the Jews crucifying Christ their King* (1649) or John Warner's *The devilish conspiracy, hellish treson, heathenish condemnation and damnable murder committed and executed by the Jews against the annointed of the Lord, Christ the King* (1649).[120] The most systematic of such works was Henry Leslie's *The martyrdom of King Charles or his conformity with Christ in his sufferings*. It identified the Scots who sold Charles to parliament with Judas, Cromwell and Ireton with Annas and Caiphas, Bradshaw and Cook with the scribes and the pharisees and Fairfax with Pilate. It also devoted over thirty pages to setting forth the exact parallels between Charles's martyrdom and Christ's passion. If some of these comparisons are rather strained – at the crucifixion darkness fell over the land, the earth shook and graves were opened; at Charles's execution the ducks mysteriously left their pond in St James's Park and began fluttering around the king's scaffold – this demonstrates Leslie's determination to make the identification of Charles with Christ as complete as possible.[121] The famous frontispiece to *Eikon basilike* says it all. Here Charles, having laid aside his earthly crown, clutches a crown of of thorns while contemplating his heavenly crown.[122] Charles is Christ, Cromwell and the regicides are evil and these works are consequently intensely political and unmistakably partisan.

VII

Earlier, I suggested that the tendency to equate the martyr with Christ may have been particularly strong in England because it was one of the few ways left to express the traditional, but increasingly illicit, devotion to the traditional signifiers of the passion of Christ. Now I would like to suggest a number of additional reasons why the Christ-like martyr was particularly well suited to the English experience and why this model remained particularly potent in England, and later the English-speaking world.

John Morrill has famously declared that the English Civil War was 'the last of the Wars of Religion'.[123] In one important respect, however, the Civil Wars differed from the Continental religious wars – it lacked massacres.[124] In fact, the

explicit identification of Charles with Christ is virtually unique in the annals of martyrology' (*Cult of King Charles*, p. 15) is an exaggeration.

[120] These works are STC [Wing] W1093 and STC [Wing] W902 respectively.

[121] Henry Leslie, *The martyrdome of King Charles or his conformity with Christ in his sufferings* (The Hague, 1649), STC [Wing] L1163, pp. 19 and 25. For the prodigies attending Christ's crucifixion see Matthew 27: 45 and 50–1, Mark 15: 38 and Luke 24: 44–5.

[122] On this frontispiece and on *Eikon basilike* itself, see Andrew Lacey's chapter in this volume.

[123] John Morrill, 'The Religious Context of the English Civil War', *Transactions of the Royal Historical Society*, fifth series 34 (1984), p. 178.

[124] Not surprisingly, such a generalisation requires some qualification. Will Coster has listed eighteen massacres that occurred during the First Civil War (Will Coster, 'Massacres and Codes of Conduct in the English Civil War', in *The Massacre in History*, ed. Mark Levene and Penny Roberts (New York, 1999), pp. 89–105, also see his list of these massacres on p. 92). However, fifteen of the eighteen took place during

urban violence and riots so typical of the French religious wars were unknown in England. There was no English equivalent of St Bartholomew's day or the slaughter of Waldensian communities in the Piedmont and Provence. (In fact, the word massacre, derived from a French word for a butcher's chopping block – the butcher's knife was the 'massacreur' – acquired its modern meaning when applied to the purges of Waldensians in Provence in 1545.)[125] Nor was there anything resembling the extermination of Anabaptists in Germany, Switzerland and eastern Europe.

The massacres of religious dissidents were a new, blood-red wine, which burst the old wineskins of traditional martyrology. In 1582, Simon Goulart, the continuator of Crespin's martyrology, apologised to his readers for having to devote the later sections of his work to the anonymous victims of mass slaughters rather than to the individual champions of Christ.[126] In particular, while it was relatively easy to identify the sufferings of an individual martyr, whose trial and execution could be described in detail, with Christ's, it was much harder to do this for the anonymous victims of a massacre. It was hard for contemporaries, even (or perhaps especially) the survivors of one, to appreciate the extent of a massacre and thus to empathise with the sufferings of its victims.[127] It has been argued that that the decline of French Protestant martyrologies occurred precisely because of their inability to adequately chronicle persecutions which took place by means of riot and massacre rather than trial and judicial execution.[128] The English experience of judicial execution rather than wholesale slaughter ensured that the model of Christ's passion remained relevant.

At the same time, the blood spilled in riot and massacre ate like acid into the stoicism and passivity expected of the Christ-like martyr. Denis Richet has analysed insightfully the shift in French Protestant attitudes after 1559, when the passive, stoical acceptance of martyrdom was replaced by exhortations to resistance. Richet argues that the Huguenots abandoned their 'martyr complex' (his phrase) and became militant fighters for their cause.[129] Such a transformation

or after an attack on a garrison, and are not analagous to religious riots or massacres (even the notorious massacres at Drogheda and Wexford in 1649 occurred in the aftermath of protracted sieges and the equally notorious massacre of Montrose's army and its camp followers at Philiphaugh followed a battle). Moreover, none of these massacres in England during the First Civil War involved more than about 120 casualties, and thus are dwarfed in comparison to the riots and massacres on the Continent. Only the massacre of English settlers in Ireland in 1641 provides some comparison to religious violence on the Continent.
[125] Mark Greengrass, 'Hidden Transcripts: Personal Testimonies of Religious Violence in the French Wars of Religion', in *The Massacre in History*, pp. 69–70.
[126] Quoted in Gregory, *Salvation at Stake*, pp. 191–2.
[127] Greengrass, 'Hidden Transcripts', pp. 69–88, especially p. 80.
[128] Kenz, *Les bûchers du roi*, pp. 202–33.
[129] Denis Richet, 'Aspects socio-culturels des conflits religieux à Paris dans le seconde moitié du XVIe siècle', *Annales E S.C.* 32 (1977), pp. 764–89, especially pp. 768–9 and 785. Barbara Diefendorf has commented on the passivity of Huguenots faced with persecution in an earlier period, although she has also observed an ambivalence among French Protestants in this earlier period as to whether armed resistance to persecution was justifiable (Barbara Diefendorf, *Beneath the Cross: Catholics and Huguenots in Sixteenth-Century Paris* [New York and Oxford, 1991], pp. 107–8 and 136–42).

never took permanent root in England, where even in the present day, the common perception of martyrdom demands that the martyr be a passive sufferer, not a violent militant.

Finally, the circumstances of persecution in England, in which Thomas More and John Fisher were executed for treason under Henry VIII, George Eagles was executed for treason under Mary, and Campion, and the other mission priests, were executed for treason under Elizabeth and the early Stuarts, contributed powerfully to undermining the distinction between religious and political offences.[130] Later victims of political authority in England contributed to this process by invoking the moral authority of martyrdom. Several factors made this particularly easy in England. One was the importance of anti-Catholicism in the political struggles of the seventeenth century. This permitted opponents of the later Stuarts, such as Lord William Russell, to be portrayed as martyrs for the Protestant cause. It also worked in reverse, allowing, not without reason, victims of anti-papist hysteria, such as Oliver Plunkett, the archbishop of Armagh, to be depicted as sufferers for religion.[131] Anti-Catholicism was fed by martyrological works, especially Foxe's *Acts and Monuments* and the numerous abridgements of it, and in a circular process, anti-Catholicism also increased the esteem of both martyrologies and martyrs. And as the Church of England basked in the warmth of the fires of Smithfield, other English denominations, notably, but by no means exclusively, the Catholics, took increasing comfort in their own martyrological traditions. The stronger the hold of martyrdom on the popular imagination, the more desirable it was for the victims of political authority, and their supporters, to depict them as martyrs. And to do this convincingly they needed to cast them in the mould of the Christ-like martyr already created by Tyndale, More, Hogarde, Bale, Foxe, Harpsfield, Persons and the other English Reformation martyrologists and anti-martyrologists.

VIII

Charles I is an outstanding example of the politicisation of martyrdom, but he was far from the last. One case is particularly striking in its successful blurring of the distinction between religious martyrdom and death for a political cause. In 1651, Christopher Love, a Presbyterian minister, was executed for his involvement in a plot to assist Scottish Covenanters in bringing the future Chares II to the throne.

---

[130] For the impact of charges of treason on Catholic conceptions of martyrdom see Victor Houliston's chapter in this volume.

[131] Plunkett provides a good example of how nebulous the boundaries between religious and political martyrdom could be. On the one hand, Plunkett was clearly singled out because of his office and was certainly, in the broadest sense, a victim of anti-Catholic bigotry. But the decision to try him was made in order that Charles II's government might use the trial to establish the credibility of witnesses it planned to use against the earl of Shaftesbury and other Whigs (John Miller, *Popery and Politics in England, 1660–1688* [Cambridge, 1973], p. 190).

Love was quite concerned to present himself as a martyr and well aware that the political nature of his offence potentially prevented his being perceived as one. In his scaffold speech Love declared, in words which, ironically, many executed Catholic priests would have endorsed, that

> herein is the disadvantage which I am in, in the thoughts of many who judge that I suffer not for the Word, or for conscience, but for meddling with state matters. To this I shall briefly say, that it is an old game of the devil, to compare the cause of God's people's sufferings to be contrivances against the state, when in truth it is their religion and conscience they are persecuted for . . . Upon a civil account my life is pretended to be taken away, whereas indeed it is, because I pursue my Covenant and will not prostitute my principles and conscience to the ambition and lusts of men.[132]

Love was also acclaimed as a martyr by his supporters, notably the Nonconformist minister and poet Robert Wild.[133] And Love's wife not only extolled him as a martyr, she compared him to Christ. According to her account, Christopher assured well-wishers at his execution, in another clear echo of Christ at Gethsemane, that 'he was but drinking the cup which his Father had invigled'. And, in a more personal note, she exclaimed, invoking Mary Magdalene at Christ's tomb: 'Give me now leave with Mary to sit down and weep at his sepulchre'.[134]

Later the regicides would be considered martyrs and compare themselves, or be compared by their own supporters with the most apocalyptically significant martyrs of them all, the two witnesses prophesied in Revelation.[135] Burton, Bastwick, Prynne, Charles I and the regicides were all persecuted for political rather than strictly religious causes and each successfully wore the mantle of Christ. They were followed by figures such as Algernon Sidney and, most spectacularly, Lord William Russell, who despite being unambigiously political figures, were honoured as religious martyrs by their supporters. Gilbert Burnet, whose devotion to the Whig cause was eventually rewarded with his elevation to the bishopric of Salisbury, preached a sermon on the morning of Russell's execution, in which he came close to comparing the condemned peer to Christ.[136] Sir

---

132 Christopher Love, *Mr Love's case* (1651), STC [Wing] L3143, pp. 15–16. In his speech, Love also compared himself to the Marian martyr Rowland Taylor (p. 15). For a contemporary attack denying that Love was a martyr because he died for secular offences, see pp. 35–8.

133 Robert Wild, *The tragedy of Christopher Love* (1651), STC [Wing] W2151, pp. 5–6.

134 Dr Williams's Library MS PP.12.50.4 (21), p. 139; also see pp. 136 and 138.

135 See Blair Worden, *Roundhead Reputations: The English Civil Wars and the Passions of Posterity* (2001), p. 52, and John Coffey's chapter in this volume.

136 Lois G. Schwoerer, *Lady Rachel Russell: 'One of the Best of Women'* (Baltimore and London, 1988), p. 129. On the construction of Russell as a martyr see Lois G. Schwoerer, 'William, Lord Russell: The Making of a Martyr, 1683–1983', *Journal of British Studies*, 45 (1985), pp. 41–71. Russell appeared as a martyr in at least one abridged edition of Foxe's martyrology (*The new and complete Book of Martyrs . . . being Foxe's Book of Martyrs, revised and corrected with additions and great improvements*, ed. Paul Wright (1784), p. 768). For the veneration of Algernon Sidney as a martyr see Blair Worden, 'The Commonwealth Kidney of Algernon Sidney', *Journal of British Studies*, 24 (1985), pp. 1–46. For an attack

Roger L'Estrange, Charles II's licenser for the press, sourly observed that if the arguments of Russell's apologists were to be accepted, 'every man that suffers for treason, shall presently at this rate be made a martyr for the Reformation'.[137]

The glorification of political martyrs was not a Whig monopoly; during the Restoration several martyrologies were written extolling fallen royalist soldiers.[138] In these works, the boundary between military and political casualty and martyr of God all but disappeared. The earl of Strafford was hailed – in terms invoking both St Stephen and John Rogers, the first Marian martyr – as the 'proto-martyr' of the royalist cause.[139] Two men executed for leading an uprising against the parliamentary garrison in Bristol in 1643 were hailed as 'glorious martyrs now lying under the altar'.[140] Nor were such comparisons left to the martyrologists; James Stanley, the earl of Derby, a royalist commander captured and executed in the aftermath of the battle of Worcester, exclaimed as he was led past the market cross in Bolton, 'This scaffold must be my cross. Blessed Saviour, I take it up willingly and follow thee'.[141] Eusebius Andrews, a London barrister executed in 1650 for his involvement in a conspiracy to foment rebellion, also compared his sufferings to those of Christ, writing on the eve of death that God 'is resolved not to let me be less than a Son beloved, and I am content to bear stripes and kiss the instrument'.[142]

Whig martyrology, moreover, hardly ceased in the reign of Charles II. A stream of martyrological works, compiled or published by John Tutchin, appeared after the Glorious Revolution. Initially these works dealt with those punished for involvement in Monmouth's rebellion, but soon they began to include those 'martyred' in the reign of Charles II as well.[143] Tutchin admitted that some readers might

---

on the 'multitudes' who honoured Sidney as a saint and martyr see [Edmund Bohun], *A defense of Sir Robert Filmer against the mistakes and misrepresentations of Algernon Sidney* (1684), STC [Wing] B3450, p. 16.

[137] Roger L'Estrange, *Considerations upon a printed sheet entituled the Speech of the late Lord Russell to the Sheriffs* (1683), STC [Wing] L1233, p. 18.

[138] James Heath, *A new book of loyal English martyrs and confessors . . . for the maintenance of the just and legal government of these kingdoms in Church and State* (1663), STC [Wing] H1336, and William Winstanley, *The Loyall martyrology or, brief catalogues and charactes of the most eminent persons who suffered for their conscience during the late times of rebellion* (1665), STC [Wing] W3066.

[139] Heath, *New Book*, pp. 15, and Winstanley, *Loyall martyrology*, p. 5.

[140] Heath, *New Book*, p. 105. Royalist casualties of the war hailed by Heath as martyrs include Sir George Lisle and Sir Charles Lucas, who were executed by firing squad after the their stubborn defence of Colchester in the Second Civil War (pp. 126–40) and the officers of the royalist garrison at Pontefract, summarily executed in 1649, for their dogged defence of the castle (pp. 247–53).

[141] Ibid., p. 338.

[142] Ibid., p. 297.

[143] They began with Tutchin's sixteen-page pamphlet, *The Protestant Martyrs or the Bloody Assizes* (1689), STC [Wing], T3382aA. This was followed by a string of martyrological works printed in the same year: *The Bloody Assizes or the compleat history of the life of George, Lord Jeffreys* (1689), STC [Wing] T3370A; *The dying speecches, letters and prayers of those eminent persons who suffered in the West* (1689), STC [Wing] T3372A; *The second and last collection of dying speeches* (1689), STC [Wing] T3383A; *The first and second collection of dying speeches, letters and prayers* (1689) (not listed in Wing); *The dying speeches of several excellent persons who suffered for their zeal against popery and arbitrary*

be offended with the title of martyrs and martyrdom, which so often occur in the following paper [*sic*]; both because some of those concerned were accused for plots against the government and others were in actual arms. But 'tis possible for a person at the same time to be a Church and State martyr.[144]

Tutchin worked to erase what little remained of the idea that only those who died in a religious cause were martyrs by sedulously forging links between the victims of papist cruelty under the later Stuarts and the martyrs described by 'that great man' John Foxe.[145] Thus Tutchin extolled the London alderman Henry Cornish, executed in 1685 as a conspirator in Monmouth's rebellion, for displaying 'a bravery rarely to be met with, unless among those who suffered in the same age, or their predecessor's Queen Mary's martyrs'.[146] And Tutchin was also as systematic as Foxe had been in comparing his martyrs to Christ. In doggerel verses he depicted the punishment of Thomas Dangerfield (who had been sentenced to stand in the pillory and receive four hundred lashes for libelling James II) to Christ's passion:

> Pray on great soul! and like thy Master be,
> For those that now begin to murder thee,
> Thy Master thus, thus thy Lord Jesus dy'd,
> He must be scourg'd before he's crucify'd.
> Though milder Jews far more good nature have,
> They forty stripes, Jeffrey's four hundred gave.[147]

Yet the secularisation of martyrdom proceeded even further than this. In 1651, when English merchants at Ambonya were slaughtered by the Dutch, they were hailed by English pamphleters as martyrs and their deaths were described in Foxean language and according to Foxean paradigms; the pamphlets even described the providential punishments inflicted on the 'persecutors' of these English saints.[148] Eventually, even innocence was no longer a prerequisite for martyrdom. Andrea McKenzie has recently observed that the virtues and even sanctity of religious martyrs came to be attributed to criminals condemned for non-political offences such as robbery and murder. Such criminals, when they displayed sufficient courage and fortitude, were even credited with having been inspired by the Holy Spirit.[149]

---

government (1689), STC [Wing] T3372B and *The new martyrology or the Bloody Assizes* (1689), T3379. This last work was enlarged and republished (under Tutchin's *nom de plume* of 'Thomas Pitts') in 1693 (STC [Wing] T3380). In 1705, the final version of Tutchin's martyrology was published anonymously as *The Western Martyrology or the Bloody Assizes*. This work, despite its title, included earlier Whig 'martyrs' such as Sidney, Lord Russell and Titus Oates.

[144] *Western Martyrology*, sig. a1v.
[145] Ibid., sig. a1r, also see sig. a2r.
[146] Ibid., p. 78. Tutchin also compared Justice Jeffries to the persecutors of the Waldensians (p. 104).
[147] Ibid., p. 90.
[148] Steven C. A. Pincus, *Protestantism and Patriotism: Ideologies and the Making of English Foreign Policy, 1650–1668* (Cambridge, 1996), pp. 59–60.
[149] McKenzie, 'Martyrs in Low Life?', pp. 167–205, especially p. 193. McKenzie attributes this

The increasing politicisation, even secularisation, of martyrdom in the late seventeenth century was further augmented by an increasing classicism. Like two rivers flowing together, the two traditions merged at floodtide, sweeping all before them. At times these traditions competed, as when the writings of figures such as Edmund Ludlow, Richard Baxter, Thomas Fairfax and Henry Vane the Younger were printed, stripped of their religious, indeed apocalyptic, sentiments and 'Protestant martyrs' such as Vane and Algernon Sidney were recast as classical heroes and republican patriots.[150] The reputation of William Russell bobbed to and fro on the waves of both traditions; in 1784, the same year in which Russell was glorified as a Protestant martyr 'sacrificed to cruelty and revenge of his popish enemies', he was also portrayed in a play as a classical champion and compared to the Spartans who died at Thermopylae to save their homeland.[151]

But more often the two traditions buttressed each other because they both emphasised the same virtues of stoicism and fortitude. One of the many ways in which Christianity intertwined with the classical tradition was in the influence which Plutarchan biography and the lives of classical philosophers, with their celebration of *apatheia* (the superiority of reason to pain and fear), had on early Christian martyrology.[152] Initially patristic writers such as Tertullian and Clement of Alexandria regarded pagan martyrs as worthy of emulation although by the early Middle Ages sharp distinctions were drawn between pagan and Christian martyrs – invariably to the detriment of the former.[153] This attitude changed in the Renaissance as classical models and standards were deployed in praise of Christian martyrs. A striking, and famous, example of this is the letter of the celebrated humanist Poggio Bracciolini to Leonardo Bruni, recounting the execution of Jerome of Prague and comparing the heresiarch to Socrates.[154] Later

phenomenon to changes in ideas of masculinity and ignores its roots in confessional debates about martyrdom. Yet even the arguments that she cites being used by contemporaries to undermine the heroic reputation of condemned criminals – that their fortitude at their executions was due to their being drunk (pp. 197–8) or a desire for popular applause (pp. 198–201) – recapitulate exactly the arguments used earlier to undermine the heroic reputations of religious martyrs.

[150] See Worden, *Roundhead Reputations*, pp. 44–6, 52–9 and 63–4 as well as Jonathan Scott, *Algernon Sidney and the English Republic, 1623–77* (Cambridge, 1988), p. 4. On Vane see John Coffey's chapter in this volume.

[151] Schwoerer, 'William, Lord Russell', pp. 64–5.

[152] See in particular, Patricia Cox, *Biography in Late Antiquity: A Quest for the Holy Man* (Berkeley and Los Angeles, 1986), pp. 25–30. On the influence of classical biographies on Eusebius's paradigmatic ecclesiastical history, see Gustave Bardy's introduction to his edition of the *Historia ecclesiastica*, Sources Chrétiennes 73 (Paris, 1987), pp. 79–80, and Robert M. Grant, *Eusebius as Church Historian* (Oxford, 1980), p. 46.

[153] Thomas J. Heffernan, *Sacred Biography: Saints and their Biographers in the Middle Ages* (New York and Oxford, 1998), p. 219.

[154] Renee Neu Watkins, 'The Death of Jerome of Prague: Divergent Views', *Speculum*, 42 (1967), pp. 118–24. On the popularity and wide dissemination of this letter see Siegfried Hoyer, 'Jan Hus und der Hussitismus in den Flugschriften des ersten Jahrzehntens der Reformation', in *Flugschriften als Massenmedia der Reformationszeit*, ed. Hans-Joachim Köhler (Stuttgart, 1981), pp. 291–307. Poggio's letter is printed in *Documenta Mag. Joannis Hus vitam, doctrinam, causam in Constantiensi concilio . . .*, ed. František Palacky (Prague, 1869), pp. 624–6; for an English translation see *The Portable Renaissance Reader*, ed. J. B. Ross and M. M. McLaughlin (New York, 1953), pp. 623–4. For classical models in early

martyrologists were no less adept at comparing Christian martyrs with classical heroes. Foxe praised the constancy of the Marian martyr Thomas Tompkins, comparing him to the legendary Roman champion Gaius Mucius Scaevola, while Harpsfield compared Thomas More to Cicero.[155] William Winstanley neatly combined both traditions when he praised Peter Vowel, executed for plotting the overthrow of Oliver Cromwell, for displaying 'a Roman spirit temper'd with Christian patience' at his 'martyrdom'.[156] Tutchin similarly claimed that there was nothing 'more Roman and yet truly Christian' than Algernon Sidney's behaviour on the scaffold and also compared Sir Thomas Armstrong, one of the Rye House Plotters, to Brutus and Cato.[157]

IX

There is not enough space in this chapter to trace completely the development of the idea of the Christ-like political martyr, but it might be worth looking briefly at the American Civil War to see the strength of this tradition in another country in the English-speaking world, over two centuries after Charles I's death. John Brown, the fiery abolitionist leader, whose attempt to incite a slave rebellion helped to trigger the war, was not only hailed as a martyr, but was compared to Christ by his supporters. One abolitionist author, Lydia Child, wrote when she heard the news that Brown had been sentenced to death: 'What a splendid martyrdom. The scaffold will be as glorious as the cross of Calvary.'[158] Ralph Waldo Emerson used the same phrase, declaring publicly on the afternoon of Brown's execution that his imminent death 'will make the gallows as glorious as the cross'.[159] And since John Wilkes Booth, with a maladroit sense of timing ill-suited to a thespian, killed Abraham Lincoln on Good Friday, he ensured that the slain president would be compared to Christ. When Herman Melville, the novelist and poet, wrote that

> Good Friday was the day
> of the prodigy and crime
> When they killed him in his pity
> When they killed him in his prime
> Of clemency and calm –

modern martyrology see A. Prosperi, 'L'elemento storico nelle polemiche sulla santità', in *Finzione e santità tra medievo ed età moderna*, ed. G. Zarri (Turin, 1991), pp. 88–118, especially pp. 89–91.
[155] *A&M [1563]*, p. 1102. Interestingly Poggio had compared Jerome of Prague to Scaevola (Watkins, 'Death of Jerome of Prague', p. 124). For the comparison of More to Cicero see Nicholas Harpsfield, *The Life and Death of Sir Thomas Moore, Knight . . .*, ed. E. V. Hitchcock, EETS, o.s. 186 (Oxford, 1963), p. 217.
[156] Winstanley, *The Loyall martyrology*, pp. 35–6.
[157] Tutchin, *Western Martyrology*, pp. 61 and 74.
[158] *Lydia Maria Child, Selected Letters, 1817–1888*, ed. Milton Meltzer and Patricia Holland (Amherst, MA, 1982), p. 329.
[159] Robert D. Richardson, *Emerson: The Mind on Fire* (Berkeley, CA, 1995), p. 545.

> When with yearning he was filled
> To redeem the evil willed . . .

he was describing the son of Thomas Lincoln, not the Son of God.[160]

But the Union side had no monopoly on the Christ-like political martyrs. Defeat provided an ideal climate for fostering a sense of victimisation and collective martyrdom. In 1873, Robert Dabney, who had been a chaplain and chief of staff to 'Stonewall' Jackson, wrote to D. H. Hill, a former Confederate general, declaring that 'The South needs a book of "Acts and Monuments" of Confederate martyrs' that would depict 'Southern martyrdom under ruthless abolition outrages'.[161] This project was never fulfilled, but in the aftermath of the war, the Confederate leaders were extolled as martyrs who embodied the divine.

On 1 May 1886, Jefferson Davis, the former president of the Confederacy, who had been incarcerated for two years after the war, was introduced to a cheering crowd in Atlanta by a speaker who declared that his appearance there has 'given us the best Easter we have seen since Christ was risen from the dead'. The next day, Davis rode to the unveiling of a memorial in Savannah in a railroad car which bore a banner with the inscription: 'He Was Manacled For Us'.[162] In 1903, William Dame, the rector of Baltimore's Memorial Protestant Church, gave a semon on the 'Passion' of Jefferson Davis in which he explicitly compared Davis to the crucified Christ, calling him 'the chosen vicarious victim' who stood silent while the Notherners 'laid on him the falsely alleged iniquities of us all'.[163] And as late as 1923, the following hymn was composed in Davis's honour:

> Jefferson Davis! Still we honor thee!
> Our lamb victorious, who for us endured
> A cross of martyrdom, a crown of thorns,
> A soul's Gethsemane, a nation's hate,
> A dungeon's gloom! Another God in chains.[164]

Admirers of Davis were, however, positively tongue-tied in comparison with the eulogists of his great general Robert E. Lee. Randolph McKim, a leading Episocopalian priest, who had served as an aide to one of Lec's generals, wrote of the Confederate commander that 'the sign of the cross was upon his life'.[165] At the

---

160 Herman Melville, 'The Martyr', in *The Battle-Pieces of Herman Melville*, ed. Hennig Cohen (New York, 1963), p. 130. For contemporaries drawing parallels between Christ and Lincoln, in the aftermath of the latter's assassination, see Thomas Reed Turner, *Beware the People Weeping: Public Opinion and the Assassination of Abraham Lincoln* (Baton Rouge, LA, and London, 1982), pp. 82–3 and Richard Carwardine, *Lincoln: A Life of Purpose and Power* (New York, 2006), p. 320.

161 Quoted in David W. Blight, *Race and Reunion: The Civil War in American Memory* (Cambridge, MA and London, 2001), p. 263.

162 Donald E. Collins, *The Death and Resurrection of Jefferson Davis* (Lanham, MD, 2005), pp. 34–5.

163 Lloyd A. Hunter, 'The Immortal Confederacy: Another Look at Lost Cause Religion', in *The Myth of the Lost Cause and Civil War History*, ed. Gary W. Gallagher and Alan T. Nolan (Bloomington and Indianapolis, 2000), p. 198.

164 Hunter, 'The Immortal Confederacy', p. 198.

165 Ibid., p. 197.

dedication of Lee's tomb in the Lee Chapel at Washington and Lee University, in 1880, John Daniel, who had been the chief of staff to Confederate general Jubal Early, delivered the main address. In it, he claimed that Seminary Ridge (the site from which Lee observed the battle of Gettysburg) was Lee's Mount of Transfiguration, 'where, sublimating all earthly instincts, the Divinity in his bosom shone translucent through the man, and his spirit rose up into the Godlike'.[166] To modern readers, this may seem ridiculous, even sacrilegious, but at the time of its delivery, this oration was a considerable success, which garnered Daniel national praise and revitalised his flagging political career.[167]

The veneration of Charles I, Jefferson Davis, Robert E. Lee and Abraham Lincoln as Christ figures points to one important consequence of the Christ-like political martyrs. Simon Walker has argued that political saints of medieval England, such as Thomas of Lancaster, Richard Scrope and Henry VI, served as figures of reconciliation, allowing the losers in a struggle to accept defeat in the knowledge that right, if not might, had been on their side.[168] There is truth to this, but with these medieval figures this political aspect of their cults was rapidly subsumed by the thaumaturgic aspects.

The post-Reformation Christocentric model, however, fulfilled this function perfectly. Jesus had died in expiation of the sins of the world and figures such as Charles I, Lincoln and Lee were seen to have suffered in expiation of the sins of their nations or regions. (The fact that these martyrs could be religious as well as political figures broadened the range of conflicts in which they could act as symbols of mediation.) The perceived innocence of these figures, and the undeserved nature of their sufferings, won admiration and sympathy from those on opposing sides or causes. At the same time, the prospect of representing defeat as spiritual victory consoled the vanquished and made it easier for them to resign themselves to defeat. The veneration of such figures brought former adversaries together in cathartic observances of shared grief and guilt. At the same time, the forgiveness of sin inherent in the emulation of Christ increased the ability of these figures to foster rapprochement. However, while the veneration of martyrs as Christ figures could significantly advance reconciliation and reunion, this was not inevitable. This veneration could also be used, as it was with the martyrs whose sufferings were described and depicted in Foxe's 'Book of Martyrs', to foster confessional, national or sectarian hatred. But where there was a desire for harmony and the forgiveness of old grievances, the existance of Christ-like political martyrs could powerfully facilitate the process.

The diminution of the evangelical culture which spawned this model of the Christ-like political martyr has caused a weakening of its impact. But it is still with us and it still has potency. Martin Luther King and Nelson Mandela achieved

---

[166] Ibid., p. 197.
[167] Thomas L. Connelly, *The Marble Man: Robert E. Lee and his Image in American Society* (Baton Rouge, LA, 1977), pp. 97–8.
[168] Walker, 'Political Saints', pp. 95–8.

major political triumphs partly because of their sufferings for a cause and partly because of international sympathy for these causes but also because they both conformed closely to the idea of the pacific, suffering, Christ-like martyr. Even Bobby Sands, an admittedly more controversial figure, was still able, through his sacrifice of his own life in a manner consonant with the image of the Christ-like political martyr, to embarrass and frustrate his political adversaries.

And this is the primary, although not the sole importance, of the politicisation of martyrdom: it valorised political dissent. There had been no equally effective means of legitimating political dissent in Europe since the fall of the Roman Empire. Classical models of republicanism and tyrannicide were ambiguous and controversial, and lacked popular appeal. The image of the suffering Christ, a lone figure persecuted unjustly by the rulers and magistrates of his era, was superbly relevant to the needs of political martyrdom. It provided one of the few ways to undermine the allegiance subjects owed to their superiors. It not only glorified the dissenter and martyr, it damned the regime which made him or her a martyr and robbed it of its legitimacy. It gave sanctity to those who would otherwise be vilified as rebels and traitors.

The model of Christ did more than legitimate dissent, however; it also democratised it. Through it effective opposition was open to the weak and the powerless, in fact powerlessness became an asset. It also magnified the power of the individual dissenter. Paradoxically an individual martyr, or at best a small number of individual martyrs, was far more effective than a large group of them. An individual willing to suffer the consequences, and able to present his or her sufferings in a way which conformed to the model of Christ, could galvanise resistance and destabilise the most authoritarian regimes. If you were willing to lose your life, you might gain the whole world thereby.

2

'Thus may a man be a martyr': The Notion, Language and Experiences of Martyrdom in Late Medieval England*

DANNA PIROYANSKY

The language of martyrdom was common in late-medieval England.[1] Contemporary people – men and women, rich and poor, lay and religious, literate and illiterate – used it in their contemplative and active lives, and in diverse ways. This could be as mimesis, as metaphor, as pedagogic example, as an inspiration, or as an explanation. The language of martyrdom not only constructed the worlds of contemporary men and women but also reconstructed them. The idea of martyrdom was more than just the religious or cultural legacy from earlier generations: it was a means for contemporary people to interpret their own world.[2] The anthropologist Victor Turner has suggested that we see martyrdom as a 'root paradigm' for Christians, because from the early days of Christianity, through text and iconography, martyrological traditions were made and remade, that of Christ's passion being the most prominent among them.[3]

In this chapter I shall explore the use of the traditional and paradigmatic language of martyrdom in late medieval England in the practices and utterances through which people created their own unique understandings of the world. The objective, therefore, will be to map the uses of the notion, language and

---

* I wish to thank Miri Rubin and the European History 1150–1550 seminar at the Institute of Historical Research for their helpful and encouraging comments.

[1]   As in the Continent in the period, although with some different emphases, derived from differing circumstances. See Miri Rubin, 'Choosing Death? Experiences of Martyrdom in Late Medieval Europe', in *Martyrs and Martyrologies*, ed. Diana Wood, Studies in Church History 30 (Oxford, 1993), pp. 153–83; also Brad S. Gregory, *Salvation at Stake: Christian Martyrdom in Early Modern Europe* (Cambridge, MA, and London, 1999), ch. 2.

[2]   Gunter Gebauer and Christoph Wulf, *Mimesis: Culture, Art, Society* (Berkeley, Los Angeles and London, 1995), p. 61.

[3]   'Root paradigms' being 'the cultural transliterations of generic codes – they represent that in the human individual as a cultural entity'. Victor Turner, *Dramas, Fields, and Metaphors: Symbolic Action in Human Society* (Ithaca and London, 1975), p. 67.

experiences of martyrdom in later medieval England, in contemplative, active, and 'mixed' lives. I shall begin with the most central theme of Christian sufferings, Christ's passion, and discuss how people understood and co-experienced it in the period, then proceed with the linking of past martyrdoms and contemporary understandings and recreations of them, and conclude with the daily and mundane ways in which martyrdom has been discussed and practised in later-medieval England. For lack of space, another martyrological discourse of the period, that created with the Lollards, will not be discussed here.

I

Compassionate suffering with Christ and his mother offered, through the use of imagination and intellect, an experience of martyrdom. Although in nature an affective and cognitive auto-suggestive suffering, it sometimes resulted in physical pain. The model of this type of spiritual martyrdom was Mary, the mother of Christ. Her compassionate suffering with her son at the foot of the cross was seen as a form of martyrdom, 'for so much as she louyd [loved] hym more then alle other, her peyne passyd [passed] alle other'.[4] The *Mater dolorosa* became a theme of devotion in itself in the later Middle Ages.[5] Mary's martyrdom was believed to have been predicted in Luke 2: 35, 'and a sword will pierce through your soul also', an image which provided a central theme for devotional and liturgical texts. In the Mass of Compassion or Lamentation of the Blessed Virgin Mary which is part of the Sarum Use Missal the sword that pierces Mary's heart inflicts collective pain, by which believers share Mary's suffering.[6] A meditative experience of the passion through Mary's martyrdom may therefore 'count as a form of self-martyrdom'.[7] Mary was thus not only a focus of devotion because of her sufferings, but a martyrological model, and a channel through which one could identify in new ways with Christ's sufferings. Albeit a distinction between Christ's passion of body and Mary's compassion of soul did exist, the difference between the two became less discernible in the later Middle Ages.[8]

---

4   Julian of Norwich, *A Book of Showings to the Anchoress Julian of Norwich*, ed. Edmund Colledge and James Walsh, 2 vols, Studies and Texts 35 (Toronto, 1978), II, ch. 18, p. 366, lines 7–8.

5   Duffy, *The Stripping of the Altars: Traditional Religion in England c.1400–c.1580* (New Haven and London, 1992), pp. 259–65; Marina Warner, *Alone of All Her Sex: The Myth and the Cult of the Virgin Mary* (1976), ch. 14, especially pp. 210–18.

6   *Missale ad usum insignis et praeclarae ecclesiae Sarum*, ed. F. R. Dickinson (Oxford and London, 1861–83), 'Missa compassionis sive lamentationis Beate Mariae Virginis', cols. 919–24, especially col. 923.

7   R. N. Swanson, 'Passion and Practice: The Social and Ecclesiastical Implications of Passion Devotion in the Late Middle Ages', in *The Broken Body: Passion Devotion in Late-Medieval Culture*, ed. A. A. MacDonald, H. N. B. Ridderbos and R. M. Schlusemann (Groningen, 1998), pp. 1–30, see pp. 8–9, n. 18.

8   Mainly 'because of the propensity . . . to stress the bodily ties between Mary and Jesus and to see the Virgin mother and Divine son as almost equal' (Donna Spivey Ellington, 'Impassioned Mother or Passive Icon: The Virgin's Role in Late Medieval and Early Modern Passion Sermons', *Renaissance Quarterly*, 48 [1995], pp. 227–61, at p. 237).

Devotional writers in fourteenth- and fifteenth-century England, as on the Continent, experienced, through visions of suffering with Christ's passion, a spiritual experience of martyrdom. Julian of Norwich, the anchoress who wrote her *Book of Showings* after a series of mystical visions during May 1373, commented, after a vision of Christ's crucifixion, on the suffering she experienced – like Mary – for loving him and seeing his pain:

> Here I felt steadfastly that I loved Christ so much above my self that there was no pain that might be suffered like to that sorrow that I had to see him in pain.[9]

Margery Kempe (b. *c.*1373), the pious laywoman from Lynn, was so dedicated to Christ's and Mary's sufferings, so eager to share them, that she reacted dramatically to any passion-related stimulus. During a sermon in Germany, for example, she suddenly felt sudden sorrow and heaviness occupying her heart, and started weeping and sobbing. When asked what was wrong, she cried 'with loud voice': 'the Passion of Christ slays me'.[10]

The line between a contemplative martyrdom for the love of God, and self-afflicted physical suffering for the same purpose was blurred sometimes. Walter Hilton (d. 1395–6), an Augustinian Canon at Thurgarton (Nottinghamshire) and author of *Scale of Perfection*,[11] rebuked as 'hypocrites and heretics' those who endured great bodily pain with great joy,[12] but who carried it out without humility and discretion.[13] The 'right' type of pain was not necessarily a visible one, and certainly not a goal in itself, but a means towards unification with God.[14]

The fact that these sufferings originated in the mind and spirit did not make them any less real, painful or rewarding than those of a 'real' martyrdom. Imagined sufferings, for and with Christ, were, at least for some, a way of being martyred. Margery Kempe illustrated it best in her *Book*, when describing her own imagined martyrdom: 'to be bound at her head and her feet to a stake, and her head to be struck off with a sharp axe, for God's love'.[15] Although she feared the point of death, the willingness to be martyred for Christ's love, and the imagined

---

[9] Julian of Norwich, *A Book of Showings*, II, ch. 17, p. 365, lines 61–3. My modernisation of the original Middle English.

[10] *The Book of Margery Kempe*, ed. Sanford Brown Meech and Hope Emily Ellen, EETS, o.s. 212 (1949), ch. 41, p. 98. My modernisation of the original Middle English.

[11] Marion Glasscoe, *English Medieval Mystics: Games of Faith* (London and New York, 1993), p. 116.

[12] Walter Hilton, *The Ladder of Perfection*, trans. Leo Sherley-Price (1988) (first printed in 1957), book II, ch. 38, p. 218.

[13] Ibid., Book II, ch. 35, p. 206.

[14] Ellen Ross, ' "She Wept and Cried Right Loud for Sorrow and for Pain": Suffering, the Spiritual Journey, and Women's Experience in Late Medieval Mysticism', in *Maps of Flesh and Light: The Religious Experience of Medieval Women Mystics*, ed. Ulrike Wiethaus (Syracuse, New York, 1993), pp. 45–59, see pp. 51–8. See Domenico Pezzini, 'The Theme of the Passion in Richard Rolle and Julian of Norwich', in *Religion in the Poetry and Drama of the Late Middle Ages in England*, ed. Piero Boitani and Anna Torti (Cambridge, 1990), pp. 29–66, especially pp. 47, 59.

[15] 'to be bowdyn hyr hed & hir fet to a stoke & hir hed to be smet of with a scharp ex for Goddys lofe *'. The Book of Margery Kempe*, ch. 14, p. 30. My modernisation.

experience of martyrdom were enough to please God, who promised her that for this readiness she will be rewarded in heaven 'as þow þu suffredyst þe same deth' ('as if you suffered the same death').[16] Even if Margery was not seen by society as a martyr because of the martyrdom she was *willing* to undergo, Margery believed that to her God it was enough: she was a martyr.

By imitating Christ's suffering, and experiencing it with him or for him, these writers expressed their love, so that 'the distance between oneself and the suffering Christ' could diminish.[17] Christ's humanity, emphasised throughout his suffering, also made him a kinsman – father, mother, husband or brother – and enabled a higher degree of intimacy between God and man.[18]

II

Although visionary encounters with God were available only to a small minority, meditating on and identifying with Christ's sufferings, together with repentance and confession, were ways in which men and women could approach the divine God, through a martyrdom of sorts. This co-suffering with Christ and his mother was discussed, instructed and encouraged in countless texts and visual representations related to Christ's passion: prayers, sermons, poems, devotional treatises, mystery plays and images. New cults developed in the later Middle Ages around themes of the passion, such as the *Arma Christi* or The Five Wounds, and these also produced prayers, poems and iconography.[19]

This devotional literature and imagery aimed at creating an affective reaction to Christ's sufferings as a man, and were 'often not concerned at all with the niceties of dogmatic theology, but with vivid emotion and immediate effect'.[20] The desired emotional response was created by various means, such as minutely lingering on details of the passion, or instructing the reader or listener to use all senses while meditating. The employment of the present tense to stress the immediacy of the experience contributed to linking past and present. Richard Rolle (d. 1349), the hermit from Hampole, who composed many devotional treatises and poems in Latin and the vernacular, elaborately described in his *Deuout meditacioun vp þe passioun of Crist* the details of Christ's passion. The people

---

[16] Ibid., My modernisation.

[17] Richard Kieckhefer, *Unquiet Souls: Fourteenth-Century Saints and their Religious Milieu* (Chicago and London, 1984), p. 105.

[18] Duffy, *The Stripping of the Altars*, p. 236.

[19] All these genres borrowed from one another. The poems, for example, could have been used in prayers and sermons. Douglas Gray, *Themes and Images in the Medieval English Religious Lyric* (1972), p. 37. For summary and examples of the genres (textual and visual), see Kieckhefer, *Unquiet Souls*, pp. 98–113. For the cult of the *Arma Christi*, see R. H. Robbins, 'The "Arma Christi" Rolls', *The Modern Language Review*, 34 (1939), pp. 415–21; For the cult of Five Wounds see Douglas Gray, 'The Five Wounds of Our Lord', *Notes and Queries*, 208 (1963), pp. 50–1, 82–9, 127–34, 163–8, and Duffy, *The Stripping of the Altars*, pp. 238–48.

[20] Gray, *Themes and Images*, p. 36.

chosen to scourge Christ, for example, are described as 'stronge and stalwarth and willy to slee þe' ('strong and stalwart and willing to slay you').[21] Walter Hilton instructed his meditative reader or listener to see, feel and weep in the heart. By using the 'dramatic present',[22] the emotional result was meant to be even more affective:

> You see the crown of thorns . . . you feel your heart stirred to such compassion and pity towards your Lord Jesus that you mourn, weep, and cry out with every power of the body and soul.[23]

The writers of texts describing spiritual co-suffering with Christ which often enabled identification with his humiliation and pain were men and women who practised religion in a variety of ways. Although some of them experienced mystical visions, their writings were aimed at any Christian aspiring to come closer to God. While Richard Rolle, for example, wrote for 'mystic beginners',[24] Julian of Norwich emphasised that meditation on Christ's humanity was not a religious privilege or a special calling, but a practice aimed at all Christians, regardless of their status.[25]

Passion-related texts and images could have been used in the sacred space of the church or in a private room, as part of a shared public experience or in personal devotion. Themes of the passion were preached from the pulpit, and mystery plays which re-enacted the passion and crucifixion reached large audiences in English towns and even villages. The devotional practice of co-suffering with Christ was not, therefore, a monopoly of the religious, rich or literary. On the contrary, the growing accessibility and popularity of the affective meditation on the passion reflected rather its widening democratisation.[26]

III

Past sufferings were remembered and shared through new accounts of the old martyrs and their anguish. The theme of martyrdom was elaborated, and devotion to the martyrs was expressed and constructed, through the production and use of hagiography: in sermons, lyrics, *Vitae*, liturgy and visual imagery, which constantly reminded Christians of the sufferings the martyrs had experienced for

[21] *Richard Rolle: Prose and Verse*, ed. S. J. Ogilvie-Thomson, EETS, o.s. 293 (Oxford, 1988), p. 73, lines 189–90. My modernisation.
[22] J. A. W. Bennett, *Poetry of the Passion: Studies in Twelve Centuries of English Verse* (Oxford, 1982), p. 36.
[23] Walter Hilton, *The Ladder*, Book I, ch. 35, p. 39.
[24] Mary Felicitas Madigan, *The* Passio Domini *Theme in the Works of Richard Rolle: His Personal Contribution in its Religious, Cultural, and Literary Context*, Salzburg Studies in English Literature 79 (Salzburg, 1978), p. 125.
[25] Mark S. Burrows, ' "Yett he sufferyth with vs": Divine Asceticism in Julian of Norwich's *Revelation of Love*', *Studies in Spirituality*, 7 (1997), pp. 99–112, see p. 109.
[26] Duffy, *The Stripping of the Altars*, p. 265.

God's love. The opening lines of the *Speculum sacerdotale*, a fifteenth-century collection of vernacular sermons, many of them on martyrs, explained the intent in celebrating the martyrs and their days:

> that we, the hearers of their blessed commemorations ... might be stirred to follow them in the same way, and also that we might, through their prayers and merits, be in their everlasting fellowship, and help here in earth.[27]

Several writers – known as well as anonymous – narrated the martyrs' legends and 'translated' them from Latin into the vernacular. Collections of such legends, whether intended for preaching or reading,[28] appeared in Middle English compilations such as the *South English Legendary*,[29] the *North English Legendary*, dating from the end of the fourteenth century,[30] the *Festial* of John Mirk, an Austin canon and later prior of Lilleshall (Shropshire), published probably during the 1380s,[31] Osbern Bokenham's *Legendys of Hooly Wummen*, completed in 1447,[32] and the *Speculum sacerdotale* mentioned earlier. These homiletic and literary sources treated, along with lives of other saints and celebrations of the Church, different types of martyrdoms, those of men, boys and virgins.

---

[27] 'That we, the herers of here blessid commemoracions ... my3t be stired forto folowe hem in the same wey and also that we my3te þrou3 here prayers and medes be in here euerlastynge fellaschip and holpen her in erþe', *Speculum Sacerdotale*, ed. Edward H. Weatherly (London, 1936), EETS, o.s. 200, p. 1. My modernisation.

[28] For example, whereas Mirk's *Festial* was intended for preaching, and the *North English Legendary* for reading, it is not clear whether the *South English Legendary* was originally intended for preaching or reading. Karen A. Winstead, *Virgin Martyrs: Legends of Sainthood in Late Medieval England* (Ithaca, NY and London, 1997), pp. 72, 78.

[29] *The South English Legendary*, ed. Charlotte D'Evelyn and Anna J. Mill, EETS, o.s. 235, 236 and 244 (1956 and 1959). The *South English Legendary* was popular during the later thirteenth and the fourteenth century, whereas in the fifteenth century single legends from the collection were still occasionally copied. Manfred Görlach, *The Textual Tradition of the South English Legendary* (Leeds, 1974), pp. 1, 60–2. For the text's potential and actual users see ibid., pp. 45–50.

[30] 'Die nordenglische Legendensammlung', in *Altenglische Legenden Neue Folge*, ed. C. Horstmann (Henninger, 1881), pp. 1–173. The *North English Legendary* was intended for reading, perhaps by a middle-class audience (Winstead, *Virgin Martyrs*, pp. 78–80).

[31] John Mirk, *Mirk's Festial: A Collection of Homilies*, ed. Theodor Erbe, EETS, e.s. 96 (1905). For dating and popularity of the *Festial* see Susan Powell, 'John Mirk's Festial and the Pastoral Programme', *Leeds Studies in English* n.s. XXII (1991), pp. 85–102, especially pp. 85 and 94, n. 3.

[32] Osbern Bokenham, *Legendys of Hooly Wummen*, ed. Mary S. Serjeanston, EETS, o.s. 206 (1938). For dating see Osbern Bokenham, *A Legend of Holy Women*, trans. and introduction Sheila Delany (Notre Dame, 1992), p. ix.

IV

Legends of virgin-martyrs were retold in later-medieval English collections of legends, and by several prominent writers of the period.[33] Chaucer 'translated' St Cecily's story in *The Second Nun's Tale* in his *Canterbury Tales*;[34] William Paris, an esquire of the exiled earl of Warwick, Thomas Beauchamp, depicted St Christine's life and death in 1398/9;[35] John Lydgate wrote a life of St Margaret between 1415 and 1426 for Ann Mortimer, Lady March;[36] Osbern Bokenham composed the lives of Saints Margaret, Christine, Agnes, Catherine, Cecelia, Agatha and Lucy (among others) in his *Legendys of Hooly Wummen*, which was presumably completed in 1447;[37] and John Capgrave, the Austin friar and later prior, wrote a life of St Katherine *c.*1445.[38]

The virginity in these legends is 'menaced', to use Kathleen Coyne Kelly's term,[39] by frustrated rulers, such as Quintianus, the consular official in Sicily, in the legend of St Agatha, or Eulogius, the prefect of Nicomedia, in St Juliana's legend.[40] The virgin martyrs suffered at the hands of their adversaries because they wished to preserve their virginity and refused to worship idols. In these ways they preserved their love of Christ: by avoiding idolatry (spiritual infidelity), they avoided adultery (carnal infidelity) too.[41] As John Capgrave's Catherine explains to the tyrant Maxentius who tries to persuade her to worship his gods: ' "I shal keepe that truthe whiche þat I [made]/ Onto myn husbond, though I shulde be

---

[33] For a thorough study of legends of virgin martyrs in the later Middle Ages and their changing emphases see Winstead, *Virgin Martyrs*. For a study of fifteenth-century collections of female saints' lives, their mainly East Anglian origin and circulation, and laywomen's audience, see A. S. G. Edwards, 'Fifteenth Century English Collections of Female Saints' Lives', *The Yearbook of English Studies*, 23 (2003), pp. 131–41.

[34] Chaucer's translation of Cecily's legend may have been done 'in commemoration of the appointment in the early 1380s of the English prelate Adam Easton to the post of Cardinal Priest of the Church of Saint Cecilia in Trastevere by Pope Urban VI' (David Raybin, 'Chaucer's Creation and Recreation of *The Lyf of Seynt Cecile*', *The Chaucer Review*, 32 [1997], pp. 196–212, at p. 196).

[35] For the text see William Paris, 'Christine', in *Sammlung Altenglischer Legenden*, ed. C. Horstmann (Heilbronn, 1878), pp. 183–90. For dating and the identity of the writer see Gordon Hall Gerould, 'The Legend of St. Christine by William Paris', *Modern Language Notes*, 29 (1914), pp. 129–33; Mary-Ann Stouck, 'A Poet in the Household of the Beauchamp Earls of Warwick, *c.*1393–1427', *Warwickshire History*, 9 (1994), pp. 113–17.

[36] John Lydgate, *The Minor Poems of John Lydgate*, ed. Henry Noble MacCracken, EETS, e.s. 107 (1911), pp. 173–92. See Winstead, *Virgin Martyrs*, p. 119.

[37] Osbern Bokenham, *A Legend of Holy Women*, trans. Sheila Delany (Notre Dame, 1992), p. ix.

[38] John Capgrave, *The Life of St Katharine of Alexandria*, ed. Carl Horstmann, EETS, o.s. 100 (1893). For Capgrave's biography see J. C. Fredman, 'The Life of John Capgrave, O.F.S.A. (1393–1464)', *Augustiniana: Revue pour l'étude de Saint Augustine et de l'Ordre des Augustins*, 29 (1979), pp. 197–237.

[39] For the use of this term see, Kathleen Coyne Kelly, *Performing Virginity and Testing Chastity in the Middle Ages* (2000), for example, p. 42.

[40] Jacobus de Voragine, *The Golden Legend: Readings on the Saints*, trans. William Granger, 2 vols (Princeton, 1993), I, pp. 154–7, 160–1.

[41] Thomas Freeman stresses the link between the two: ' "The Good Ministrye of Godlye and Vertuose Women": The Elizabethan Martyrologists and the Female Supporters of the Marian Martyrs', *Journal of British Studies*, 39 (2000), pp. 8–33, at p. 13.

ded." '[42] Their torments were corporeal and physical, so substantial to their virginity that they 'can be understood as a virginity test, simultaneously producing and displaying the virgin body'.[43] Whatever afflictions the virgins experienced, the story usually ended, as in John Lydgate's legend of St Margaret, with 'the chaste lely [lily] of whos maydenhede [virginity]/ Thorugh martyrdam was spreynt with roses rede'.[44]

Although the popularity of these virgin-martyrs in late-medieval England is well established, their religious and social significance is disputed. Whereas Katherine J. Lewis, among others, argues that virgin-martyrs were used as 'model girls' in training of young women,[45] Eamon Duffy suggests that 'what it [devotion to virgin-martyrs] gave to the ordinary Christian man and woman was not so much a model to imitate, something most of them never dreamt of doing, but rather a source of power to be tapped'.[46] Perhaps we need not restrict the meaning which virgin-martyrs encompassed for later-medieval contemporaries, and instead see them as functioning in manifold ways, be it as a behavioural model, an encouraging influence, or an instrumental cure invoked for ailments and pains.

In the contemporary experiences of real-life virginity the language of martyrdom was central, too. In later-medieval England several ways of practising virginity existed, either physical or 'honorary',[47] religious or lay, in enclosed solitude, or as part of a community.[48] Circumstances that enabled martyrdom for virginity as represented in the legends of the virgin-martyrs seem to have been related to historical events. Waves of anti-Christian persecution in the first centuries of Christianity created opportunities for virgins to undergo martyrdom.[49] But such opportunities no longer existed in later-medieval England; marriage plans were the sole real threat to the wish to live in chastity.[50] The virgin-martyr legends

---

42 John Capgrave, *The Life of St. Katharine*, p. 277, lines 505–6.

43 Sarah Salih, *Versions of Virginity in Late Medieval England* (Cambridge, 2001), p. 96.

44 John Lydgate, *The Minor Poems*, p. 174, lines 27–8.

45 Katherine J. Lewis, 'Model Girls? Virgin-Martyrs and the Training of Young Women in Late Medieval England', in *Young Medieval Women*, ed. Katherine J. Lewis, Noël James Menuge and Kim M. Phillips (Stroud, 1999), pp. 25–46.

46 Eamon Duffy, 'Holy Maydens, Holy Wyfes: The Cult of Women Saints in Fifteenth- and Sixteenth-Century England', in *Women in the Church*, ed. W. J. Sheils and Diana Wood, Studies in Church History 27 (Oxford, 1990), pp. 175–96, p. 189.

47 The term 'honorary virginity' is used by Jocelyn Wogan-Browne, and relates to virginity practised by wives, mothers and widows. See Jocelyn Wogan-Browne, *Saints' Lives and Women's Literary Culture c.1150–1300: Virginity and its Authorization* (Oxford, 2001), for example, pp. 41 and 48.

48 For a discussion of the historical and religious background leading to the growing numbers of people practising virginity and anchoritism from the thirteenth century on see, for example, Clarissa W. Atkinson, ' "Precious Balsam in a Fragile Glass": The Ideology of Virginity in the Later Middle Ages', *Journal of Family History*, 8 (1983), pp. 131–43, at p. 139, or Ann K. Warren, *Anchorites and their Patrons in Medieval England* (Barkley, Los Angeles and London, 1985), p. 22.

49 Wogan-Browne, *Saints' Lives*, p. 116.

50 The opportunity for virgin-martyrdom would arise again after the Middle Ages, for example during the Spanish Civil War, although mainly for men. Mary Vincent, 'The Keys of the Kingdom: Religious Violence in the Spanish Civil War, July–August 1936', in *The Splintering of Spain: Cultural History and the Spanish Civil War*, ed. Chris Ealham and Michael Richards (Cambridge, 2005), pp. 68–89.

offered, therefore, to late-medieval English virgins a way of practising virginity that, at the practical level, was no longer available for emulation. The legends were, therefore, 'customised' for present needs, not only as reading material for virgins, but also as more general models of chastity, resolve, humility, charity, and patience.[51] Miri Rubin concludes: 'Martyrs were good to think with, and above all to learn from. They were not meant to be emulated literally, but rather to give occasion for disciplined reflection and improvement.'[52]

Inner suffering caused by the practising of virginity included the struggle against sexual temptation, and could make a devoted virgin into a martyr of sorts. This element of inner pain in virginity was stressed in a guide for anchoresses, *Ancrene Wisse*, written *c.*1220 for three sisters by an anonymous Augustinian canon.[53] In this guide virgin anchoresses were directed to hang in their chambers black curtains marked by a white cross, in order to symbolise 'the keeping of pure chastity, which is guarded with much pain'.[54] The virgin fights inwardly against devilish desires in order to produce and preserve her mental state of virginity. If she finds it difficult, she is instructed to 'turn the sweet pleasure into smarting pain', to imitate the agonising experiences which produced the martyrdom of the virgin-martyrs of old.[55]

V

A life of enclosure offered some later-medieval English people – especially women[56] – another way of experiencing martyrdom, one traditionally reserved for religious men and women. The anchoress, who wished to live a solitary life, was pronounced dead to the world through her own choice. This symbolic death was liturgically celebrated in a ceremony that sealed the anchoress in her cell, encompassing liturgical elements of death, such as the singing of antiphons and psalms from the Office of the Dead, or receiving the sacrament of extreme unction.[57] The 'funerary tones of the ceremony' and its ending in the grave-like

[51] Winstead, *Virgin Martyrs*, pp. 112, 141.
[52] Miri Rubin, 'Religious Symbols and Political Culture in Fifteenth-Century England', *The Fifteenth Century*, 4 (2004), pp. 97–111, quotation on p. 105.
[53] Warren, *Anchorites and their Patrons*, p. 295. The *Ancrene Wisse* is one of the English anchorite rules listed in appendix 2.
[54] *Ancrene Wisse: Edited from MS. Corpus Christi College Cambridge 402*, ed. J. R. R. Tolkien (Oxford, 1962), EETS, o.s. 249, p. 30. Translation in *The Ancrene Riwle*, trans. M. B. Salu (1955), p. 22, with my correction: while the translator translated *pine* as *difficulties*, I preferred leaving it as *pain*, which, according to the *Middle English Dictionary*, could mean injury resulting from punishment, physical pain or discomfort (like disease), or a mental suffering.
[55] *Ancrene Wisse*, p. 152; *The Ancrene Riwle*, p. 131. The quote and discussion appear in Salih, *Versions of Virginity*, pp. 98–9.
[56] From the thirteenth century on there is an increase in the numbers of female anchoresses (Warren, *Anchorites and their Patrons*, table 1, p. 20).
[57] For the ceremony of sealing the cell, see Warren, *Anchorites and their Patrons*, pp. 97–9. For a discussion on anchoritism as an ongoing liminal state see ibid., pp. 95–7.

'dark and narrow space of the anchorhold'[58] symbolised that death to the world which was also the beginning of new life for the anchoress.

Paradoxically, physical enclosure and symbolic death made the anchoresses, like the early stylitic saints 'at once remote on the pillars and yet highly visible in the center of their communities'.[59] Like martyrs, the enclosed recluses acquired new religious, social and cultural recognition, and significance – a 'symbolic capital'[60] – after, and because of, their 'death'.

But elements of death to the world were not the only martyrological motifs to be found in the enclosed life: enclosure symbolised the *mental* state of martyrdom *in life*. Just as the Desert Fathers had developed their type of martyrdom after the age of persecution, living in a cell was a 'modern' way towards a life – not death – of martyrdom.[61] This was achieved, for example, through resistance, not only to sexual desires, but also to cravings for food. Rather than asking for more palatable food the anchoress was instructed to 'die like a martyr in her suffering'.[62] The anchoress's practice of martyrdom could commence after her ceremonial death to the world, but grew into a continuous state of martyrdom, much like that of virginity.

VI

In the collections and single texts which described the sufferings of the martyrs not only the anguishes of the virgin-martyrs were narrated, but also the martyrdoms of Christ's apostles, other early Christian martyrs and royal martyrs. All these represented a wide range of virtues, some of which were occasionally interwoven: Archbishop Thomas Becket's humility and faith, St George's knightly prowess and heroism and King Edmund's regality and chastity.[63]

In the sufferings experienced by boy-martyrs, the victims of alleged Jewish crimes, however, virginal qualities and innocence were the central themes. Although historically these 'martyrdoms' occurred in earlier generations (the twelfth and thirteenth centuries), the martyrological model of the boy-martyr is to be found in later-medieval England. Their martyrdoms were celebrated, as in the

---

58 Miri Rubin, 'An English Anchorite: The Making, Unmaking, and Remaking of Christine Carpenter', in *Pragmatic Utopias: Ideals and Communities, 1200–1630*, ed. Rosemary Horrox and Sarah Rees Jones (Cambridge, 2001), pp. 204–23, at p. 209.

59 Wogan-Browne, *Saints' Lives*, p. 29.

60 See Nancy Bradley Warren's discussion on 'female saints, nuns, and holy women' as sources of 'symbolic capital' (Nancy Bradley Warren, *Spiritual Economies: Female Monasticism in Later Medieval England* [Philadelphia, 2001], especially ch. 5).

61 Warren, *Anchorites and their Patrons*, pp. 8–9.

62 *Ancrene Wisse*, p. 57, translation in *The Ancrene Riwle*, p. 46.

63 See, for example, John Lydgate's depiction of St Edmund in the legend composed following a visit of Henry VI to Bury St Edmund in 1433–4. In the legend the saint is repeatedly hailed as 'Blyssyd Edmund, kyng, martir, and vyrgyne'. 'S. Edmund und Fremund', in *Altenglische Legenden*, pp. 376–445. For a treatment of male virginity see Kelly, *Performing Virginity*, ch. 4.

case of little St Hugh of Lincoln, a boy who had been allegedly murdered by Jews in 1255, and whose feast day, according to the use of Lincoln, was celebrated on 27 August. This boy-martyr produced miracles, and was translated to a new shrine in Lincoln cathedral during the 1290s, which attracted the most prominent men of the kingdom: King Edward I left alms for Little Hugh of Lincoln's shrine in 1299–1300.[64] Some of the boy-martyrs were visually depicted, as in the rood screen in Litcham church, Norfolk, which depicts William of Norwich, said to have been crucified by Jews in 1144, holding three nails and a knife.[65] Boy-martyrs were remembered not only through cults and iconography, but also in contemporary literature, narrated by writers such as Geoffrey Chaucer and John Lydgate. Chaucer linked the story of little St Hugh of Lincoln with the tale of the boy-martyr in his *Prioress's Tale*.[66] Chaucer's prioress refers again and again, with great pathos, to the martyr's young age and tenderness, his purity and inno-cence. He was 'the white Lamb celestial', expressing an anguished reaction to the boy's death.[67] John Lydgate (d. 1449–50), a monk of Bury St Edmunds, composed a prayer to his local boy-martyr, Robert of Bury, a child who was supposedly crucified by Jews in the twelfth century.[68] Like Chaucer, Lydgate elaborated in the prayer the child's purity and innocence, inquiring, in the dramatic climax of the poem: 'Was it not pitiful to see your veins bleed?'[69] Later-medieval treatment of boy-martyrs helped crystallise the notion of martyrdom as an injustice done to an innocent victim, and the child-martyr offered, therefore, an ultimate representation of the sufferings experienced by a faultless being.

[64] For a general discussion of ritual child murder, its sources and models, see Joe Hillaby, 'The Ritual-Child-Murder Accusation: Its Dissemination and Harold of Gloucester', *Jewish Historical Studies*, 34 (1994–6, 1997), pp. 69–109. For the case of little St Hugh of Lincoln see ibid., pp. 90–6. See also J. W. F. Hill, *Medieval Lincoln* (Cambridge, 1948), pp. 228–9, and Joseph Jacob, 'Little St Hugh of Lincoln', in *Jewish Ideals and Other Essays* (1896), pp. 192–224.
[65] W. W. Williamson, 'Saints on Norfolk Rood-Screens and Pulpits', *Norfolk Archaeology*, 31 (1955–7), p. 332. It has been dated to 1436. Nikolaus Pevsner and Bill Wilson, *The Buildings of England: Norfolk*, 2 vols (London, 1999), II, pp. 517–18. See also John M. McCulloh, 'Jewish Ritual Murder: William of Norwich, Thomas of Monmouth, and the Early Dissemination of the Myth', *Speculum*, 72 (1997), pp. 698–740.
[66] For a summary of criticism on the *Prioress's Tale*, see Carolyn Collette, 'Critical Approaches to the *Prioress's Tale* and the *Second Nun's Tale*', in *Chaucer's Religious Tales*, ed. C. David Benson and Eliza-beth Robertson (Cambridge, 1990), pp. 95–107, especially pp. 96–100. For discussion of the importance of the historical layers of the story to the understanding of the *Prioress's Tale* as a whole, see Lee Patterson, ' "The Living Witnesses of Our Redemption": Martyrdom and Imitation in Chaucer's Prioress's Tale', *The Journal of Medieval and Early Modern Studies*, 31 (2001), pp. 507–60.
[67] For the use of pathos in the story and its intention, see Robert Worth Frank, 'Pathos in Chaucer's Reli-gious Tales', in *Chaucer's Religious Tales*, pp. 39–52, especially pp. 43, 45–6.
[68] For the text of the prayer to St Robert of Bury see Lydgate, *The Minor Poems*, pp. 138–9. For a discus-sion on the possible influence of Chaucer on Lydgate, see, for example, Walter F. Schirmer, *John Lydgate: A Study in the Culture of the XVth Century* (1961), trans. Ann E. Keep (first published 1952), p. 187; Lois A. Ebin, *John Lydgate* (Boston, MA, 1985), p. 125.
[69] 'Was it nat routhe to se þi veynes bleede?', Lydgate, *The Minor Poems*, p. 138, lines 17–18. My modernisation.

VII

This type of martyrdom, of suffering caused by evil wrongdoing, was broadened to include other victims. These were the victims not of allegedly murderous Jews but of political events, especially people who were executed by the state, and which we may call 'political martyrs'. Such examples of what André Vauchez called 'suffering leaders'[70] include, for example, the archbishop of York Richard Scrope, executed in 1405 for his part in the rebellion against King Henry IV. Scrope was described by his adherents, in a contemporary poem written in his honour, as a dove, and, in the account of his martyrdom, as a lamb, led to be slaughtered.[71] Another such innocent victim was the Lollard preacher Richard Wyche, burnt for heresy in 1440, whose case is studied elsewhere in this volume. King Henry VI, who was murdered in the Tower in 1471, was also depicted in his posthumous *Vita* as an innocent sufferer. He was depicted as a holy martyr not only because of his death, but due to his saintly and innocent life, as well as his meek acceptance of sufferings and tribulations while alive. In a Book of Hours of 1409 a later hand added a prayer, of which a few lines read:

> Your troublous life and great suffering
> With patience that you had therein
> And your constant contemplation
> Has made the heaven for to win.[72]

This type of 'political martyrdom' has been hitherto discussed in a restricted political context, and has been interpreted as a product of a manipulative political propaganda by partisans of the dead political actor.[73] Although elements of political manoeuvres may have been present at the emergence and in the activity of the cults which evolved around such martyrs, these cults nevertheless formed an organic part of the devotional and social fabric of late-medieval life. Adherents interpreted a death as martyrdom since they saw it as unjust death, the killing of an innocent. It required, therefore, not only an explanation but also expiation.

In a period of political violence in the fourteenth and fifteenth century – private wars between magnates, the civil war in the period of Edward II, Henry IV's usurpation of the crown, and the Wars of the Roses – several occasions led to death

---

[70] André Vauchez, *Sainthood in the Later Middle Ages*, trans. Jean Birrell (Cambridge, 1997), pp. 158–73.

[71] 'Flexis poplitibus post pacis osculum/ Offert carnifici columba jugulum', *Political Poems and Songs Relating to English History*, ed. Thomas Wright, 2 vols (1861), II, p. 116; 'Et sic . . . ductus est, sicut ovis ad victimam', *The Historians of the Church of York and its Archbishops*, ed. James Raine, 3 vols (1879–94), Rolls Series 71, II, p. 307. See also Thomas Gascogine, *Loci e Libro Veritatum*, ed. J. E. T. Rogers (Oxford, 1881), p. 227.

[72] 'Thy trowbulas lyf and grett vexacion/ With pacyens that thu had therein/ And thi constans in contemplacion/ Has mad the hevyn for to wyne'. Durham, Usahw College MS 10, fo. 1v. My modernisation.

[73] See, for example, J. W. McKenna, 'Popular Canonization as Political Propaganda: The Cult of Archbishop Scrope', *Speculum* XLV (1970), pp. 608–23.

and state trials. Although only a few of the people killed in this period were venerated by their contemporaries as martyrs, the ones who were corresponded to the
model of the innocent victim.

Another model, that of God's warrior as martyr, reached its peak during the
Crusades. The first Crusade (1096) created 'a new route to the status of martyr,
which could be earned by those who fell in battle against the unbeliever, fighting
for Christ and for his people'.[74] *Chansons de geste*, like the French *Chanson de
Roland*, intermingled martyrological ideas with heroic deeds.[75] The later-
medieval *Christi miles* offered, however, a slightly different typological model.
As with the virgin-martyrs, the historical circumstances of inception had changed
by the later Middle Ages: there were few infidels to be fought in later-medieval
England, only political opponents. The later-medieval *Christi miles* was therefore, as in contemporary romance, an ideal knight, descended from a noble
lineage, skilled in the art of war, gentle in his behaviour, pious and generous, and
fighting for God's cause. The later-medieval image of Christ's knight was utilised
as a model during Edward III's reign, when knighthood was of core value, not
only in literature but also in court life, which aimed to recreate the legendary
Arthurian court.[76]

Thomas, earl of Lancaster, who was executed by King Edward II in 1322 for
treason,[77] and who was posthumously venerated as a martyr, was represented in
hagiography, liturgy and iconography as the ideal *Christi miles*. Lancaster's prestigious lineage was central to his representation as a knight-martyr, and we come
across it several times in the liturgical office in his honour.[78] He was depicted as
generous, a desirable quality not only in secular literature, but in religious texts
too: one of the prayers to Lancaster describes him as 'generose miles Christi',[79]
and his *Vita* further elaborates the theme of kindness.[80] Fighting prowess was
most important to a knight, accompanied by courage, and the willingness and
ability to protect the people dependent on him. The deceased earl was indeed
depicted as a warrior not only in texts, which name him *Christi miles*, or 'flower
and gem of knighthood' ('gemma que flos militie'),[81] but also in a Book of Hours
dated to *c*.1325–30, where he is juxtaposed with the ultimate saint-knight, St

---

[74] Colin Morris, 'Martyrs on the Field of Battle before and during the First Crusade', in *Martyrs and Martyrologies*, pp. 93–104, p. 93.

[75] Rubin, 'Choosing Martyrdom?', pp. 155–6.

[76] See Hugh E. L. Collins, *The Order of the Garter 1348–1461: Chivalry and Politics in Late Medieval England* (Oxford, 2000), pp. 6–14. For Edward III's attitude towards Arthurian traditions, see W. M. Ormrod, *The Reign of Edward III: Crown and Political Society in England 1327–1377* (New Haven, CT, and London, 1990), p. 45.

[77] The most complete study of Lancaster's life and activity is, of course, John Robert Maddicott's biog-raphy, *Thomas of Lancaster, 1307–1322: A Study in the Reign of Edward II* (1970).

[78] He is described, for example, as a royal vessel, as being of an illustrious pedigree, and born from a royal bed, BL, MS Royal 12 C XII, fo. 1r.

[79] Norfolk Museums and Archaeology Service MS 158.926/4f, fo. 152r.

[80] *Anecdota ex codicibus hagiographicis Iohannis Gielemans canonici regularis in Rubea*, Société des Bollandistes, Subsidia hagiographica 3 (Brussels, 1895), p. 94.

[81] Cambridge, Clare College MS 6, fo. 145r.

George.[82] More than anything, the link between knighthood and martyrdom is to be found in the shared willingness to fight till the end, and even die, for a just cause. The cause for which Lancaster died is therefore always explained in altruistic terms – it was for justice and the peace and tranquility of England's inhabitants[83] – making Lancaster's struggle and death both martyr-like and chivalric. He was a true *Christi miles*.

VIII

The language of martyrdom was also deployed in contexts which can only be called everyday and mundane. Difficulties of daily lives – disease, loss, betrayal – were occasionally articulated by using the theme of martyrdom metaphorically. Although at times the symbolic use of a martyrological terminology could have been sardonic or humorous, most of the times it was rather a way for people to interpret life's hardships in a manner that would provide them with comfort and strength.

As Caroline Walker Bynum has shown, from the twelfth century onwards enduring disease was sometimes seen as holy suffering, even martyrdom, especially when experienced by women.[84] In the *Ancrene Wisse*, for example, a disease sent by God is interpreted as resulting in, among other beneficial consequences, putting the sufferer close to the martyrs:

> Illness which is sent by God, and not that which is caught by some through their own foolishness, does these six things: washes away sins previously committed; protects against those that were threatening; tests our patience; keeps us humble; increases our reward; puts the patient sufferer on a level with the martyrs.[85]

In this genre of guidance literature, the likening of disease to martyrdom is a way of interpreting and even manipulating the sickness that God sent. It is seen as an opportunity for advocating not only the sick sufferer's salvation, but that of other people too.[86]

---

[82] Norfolk Museums and Archaeology Service MS 158.926/4f, fo. 152r; BL, MS Royal 12 C XII, fo. 1r; Baltimore Walters Art Gallery MS W. 105, fo. 13v; Bodleian MS Douce 231, fo. 1r. *Illuminated Manuscripts in the Bodleian Library*, ed. Otto Pacht and J. J. G. Alexander, 5 vols (Oxford, 1966–73), III, p. 53. For the dating see *Age of Chivalry: Art in Plantagenet England 1200–1400*, ed. Jonathan Alexander and Paul Binski (1987), pp. 254–5.

[83] Baltimore Walters Art Gallery MS W. 105, fo. 13v; Bodleian MS e. Mus 139, fo. 85r; BL, MS Royal 12 C XII, fo. 1r.

[84] Caroline Walker Bynum, *Fragmentation and Redemption: Essays on Gender and the Human Body in Medieval Religion* (New York, 1991), p. 186.

[85] 'Secnesse þet godd send nawt þet sum lecheð þurh hire ahne dusischipe. deð þeose six þinges. wescheð þe sunnen þe beoð ear iwrahte. wardeð to ȝein þeo þe weren towards. Pruueð pacience. Halt in ead modnesse. Muchleð þe mede. Eueneð to martir þene þole mode.' *Ancrene Wisse*, pp. 94–5, translation in *The Ancrene Riwle*, p. 80.

[86] Bynum, *Fragmentation and Redemption*, p. 188. For examples of patient suffering of illness as sacred see Kieckhefer, *Unquiet Souls*, pp. 57–8.

Social marginality and the slander which occasionally accompanied it were also seen as martyrdom on occasion. It could result from either chosen or enforced seclusion, as in the cases of Margery Kempe or Thomas Hoccleve.

Margery Kempe's social martyrdom is described in her *Book* not only as chosen, but also as wilfully embraced.[87] Margery preferred social and public martyrdom over physical pain.[88] She participated in Christ's sufferings,[89] not only through affective contemplations on his passion and death, but also in mimetic recreation of the social humiliation he experienced.[90] So, for example, one of the rebukes, to which 'she said no word', calls to mind the rebukes Christ suffers on the way to be crucified.[91] Margery received God's encouragement in the martyrdom she chose. The gap between this social martyrdom and the 'traditional' martyrdom was narrowed when she declared that it is more pleasing for him to see her going through these sufferings, rather than being beheaded three times a day for seven years.[92] The obvious fact that one's head can be smitten off only once emphasises therefore Margery's daily suffering, and makes it, in a way, even more prestigious than a 'simple' traditional martyrdom.

In the case of Thomas Hoccleve (d. 1430?), the court poet who worked as a clerk in the Office of the Privy Seal, however, this question of choice does not rise. Hoccleve described another martyrdom by society in his *Complaint* from 1421–2.[93] After recounting a mental crisis he had experienced, in which, as he described, 'my witt/ were a pilgrime,/ and went fer from home' ('my mind was a pilgrim and went far from home'),[94] he refers to his martyrdom. Although official documents which could testify to Hoccleve's illness do not survive,[95] the suffering which resulted from this crisis seems very real. This martyrdom was not, as may have been expected, caused directly by the disease. He 'lived in great torment and martyrdom' only after he was recovered from his mental illness.[96]

---

[87] Gail McMurray Gibson, 'St. Margery: *The Book of Margery Kempe*', in *Equally in God's Image: Women in the Middle Ages*, ed. Julia Bolton Holloway, Constance S. Wright, and Joan Bechtold (New York, 1990), pp. 144–63, at p. 144.

[88] '"A, blissful Lord, I had leuyr suffyr alle þe schrewyd wordys þat men myth seyn of me & alle clerkys to prechyn a-ȝens me for thy lofe, so it were no hyndryng to no mannys sowle, þan þis peyne þat I haue."' *The Book of Margery Kempe*, ch. 56, pp. 137–8.

[89] Gibson, 'St. Margery', p. 145.

[90] For Margery's two narratives of martyrdom, through her visions and public slander, see Joel Fredell, 'Margery Kempe: Spectacle and Spiritual Governance', *Philological Quarterly*, 75 (1996), pp. 137–66, especially pp. 156–8.

[91] *The Book of Margery Kempe*, ch. 53, p. 129. My modernisation.

[92] *The Book of Margery Kempe*, ch. 54, p. 131.

[93] Hoccleve's *Complaint* is part of his *Series*, written between 1419 and 1422. See James Simpson, 'Madness and Texts: Hoccleve's Series', in *Chaucer and Fifteenth-Century Poetry*, ed. Julia Boffey and Janet Cowen (1991), pp. 15–29.

[94] *Hoccleve's Works: The Minor Poems*, ed. Frederick J. Furnivall and I. Gollanez, EETS, e.s. 61, 73 (revised reprint in one volume, 1970), p. 103, lines 232–3.

[95] Jerome Mitchell, *Thomas Hoccleve: A Study in Early Fifteenth-Century English Poetic* (1968), p. 4.

[96] 'lyved in great torment/ and martire', *Hoccleve's Works*, p. 97, lines 62–3. My modernisation.

This martyrdom was social in nature: people did not realise he was no longer ill, and therefore disdained him.[97]

The juxtaposition of unkindness, rejection suffered and martyrdom is implied by Hoccleve in his *Complaint* and found also in representations of boy-martyrs and several political martyrs. It was treated more explicitly in another literary genre. The *Festial* of John Mirk, a collection of homilies for the use of preachers, has already been mentioned. In the homily for St Stephen, the first martyr, Mirk elaborates the idea of martyrdom, and reaches a social understanding of it. After preaching on St Stephen's passion Mirk illuminates the three ways in which martyrdom is practised: by passion and will, by will without passion, by passion without will.[98] It seems that Mirk was trying to replace the physical sufferings of the ancient martyrs – such as St Stephen, or the Holy Innocents – with a more mundane understanding of martyrdom. This martyrdom could be reached by offering prayers for an enemy: 'For he that prays devoutly for his enemy, he is in that a martyr.'[99] Another way was by suffering willingly the wrong done to a person, not to the point of death, but through active daily life:

> Thus may a man be a martyr, although he shed no blood: that is when he suffers wrong and is pursued by evil men, and thanks God for it, and takes it with good will, and prays God for his enemies in full charity.[100]

By using the language of martyrdom, Mirk encouraged men and women to seek out the potential for the experience of martyrdom in their own lives.

IX

The language of martyrdom was widely used as a metaphor to describe common-place sufferings caused by marriage. Marriage was sardonically seen as a contin-uing state of martyrdom through life. In a satirical poem discussing the pain and sorrow of marriage, John Lydgate described wedlock not only as endless penance, but also as 'martirdome and a contynuaunce/ Of sorowe ay lasting [ever-lasting]'.[101] In a marginal image in the Luttrell Psalter, a manuscript written and

---

97 Ibid., p. 97, lines 64–6.
98 *Mirk's Festial*, part 1, pp. 28- 29.
99 'For he þat praythe deuotly for his enmy, he ys yn þat a martyr.' Ibid., part 1, p. 28. My modernisation.
100 'Þus may a man be a martyr, þagh he sched no blod, þat ys when he suffereth wrong, and ys pursued of euell men, and þonketh God þerfor, and taketh hit with good wyll, and prayth for his enmyes to God yn full scharyte.' Ibid., part 1, p. 29. My modernisation.
101 Lydgate, *Minor Poems*, II, pp. 456–61, quotation on p. 458, lines 64–7. This is a version of a Latin poem by Walter Mapes (Map), titled *De conjuge non ducenda*. Schirmer, *John Lydgate*, p. 97. For the Latin text see *The Latin Poems Commonly Attributed to Walter Mapes*, ed. Thomas Wright (1841), pp. 77–85. In the Latin text the word martyrdom is not mentioned. I could not find out when Lydgate's version was written. For Lydgate's attitudes towards women as conditioned by audience, see Anthony S. G. Edwards, 'Lydgate's Attitudes to Women', *English Studies: A Journal of English Letters and Philology*, 51 (1970), pp. 436–7.

illuminated *c.*1340 for Geoffrey Luttrell of Irnham, Lincolnshire,[102] a woman beats with her distaff a man kneeling before her with hands held jointly in suppli-cation. Michael Camille's reading of this scene as making a point about mastery in marriage[103] can be further interpreted as a satirical comment on the daily martyrdom which marriage is. This image is iconographically similar to three previous martyrdom-by-execution scenes in the manuscript, those of Thomas Becket, John the Baptist and Thomas of Lancaster (on folios 51r, 53v and 56 respectively).[104] A reading of the image with the text in the folio, Psalm 32: 4–5 ('For day and night thy hand was heavy upon me'), further highlights the image's satirical emphasis on the husband who is daily martyred by his wife.

Martyrdom imagery was also used in the later Middle Ages to describe suffer-ings caused by love. Lovesickness (*amor hereos*) was treated extensively in con-temporary literature, but was also seen as a medical condition of which mainly noble men suffered.[105] Even though lovesickness was mainly discussed in literary and medical texts, it was cultivated in the later Middle Ages in relation to the growing devotion to Christ's passion.[106] The link between sacred and secular love reached a peak in the 'pierced and broken body of Christ [that] was both a cultur-ally sanctioned image of masculine suffering for love and a psychological model for the individual'.[107] The mid-fifteenth-century *Lover's Mass* explored this rela-tion between the sacrifice and sufferings of Christ, and those of the lover.[108] In this anonymous text,[109] the structure and style imitate the Mass.[110] It emphasises the affinity between human suffering (including that for earthly love), the torments suffered by Christ for humanity, and its daily repetition in the liturgy of the Mass.

Martyrdom was a central theme in the lives of late-medieval English people. Their world was marked by it, and gradually signified not necessarily sufferings that ended in death, but many types of sufferings in life. Martyrdom could be

---

[102] BL, MS Add. 42130, fo. 60r. For the Luttrell Psalter see Eric George Millar, *The Luttrell Psalter* (1932); Janet Backhouse, *The Luttrell Psalter* (1989); Michael Camille, *Mirror in Parchment: The Luttrell Psalter and the Making of Medieval England* (1998). For a reproduction of this image see Backhouse, *The Luttrell Psalter*, p. 49, illustration no. 59; Camille, *Mirror in Parchment*, p. 300, illustration no. 139.
[103] Camille, *Mirror in Parchment*, p. 299. For the symbolism of the distaff and knife in this image and in general see Ibid., p. 301.
[104] Michael Camille has commented that 'another important aspect of the way marginal motifs work is not by reference to the text, but by reference to one another – the reflexivity of imagery . . . in chains of linked motifs and signs that echo throughout a whole manuscript or book'. Michael Camille, *Image on the Edge: The Margins of Medieval Art* (1992), p. 42.
[105] Mary Frances Wack, *Lovesickness in the Middle Ages: The* Viaticum *and its Commentaries* (Philadel-phia, 1990). For possible etymological origins of the Latin name, see pp. 60, 88–9, 182–5.
[106] Wack, *Lovesickness*, p. 25.
[107] Wack, *Lovesickness*, pp. 26, 171.
[108] 'The Lover's Mass', in *English Verse between Chaucer and Surrey*, ed. Eleanor Prescott Hammond (Durham, 1927), pp. 207–13.
[109] Eleanor Prescott Hammond, an editor of this composition, has rejected the suggestion that John Lydgate was the author of this text, mainly on stylistic grounds (*English Verse*, pp. 208–9).
[110] Ibid., p. 207.

willfuly embraced, as it was by anchoresses and visionaries, but it could also be used as an explanation of traumatic deaths and executions, as with political martyrs. More than anything, perhaps, martyrdom enabled men and women to make sense of suffering encountered in their own lives, giving it value, and providing steadfastness.

The interpretation of the world through a martyrological prism was available, in essence, to anyone, whether man or woman, religious or lay, magnate, merchant or peasant, well-read or illiterate. The ultimate martyrological model, that of Christ, was always near, and the richness of the martyrological language, as well as the manifold martyrological models which were available, offered comfort, consolation and hope.

The other chapters in this volume will show that the various late-medieval 'martyrdoms' were later amalgamated during the period of religious persecution in the sixteenth and seventeenth centuries, into a more uniform model. This saw a return to the Christian 'root paradigm' of martyrdom: Christ's passion and death.

3

Which is Wyche?
Lollardy and Sanctity in Lancastrian London

RICHARD REX

'I should have more faith,' he said; 'I ought to know by this time that
when a fact appears to be opposed to a long train of deductions, it invariably proves to be capable of bearing some other interpretation.'
     Sherlock Holmes, in *A Study in Scarlet*, by Sir Arthur Conan Doyle[1]

Richard Wyche is unique among Lollard martyrs for the display of popular
sympathy which followed his death. Burned alive on Tower Hill on 17 June 1440,
he rapidly became the focus of intense devotional activity. The ashes of his pyre
were sought as relics, and the site itself became a shrine, with pilgrimages, votive
offerings and reports of miracles. In the context of a sect or movement which,
despite furnishing several dozen martyrs to the pages of Foxe's *Acts and Monuments*, did not generate much in the way of cult or martyrology of its own, this
lends the case of Wyche particular importance. The degree of support shown after
his death has been adduced as evidence for the abiding strength of Lollardy in
London.[2] However, the fact that it was somewhat odd for Lollards to venerate one
of their number with the full panoply of a medieval saint's cult has not passed
unnoticed. This observation can lead to very different conclusions about the
meaning of the events. On the one hand, Anne Hudson has judged that those
involved were simply showing a 'blatant disregard for consistency'.[3] On the

---

[1] I owe this reference to that incomparable Holmesian, R. A. Knox, *Some Loose Stones* (1913), p. 87. The
first version of this paper was read on 1 July 2002 at the interdisciplinary conference 'Suffering History:
Martyrdom in Britain, 1401–1570' convened by Professor James Simpson at Queens' College, Cambridge,
under the auspices of the University of Cambridge's Centre for Research in the Arts, Social Sciences and
Humanities. It has benefited immeasurably from the lively discussion it received there and likewise at the
Seminar in Medieval and Tudor London History held under the auspices of the Institute of Historical
Research (22 May 2003).
[2] J. A. F. Thomson, *The Later Lollards, 1414–1520* (Oxford, 1965), p. 149. For a less cautious reformula-
tion of this claim, in a paragraph on Wyche littered with errors and liberally embroidered, see Derek
Wilson, *The Tower of London: A Thousand Years* (1998), p. 66.
[3] Anne Hudson, *The Premature Reformation* (Oxford, 1988), p. 172.

other, Christina von Nolcken has suggested that the events following Wyche's death show that 'Lollard discourse here has become almost entirely indistinguishable from some of the discourses which it had once opposed'.[4] Either way, in terms of an analysis of Lollardy which concludes that Lollards were generally few and quiet after the Oldcastle Rising and that the boundary between orthodoxy and heresy was in fact generally clear,[5] and in terms of a historical approach which assumes that in our investigations historical agents should be allowed at least an initial presumption of rationality,[6] the martyrdom and cult of Richard Wyche cry out for the kind of close investigation which they have not hitherto been given.[7]

Richard Wyche had long been associated with Lollardy. He was presumably a student at Oxford in the late fourteenth century, as were a few others of his surname and from his native county of Hereford in the fourteenth and fifteenth centuries.[8] He first appears in the historical record over the winter of 1402–3, charged with heresy before Bishop Walter Skirlaw of Durham, having been preaching Wycliffite doctrine in the region. Although no Durham diocesan register survives for Skirlaw's episcopate, we know of these proceedings from three documents: a written response to various articles alleged against him, an account of his conversations with Skirlaw that Wyche himself composed in the form of a letter to an unnamed man, and a subsequent abjuration.[9] The letter and the written response reveal that Wyche was a shrewd and learned man, and it is the quality of learning and argument on show in them that makes it impossible to doubt that he enjoyed a university education. It was perhaps Wyche's intransigent refusal to recant, despite the efforts of the bishop and his staff, that resulted in his

---

[4]   Christina von Nolcken, 'Richard Wyche, a Certain Knight, and the Beginning of the End', in *Lollardy and the Gentry in the Later Middle Ages*, ed. Margaret Aston and Colin Richmond (Stroud, 1997), pp. 127–54, at p. 143.
[5]   Richard Rex, *The Lollards* (Basingstoke, 2002).
[6]   This approach is laid out and justified in characteristically lucid and rigorous fashion by Quentin Skinner, 'Interpretation, Rationality and Truth', in his *Visions of Politics*, 3 vols (Cambridge, 2002), I, pp. 27–56, esp. pp. 38 and 54.
[7]   Richard Wyche has, of course, frequently figured in historical accounts and investigations of Lollardy. Most recently, he is the subject of a chapter in Rita Copeland's study, *Pedagogy, Intellectuals, and Dissent in the Later Middle Ages: Lollardy and Ideas of Learning* (Cambridge, 2001), pp. 151–90. But while Copeland finishes her chapter with a good account of Wyche's execution and its aftermath (pp. 188–90), and notes the difficulty of tracing any causal link between those events and the much earlier proceedings against him, her main interest is in elucidating the narrative and evasive strategies he implemented in his own account of his first trial.
[8]   For the other Richard Wyches at Oxford, see A. B. Emden, *A Biographical Register of the University of Oxford to 1500*, 3 vols (Oxford, 1957–9), III, p. 2101. Emden includes the Lollard Richard Wyche in his register.
[9]   F. D. Matthew, 'The Trial of Richard Wyche', *English Historical Review*, 5 (1890), pp. 530–44; *Fasciculi Zizaniorum*, ed. W. W. Shirley (1858), pp. 370–82 (response) and 501–5 (recantation). The response is undated, but seems to belong to these proceedings. Wyche's appearances before Skirlaw were definitively dated by M. G. Snape, 'Some Evidence of Lollard Activity in the Diocese of Durham in the Early Fifteenth Century', *Archaeologia Aeliana*, 4th series 39 (1961), pp. 355–61, which convincingly dates the start of the proceedings Wyche describes to 7 Dec. 1402, and his conviction as a heretic to March 1403.

being sent down to Westminster as a prisoner, where he was released in Chancery.[10] It is merely speculation, but tempting nonetheless, to suggest that he may have benefited from some connections at Court. There was a king's clerk, also named Richard Wyche, a canon of Salisbury, who might perhaps have been a relative. There was also a king's serjeant of the same name.[11] And the status of the family is confirmed by the fact that a John Wych was MP for Hereford in the 1390s.[12] However, if influence was exercised on his behalf, it probably worked in both directions. For Wyche was now induced to make a formal recantation some time between October 1404 and November 1406.[13]

In understanding Wyche's position at this time and his ultimate fate, it is important to note his connections with Sir John Oldcastle. The Oldcastles were a leading Herefordshire family. Moreover, these connections may perhaps explain Wyche's presence in Durham in 1401. As McFarlane observed, 'It may have been a mere coincidence that Oldcastle was in that area in the same year.' But some thought should be given to the unmistakable implication that it was not a coincidence at all. Richard Wyche's letter reporting his troubles is written to someone he addresses as 'Reverend Lord and Brother', and it later extends greetings to the addressee's wife and mother-in-law – which would at least be consonant with the conjecture that it was written to Oldcastle, who was already a knight, married and with children.[14] Moreover, a few years later, in 1410, Wyche was evidently in Oldcastle's company, for they both wrote letters to the Hussites of Bohemia on the same day, 8 September, during a tour of England by a couple of Hussite brethren who took the letters back with them.[15] Eventually, some time after the

10 *The Register of Henry Chichele, Archbishop of Canterbury, 1414–1443*, ed. E. F. Jacob, with the assistance of H. C. Johnson, 4 vols (Oxford, 1938–47), III, pp. 56–7.
11 For the other Richard Wyches see, for example, *Calendar of Close Rolls Richard II. Vol. V. 1392–1396*, pp. 302 ('the king's serjeant') and 397, 480, 530, and 543 (the canon of Salisbury).
12 For John Wych MP see *The House of Commons 1386–1421*, ed. J. S. Roskell, Linda Clark and Carole Rawcliffe, 4 vols (Stroud, 1992), IV, p. 912. He may well have been the father of the Lollard Richard Wyche. *A Descriptive Catalogue of Ancient Deeds*, 6 vols (1890–1915), I, C.1756, summarises a grant of land made on 3 Jan. 1409 by Richard Wyche, chaplain, and John Wyche, sons of John Wyche of Hereford, in their capacity as executors of his will. It is interesting to note that one of the men to whom they grant the land (to be sold for the benefit of their father's soul) is John May, mayor of Hereford. A John May is named in Wyche's letter (Matthew, 'Trial of Richard Wyche', p. 541), which may suggest a connection, although it is a common enough name. The Richard Wyche of this land grant is almost certainly not the canon of Salisbury, who is usually described around this time as 'parson of Tredington' or 'clerk', and was probably a son or relative of John Cassy of Wych. *Descriptive Catalogue of Ancient Deeds*, I, C.326, is a reference from 22 Edward III (1348) to one 'Robert', son of John Cassy of Wych; and the *Calendar of Close Rolls Richard II. Vol. III. 1385–1399*, p. 35, refers as of 21 Jan. 1386 to the Richard Wyche, clerk, who is overseas on royal service (and can therefore be identified with the canon of Salisbury) as 'alias R. Cassy'. The two later clerical Richard Wyches (see above, n. 8) were too young to be appearing in a land grant in 1409.
13 *Fasciculi Zizaniorum*, pp. 501–5. The recantation was dated by James Gairdner, *Lollardy and the Reformation in England*, 4 vols (Oxford, 1908–13), I, p. 183, between the election of Pope Innocent VII and the death of Bishop Skirlaw.
14 Matthew, 'Trial of Richard Wyche', pp. 531 and 543. Wyche's reference to a third person as 'my brother' later in the letter (p. 544) suggests that the 'brother' of the address is metaphorical. K. B. McFarlane, *Wycliffe and English Non-Conformity* (Harmondsworth, 1972), p. 144, for Oldcastle's early career, and p. 146 for his presence in the north around that time.
15 McFarlane, *Wycliffe*, p. 146. See also Nolcken, 'Richard Wyche', pp. 143 and 153, n. 100.

Oldcastle Rising of January 1414, Wyche was arrested and imprisoned again, apparently in Hampshire, for he was brought to Westminster, in company with another captured Lollard chaplain named William Brown, by a sergeant of the sheriff of Hampshire in autumn 1417, in order to face questioning before the King's Council over the fate of certain monies which Oldcastle had forfeited.[16] This again suggests a close connection between Wyche and Oldcastle, and it may not be going too far to conclude that Wyche – who at this stage is not known to have held any benefice – had been a chaplain in Oldcastle's household.

In 1419 he appeared before the archbishop of Canterbury, Henry Chichele, and made a full confession of his chequered past and his suspect present status. His case was discussed at Convocation on Tuesday 20 November 1419, and he was gaoled in the Fleet pending judgement.[17] It would appear, however, that no evidence was forthcoming to convict him of relapse, for on 15 July 1420 the King's Council sent an order to the keeper of the Fleet prison ordering the release of 'Richard Wyche, clerk, alias Richard Godwote', on bail to appear before the Council again at Michaelmas.[18] The five men who stood bail for Wyche included two London citizens (one of them, John Clement, was a business associate of another Mr Richard Wyche, rector of Cadbury in Wiltshire[19]) and two Hereford-shire gentlemen – Richard Wynnesley and Edmund Morys (the latter a trusted royal agent in the county who had some links with the Oldcastles).[20]

At this point the course of Wyche's career changed. Hitherto the youthful radical dissident, he now settled down in middle age to a clerical career which, apart from its spectacular end, was firmly in the mainstream. In 1423 he was presented to the living of St Nicholas, Deptford, which was in the gift of the obscure Premonstratensian abbey of Bayham in Sussex.[21] Abbeys and priories, especially smaller ones, often presented candidates for livings at the instigation of

---

[16] *Issues of the Exchequer . . . from King Henry III to King Henry VI*, ed. F. Devon (1837), pp. 352–3, transcribes an entry on the Exchequer Rolls recording the payment of the sergeant's expenses in late October or very early November 1417. I owe this reference to Nolcken, 'Richard Wyche', pp. 143 and 153, n. 102. TNA E404, Box 33/168, is a warrant for an issue on the Exchequer paying the costs of the sheriff's sergeant, one William Wykeham. See *List and Index of Warrants for Issues 1399–1485*, Lists and Indexes Supplementary Series IX. 2 (New York, 1964), p. 302. Nolcken's suggestion that William Brown might be identified with a Woodstock glover of the same name who was involved in the Oldcastle Rising does not seem to fit with his description as a chaplain in both the sources regarding Wyche's arrest. It was a common enough name.

[17] *The Register of Henry Chichele*, vol. III, pp. 56–7.

[18] *Calendar of Close Rolls. Henry V. Vol. II. 1419–1422*, p. 82.

[19] *Calendar of Close Rolls. Henry VI. Vol. I. 1422–1429*, p. 81, 8 Dec. 1423, links a Richard Wyche with John Launoy in regard to the lands of William, Lord Clynton. See also *Calendar of Close Rolls Henry VI. Vol. III. 1435–1441*, pp. 168 and 170.

[20] *Calendar of Fine Rolls. Vol. XIII. 1405–1413*, p. 148, notes that Edmund Morys and Richard Oldcastell of Herefordshire had custody of the alien priory of Carswell in Wales on 21 May 1409. *Calendar of Patent Rolls. Henry VI. Vol. IV. 1441–1446*, p. 466, sees Morys with Henry Oldcastell, Esq., on a commission regarding the duke of Warwick's lands in the Marches, 12 July 1445. Wyche's fifth surety was one Roger Wynter of Worcestershire.

[21] C. H. Fielding, *The Records of Rochester* (Dartford, 1910), pp. 80–1. Other possible candidates for recommending him to the abbey would be John Langdon (bishop of Rochester, 1421–34), or more plausibly the lord chancellor, Thomas Langley (bishop of Durham, 1406–37). Langley was lord chancellor

bishops and other powerful men, and it seems likely that Bayham was acting here at the instigation of another – most probably Chichele himself. In 1434, Wyche was appointed to the rectory of Leaveland in Kent.[22] It was presumably the lord chancellor who made this presentation, as one of the perquisites of that office was the administration on the king's behalf of the patronage of benefices worth less than £10 a year: Leaveland was worth a mere £4. Finally, in 1437, Wyche exchanged this benefice for the far better berth of Harmondsworth in Middlesex, worth £16 a year.[23]

Then, after nearly two decades of mainstream ministry, having survived a major Lollard panic in the years 1428–31, Wyche suddenly fell from grace in 1440. There are many chronicle accounts of this event. It is more widely reported than any other Lollard execution with the possible exception of Oldcastle's, and in greater detail. No one account is exhaustive, and it is necessary to draw on many separate sources in order to obtain as complete a version of the story as possible. Perhaps the account from the Trinity College manuscript of the *Brut* will stand for the dozen or more versions that appeared in due course, as it mentions most of the salient features of the episode:

> And in the same yere, Sir Richard Wyche, vicar of Hermondesworth in Middlesex, that somtyme was vicar of Depford in Kent; and oon Roger Norman, of Normandy born, was take and brought before the Bisshop of London, and tofore the clergie, in the Chapitre hous of Seint Paules; and there they bothe were conuicte in heresye. And then there come a writte from the Chaunceller to the Maire and Shirrefs of London, to do execucion on theym; and so they were brought to the Towre Hill on Seint Botulphes Day, and there brent, bothe in oon tonne; and thus they ended theire lives in this world. And the peple that sawe theym dye, had greate compassion on theym, for the confession and ende that they made in theire good byleue, and thanked God of his sonde.[24]

Wyche was, of course, formally degraded from the priesthood before being committed to the 'secular arm', and was burned with his companion (identified in one source as Wyche's servant) 'be the morne at vi of the clok'.[25] What gave

1417–24 (the period during which Wyche was released from the Fleet) and had also been lord chancellor 1405–7, very probably when Wyche was released from custody after his recantation.
22 *Calendar of Patent Rolls, Henry VI. Vol. II. 1429–1436*, p. 342, 7 June 1434. For the institution, on the same date, see *The Register of Henry Chichele*, vol. I, p. 284.
23 These valuations are taken from the *Valor ecclesiasticus*, ed. J. Caley and J. Hunter, 6 vols (1810–34), I, pp. 70 (Leaveland), 118 (Deptford) and 434 (Harmondsworth).
24 *The Brut*, ed. F. W. D. Brie, 2 vols, EETS, o.s. 131 and 136 (1906–8), p. 476, citing Trinity College Cambridge MS O.9.1. The obsolete substantive 'sonde' (or 'sound') bears the sense of health, safety or salvation. The meaning here seems to be to thank God for his gift of salvation to the two victims. It is worth noting that although there were two victims, only one of them was the focus of subsequent veneration.
25 *The Brut*, p. 508, and many other sources report Wyche's degrading. *Chronicles of London*, ed. C. L. Kingsford (Oxford, 1905), p. 147, makes it 6 o'clock. *A Chronicle of London from 1089 to 1483*, [ed. H. Nicolas] (1827), p. 173, citing a variant in BL, MS Julius B. I, makes it 'in a morning at vij of the belle'. *William Gregory's Chronicle of London*, in *The Historical Collections of a Citizen of London*, ed. James

Wyche's burning its contemporary importance was the extraordinary, indeed unique, reaction to it: a display of spontaneous popular sympathy verging on worship, or, from the jaundiced point of view of the authorities, upon idolatry. A chronicle which formed the basis of the later account of John Stow gives us the fullest account of the aftermath:

> . . . a prest callid ser Richard Wyche . . . was brend on the Tourhille for heresie, for whoos deth was gret murmur and troubil among the peple, for some said he was a good man and an holy, and put to deth be malice; and some saiden the contrary; and so dyuers men hadde of him dyuers oppinions. And so fer forth the comune peple was brought in such errour, that meny menne and wommen wente be nyghte to the place where he was brend, and offrid there money and ymages of wax, and made thair praiers knelyng as they wolde haue don to a saynt, and kiste the ground and baar away with thaym the asshis of his body for reliques. . .[26]

Other chronicles fill in more details. The pilgrims erected a cairn of stones with a makeshift cross at the site of Wyche's execution.[27] One story went around to the effect that he had prophesied the collapse of the postern gate at the Tower of the London, and that this duly occurred.[28] The images of wax represent votive offerings, and other sources confirm that miracles were soon being reported.

This burgeoning devotion caused considerable anxiety to the authorities in Church and kingdom. The first sign of this can probably be seen in the writ despatched to the mayor of London on 23 June 1440 instructing him to act decisively against breaches of the peace in the city and its suburbs, and to summon home any aldermen then absent from the city in order to assist in the task. The writ offers no specific explanation of how the king's peace is threatened, but its date and its vague attribution of the trouble to 'the author of all disturbance and wickedness' (i.e. the devil) point towards the Wyche affair.[29] If any immediate measures were taken, they have left no mark in the city records. But on Wednesday 13 July the Common Council ordained that a proclamation should be published 'for the peace and against congregations and conventicles'. This is doubtless the proclamation whose text is found in the corporation's Letter-Book.[30] That same day the Common Council handed down an injunction to one

---

Gairdner, Camden Society, new series 17 (1876), pp. 55–239, at p. 183, made the other man Wyche's servant.

[26] *An English Chronicle of the Reigns of Richard II, Henry IV, Henry V, and Henry VI*, ed. J. S. Davies, Camden Society, o.s., 64 (1856), p. 56. Its frequent references to Franciscans would suggest a provenance within that order. For Stow, see below n. 36.

[27] *The Brut*, p. 508.

[28] Robert Fabyan, *The New Chronicles of England and France*, ed. Henry Ellis (1811), p. 613. It has not proved possible to verify this story in any particular. The postern gate, which was on Tower Hill, was the gate in the city walls just outside the moat of the Tower of London.

[29] Corporation of London Records Office (CLRO), Letter-Book K, fo. 187v.

[30] Ibid., fo. 188r. Falling between items respectively dated 6 July and August, it forbids anyone 'to gader eny congregacions or companys to gedre within this cite or the Suburbes of the same at eny tyme be day or be nyght in places priuat or opyn'.

William Illage, forbidding him to encourage 'conventicles' with mendacious claims to have been healed.[31] However, higher authorities may not yet have been fully satisfied with the Common Council's measures. A royal proclamation was issued on 15 July to the sheriffs of London and Middlesex instructing them to suppress the incipient cult of Richard Wyche as the fruit of idolatry and sedition. Similar instructions were despatched to all the sheriffs of the Home Counties, East Anglia, the Midlands, the southern counties, and Yorkshire.[32] Interestingly, one source states very specifically that these instructions were issued 'by the commaundement of the Chaunceler & othir Bysshopis', suggesting that the campaign against Wyche and his memory was seen as a particularly ecclesiastical initiative.[33]

In the meantime, the mayor and Common Council had begun to act firmly, and for the next few days the Wyche affair shut out all other business. On Thursday 14 July they examined three more men on activities connected with the cult of Wyche: John Copyn, Richard Norton, and William Brigge. Moreover, owing to the illness of the mayor (which may perhaps explain why little had hitherto been done), they appointed a former mayor, William Estfield, as his lieutenant for the purpose of dealing with the crisis. Fortified with the royal proclamation, they convened the wardens of all the craft guilds on Saturday 16 July, instructing them to deliver to all their members the message against illegal conventicles and any display of 'help and favour' to Lollards.[34] By now the net was also closing on the key figures in the cult. On Friday William Walton, a cleric who was a servant of the vicar of Barking, had stated under questioning that he had been given a pyx by William Bole (or Bele). In addition, his master, the vicar of Barking, had told him to compile a list of all the miracles performed at the place of Wyche's execution, which lay within their parish.[35] Saturday saw Bole examined, and he said that he had been told by the vicar to give the pyx to Walton for collecting the offerings at Smithfield.[36] Alice Wareyn was questioned the same day about her claim to have

---

[31] CLRO, Journal of the Common Council 3, fo. 48r (cited by the later pencil foliation: for the earlier ink foliation, subtract 2). I must thank Professor Paul Strohm for bringing to my attention this crucial source, of which I was previously unaware, and Professor Caroline Barron for her advice in interpreting it.
[32] TNA C54/290, Close Roll 18 Henry VI, membrane 3 dorso. For a summary, see *Calendar of Close Rolls. Henry VI. Vol. III. 1435–1441*, pp. 385–6.
[33] *The Great Chronicle of London*, ed. A. H. Thomas and I. D. Thornley (Gloucester, 1983), p. 174. This would therefore sit very well with the argument of John Watts that a clerical clique around the young king was particularly influential at this time, when the royal foundations of Eton and King's College, Cambridge, were being undertaken. See John Watts, *Henry VI and the Politics of Kingship* (Cambridge, 1996), pp. 167–71. The lord chancellor at this point was John Stafford, bishop of Bath and Wells.
[34] CLRO, Journal of the Common Council 3, fo. 49r: 'Isto die conuocati fuerunt Custodes omnium misterarum Et iniungebatur eis quod ipsi dicerent omnibus de misteriis suis quod non faciant conuenticla & non prestent auxilium vel fauorem lollardis seu erreticis quouismodo sub pena & id pro uxoribus & famulis suis & apprentic'.'
[35] For the location of the place of execution in the parish of Barking, see John Stow, *The Chronicles of England, from Brute vnto this present yeare of Christ. 1580* (1580), p. 642, RSTC 23333.
[36] The chronicles unanimously locate Wyche's execution on Tower Hill, while the Journal of the Common Council refers to the place of execution three times as West Smithfield, and once each as Smithfield and East Smithfield. This apparently considerable discrepancy is explicable. Although West

seen three rays of light shining down from heaven upon the site of the burning, but now said that she had made this claim while drunk. The Church authorities were also doing their part, and on Sunday 17 July a friar was put up at Paul's Cross to preach against the cult of Wyche. John Kyxe, a labourer, was arrested next day for having heckled him, yelling out that it would be a great almsdeed ('magnam fore elemosinam') to drag the preacher down out of his pulpit.[37]

Monday 18 July saw the campaign against the cult reach a dramatic climax, and the Common Council dealt with no other business that day. The Council mounted a round-the-clock guard on the site of the execution, calling on the aldermen and the under-sheriffs to make themselves and their servants available for the task. Twelve people were arrested for offences relating to the cult, most or perhaps all of them at Smithfield. Among the first to be dealt with was the man who had provided the pyx in which to collect the offerings of the pilgrims, Thomas Virley, the vicar of All Saints', Barking. According to one chronicle he had also feigned a miracle to sustain the odour of sanctity:

> for to excite and stire thaym to offre the more feruently, and to fulfille and satisfie his fals couetise, he took asshis and medlid thaym with powder of spices and strowed thaym in the place where the said heretic was brend; and so the symple peple was deceyued, wenyng that the swete flauour hadde comme of the asshis of the ded heretic. . .[38]

The 'swete flauour' was dealt with by the simple expedient of defiling the site with dung.[39] The fact that Virley had used, or was alleged to have used, a pyx (a word which denoted very specifically a receptacle for the blessed sacrament) for collecting the offerings may have added to the sense of desecration and sacrilege with which the authorities were keen to invest these events. William Walton and William Brigge were both arrested for having held the pyx to solicit offerings. Walton's list of miracles may have led the authorities to some of the others pulled in. Richard Norton was arrested for saying he had seen someone there miraculously cured of a swollen throat. This was probably Alice Dauntre, whose husband John was arrested for reporting that she had been cured of some affliction of the throat. Alice herself had been arrested the previous Friday, and one John Holderness was taken at the same time for assaulting the city officer who

Smithfield lay to the north-west of the city, outside St Bartholomew's Priory and Hospital, the street which led eastwards from Tower Hill outside the city walls, passing between the north-east corner of the moat and the south-west corner of the abbey of St Mary Graces, was called East Smithfield. For the geography, see *The City of London from Prehistoric Times to c.1520*, ed. Mary D. Lobel (Oxford, 1989), Maps 2 and 4. The descriptions of the place of execution as Tower Hill and East Smithfield can be regarded as interchangeable. The use of 'West Smithfield' in the Journal must be put down to scribal error: presumably the scribe was more used to talking and writing of West Smithfield than of East Smithfield. I am grateful to Professor Caroline Barron for her advice in clarifying this issue.

[37] CLRO, Journal of the Common Council 3, fos 49v and 51r. The entries do not actually say that the friar was preaching against Wyche, but under the circumstances this seems a reasonable conclusion.

[38] *An English Chronicle*, ed. Davies, p. 56. Several later chronicles repeat this story.

[39] *Six Town Chronicles of England*, ed. Ralph Flenley (Oxford, 1911), p. 101: 'cum fumo animalium deturpaverunt locum ne ibi ulterius fieret ydolatria'. See also the *Great Chronicle of London*, p. 174.

was arresting her. Christina Kendale was taken into custody for having allegedly feigned first lameness and then a miraculous cure, leaving her crutches to be made into a cross to mark the 'profane place'. John Petter also claimed to have witnessed a miracle. John Thomson, Thomas Whitway, William Mason and John Highholme (or Higham) were all arrested for making violent disturbances at the site of the execution, and Highholme was also charged with building the stone cairn there.[40]

This was not quite the end of the story. On the day of the arrests a man named James Johnson was wandering around saying that Richard Wyche had been seen vested in an alb, and that there was likely to be a popular rising in Brent, Kent and Essex on account of his death. Johnson was brought before the mayor's lieutenant and the aldermen on Thursday 21 July, and witnesses testified to his remarks. He had also declared himself willing to undergo the same death as Wyche himself, adding that nobody would infer any harm from his words except for 'false priests, for whom he stated that he did not care'.[41] But by the end of the week the fuss was dying down. On Saturday half a dozen men were summoned to appear before the mayor to answer for refusing to take their turn on guard.[42] Perhaps by now they felt it was a pointless exercise. Certainly the Wyche affair, which was almost literally a nine days' wonder, makes no further appearance in the city archives, and by Lammas day (1 August) the authorities felt secure enough to stand down the guard.[43]

This short-lived display of popular veneration is, of course, most unlollardly behaviour. Lollards were notoriously scornful of the cult of the saints and its popular manifestations. Yet if Wyche was a Lollard, and if the people who venerated him with such enthusiasm did so because they sympathised with the doctrines for which he was condemned, then Lollardy must have been both more complex and more popular than certain unsympathetic historians believe.[44] For if Lollards were capable, despite their theological principles, of immersing themselves so completely and enthusiastically in the structures of orthodox devotion, then 'Lollardy' itself becomes such a numinous phenomenon, with such fluid or porous boundaries, that the intellectual attempt to distinguish between Lollards and Catholics becomes so much wasted time, and the position that Lollardy, in some sense, was a widespread phenomenon becomes easy to advance and difficult to resist. After all, people's beliefs are not always consistent, nor are their actions always consistent with their beliefs. On the other hand, the actions in this case are in such blatant contravention of Lollard doctrines then widespread among even the humblest adherents of the movement that consideration should

---

[40] CLRO, Journal of the Common Council 3, fos 50r–51r.
[41] Ibid., fo. 52r: 'quod nullus inferret lesionem taliter loquentibus nisi solum falsi sacerdotes de quibus asseruit se non curare'.
[42] CLRO, Journal of the Common Council 3, fo. 52v.
[43] *Chronicles of London*, ed. C. L. Kingsford (Oxford, 1905), p. 153, printing a chronicle found in BL, Cottonian MS Vitellius A. xvi.
[44] Notably Richard Rex, *The Lollards* (Basingstoke, 2002).

surely be given to the possibility of an alternative explanation of the facts that would make the actions of those involved less radically irrational.

A close reading of the surviving documents, which are relatively plentiful, does indeed suggest the possibility of an alternative explanation. For by attending both to what the documents say and to what they do not say, we are led towards some surprising conclusions about Richard Wyche: first, that the specific beliefs or utterances for which he was put to death should not be construed as 'Lollardy' in the narrow sense of Wycliffism; and second, that the burgeoning cult that followed his execution represented in the minds of its devotees not endorsement of heresy, but fellow feeling for an innocent man wrongfully convicted and the belief that his victimisation and Christian death had earned him a place in heaven. The contention of this chapter is, therefore, that those who venerated Richard Wyche were not Lollards but Catholics.

Of course, in the simple sense Wyche was by definition a Lollard. He was charged with heresy, convicted, condemned and burned. But it is the cause which makes the martyr, and not the death. And this is where we find our first serious problem. For notwithstanding the undoubted facts that earlier in his career Wyche had held, preached and subsequently abjured Wycliffite doctrines, there is nothing in the considerable corpus of evidence about his condemnation and burning to indicate that he met this fate as a result of once more affirming the views he had previously recanted. Research here is hampered by the absence of any formal records of his trial. Although, as we learn from the Trinity *Brut* (corroborated in other sources), Wyche was tried before the bishop himself, in what must therefore have been the London Consistory Court, records of the proceedings have long since disappeared. The bishop's register makes no mention of the case. As it contains only one or two judicial records, it is evident that there were court books which no longer survive.

However, we are not entirely without light on this subject. Turning to the chronicles, we find them almost unanimous in their silence as to the actual heresy with which Richard Wyche was charged. No less an authority than John Foxe was the first to notice this: 'What his opinions were, they do not expresse.'[45] It is their very silence which is deafening, and it is echoed in the silence of the official documents regarding the suppression of Wyche's cult. An illuminating contrast is provided by the propaganda against Oldcastle which was circulated on the orders of Archbishop Arundel in October 1413, and which was careful to spell out Oldcastle's unsoundness on Eucharistic doctrine.[46] Yet even the royal procla-

---

[45] *A&M [1570]*, p. 830.
[46] See *The Episcopal Register of Robert Rede . . . Bishop of Chichester, 1397–1415*, ed. Cecil Deedes, 2 vols, Sussex Record Society 8 and 11 (1908–10), I, pp. 151–6. See also *The Register of Edmund Stafford (A.D. 1395–1419)*, ed. F. C. Hingeston-Randolph (1886), pp. 268–70 for Exeter diocese; *The Register of Nicholas Bubwith, Bishop of Bath and Wells, 1407–24*, ed. T. S. Holmes, 2 vols, Somerset Record Society, 29–30 (1914), I, pp. 154–64; and *The Register of Philip Repingdon, 1405–1419*, ed. Margaret Archer, 3 vols, Publications of the Lincoln Record Society, 57–8 and 74 (1963–82), III, pp. 10–12, for Lincoln diocese.

mation against Wyche's cult, which might have found it useful to discredit him by detailing the heinous crimes with which he was charged, remains coy about the content of his beliefs. The best it can do is denounce him as a relapsed Lollard, invoking the inevitable cliché 'tanquam canis ad uomitum rediens' ('like a dog returning to its vomit').[47]

In this silence there are two faint whispers, both heard in chronicles, as to the precise nature of Wyche's offences. The clearest comment comes from John Benet's chronicle. The work of a clergyman of some education, it relates that

> A vicar of Middlesex, near Hounslow, was taken and burned in London, having preached against clerical pluralism, saying that a layman might as well have two wives as a priest have two benefices with cure of souls.[48]

The second, an English chronicle running roughly from the decline and fall of Richard II to the accession of Edward IV, and evidently written by a friar, probably a Franciscan, adds the following parting shot to the story:

> And the said heretic cesid nevir vnto the laste breth forto blaspheme and desclaundre then iiij ordris of freris, the whiche was no token of perfeccion ne of charite.[49]

This is somewhat less specific, and to some extent contradicts other evidence that Wyche made a pious and Christian end. Nevertheless, it may well reflect a current of anti-fraternalism in Wyche's preaching. A more distant echo of this may perhaps be found in the aftermath of his death. Perhaps a friar was chosen to preach against him at Paul's Cross not just because friars were the main popular preachers but also because they had a particular interest in discrediting him.

Nowhere in the records, however, is there any hint of the kind of characteristic Lollard teachings which tended to attract the unwelcome attention of the ecclesiastical authorities: nothing about the Eucharist, the cult of the saints, pilgrimage or confession. John Benet's chronicle, for example, is very specific about John Cardmaker of Coventry, burnt nearly ten years later, like Wyche, at the Tower of London. It notes his insistence on the remanence of bread in the consecrated Eucharistic host, and his claim that the children of baptised parents did not themselves require baptism.[50] As we shall see, the London clergy were particularly interested in destroying Wyche's reputation, so the fact that neither of the two clerical and metropolitan sources to discuss his beliefs suggests that his errors

---

[47] See above, n. 32.

[48] 'John Benet's Chronicle for the Years 1400 to 1462', ed. G. L. and M. A. Harriss, in *Camden Miscellany 24*, Camden Society, 4th series, 9 (1972), pp. 151–233, at p. 187: 'Et Anno Domini MCCCXL post festum Pentecostes captus et crematus est Lundon unus vicarius de Mydylsex iuxta Howndysley qui predicavit contra pluralitates ecclesiarum dicens quod laicus tam bene posset habere duas uxores sicut presbiter duo beneficia curata.' This entry does not seem to have been noticed in previous accounts of Wyche.

[49] *An English Chronicle*, ed. Davies, p. 56.

[50] 'John Benet's Chronicle', p. 194; and for similar details regarding the recantation of a Lollard from Essex, see pp. 220–1.

were typical of mainstream Lollardy is highly significant. As Paul Strohm has pointed out, Eucharistic heresy was the preferred killing field on which to entice and then implicate and discredit Lollards. So the fact that this strategy was not attempted in this case suggests precisely that it would not have been credible to employ it.[51]

In short, Richard Wyche's actual offence, as far as we can tell, was to preach sermons in a vein of reformist 'anticlericalism' and anti-fraternalism. If so, then he was probably hounded to death by a clerical interest group which had taken offence at his vigorous critique of pluralism – and, no doubt, of other ecclesiastical abuses. While such preaching clearly reflected some of those reformist inclinations which had originally taken him into Lollardy at Oxford in the late fourteenth century, the sentiments which finally cost him his life were by no means exclusively Wycliffite. They were the common coin of reformist clergy of any age. At almost the same time as Wyche was being condemned, Thomas Gascoigne was busy at Oxford compiling his *Libri veritatum*, what a later age would call a theological commonplace book. In a sermon found in that book on 'the seven rivers of Babylonian confusion in the Church', Gascoigne described pluralism as 'the third river of Babylonian confusion, drowning and destroying most works of virtue'. He did not himself invoke the parallel between pluralism and bigamy, though that too was a commonplace of reformist preaching. But he did deliver himself of a similar aphorism, noting of the parable of the vineyard that 'the master sent many labourers into one vineyard, not one labourer into many'.[52] He went on to describe pluralists as 'devourers and destroyers of the salvation of souls and of divine worship'.[53] What mattered, of course, about such comments was not their substance, but from whose lips and for whose ears they were uttered. Thomas Gascoigne was a pillar of orthodoxy writing a Latin sermon 'ad clerum'. Likewise, in the early sixteenth century, John Colet's scathing indictment of clerical failings was delivered in Latin to a convocation which was addressing a reformist agenda. Colet's sermon was published in English only rather later, when Henry VIII was out to undermine clerical morale and credibility.[54] Similar concerns were evident in John Fisher's response to a remark made in a sermon by Robert Barnes, namely that he would not define it as heresy for a hundred pounds, but that Barnes was foolish to raise the matter 'afore the

---

[51] Paul Strohm, *England's Empty Throne* (New Haven, CT, and London, 1998), pp. 45–9. I should register my disagreement with his implications that this ground was selected cynically and for no other reason, that Eucharistic doctrine was not seen by the ecclesiastical authorities as intrinsically important, and that it was in effect impossible to avoid conviction for Eucharistic heresy irrespective of guilt or innocence.

[52] Thomas Gascoigne, *Loci e libro veritatum*, ed. J. E. T. Rogers (Oxford, 1881), p. 67: 'dominus vineae . . . misit plures operarios in vineam suam, et non unum operarium ad operandum in diversis vineis'.

[53] Gascoigne, *Loci e libro veritatum*, p. 68: 'Tales, pluralitates habentes, merito suo malo vocantur devoratores, et destructores salutis animarum, et cultus Dei'. See also W. A. Pronger, 'Thomas Gascoigne', *English Historical Review*, 53 (1938), pp. 606–26, and 54 (1939), pp. 2–37, at pp. 616 and 31–2.

[54] See John Colet, *Oratio habita a D. Ioanne Colet decano Sancti Pauli ad clerum in conuocatione. Anno. M.D.xj* (1512), RSTC 5545, and the later translation, *The sermon of doctor Colete, made to the conuocacion at Paulis* (1530), RSTC 5550.

bodchars off cambryge'.[55] In the fifteenth century, it was the fact that Reginald Pecock was opening up for the laity matters which his colleagues felt were best reserved for the clergy that played a large part in his own condemnation for heresy, in a case which exhibits some parallels with that of Wyche.[56] Richard Wyche's tragedy was that comments which were merely reformist rhetoric from the lips of a chancellor of Oxford of impeccable orthodoxy, could be construed as radical heresy from the lips of an abjured Wycliffite.

The second surprise which emerges from the stories of Wyche's burning is that although he died as a condemned heretic, this was not how people saw him. The chronicles imply that many people thought him genuinely innocent. As the Trinity *Brut* said, 'And the peple that sawe theym dye, had greate compassion on theym, for the confession and ende that they made in theire good byleue, and thanked God of his sonde'. A British Library *Brut* is even more explicit: 'how-be-it, at his deth he died a gode Cristen man'.[57] For the *Great Chronicle*, Wyche 'took such Repentaunce that he dyed a trewe Crystyn man'.[58] Sympathy for him seems not to have been sympathy for heresy or a heretic – and there is, after all, little evidence of sympathy for condemned heretics in any other case in the fifteenth century – but sympathy for an innocent man unjustly killed. The English chronicle by the anonymous friar, hardly a favourable source, reports the feeling of some people that Wyche was 'put to deth be malice'.[59] The royal proclamation against the cult offers some support for this account of popular attitudes. According to that document, various of the king's subjects, 'seduced by a diabolical spirit into an attempt to sow sedition and idolatry in the realm, are not ashamed to claim openly that the aforesaid Richard was altogether innocent of heretical depravity'.[60]

Of course, Lollards might equally well have claimed that one of their own number was altogether innocent of heretical depravity, meaning that his beliefs were not heretical, rather than that he did not hold beliefs which the authorities denounced as heretical. Yet in this case that does not seem to be what the proclamation intends. For it treads carefully in dealing with the people involved. In denouncing them as misguided subjects, it does not assume that they are actually Lollards, as recent historians have tended to do. On the contrary, it informs them

---

[55] Richard Rex, 'The Early Impact of Evangelical Theology at Cambridge University, 1521–1547', *Reformation and Renaissance Review*, 2 (1999), pp. 38–71, at p. 44, citing *A supplicatyon made by Robert Barnes* ([1531]), RSTC 1470, fo. XXIIIv.

[56] For the involvement of an influential clerical clique in Pecock's destruction, see J. I. Catto, 'The King's Government and the Fall of Pecock', in *Rulers and Ruled in Late Medieval England*, ed. R. E. Archer and S. Walker (1995), pp. 200–22, at pp. 207 and 211, though Catto also emphasises the role of the laity and of the government in this process, and notes the reluctance of the bishops to act against one of their own.

[57] *The Brut*, pp. 476 and 508.

[58] *Great Chronicle of London*, p. 174.

[59] *An English Chronicle*, ed. Davies, p. 56. It also notes that 'some saiden the contrary'.

[60] TNA C54/290, Close Roll 18 Henry VI, membrane 3 dorso: 'quidam . . . subditi nostri diabolico spiritu instigati nedum sedisicionem set & ydolatriam in regno nostro suscitare verissimiliter satagentes prefatum Ricardum heretice prauitatis fuisse omnino innocentem palam dicere non formidant'.

that the king can 'probably reckon them not only favourers, accomplices, and maintainers of heretical depravity and heretics, but also guilty of treason against us and the peace of our kingdom'.[61] The attitude of the authorities is not so much to assume that these people are heretics and traitors, as to warn them that by acting in this way they are in danger of being regarded as 'fautores' of heresy – a distinct offence in canon law. The clear lead of the king's proclamation was followed religiously by the London authorities as they clamped down on the cult. The records of their swoop against the leading figures in the cult on Monday 18 July first detail the precise offences of each individual and then, to make sure that nobody misses the point, in each case conclude that the guilty party has thus 'shown favour and goodwill to heresy, in breach of the king's peace and contrary to the determination of the church'.[62] Similar views can be seen in the London chronicles, several of which categorise the devotees of Richard Wyche as 'symple peple' and 'common people'.[63] Simplicity, associated with innocence, is for such authors the explanation of their behaviour – not heretical depravity. Moreover, the simplicity of the common people here is not being led astray by doctrinal error: they are not venerating Wyche because of what he taught, nor are they espousing what he taught because of his admirable death; the simplicity of the people is being imposed upon by a trick and their good intentions are being abused by a greedy fraudster.

The fate of the fraudster himself is also revealing. Although there seems to have been a tradition current to the effect that he had followed Wyche to the stake (John Stow notes this to refute it), Thomas Virley seems otherwise to have been an unremarkable parish priest.[64] Presented to the benefice of All Hallows', Barking, in 1435, he was still the incumbent when he died in December 1453 and was buried in the north chapel of the church beneath a slab which depicted him as a priest and made the usual request for prayers for his soul.[65] His will, leaving his worldly goods to the disposal of a group of clerical friends, makes no provision for his soul, but given the nature of his monument in the church and the priestly status of his friends, it is likely that he had seen to this beforehand.[66] There is no evidence that he was regarded or treated as a heretic, as he certainly would have

[61] TNA C54/290, Close Roll 18 Henry VI, membrane 3 dorso: 'quos non solum heretice prauitatis set & hereticorum fautores complices & manutentores atque inimicos lese mages[tatis] culpabiles nobis & paci regni nostri possumus probabiliter arbitrari'.

[62] CLRO, Journal of the Common Council 3, fos 50r–51r.

[63] See above, n. 39. See also *Chronicles of London*, ed. Kingsford, p. 147, for 'common people', and the *Great Chronicle of London*, p. 175, for 'many unlernyd, as specyally women'.

[64] John Stow, *The Chronicles of England* (1580), p. 642: 'some haue writen the Vicare of Berking to bee brente, whiche is false, for hee was not brente, thoughe he better deserued than the other'. I have not so far found any printed or manuscript chronicle to substantiate Stow's observation, though I am nevertheless inclined to credit it. Presumably some later chronicler misinterpreted earlier material to create this confusion. Had Virley been condemned for heresy, his goods would have been forfeit and his testamentary dispositions would not have been granted probate.

[65] *Novum repertorium ecclesiasticum parochiale Londinense*, ed. G. Hennessy (1898), p. 74, where he appears as 'Vyrby'. I owe the information about Virley's burial to the kindness of Mr Christian Steer.

[66] Guildhall Library, MS 9171/5, London Commissary Court, Register of Wills 5, fo. 141r–v (I owe this

been if the authorities had felt his involvement in the cult of Wyche reflected Lollard sympathies.

The nature of the cult in itself demonstrates that Wyche's following was among the conventionally devout. For the proper context of his shortlived cult is not that of Lollardy but of popular piety. It represents not sympathy with Lollard dissent, but the normal functioning of Catholic devotion, focusing in one and the same person on two typical models of Catholic cult in fifteenth-century England: firstly, the martyr considered not as witness to dogma but as victim of injustice; and secondly the poor parson, the good parish priest. The suspicion of Lollardy which attached to Wyche's name at the end was akin that jocularly imputed to the poor parson by Chaucer's host – except that in Wyche's case it was no joke. Popular reaction seems to have cast Wyche in the role of such saintly parish priests as Richard Caistor of Norwich (himself suspect in some quarters of Lollardy) or Master John Schorne, who were venerated because of their humble dedication to the spiritual welfare of their parishioners.[67] André Vauchez has remarked upon the emergence of the cult of the 'simple priest' in Tuscany and western France from the late thirteenth century, noting that those venerated in this way were usually educated yet humble men, characterised by 'tireless pastoral zeal'.[68] Although Vauchez did not spot the English examples, presumably because they never got as far as the formal canonisation proceedings on which his research was based, the cult of the 'simple priest' seems to have been developing in England through the fourteenth and fifteenth centuries alongside the rather older tradition of the saintly bishop.[69] It is clear that Richard Wyche was a precise fit for the model of simple priestly sanctity which Vauchez has identified. The importance of Wyche's priestly status in his cult is suggested by a couple of rumours in circulation, one that since his death Wyche had been seen 'vested in an alb', and the other that he had been seen 'in the form of a priest'.[70]

Equally, Wyche's status as an innocent man unjustly killed made him a powerful intercessor according to another prevalent model of sanctity. For

reference also to the kindness of Mr Christian Steer). Virley may well have expected, or even have arranged, for his priestly friends to offer Masses for him.

[67] Richard Rex, *Henry VIII and the English Reformation* (Basingstoke, 1993), pp. 84–5.

[68] André Vauchez, *Sainthood in the Later Middle Ages*, trans. Jean Birrell (Cambridge, 1997), pp. 310–15. I should like to thank Melanie McDonagh for drawing my attention to the significance of Vauchez's work for this article.

[69] The fact that such 'simple priests' were attracting popular veneration in late-medieval England suggests the need for some modification to Vauchez's comment that nearly all English saints at this time 'were persons of aristocratic rank – prelates and great laymen – who had opposed royal power' (*Sainthood*, p. 169).

[70] CLRO, Journal of the Common Council 3, fo. 52r. The relevant phrases in the Latin are 'visus fuit albu indutus' and 'videbatur in forma sacerdotali posterius eius mortem'. In this latter case, the word here rendered as 'posterius' is nothing more than a 'p' with a large apostrophe (as an abbreviation for 'us' or 'ius') after it. The rendering 'prius' would be the first choice for this: but there would not normally be anything worthy of remark in a priest appearing dressed as a priest before his death. It might be referring to the interval between his degradation and his execution, but visions of people are more commonly reported after their deaths than before.

popular devotion seems also to have cast him in the role of such innocent victims of malice as Archbishop Scrope, King Henry VI himself, and even Prince Edward of Lancaster. Such victims were often seen as, in effect, martyrs.[71] As Vauchez has remarked in general of those medieval persons who came to be venerated at the time as martyrs, 'The contrast between the severity of the punishment inflicted and its iniquitous character gives rise to an emotion which, immediately transposed onto the religious register, develops into a devotion'.[72] As has been suggested with the so-called 'political saints' of late-medieval England, Wyche's cult may additionally have expressed popular disquiet with the regime in power.[73] The step from victim to posthumous symbol of opposition seems to have been a short one – victimhood was in any case usually predicated on behaviour which would already classify the agent as in some sense a figure of opposition or dissent.

It is worth remarking that the next entry on the Close Rolls after the proclamation against the cult is another proclamation to most of the sheriffs of England to clamp down on disorder and riotous assembly.[74] One of those men who appeared before London's Common Council in connection with the Wyche affair, James Johnson, was predicting that the attempts to suppress the cult would provoke risings in the volatile counties of Essex and Kent.[75] And one of the London chronicles reports that 'the same yere there were men taken that were named Risers of ffernam [Farnham] in Sotherey [Surrey]; and some were hangid, and some were brent'.[76] The King's Council seems to have been in a state of particular anxiety about popular disorder and rebellion in the summer of 1440, and their anxiety over the cult of Wyche clearly had a significant political dimension to it. It posed an intrinsic challenge to royal and ecclesiastical authority (although its practitioners may or may not have seen it primarily in this light) which an insecure regime – insecure chiefly because of the growing realisation that the king, though no longer a child, was showing no signs of having reached or of ever reaching political maturity and capacity[77] – simply could not tolerate.

Further political ramifications of the Wyche case can perhaps be discerned in one of the lesser documents in the case. On 2 July 1440, a fortnight before the proclamation against Wyche's cult, and a fortnight after Wyche's execution,

---

[71] On innocent victims as martyrs see the Introduction and Danna Piroyansky's piece in this volume. In the context of the Counter-Reformation, this capacious sense of the innocent victim as martyr was repudiated by Catholic theologians anxious to police more strictly the boundaries of both sanctity and martyrdom. Nicholas Harpsfield was at pains to emphasise that Abel himself was merely a victim, not a martyr; and that, assuming Richard Hunne had really been murdered (which he denied was in fact the case), this no more made him a martyr than anyone who was simply killed by thieves on the highway (Nicholas Harpsfield, *Dialogi sex contra Summi Pontificatus, monasticae vitae, sanctorum, sacrarum imaginum oppugnatores, et pseudomartyres* (Antwerp, 1566), pp. 799–800 and 847).

[72] Vauchez, *Sainthood*, p. 151.

[73] Vauchez, *Sainthood*, pp. 155 and 169–70, notes the oppositional connotations of martyr cults in England.

[74] TNA C54/290, Close Roll 18 Henry VI, membrane 2 dorso.

[75] CLRO, Journal of the Common Council 3, fo. 52r.

[76] *Chronicles of London*, ed. Kingsford, p. 153.

[77] I follow here the persuasive analysis in John Watts, *Henry VI and the Politics of Kingship* (Cambridge, 1996).

letters patent were issued making over all the goods and chattels of the late vicar of Harmondsworth to 'our most dearly beloved John Somerset', who was both physician and tutor to Henry VI.[78] Though a layman (he was twice married), John Somerset was a very clerkly layman, having been a fellow of Pembroke College, Cambridge. He played a prominent part in the foundation of King's College, Cambridge,[79] and had very close links to the influential grouping of bishops and clerics which surrounded the young king at this time.[80] The fact that a member of this group should have benefited from Wyche's destruction even before the cult of the victim assumed disturbing dimensions suggests that this group was already closely involved with the case. If so, then the proceedings against Wyche may look a little less like those against 'Lollards' as commonly understood, and a little more like the proceedings against Reginald Pecock. It may be that Wyche's 'anticlerical' reformism, like Pecock's rationalism after it, made him powerful enemies amongst the nexus of senior clergy prominent at the king's court and in the city of London.[81]

The problems of order and disorder associated with Wyche's case account for the remarkable frequency and detail with which it is related in the various manuscripts of the London chronicles. In a penetrating study of the London chronicle tradition, Mary-Rose McLaren has recently presented a persuasive analysis of the chronicles as texts which depend heavily on the London civic archives (the Wyche narratives are clearly based to a greater or lesser extent on the minutes of the Common Council proceedings) and which reflect a desire by their owners, readers, and writers – predominantly men from the aldermanic elite of London society – to reflect and record 'their control over the affairs of the city'.[82] From the point of view of the chronicle texts themselves, the meaning of the Wyche affair is crucially bound up with problems of order and disorder. The events following Wyche's execution assumed particular importance to the civic elite in the dual challenge they posed to the established civic order. While the outburst of popular sympathy for Wyche constituted an implicit populist challenge to the patrician elite, at the same time the heavy-handed response from higher authorities in Church and kingdom called into question that elite's ability to maintain the order on which it prided itself. The vigorous police action recorded in the archives and the chronicles was a highly successful exercise in the restoration of order, and at the interpretative level the chronicles also endeavour to restore order by identifying themselves firmly with the official ecclesiastical condemnation of Wyche as a Lollard. This condemnation implied an identification of his sympathisers as

---

[78] TNA C66/447, Patent Roll 18 Henry VI, part 3, membrane 21. *Calendar of Patent Rolls. Henry VI. Vol. III. 1436–1441*, p. 426.

[79] See the entries on John Somerset in the *ODNB* and A. B. Emden, *Biographical Register of the University of Cambridge to 1500* (Cambridge, 1963), pp. 540–1.

[80] Watts, *Henry VI and the Politics of Kingship*, pp. 167–71.

[81] See above, n. 33, for the role of the bishops, and n. 56 for the parallel with Pecock.

[82] Mary-Rose McLaren, *The London Chronicles of the Fifteenth Century: A Revolution in English Writing* (Cambridge, 2002), p. 141. See appendix 6, pp. 268–75 for the 'significant events'.

heretics or at least favourers of heretics, evident in those chronicles which categorise them as people of his 'secte' or 'affinite'. But the evident discomfort of other chroniclers with this cavalier condemnation of their fellow Londoners exposes some of the tensions generated by the official interpretation of events. By reading between the lines of the various texts we are able to read them to some extent against themselves and thus to tell rather a different story about Wyche, a story perhaps closer to that which his sympathisers told.

Richard Wyche, if the account proposed here can be accepted, was not in any useful sense a 'Lollard martyr'. It is the cause which makes the martyr, and Wyche did not die for any distinctively Wycliffite or indeed unequivocally heretical tenet. He died reconciled to the Church. The fascinating information which the judicial records of London yield as to the nature of the cult of Wyche in its earliest stages therefore gains an additional value. For it offers us a rare glimpse into the birth of a Catholic saint's cult. In most cases, the records which we have of such cults come to us filtered through years, or perhaps decades, of clerical vetting and editing, often in the form of tidy dossiers for advancing the cause of canonisation at Rome. But here, precisely because the authorities acted to suppress the cult, we have the very first shoots plucked up by the root and preserved between the pages of a book. Visions and healings, rumours and testimonies, avarice, credulity and faith are on show together in a messy mixture which perhaps gives us an insight into how cults began.

What this interpretation of the Wyche case throws into even higher relief is the lack of any kind of martyrological tradition in Lollardy, and the lack of any cult. The only Lollard for whom Lancastrian Lollards often expressed respect was John Wyclif himself – and he was no martyr. Margery Baxter famously announced to her interrogators that she prayed to William White, whom she regarded as a great saint in heaven. Yet while she admitted that she had gone to witness his burning because he had predicted to her that 'mirabilia' would occur there, the promised wonders were mass conversions through his preaching, followed by a rising against his persecutors – predictions which failed to materialise. She does not seem to have expected the kind of wonders associated with the shrines of 'that cursed Thomma of Canterbury' or 'Mariam de Falsyngham' (as she called them), and she was adamant in her repudiation of pilgrimages to saints and shrines.[83] Lollards produced testimony, not martyrology. William Thorpe and John Oldcastle both wrote accounts of their discussions with Archbishop Arundel, akin to Wyche's letter recounting his dealings with Bishop Skirlaw (and both men can be associated with Wyche).[84] But there is nothing recorded in the

---

[83] *Heresy Trials in the Diocese of Norwich*, ed. N. P. Tanner, Camden Society, 4th series, 20 (1970), pp. 45–7.

[84] *The examinacion of Master William Thorpe* (n.p., n.d. [Antwerp, 1530]), RSTC 24045, also includes *The examinacion of . . . syr Ihon Oldcastell*. The former is now available in a critical edition in *Two Wycliffite Texts: The Sermon of William Taylor, 1406; The Testimony of William Thorpe, 1407*, ed. Anne Hudson, EETS, o.s. 301 (Oxford, 1993). At pp. lvii–lix Hudson points out that the William 'Corpp'

theology or practice of Lollardy to lead us to expect that its adherents would react to the execution of one of their number in the way that Londoners reacted to the death of Richard Wyche.

Richard Wyche, then, had been a Lollard. In the eyes of highly placed clergymen in London he had reverted to type. But for the common people of the city, he was 'a good Christen man' and a good parish priest, 'put to deth be malice'. In our terms, we might call him the victim of a witch hunt. In their terms, he was a saint. They were probably right.

mentioned in Wyche's letter (Matthew, 'Trial of Richard Wyche', p. 543) is probably a scribal error for 'Thorpe'.

4

Saints and Martyrs in Tyndale and More

BRAD GREGORY

Before Nicholas Harpsfield attacked John Foxe's *Acts and Monuments*, before John Bale exalted John Oldcastle as a martyr and denigrated medieval Catholic saints, before Henry VIII dissolved the monasteries or razed the shrine to St Thomas of Canterbury, William Tyndale and Thomas More squared off in rancorous dispute about saints and martyrs. Their wrangling was symptomatic of disagreements about Christian truth that characterised the Reformation era from its inception. As part of the most visible religious controversy in England carried on in print during the later 1520s and early 1530s, the conflict between More and Tyndale would prove to be a fountainhead in the contestation over sanctity and martyrdom in Britain, one that would persist throughout and long outlive the early-modern period, a clash interwoven with the formation and reformation of Christian identities. Not only did Tyndale and More dispute what sanctity was and whether, for example, saints ought to be invoked as intercessors by Christians. The two men also quarreled about true and false martyrs; they shared a deep biblicism in their own attitudes toward persecution, suffering and martyrdom; and both men were ultimately put to death for persisting in their respective religious convictions. They wrote about martyrs and they themselves became martyrs, a combination that would prove to be relatively unusual in England in the subsequent decades of see-saw religious polities and conflicts between Protestants and Catholics.[1] By enacting their respective attitudes about the willingness to die for Christ, they ensured that they themselves would become the subject matter of subsequent disputes of the sort in which they had participated. Just as Tyndale would be for Foxe such an important Henrician evangelical

---

[1] Most English martyrological writers (e.g. Bale, Foxe, Harpsfield, Allen, Persons) were not executed for their faith, whereas most of those put to death did not publish works about martyrs, martyrdom or the endurance of persecution. Examples of martyrs in the same category as Tyndale and More, however, include the seminary priest Thomas Alfield, whose *True reporte of the death and martyrdome of M. Campion* appeared in 1582 and who was executed in July 1585, and the Jesuit Robert Southwell, whose *Epistle of Comfort* (1587/8) is the most extensive Elizabethan work of consolation for persecuted Catholics, and who was put to death in February 1595.

witness, so More would be for Marian apologists and Elizabethan recusants the great Henrician lay Catholic martyr, a meet parallel to the bishop of Rochester, John Fisher.[2] Having argued about saints and martyrs while they were alive, by dying for their incompatible beliefs Tyndale and More would be respectively esteemed by sympathisers and denounced by detractors in later decades, and indeed, centuries. Hence their unresolved disagreements were inadvertently deepened by their deaths.

This disaccord between Tyndale and More – and much more broadly, the contestation over Christian sanctity and martyrdom throughout the early-modern era – was not a self-standing debate. Rather, it was one corollary of a logically (if not always experientially) prior disagreement about the content of Christian truth, itself the most fundamental religious issue at stake in Western Christianity during the Reformation era. *Because* people disagreed about what God's truth was, *therefore* they disputed who was saintly, how one identified a martyr, and what sorts of human characteristics and behaviours made for holiness. One cannot separate sanctity disputes from doctrinal disputes, because the former derived from competing claims about what God had revealed and what it meant for men and women to be Christian. In the final analysis, Tyndale and other Protestant reformers rejected traditional beliefs and practices associated with sanctity because they considered them incompatible with true Christianity, whereas More and others who defended the Roman Church upheld the same beliefs and practices because they considered them as an expression of true Christianity.

From Tyndale's *Parable of the Wicked Mammon* and *Obedience of a Christen man* in 1528 to More's Tower works in 1534–5, this chapter investigates their controversy about saints and martyrs in three distinct yet related areas: prayer and devotion to traditional saints as understood in late-medieval Catholicism, the

[2] For Foxe on Tyndale, see *A&M [1563]*, pp. 513–22. Foxe was also a principal editor of the deluxe Elizabethan collected writings of Tyndale, John Frith and Robert Barnes; see *The whole workes of W. Tyndall, Iohn Frith, and Doct. Barnes, three worthy martyrs, and principall teachers of this Churche of England collected and compiled in one tome togither, . . .* (1573), RSTC 24436. For Marian and Elizabethan Catholic works about More, see for example Nicholas Harpsfield, *The Life and Death of Sir Thomas Moore, Knight, Sometime Lord High Chancellor of England, . . .* ed. Elsie Vaughan Hitchcock, EETS, o.s. 186 (1932); William Roper, *The Lyfe of Sir Thomas Moore, Knighte*, ed. Elsie Vaughan Hitchcock, EETS, o.s. 197 (1935); and Thomas Stapleton, *Tres Thomae: seu de S. Thomae Apostoli rebus gestis. De S. Thomas archepiscopo Cantuariensi et martyre. D. Thomas Mori Angliae quondam cancellari . . .* (Douai, 1588). See also the prominent place given to More and the other Henrician martyrs of 1535 by Reginald Pole in both his St Andrew's day sermon of 1557 as Mary's archbishop of Canterbury, in *Ecclesiastical Memorials*, ed. John Strype, vol. III, pt. 2 (Oxford, 1822), pp. 482–510 at pp. 490–3, 495–6, and in his *Pro ecclesiasticae unitatis defensione* (Rome, c.1538), esp. fos. 89–95, 98v–100, written during his Italian exile. On the English Catholic understanding of More in the generations following the Henrician Reformation, see Michael A. Anderegg, 'The Tradition of Early More Biography', in *Essential Articles for the Study of Thomas More*, ed. R. S. Sylvester and G. P. Marc'hadour (Hamden, CT, 1977), pp. 3–25; James K. McConica, 'The Recusant Reputation of Thomas More', repr. in *Essential Articles*, ed. Sylvester and Marc'hadour, pp. 136–49; Brad S. Gregory, *Salvation at Stake: Christian Martyrdom in Early Modern Europe* (Cambridge, MA, 1999), pp. 268–72; and Anne Dillon, *The Construction of Martyrdom in the English Catholic Community, 1535–1603* (Aldershot and Burlington, VT, 2002), pp. 38–47, 197, 215.

criteria for telling true from false martyrs, and finally the biblical foundations on which both men stood as each readied himself for death by execution. Throughout the remainder of the sixteenth century, all three domains would remain important in England's religious strife.

The Saints: Friends or Usurpers of Christ?

The ubiquity of the saints and devotion to them by men and women, clergy and laity, was throughout Europe one of the most conspicuous features of late medieval Christianity. Understood above all as merciful helpers to devotees in need, in England the saints were painted on rood screens, carved as church statues, rendered in stained glass, mass-produced in woodcuts, celebrated in the liturgy, implored in prayers, chosen as names for infants, narrated in stories, and preached about in sermons. Their nearness to Christ, bewildering in its variety, made them powerful, specialised intercessors for Christians in need of everything from protection during childbirth, to relief from toothaches, to strength in the face of imminent death. Particular cults waxed and waned, varying according to local circumstances and pious preferences, but that all Christians should cultivate supplicatory relationships with *some* saints was a fundamental assumption that had been built up over many centuries of religious practice.[3] In addition to supplicatory prayer, such practices included the veneration of saints's relics and other material objects that they had touched, or pilgrimage to places where they had been present. Such behaviours in turn reflected a wider sensibility about sacramentality, the belief that God, according to his will, manifested his supernatural presence in and through created, natural reality, as an extension of his once having become incarnate in a human being.

Hence when Tyndale and other early evangelical reformers attacked the cult of the saints, they struck at a central pillar of late-medieval Christianity. In certain respects they extended Erasmian criticisms of allegedly unthinking piety, a dubious substitute, it was argued, for the deliberate imitation of the saints's virtuous example. But the evangelical critique went further, inferring from the purportedly intercessory function of the saints the scandalous implication that Christ's unique, once-for-all sacrifice as redeemer, plus his continuing role as the sole, salvific intercessor, were somehow incomplete. To seek help from the saints was necessarily an affront to the Lord and an act that reflected an erroneous theology. Why pursue in piecemeal fashion from specialised wonder-workers what Christ alone could and did offer all at once? Christ's atonement as understood by Luther and his followers, such as Tyndale, was the very thing that made possible the cornerstone teaching of justification by faith alone and the conscience-quieting, existential certainty of salvation that it was meant to

---

[3] On the saints and devotion to them in late-medieval England, see Eamon Duffy, *The Stripping of the Altars: Traditional Religion in England, c.1400–c.1580* (New Haven, CT, 1992), pp. 155–205.

provide.[4] Saints as intercessors therefore impinged on the heart of evangelical doctrine and had to be rejected. The repercussions of this rejection sometimes showed up in places that one might not expect. On the other side, because the intercessory role of saints was so integral to late-medieval religiosity, its defense could lead in directions that might not, at first sight, seem obvious. Hence Tyndale and More broached the issue tangentially, when touching on other matters.

Tyndale followed contemporary practice in linking the saints to fasting, for example, in his *Parable of the Wicked Mammon* (1528), an exposition of Luther's view of the relationship between faith and works in the guise of a commentary on the parable in Luke 16: 1–13. Tyndale denigrated those who fasted 'some in the honour of this saynt, some of that, and every man for a sondry purpose. Some for the toth ache, some for the hed ache, for fevers, pestielence, for soden death, for hanginge, for drounding, and to be delyvered from the paynes of hell.'[5] The true purpose of fasting was not to obtain some favor from a saint, but rather 'to tame the bodie, that the sprite may have a free course to God, and may quyetly talke wyth God'.[6] The wayward traditionalists fasted 'without conscience of God, and without knowleage of the true entente of fastinge, and do no other than honour sayntes as the gentyles and heathen worshiped ther ydolles, and ar drowned in blyndnes, and knowe not of the testament that God hath made to manwarde in Christes bloude'.[7] Apparently secondary concerns such as fasting and the invocation of saints were accordingly seen as symptomatic of fundamental errors at the core of what Tyndale, Luther and other evangelicals considered the doctrinal centre of Christianity. Honouring the saints was akin to worshipping pagan idols. Because Christ was the only savior, and 'ther ys no strength, no helpe, no succure but of God only', it made no sense to implore aid from dead saints, devotion to whom drained attention and resources away from the needy, living poor.[8]

Several months later Tyndale articulated the same sense of either/or competition between devotion to God and to the saints in his best known treatise, *The obedience of a Christen man* (1528), like *Wicked Mammon* the product of Johannes Hoochstraten's print shop in Antwerp.[9] To believe truly in Christ was to be a saint, period. Misguided pseudo-Christians missed the meaning of whatever

[4] Tyndale was deeply indebted to Luther for most of his theology, although he went his own way on numerous points, including on the critical doctrine of the Eucharist. On Tyndale's independence from Luther, see David Daniell, *William Tyndale: A Biography* (New Haven, CT, 1994), pp. 150, 224, 296–9.
[5] William Tyndale, [*Parable of the Wicked Mammon*], ([Antwerp], 1528), RSTC 24454, fo. 36v; for the same passage in the Parker Society edition, see Tyndale, *Doctrinal Treatises and Introductions to Different Portions of the Holy Scriptures* (hereafter PS, I), ed. Henry Walter (Cambridge, 1848), p. 91.
[6] Ibid., fo. 36 (PS, I, p. 90).
[7] Ibid., fo. 36v (PS, I, p. 92).
[8] Ibid., fos. 17v–18, 37v–38 (quotation) (PS, I, pp. 66–7, 93 (quotation)).
[9] For the identification of Hoochstraten as the printer, see Anthea Hume, 'English Protestant Books Printed Abroad, 1525–1535: An Annotated Bibliography', in Thomas More, *The Confutation of Tyndale's Answer* [1532–3], in *CWTM*, VIII, pt. 2, ed. Louis A. Schuster *et al.* (New Haven, CT, and London, 1973), p. 1071.

miracles God might work through saints, namely 'to move the vnbelevinge vnto the fayth, and to confirme the trouth of his promyses in Christe, whereby all that beleve are made sayntes'.[10] By contrast, those unfortunate souls caught up in traditional piety, Tyndale claimed, 'att onse turne them selves from Gods worde and put their trust and confidence in the saynt and his merites and make an advo-cate or rather a God of the saynt, and of their blinde imaginacion make a testamente or bonde betwene the saynt and them, the testamente of Christes bloude cleane forgoten'.[11] Encouraged by greedy clergy, saints led the Christian laity away from God, just as a mania for miracles led them away from the genuine knowledge of Christ and his Gospel. According to Tyndale, as he elaborated the idea in the section of the treatise entitled, 'Of miracles and worsheppinge of sayntes', the clergy compelled the faithful 'to hyre the sayntes that are deed to praye for vs' in order to make money for themselves, and to create an obstacle meant to keep lay Christians 'from knowleage of Christe'.[12] Again, the connec-tion between doctrinal claims and devotional practices was clear, insofar as those with genuine knowledge of Christ saw through clerical scams masquerading as piety. Tyndale offered his interpretation of the way in which the phrase 'Per Christum dominum nostrum' was purportedly understood in collects of the saints, 'with which we pray God to save vs thorow the merites or deservinges off the Sayntes'.[13] By Tyndale's account, the Latin phrase was understood to mean '*for* christe our lorde's sake', which he denounced for its implication that Christ was somehow in need of salvation through the saints' merits: 'We saye "save us good lorde thorow the sayntes' merites for Christe's sake." '[14] Tyndale needed to render the phrase in something like this manner, because if 'per Christum dominum nostrum' were instead taken straightforwardly to mean '*through* our Lord Christ', then it would have implied a theological understanding of Christ and the *communio sanctorum* in which the saints intercede with Christ but do not displace him as saviour. Yet such a reading would have attributed to standard, petitionary prayers to saints a theologically less objectionable view than the one imputed by Tyndale, and so would have undermined (or at least complicated) his view that devotion to the saints and to God was a zero-sum game.

Yet Tyndale did not altogether jettison a role for the saints in Christian life. In an Erasmian vein, he gestured toward them in *Obedience* as models to be imitated. This presupposed, however, that the primary lessons of the Gospel à la Luther and Tyndale had been properly absorbed, it being most important to 'set oure hertes at rest in Christ and in Gods promyses', after which one could 'take the sayntes for an ensample only and let vs doo as they both taught and did'.[15]

---

[10] William Tyndale, *The obedience of a Christen man and how Christen rulers ought to governe, . . .* ([Antwerp], 1528), RSTC 24446, fo. 36v (PS, I, p. 184).

[11] Ibid., fo. 37 (PS, I, p. 184).

[12] Ibid., fo. 117v (PS, I, p. 289).

[13] Ibid., fo. 118 (PS, I, p. 290).

[14] Ibid., fo. 118v (PS, I, p. 290); my emphasis.

[15] Ibid., fos. 117v–18 (PS, I, p. 289). In his *Exposition of the fyrst Epistle of seynt Jhon* (1531), Tyndale

What genuine saints taught, Tyndale thought, was the doctrine of justification by faith alone, and what they did was preach it. Rather than altogether rejecting a place for the saints in Christian life, then, Tyndale, like other Protestant reformers, denied their role as intercessors for Christians in need, and so repudiated their primary importance for late-medieval Christians. First and foremost, saints were instead simply all living Christians with true knowledge of Christ, understood according to Luther's paradigm of the relationship between Law and Gospel and gifted with what Tyndale called 'feeling faith'.

One living Christian who adamantly rejected Luther's as well as Tyndale's claims about sanctity was Thomas More. To be sure, More's education, legal training and political influence distinguished him from all but the tiniest fraction of his English contemporaries, yet he participated thoroughly in late-medieval Christian life, including devotion to the saints. Bishop Cuthbert Tunstall of London commissioned More to write against heresy for publication in the vernacular, the first fruit of which was his *Dialogue Concerning Heresies* (1529), a work that was in part a response to Tyndale's *Obedience of a Christen man*. In it More defended intercessory prayers to the saints as well as a host of related practices, such as the veneration of relics and the undertaking of pilgrimages and processions. Published just months before Henry VIII appointed More as Lord Chancellor, the *Dialogue* shared in both learned ecclesiastical discourse and the socially inclusive world of late-medieval religious belief and practice: More readily quoted scripture and the Church Fathers, but at the same time endorsed a wide range of traditional medieval religiosity. Just as Tyndale's critique was driven by his evangelical convictions about true Christian teaching, so More's defense derived from a lifetime of committed participation in the Catholic faith (the Romanness of which was soon to become unexpectedly important due to the king's Great Matter). According to More, saints could be and were intercessors, but this neither impinged on Christ's role as savior nor infringed upon the worship that Christians owed to God alone.

In keeping with medieval Catholicism, More believed that just as Christians asked people to pray for them in life, so ought they to ask the saints to pray for them after the saints had died. In fact, from their place in heaven, where charity had brought them to perfection, the saints were more likely to heed and to help petitioners than they had been when they were alive. How they actually managed

---

restricted any use of 'images, reliques, cerimonies and sacramentes' to 'memorialles and signes of remembraunce only', and, parallel to this, limited the saints to the role of holy exemplars who provided inspiration: 'If we went in pilgrimage to kepe the remembrance of the sainctes lyuinge in mind for oure ensample, and fasted and went barefote to tame the fleshe that it shulde not lust after suche worldly thinges which we nowe desire of the sainctes, then did oure fastynge and pilgrimage goinge serue vs, ye, and the saincte were yet oure seruaunt to edify vs in Christe with the remembrance of his life left behinde, to preache and to prouoke vs to folowe thensample.' Tyndale, *The exposition of the fyrst Epistle of seynt Jhon with a Prologe before it* [Antwerp, 1531], RSTC 24443, sigs. H1v–H2. For the same passage in the Parker Society edition, see Tyndale, *Exposition of the First Epistle of St. John*, in *Expositions and Notes on Sundry Portions of the Holy Scriptures Together with The Practice of Prelates*, ed. Henry Walter (hereafter PS, II) (Cambridge, 1849), p. 216.

to hear simultaneously so many supplicants and to respond to them was irrelevant, More claimed, considering that they answered so many prayers, which in turn proved that they could and did assist those who called on them.[16] God had deigned 'that we shall aske helpe of his holy sayntes, and praye for helpe to them', which was 'not a makynge of them equall vnto God hym selfe', because although God 'be chyef and haue no matche, yet forbedeth he not one man to praye for helpe of another'.[17] Christians were to approach God through his special friends rather than presuming to seek him directly: 'He wyll dysdayne ones to loke on vs, yf we be so presumptuous and malapert felowes, that vpon boldnes of famyly-aryte with hym selfe, we dysdayne to make our intercessours his especyall byloued frendes.'[18]

Well aware of the concern about relic fraud and the authenticity of saints that long antedated the Reformation, More conceded that God might permit some Christians to venerate a bogus relic as though it were genuine, or to honor a fictitious saint.[19] But this was hardly sufficient to undermine one's faith or to impugn the practice in general. So long as such veneration was done unwittingly, it was no more culpable than was the unknowing veneration of an unconsecrated host as Christ's body. Yet the issue of counterfeit relics and invented saints did not touch the heart of the matter, namely whether it was wrong as such to venerate *genuine* relics or to implore *true* saints to intercede for one before God. More contended that in keeping with the promise of the Holy Spirit, God would not permit his Church to err concerning universally recognised saints, nor for the same reason was it possible that praying to saints or reverencing their relics was impermissible as such.[20] 'And therwith remember that thoughe it were no dampnable errour to take one for a saynt that were none, or a bone for a relyke that were none, yet were it a dampnable erroure to worshyp any yf we sholde worshyp none at all. And therfore syth the chyrche byleueth that we sholde worshype them, that kynde of byleue can be none errour, but must nedes be trewe.'[21]

Against the allegations of Tyndale and others, More asserted that ordinary Christians did not worship God and the saints indifferently, as though they were interchangeable, nor did they confuse God's holy friends with God himself. Contrary to widespread accusations, all but 'a naturall foole' could tell images of the saints from the holy people whom they represented, just as 'they knowe quycke men from ded stones, and tre[e] from flesshe and bone'.[22] Like his

[16] Thomas More, *A Dialogue Concerning Heresies* [1529], in *CWTM*, VI, pt. 1, ed. Thomas M. C. Lawler, Germain Marc'hadour, and Richard Marius (New Haven, CT, and London, 1981), pp. 211–13.
[17] Ibid., p. 214/24–9.
[18] Ibid., p. 215/19–22.
[19] Ibid., pp. 217–19. On More's writing about feigned miracles and bogus relics as part of a longstanding medieval tradition sharpened by Erasmian criticism, see Peter Marshall, 'Forgery and Miracles in the Reign of Henry VIII', *Past and Present*, 178 (2003), pp. 44–9.
[20] Ibid., pp. 220–1, 224.
[21] Ibid., p. 239/14–20.
[22] Ibid., pp. 231/29, 231/3–4.

long-time friend, Erasmus, More acknowledged without condoning the practices of those Christians devoted to the saints in superstitious ways, condemning their actions as 'not worshyppynge, but dyspytynge and dysworshyppynge of sayntes'.[23] The real issue, however, was where genuine religion left off and super-stition began – and even more fundamentally, who had the authority to draw the line. More stood by the traditional practice of the medieval Church, in which it was not at all objectionable to pray to specific saints for particular needs. The abuse of a good practice per se was no justification for eliminating it altogether, or else, for example, one should do away with the celebration of Christmas, 'yf we consider how commonly men abuse it' as 'a tyme of liberty for all maner of lewd-ness'.[24] More argued similarly in his principled approval of the Bible in English translation, so long as it was authorised by the bishops and under their control.[25] Despite abuses, 'yet were not a good thynge to be put awaye for the mysse vse of bad folke'.[26] Correction and instruction, not elimination, were the proper means of addressing such problems.

What the matter came down to, then, as Tyndale seemed to recognise clearly in his *Answere vnto Sir Thomas More's dialoge*, published in mid-1531, was not whether some restricted role might be found for the saints (it might); nor whether abuses ought to be rectified (they should); but rather whether there was any legiti-mate place for invoking the saints as intercessors before God. Tyndale remained consistent with *Mammon* and *Obedience*, denying any such place, categorically repudiating More's position: not Christ *and* the saints, but Christ *or* the saints. 'Now in Christ we haue promises of al maner [of] help and not in them. Where then is our faith to be holpe by Christ when we hope to be holpe by the merites of saintes? So it appereth that the moare trust we haue in saintes, the lesse we haue in Christe.'[27] Tyndale referred to More's advice to call on the saints rather than directly on God as 'open blasphemy', and he mocked the alleged 'presumptuouse malapertenesse to trust in God's worde and to beleue that God is true'.[28] Spurning More's commendation of saints's statues and Christians' supposed ability to discern the difference between representations and what they represented, Tyndale struck at traditional, underlying notions of sacramentality: 'Now God is a spirite and wilbe worsheped in his worde only which is spiritual, and wil haue no bodylye seruice. . . . So that he which obserueth any ceremonie of any other purpose is an Idolater, that is, an imageseruer.'[29] Such a passage sounds more like

23 Ibid., p. 234/22–4.
24 Ibid., pp. 232–6, 236/10–12.
25 Ibid., pp. 337–9.
26 Ibid., p. 237/13–14.
27 William Tyndale, *An Answere vnto Sir Thomas Mores Dialoge* [1531], ed. Anne M. O'Donnell and Jared Wicks (Washington, DC, 2000), p. 118/12–16.
28 Ibid., p. 119/19, 21–3.
29 Ibid., p. 124/17–18, 20–2. More's implicit sacramentality in a comment on martyrs' relics is striking by contrast. After noting that the bodily remains of numerous martyrs had been discovered, he concluded, 'Wherby well appered that God wolde haue not theyr soules only, but also theyr bodyes, and in a maner the very soles of theyr shone set by for theyr sakes, and them selfe for his. Was not the woman heled by the

Zwingli than Luther, an indication that despite his heavy debt to Luther, Tyndale divined his own views as he saw fit on the basis of his reading of scripture. In the end, Tyndale's repudiation of More's defense could hardly have been clearer or sharper: 'Youre doctrine is but the opinion of faithlesse people, which to confirme the deuel hath wrought much sotilte.'[30]

More was far from persuaded, as is evident not only from the virulence of his *Confutation of Tyndale's Answer*, but also from what he wrote in the Tower of London during the final months of his life. The *Dialogue of Comfort Against Tribulation*, for example, shows that More continued to see no incompatibility between devotion to God and devotion to saints. On the contrary, just as one would pray to God if the devil tempted one to commit suicide, for instance, so one would ask others to pray to God on one's behalf, including the poor and priests, 'and not onely them, but also his own good Angell and other holy sayntes such as his devocion specially stand vnto, or yf he be lernid, vse than the letany with the holy suffrages that folow'.[31] More cited as an authority 'holy saynt Bernard' who 'geveth counsayle that euery man shuld make sute vnto Angelles and sayntes to pray for hym to God in the thynges that he wold haue sped at his holy hand'.[32] In the following paragraph, More urged one bedeviled with thoughts of suicide 'to haue recourse above all' to 'God hym self', being particularly mindful of Christ's passion, 'the ground of man's saluacion'.[33] Clearly, More rejected Tyndale's assertion that trusting in saints necessarily detracted from trusting in Christ. Devotion to the saints remained integral to devotion to the Lord, as they were those holy men and women most nearly conformed to him as members of his body, the Church, and so likelier to intercede effectively with him than were one's less holy friends and acquaintances on whom one might prevail for prayers.

In the course of their controversy, then, Tyndale and More disagreed fundamentally about the role of saints in Christian life because they disagreed about what Christianity was to begin with. For the same reason, a dispute over the saints and sanctity would run like a red thread through the religious controversy between Catholics and Protestants during the entire Reformation era and beyond. Disputed doctrines were also inseparable from the identification of true and false martyrs, another domain in which More and Tyndale tangled, and another in which they were but two early participants in a much broader phenomenon.

---

touche of our lorde's garments?' More, *Dialogue Concerning Heresies*, in *CWTM*, VI, pt. 1, p. 225/25–31, quotation at lines 28–31. The story of the woman healed by touching Jesus's garment is told in Matthew 2: 20–2, Mark 5: 25–9, and Luke 8: 44–6.

[30] Tyndale, *Answere*, p. 127/2–3.

[31] More, *A Dialogue of Comfort Against Tribulation* [1534–5], in *CWTM*, XII, ed. Louis L. Martz and Frank Manley (New Haven, CT, 1976), p. 155/15–21, quotation at lines 18–21.

[32] Ibid., p. 156/1–3.

[33] Ibid., p. 156/13–16.

True and False Martyrs, True and False Doctrine

A great many of the saints whom late medieval Christians invoked as intercessors were martyrs from the early centuries of the Church, men and women who had shed their blood (whether in fact or in legend) under the tyrannical Roman emperors by whom they had been persecuted. As Christendom was gradually created as an institutional and social reality during the Middle Ages, those who remained within the Church of their baptism had dwindling opportunities for martyrdom in Europe. The dramatic renaissance of Christian martyrdom in the Reformation era, beginning in the early 1520s, was thus a revivification of an ancient form of sanctity, awareness of which had been sustained in late medieval Europe through practices pertaining to martyr-saints, devotion to Christ's passion, and cultivation of the virtue of patient suffering in imitation of Christ.[34] In the world of ancient Christianity, the phenomenon of genuine martyrdom had been inextricable from the question of true doctrine, as in the controversy between Donatists and Catholics in north Africa.[35] With the widespread, contested revival of martyrdom in the Reformation era the same connection is apparent, because in the end, only doctrinal criteria could serve to separate true from false martyrs, despite efforts made to identify behavioural or other signs that would distinguish them.[36] Simply to die for one's convictions did not make one a martyr – one had to die for the right convictions, and the main point of religious contention in the Reformation era was precisely which convictions were the right ones.

The back-and-forth exchange between Tyndale and More concerning the identification of genuine martyrs exemplifies this debate in England in the late 1520s and early 1530s. More's *Confutation* was already a culmination of their quarrel, not simply a first major contribution to 'the pseudo-martyr debate' that would later run through Bale, Hogarde, Foxe, Harpsfield, Stapleton, Persons, and others.[37] The evangelicals' rejection of those martyrs whom they viewed as distinctively Catholic was an unavoidable corollary of their rejection of the Roman Church's authority. The same had been true of the Wycliffite repudiation of Catholic martyrs in the fifteenth century, as when Margery Baxter, an East Anglian Lollard, extolled the recently executed William White and condemned

---

[34] Gregory, *Salvation at Stake*, pp. 31–62; Berndt Hamm, 'Normative Centering in the Fifteenth and Sixteenth Centuries: Observations on Religiosity, Theology, and Iconology', *Journal of Early Modern Studies*, 3 (1999), p. 322.

[35] Hans Freiherr von Campenhausen, *Die Idee des Martyriums in der alten Kirche*, 2nd edn (Göttingen, 1964), pp. 166–75; W. H. C. Frend, *Martyrdom and Persecution in the Early Church: A Study of a Conflict from the Maccabees to Donatus* (Oxford, 1965).

[36] For this argument presented at length and with respect to Christian martyrdom in the Reformation era among Protestants, Roman Catholics and Anabaptists, see Gregory, *Salvation at Stake*, pp. 320–39.

[37] See Dillon, *Construction of Martyrdom*, pp. 18–71, who at pp. 19–27 discusses More without mentioning that he had been engaged in debate with Tyndale over the issue of true and false martyrs for several years prior to the publication of the *Confutation*.

Thomas of Canterbury.[38] Hence in his *Obedience of a Christen man*, in the midst of his section on miracles and the saints, Tyndale wrote that 'They [the members of Antichrist, i.e. those loyal to Rome] have also marters which never preached God's worde[,] nether died therefore; but for preveleges and liberties which they falsly purchesed contrary vnto God's ordinaunces[.]' By 'God's word' Tyndale meant fundamentally Luther's notion of justification by faith alone, in combination with Luther's view of the relationship between Law and Gospel; by 'God's ordinances' he meant what was clearly grounded in scripture (although the interpretative contestation over the Bible's meaning from the very outset of the Reformation revealed the deep problems inherent in such a notion). Tyndale elaborated in a marginal comment: 'All soch marters are the Pope's marters and not God's[.] For martir signifieth a wittnesberar; now is he not God's wittenes that testifieth not his worde[.]'[39] Because Catholic martyrs died for papal prescriptions rather than for God's word (again, as interpreted by Tyndale), they could not be considered genuine martyrs, and so were by implication false martyrs.

At first, writing in his *Dialogue Concerning Heresies* in 1529, More sought to differentiate Catholic from evangelical martyrs by implying that the latter did not exist – not because they were false martyrs, but rather because the recent heretics, he alleged, always recanted their views rather than dying for them. More claimed that in contrast to the many martyrs who over the centuries had witnessed to the truth of the visible, Catholic Church, in the evangelicals' 'secrete vnknowen chyrche of Cryst', More 'neuer yet founde or herde of any one in all my lyfe, but he wolde forswere your faith to saue his lyfe'.[40] At the time that More was writing, his claim was accurate if restricted to England, partly because of the relatively lenient treatment of the evangelicals investigated for heresy during the period of Wolsey's chancellorship. Apparently, More was trying to disparage the courage of the still relatively small number of evangelicals in England. Considering his many international connections and position in London, one assumes that by 1529 he was aware that unrepentant evangelicals had in recent years refused to recant their views and been executed as heretics on the Continent and in Scotland. By his remark, More presumably was not claiming that no heretics had ever displayed a willingness to die for their errors; later in the *Dialogue*, after quoting Augustine's notion that pride is the mother of all heresies, he referred to those besotted with such pride as 'the deuyls martyrs, takyngc moche payne for his pleasure, and his very apes, whom he maketh to tumble thorow the hope of that holynes that putteth theym to payne without fruyte.'[41] By

---

[38] John A. F. Thomson, *The Later Lollards, 1414–1520* (Oxford, 1965), pp. 126–7; Shannon McSheffrey, *Gender and Heresy: Women and Men in Lollard Communities, 1420–1530* (Philadelphia, 1995), pp. 113, 148.

[39] Tyndale, *Obedience*, fo. 119 (PS, I, p. 291).

[40] More, *Dialogue Concerning Heresies*, in *CWTM*, VI, pt. 1, p. 201/23, 30–2. For references to Catholic martyrs as witnesses to the truth of the Church's teaching and authority over the centuries, see ibid., pp. 89/25–6, 201/26–9, 346/26–7, 376/1, 421/31–3, 433/20–2.

[41] Ibid., p. 423/11–15.

his comment about those who abjured their beliefs rather than dying for them, More must instead have meant specifically that the recent heretics in England, when push came to shove, had been either too cowardly to stand by their convictions or insufficiently under Satan's influence to sacrifice their lives for him.[42] More's traditional category, 'the devil's martyrs', is analogous to Tyndale's rubric, 'the Pope's martyrs', in *Obedience* – both presuppose a dichotomy between true and false martyrs based on the difference between true and false doctrine.

Tyndale saw in the death of Thomas Hitton at Maidstone on 23 February 1530 a providential response to More's allegations. 'And More', he wrote later that year in his *Practice of Prelates*, 'amonge his other blasphemies in his Dialoge sayth that none of vs dare abyde by oure faythe vnto the deeth: but shortlye therafter God to proue More, that he hath euer bene, euen a false lyare, gaue strength vnto his servaunte, Syr Thomas Hitton, to confesse and that vnto the deeth the fayth of his holye sonne Jesus, whiche Thomas the bisshopes of Caunterburye and of Rochester, after they had dieted and tormented him secretlye murthered at Maydstone most cruellye.'[43] Doubtless Tyndale regarded More as 'a false liar' about many things, but it is difficult to see how the latter's failure to note before July 1529 the death of a man in February 1530 could plausibly have contributed to such a view.[44] Tyndale moderated his tone but maintained the accusation with reference to Hitton in his *Answer* the following year, at the same time expanding the geographical compass of recent evangelical witnesses to include Germanic lands on the Continent. Although More alleged that 'he neuer founde ner herd of any of vs, but that he wold forswere to saue his life', Tyndale retorted that 'Neuer theless yet it is vntrue. For he hath hearde of Sir Thomas Hitton whom the bisshopes of Rochester and Caunterbury slew at Maydstone and of the many that suffered in Braband Holland and at Colen and in all quarters of Douchlonde and doo dayly.'[45] Like More, in his *Answer* Tyndale used the term, 'the devil's martyrs', derived ultimately from the Church Fathers, which for him was a synonym for 'the Pope's martyrs', the term he had used in *Obedience*. In the *Answer*, Tyndale invoked Cyprian, along with Augustine the most important patristic author in establishing the distinction between true and false martyrs based on doctrine, in order to discredit prideful pseudo-martyrs who sought to merit heaven by their actions. Tyndale clearly approved of the way in which 'Cipriane wrote to them and called them the deuels marters and not God's', because, as Tyndale put it, they 'had a faith without faith' insofar as they wrongly sought heaven as a reward rather than dying as witnesses to the truth 'for loue of

---

[42] On this point for London in particular, see Susan Brigden, *London and the Reformation* (Oxford, 1989), p. 162.

[43] William Tyndale, *The practyse of Prelates* ([Antwerp], 1530), RSTC 24465, sig. K6 (PS, II, p. 340).

[44] For the date of publication of More's *Dialogue Concerning Heresies*, see Germain Marc'hadour, 'The Historical Context', in More, *Dialogue Concerning Heresies*, in *CWTM*, VI, pt. 2, p. 471.

[45] Tyndale, *Answere*, p. 112/8–9, 11–15.

SAINTS AND MARTYRS IN TYNDALE AND MORE

their neyboures only'.[46] Tyndale and More's knowledge of patristic authors led them to use the same argument about true and false martyrs against each other, just as more broadly it helped to shape sensibilities related to martyrdom that both men bequeathed to subsequent Protestant and Catholic writers.

That More was concerned about the evangelical martyr claims being made by Tyndale and others is evident from his extensive, angry denunciation against them at the outset of his *Confutation of Tyndale's Answer*. After lamenting the printed heretical treatises that had been appearing in England, More's first order of business was putting false martyrs in their place. He began with none other than Thomas Hitton, whom George Joye had included in the calendar of his 1530 edition of the *Ortulus anime* as a martyr, displacing Polycarp. Tyndale's and Joye's references to Hitton thus provided More with a bridge between his attacks on heretical books and on false martyrs.[47] More's logic remained that which he and Tyndale had been employing for years: because false doctrines made one a false martyr, More endeavored to 'some what shew you what holsome heresyes this holy martyr helde'.[48] Hitton's views included the rejection of confirmation, extreme unction, confession, and holy orders, the repudiation of the Mass, the denial of purgatory, the dismissal of papal and conciliar authority, and the disavowal of transubstantiation.[49] Accordingly, despite 'myche fauour shewed hym, and myche labour charitably taken for the sauynge of hym', he was 'delyuered in conclusion for his obstinacye to the seculare handes, and burned vppe in hys false faith and heresyes', and so 'the spiryte of errour and lyenge, hath taken his wreched soule with hym strayte from the shorte fyre to ye fyre euerlastyng'. The same Hitton who had 'lerned the great parte' of his heresies from 'Tyndale's holy bokes', and 'of whose burnynge Tyndale maketh boste' was according to More (the term again) 'the deuyls stynkyng martyr'.[50] And More underscored the same connection between doctrines and martyr recognition to which both men subscribed: 'Wherefore syth Tyndale aloweth his cause, he must nedes defend his artycles.'[51] This principle functioned as More's device for framing the detailed repudiations of Richard Bayfield, John Tewkesbury and Thomas Bilney that ensued, all three of whom had been executed during More's tenure as Lord Chancellor. In the course of attacking these three men and justifying their executions, More mentioned Tyndale by name no fewer than thirteen times in ten pages of the Yale edition's text, ridiculing the idea that Tyndale would celebrate any of these heretics as martyrs, denouncing 'Tyndale's heresyes' and 'Tyndale's vngracyouse bokes'. Indeed, were Tyndale to refuse to mend his heretical ways, More wrote, then like Tewkesbury in hell, 'he is lyke to

---

[46] Ibid., pp. 200/21–201/12, quotations at pp. 200/32–3, 201/1, 201/3–4.
[47] More, *Confutation*, in *CWTM*, VIII, pt. 1, pp. 11/24–8, 13/28–35; [George Joye,] *Ortulus anime. The garden of the soule: or the englisshe primers* ([Antwerp], 1530), RSTC 13828.4, sig. A3v.
[48] More, *Confutation*, in *CWTM*, VIII, pt. 1, p. 14/3–4.
[49] Ibid., pp. 15/13–16/30.
[50] Ibid., pp. 16/31–17/2.
[51] Ibid., p. 17/2–3.

fynd hym when they come togyther, an hote fyrebronde burnynge at hys bake, that all the water in the worlde wyll neuer be able to quenche'.[52] Fiery words from a fiery controversialist, one convinced, as was Tyndale, that in the dispute over true and false martyrs was embedded the issue of Christian truth itself, and so the question of eternal salvation and damnation.

When More had quit the chancellorship and left controversy behind, while he was preparing himself in the Tower of London for the ordeal of his own martyrdom, the paradigm of true and false martyrs remained with him. In the final chapter of his *Dialogue of Comfort*, More noted that a passionate lover will risk death for his beloved and that a stalwart pagan soldier will die for his country. By contrast, the fearful reluctance of Christians to endure martyrdom, especially considering the promise of eternal reward, was shameful. Perhaps even more disturbing, 'The devill hath also some so obstynate heretiques, that endure willyngly paynfull deth for vayne glory, and is it not than more than shame, that Christ shall see his Catholiques forsake his faith, rather than suffre the same for hevyn and very glory.'[53] More had inverted the scenario he had offered in his *Dialogue Concerning Heresies*: instead of English evangelicals unwilling to die for their convictions, as More had alleged in mid-1529, he proffered the prospect of cowardly Catholics unwilling to endure a loving death for the one who, through his own loving death, had made possible their salvation. No experiential wall separated More's preparation for martyrdom from mindfulness about the devil's obstinate martyrs. But a chasm existed between that for which the devil's and God's martyrs had died, a gulf between salvific truth and damning error. On this point Tyndale and More agreed.

Grounded in God's Word, Suffering and Martyrdom

Tyndale rejected the intercessory role of the saints that More defended, and he proclaimed as genuine martyrs those whom More ridiculed as justly executed heretics. As it happened, both men would be killed for their own beliefs: More beheaded as a traitor for his refusal to acknowledge Henry VIII rather than the pope as the head of the Church in England, and Tyndale burned near Brussels as a heretic for persisting in his evangelical views. Despite their bitter disagreements, however, when it came to the preparation for their respective deaths as martyrs, they shared much in common. For both men, God's word grounded the following of Christ. To be holy meant to be imbued with biblical teachings and precepts, stories and verses, and to have made them collectively constitutive of one's attitudes and actions. More and Tyndale certainly did not understand scripture identically; much of their controversy centred on discrepant readings of the Bible, and

---

[52] Ibid., pp. 17/20–1, 22/32–3, 22/35–7. For the other references to Tyndale in this discussion by More, see pp. 17/36, 18/12, 18/23, 20/27–9, 20/37–21/1, 21/4–5, 22/22–4, 25/16, 25/35–6, 26/5–6.
[53] More, *Dialogue of Comfort*, in *CWTM*, XII, pp. 313–14, quotation at p. 314/12–16.

even more fundamentally, on issues concerning its authoritative interpretation. Yet it is striking how similarly the two men understood biblical passages that bear on persecution and suffering, and the way in which they both believed that God rewards those who endure injustice for his sake.

Perhaps because scholarly stereotypes about Catholics and Protestants die hard, this might seem more surprising in the case of More than Tyndale. One would expect that Tyndale, an important biblical translator who regarded scripture alone as the authoritative source for Christian faith and life, would be deeply shaped by the Bible and that he would invoke it in times of tribulation. Yet Thomas More's knowledge of the Bible was extensive and his recourse to it pervasive, both in his controversial and consolatory writings.[54] As he put it in his *Dialogue of Comfort*, 'excepte a man first belieue, that holye scripture is the woorde of God, and that the woorde of God is true, how can a man take any coumforte of that, that the scripture telleth him therin?'[55] Because the Bible was God's word and as such was true, it could sustain one in the face of impending death, and therefore it is integral to More's prison writings: the *Dialogue of Comfort*, the *De tristitia Christi* (and the notes comprising the final gathering of the holograph manuscript), more than twenty known prison letters, and the annotations of his psalter and prayer book.

More's two major Tower treatises are in fact pastoral biblical commentaries, written in the first instance for himself. The final two-thirds of the *Dialogue of Comfort* is organised around the four different dangers mentioned in (Vulgate) Psalm 90: 5, which More, following patristic and medieval tradition, used as a framework to develop a taxonomy of temptations beginning in book two, chapter eleven, and continuing throughout the remainder of the treatise.[56] Along the way, the work is laden with scriptural quotations, allusions and paraphrases. *De tristitia Christi* is an elaborate interpretation of the end of Jesus's life that proceeds dialectically, contrasting Jesus' interior anticipation of death with that of typically fearful Christians, including More. The work – whose full title is *On the Sadness, Weariness, Fear, and Prayer of Christ before His Capture* – is based on Matthew 26, Mark 14, Luke 22 and John 18, the Gospel chapters that stretch from the end of the Last Supper to the arrest that would lead to Jesus's passion. One might consider the annotations in the margins of More's psalter as yet another, albeit sparser, form of biblical commentary – as where he wrote, for example, 'fiducia in deum aduersus tribulationem' ('trust in God against tribulation') in the margin with a bracket indicating that his comment applied to

---

[54] For the most exhaustive scholarship on More's knowledge and use of the Bible, see Germain Marc'hadour, *Thomas More et la Bible* (Paris, 1969) and Marc'hadour, *The Bible in the Work of St. Thomas More*, 5 vols (Nieuwkoop, 1969–72).

[55] More, *Dialogue of Comfort*, in *CWTM*, VI, pt. 1, p. 12/17–20.

[56] Frank Manley, 'The Argument of the Book', in ibid., pp. ci–civ. In More's English rendering of Psalm 90: 5 in the Vulgate: 'thow shalt not be aferd of the nighte's feare, nor of the arrow fleyng in the day, nor of the bysynes walking about in the darkenesses, nor of the incursion or invacion of the devil in the mydde day'. Ibid., p. 105/20–3.

(Vulgate) Psalm 45: 1–3: 'God is our refuge and strength, a very present help in trouble. Therefore we will not fear, though the earth should change, though the mountains shake in the heart of the sea; though the waters roar and foam, though the mountains tremble with its tumult.'[57]

In some ways the most revealing (and certainly the least studied) manifestation of scripture's importance to More as he prepared for death is what might be called the 'Tower notes' – the final fourteen numbered leaves of the Valencia holograph manuscript of *De tristitia Christi*. They consist almost entirely of clustered excerpts from the Vulgate. Ranging in length from a lone biblical phrase to ten verses and reminiscent of entries in a humanist commonplace book, there are, depending upon how they are counted, nearly eighty excerpts from scripture, plus four passages of independent commentary by More and one closely paraphrased passage from a sermon by Bernard of Clairvaux, all in Latin. Virtually all of the biblical passages relate in one way or another to persecution, suffering, the desire to be with Christ or obedience to God's commandments. The following excerpt of terse, one-verse quotations conveys something of their character:

> Whoever wishes to be my disciple, let him take up his cross and follow me. [Matthew 16: 24, Mark 8: 34, Luke 9: 23 and 14: 27]
>
> They have crucified their flesh with its vices and desires. [Galatians 5: 24]
>
> The world is crucified to me and I to the world. [Galatians 6: 14]
>
> Strong as death is love. [Song of Songs 8: 6]
>
> I long to be dissolved and to be with Christ. [Philippians 1: 23]
>
> For me to live is Christ and to die is gain. [Philippians 1: 21][58]

Many of the verses recorded by More in these notes are also found in the Tower treatises. For example, Luke 12: 4–5 (or its synoptic parallel in Matthew 10: 28) appears seven times in the *Dialogue of Comfort* and four in *De tristitia Christi*: 'Do not be afraid of those who can kill the body and after that have nothing more that they can do. But I will show you whom you ought to be afraid of. Fear him who, when he has killed, has the power to cast into hell.'[59] The repetition of such verses in multiple works underscores their importance to More during the fourteen months that he spent in the Tower, before his writing materials were confiscated

---

57 *Thomas More's Prayer Book: A Facsimile Reproduction of the Annotated Pages*, ed. Louis L. Martz and Richard S. Sylvester (New Haven, CT, and London, 1969), p. 84. The translation from the Psalm is taken from the new revised standard version of the Bible.

58 More, *De tristitia Christi*, ed. and trans. Clarence H. Miller, in *CWTM*, XIV, pt. 1, p. 635/1–7 (Miller's translation of More's Latin excerpts from the Vulgate).

59 Ibid., p. 635/12–15. For Luke 12: 4–5 or its Matthean parallel (10: 28–9) in the *De tristitia Christi*, see ibid., pp. 53/4–6, 133/11–135/5, 267/6–269/1, 607/8–609/3; in the *Dialogue of Comfort*, see *CWTM*, VI, pt. 1, pp. 101/5–7, 109/2–7, 165/2, 198/5–8, 247/9–10, 298/9–12, 303/7–15.

on 12 June 1535, a little over three weeks before his execution.[60] In these biblical notes, it seems to me, we get closer to More's prison experience than in any other sources with the possible exception of the scrawled annotations in his prayer book and psalter: the Tower note entries were written hastily, at different times, with different quills, without artifice, and (judging from the many minor variations in comparison to standard editions of the Vulgate) from memory. They are More's martyrological notes to himself, a lawyer's evidence in making his case, his building blocks for martyrdom. More dwelled especially on the first letter of Peter, quoting, for example, 1 Peter 2: 20–1: 'But if, when you do right, you suffer patiently, this is indeed a grace in the eyes of God. For to this you have been called, because Christ too suffered for us, leaving us an example that we might follow in his footsteps.'[61]

Tyndale was imprisoned in the Vilvoorde castle north of Brussels for more than sixteen months, from May 1535 until he was burned in early October 1536, but from him only one brief prison letter survives, written to an unidentified official. Accordingly, one cannot reconstruct the biblical character of Tyndale's prison experience per se with anything like the detail and nuance of More's. Yet neither can one reasonably doubt that Tyndale's ordeal and outlook were also deeply shaped by scripture. In his one surviving letter Tyndale requested a 'Hebrew bible, Hebrew grammar, and Hebrew dictionary', evidently hoping that he could continue the work of translating the Old Testament, which had been interrupted by his imprisonment.[62] And it seems highly likely, given his persistence in and death for his own views, that he would have concurred with the same exhortations to perseverance that he sent from Antwerp to John Frith when the latter was imprisoned, before his own execution, in 1531. Tyndale's letter to Frith, like More's Tower writings, is filled with biblical quotations and allusions. In fact, in a fashion strikingly similar to the way in which More clustered related biblical passages in his Tower notes, Tyndale clumped several together early on in his letter to Frith. He began with two verses that More himself copied in his notes and which were quoted above, 1 Peter 2: 20–1, opening in English and then (ironically, considering his importance as a biblical translator) switching to Latin: 'If when we be buffeted for well doing, we suffer paciently and endure, that is thankfull with God: Siquidem in hoc ipsum vocati estis, quoniam Christus passus est pro nobis, nobis relinquens exemplum, vt sequamur vestigia eius, qui peccatum non fecit.' ('For you are called to this very thing, since Christ suffered for us, leaving us an example, that we should follow in his footsteps, [he] who committed no sin')[63] Tyndale followed this immediately with verses from 1 John,

---

[60] For the date by which More's writing materials were taken from him in the Tower, see Miller, 'Introduction', to De tristitia Christi, in CWTM, XIV, pt. 2, p. 696.

[61] More, De tristitia Christi, in CWTM, XIV, pt. 1, pp. 655–67, quotation at pp. 657/10–659/1.

[62] See Daniell, Tyndale, p. 379, where the entire letter is translated.

[63] A&M [1563], p. 521.

Matthew and Philippians, just as More had combined verses from many different biblical books in his notes.[64]

Further, general evidence of Tyndale's heavily biblical understanding of the blessedness of persecution and suffering, which it makes sense to assume that he himself embraced during his imprisonment, comes from the preface of his *Obedience of a Christen man*. There he contrasted the 'true worde of God', which he claimed was always persecuted, with 'the Popes doctrine', which he alleged was always well received and favoured by the world.[65] He drew effortlessly on relevant biblical passages and intertwined them with his own commentary:

> Tribulacion for rigthteousnes is not a blessinge only. But also a gyfte that God geveth vnto none save his speciall frendes. The apostles, Actes. v.[: 41] reioysed that they were counted worthy to sofre rebuke for Christes sake. And Paul in the seconde pistle and thred chapter [v. 12] to Timotheum saith, 'All that will lyve Godly in Christe Jesu must sofre persecucion.' And in the first chapter of his pistle to the Philippiens [v. 29] he saith. 'Vnto you it is geven not only to beleve in Christe: But also to sofre for his sake'. Here seist thou that it is Gods gyfte to sofre for Christes sake. And Peter in the fourth Chapter [v. 14] off his first Pistle saith. 'Happy are ye, yf ye sofre for the name of Christ, for the glorious sprite of God resteth in you'. Is it not an happy thinge to be sure that thou arte sealed with Gods spirite vnto everlastynge lyfe? And veryly thou art sure therof, yf thou sofre paciently for his sake.[66]

If there was ever a fitting time for Tyndale himself to draw on such ideas, then surely it was during the sixteen months in which he sat in prison and contemplated his own death. To judge from his Tower notes and other prison writings, that is just what More had been doing in London between April 1534 and his death on 6 July 1535. However much the two men disagreed with one another about how the Bible was to be understood, and who had the authority to interpret it, they shared a keen sense of its direct applicability to afflicted Christians. For both More and Tyndale, holiness in this context meant countering the pressure to conform with confidence in the Lord's promises: 'Be faithful until death, and I will give you the crown of life' (Revelation 2: 10).

It turned out that Tyndale and More would have considerable company throughout the remainder of the sixteenth century. As devout Englishmen willing to trust God unto death, they would be followed not only by other evangelicals and Roman Catholics executed under Henry VIII, but more numerously by the Marian Protestant and Elizabethan Catholic martyrs. As committed controversialists

---

[64] The verses, also in Latin and like 1 Peter 2: 20–1 unidentified by Tyndale or Foxe, are 1 John 3: 16, Matthew 5: 12, and a paraphrase of Philippians 3: 21.

[65] Tyndale, *Obedience*, fo. 2r–v, quotation on fo. 2 (PS, I, pp. 131–3, quotation on p. 131).

[66] Ibid., fos. 7v–8 (PS, I, pp. 138–9). More also quoted 1 Peter 4: 14 in his Tower notes; see *De tristitia Christi*, in *CWTM*, XIV, pt. 1, p. 665/4–6.

concerned to defend Christian truth and to denounce rival claims to the same, hundreds of fellow writers, too, would travel on paths that they had trodden. The visibility of their controversy and the memorialisation of their respective deaths helped to establish a basic template that would persist throughout the early-modern period. Both men had renewed and so bequeathed to their successors an understanding of martyrdom that was patristic and ultimately biblical, one in which Christ's faithful followers, however maligned and mistreated, neither suicidal nor willing to deny his truth, would be rewarded by God with eternal life for their witness. This much was held in common, yet everything turned on content: who the faithful were, itself a corollary of what Christian truth was, and so related to the debate about true and false martyrs. Subsequent English martyrs would embody and martyrological writers would assume a largely shared view of Christian martyrdom paired with passionate disputes about content, a combination prominent already in the controversy between Tyndale and More.

Despite their virulent disagreements, neither More nor Tyndale nor their sixteenth-century heirs believed that sanctity was 'constructed', with the connotations of that term in current parlance. The latter is itself a peculiar construct, contingent on a cultural relativism alien to early-modern Christian martyrs and controversialists, and in part the long-term product of the era's unresolved doctrinal disagreements. In the paradigm of Christian life that they shared, genuine holiness was acknowledged, not constructed; it was given by God and lived by the godly. By contrast, bogus sanctity and its foundation, false doctrine, had indeed been 'constructed' (i.e. invented, whether by power-hungry popes or prideful heretics) and *therefore* had dutifully to be 'deconstructed' (i.e. criticised and rejected). What mattered was telling the one from the other – one more conviction that More and Tyndale shared.

5

Becket's Bones Burnt!
Cardinal Pole and the Invention and
Dissemination of an Atrocity

THOMAS F. MAYER

In September 1538 royal commissioners came to Canterbury. When they left, the shrine of Thomas Becket in the cathedral was no more. We do not know just what happened in the interval, except that whatever it was served immediately to ignite a polemic and then a mystery. The first eventually died down, but the second remains unsolved and probably will for ever. Historians in the nature of the case can have little to say about its outcome. About the polemic, on the other hand, they can and have said a great deal, usually by keeping it going. The dispute turns on a simple, concrete point. What became of Becket's bones? Rome answered almost at once. They were burnt. This invention's principal author was Reginald Pole who made of this notorious episode of Henry VIII's Reformation a key element in a much wider but largely unappreciated effort to control its historiography through the twin vehicles of martyrology and Henry's demonisation.[1] I had better say at once that I mean invention in both senses, that is, 'to find or discover' and 'to make up'. In fact the evidence is probably (although not certainly) too ambiguous to say what happened to Becket's physical remains after the desecration of his shrine. For just this reason the mystery has given much good sport to many investigators ever since. The most thorough of them, Arthur James Mason, gave due attention to Pole.[2] By contrast, the most recent student, John Butler,

---

[1] For the implications of rewriting history in the Tudor age, see D. R. Woolf, 'The Power of the Past: History, Ritual and Political Authority in Tudor England', in *Political Thought and the Tudor Commonwealth: Deep Structure, Discourse and Disguise*, ed. Paul A. Fideler and Thomas F. Mayer (London and New York, 1990), pp. 19–49. For the construction of the history of Henry's reign in polemical terms, see W. B. Patterson, 'The Recusant View of the English Past', in *The Materials, Sources and Methods of Ecclesiastical History*, ed. Derek Baker (Oxford, 1975), and more recently Peter Marshall, 'The Other Black Legend: The Henrician Reformation and the Spanish People', *English Historical Review*, 116 (2001), pp. 31–49.
[2] Arthur James Mason, *What Became of the Bones of St Thomas?* (Cambridge, 1920), pp. 133ff. Mason

plays down his involvement.[3] Both Mason and Butler agree that Pole's evidence has no independent authority, taking a soundly positivist approach in search of the facts and nothing but the facts. I shall follow their lead to a degree, while also taking a more cultural historical tack by emphasising how much Pole's writing (and writing he influenced) had to do with the 'invention' of Becket's fate. This paper will demonstrate that Pole thought he knew what had happened, had the contacts in England who could have provided the information, and was almost single-handedly responsible for propagating the tale. Mason's work, augmented by new evidence, shows that Pole coordinated a campaign designed to blacken Henry's reputation with the peculiarly heinous offense of having not merely exhumed a saint, but burned his bones and scattered the ashes.

Butler's investigation was triggered by the most recent in a long series of attempts to learn Becket's fate, the arrest in 1990 of two men in the precincts of Canterbury cathedral who had intended to open the tomb of Cardinal Odet de Coligny which they claimed really contained Becket's remains. The penultimate chapter of Butler's *Quest for Becket's Bones*, 'Five Hypotheses', leaves all securely up in the air, before ending with 'A Mystery', the only possible result of the two conclusions he draws: 1. The evidence about 1538 is too contradictory to allow a safe deduction; and 2. it is now impossible to identify a set of bones unearthed in 1888 (except that they cannot be Becket's). At this point, Butler returns to the problem of what happened when Becket's shrine at Canterbury was suppressed in 1538. Having once again cast doubt on the assertion of Pole and his circle that the bones had been burnt, little by little Butler slides in the direction of 'feeling' (p. 166) that the bones after all survived, before landing in the midst of a small group of persons assembled in front of the red martyr's lamp in the chapel of St Mary Magdalene and St Nicholas in the crypt of the cathedral, there to pray for the reconversion of England. A secret tradition is both asserted and confirmed that here is Becket's final resting place, at least for the moment. But why give any more credence to this strange group of true believers than to that other mysterious coterie assembled on Glastonbury Tor, awaiting with equal fervour (if often under more unpleasant circumstances) the return of the Druids?

The crucial phase in the plot followed almost immediately after Henry's men visited Canterbury. I have only a little new evidence about the facts of the case, but it and the other material originally assembled by H. S. Milman, amplified by Mason and recycled by Butler – neither of the two last giving due acknowledgment to their predecessors – produces a different story from that told by Butler or anybody else.[4] In fact, the tale is so seamless that, were it not well within the

ignores the earliest scholarly treatment of the problem by H. S. Milman, 'The Vanished Memorials of St Thomas of Canterbury', *Archaeologia*, 2nd ser., 53 (1892), pp. 211–28, especially p. 228.

[3] See for example John Butler, *The Quest for Becket's Bones: The Mystery of the Relics of St Thomas Becket of Canterbury* (New Haven, CT, 1995), p. 122.

[4] For a very interesting attempt to reconstruct the appearance of Becket's shrine based in part on pilgrim badges, see Sarah Blick, 'Reconstructing the Shrine of St Thomas Becket', *Konsthistorisk tidskrift*, 72 (2003), pp. 256–86.

realm of possibility that the whole thing is fabricated, the conclusion would be overwhelming: the bones were indeed burnt. On one point of great importance to the status of this evidence, however, Mason and the more cautious Butler are probably wrong. The point concerns the independent value of Pole's evidence and by implication, the nature of the pope's contacts with England.

Butler speaks of the pope and Pole, in that order, but this is almost certainly to reverse matters. Although Pole thought the pope still had a good deal of news, he was obviously forced by 1538 to rely on evidence from non-official sources.[5] One conduit is well known, Eustace Chapuys, the imperial ambassador in London, some of whose bulletins found their way to Rome. According to an anonymous report, previously overlooked, the news about Becket's shrine did indeed reach the papal court via a letter from Chapuys.[6] Just then, however, no matter what Chapuys wrote, the imperial ambassador to the pope studiously ignored most of it, since the emperor was deep in negotiations for an alliance with Henry. It is thus unclear exactly how, or even whether, the letter made it to the pope, as the anomymous report alleged. Nor does the report say *what* Chapuys said had happened. Chapuys could also have been cooperating with Pole, of whom he had a very high opinion and whom he had been trying for several years to use against England.[7] Nevertheless, the pope and cardinals had no doubts. In a consistory of 25 October, five cardinals were deputed to investigate what to do about Henry 'who ordered the body of blessed Thomas of Canterbury burned, and the ashes scattered and given to the wind'.[8] Although some later (and poorer) sources give

---

5 *The Correspondence of Reginald Pole*, ed. Thomas F. Mayer, 5 vols (Aldershot, 2002–), I, no. 172. Hereafter *CRP*.

6 *L&P*, XIII: 2, no. 686: 'Per letere dello ambasciadore Cesareo costi [in England] questa corte [the pope's] haveva inteso il successo [of Becket]'. It is difficult to explain how this document has been missed, since it is indexed in *L&P* under St Thomas. I have not been able to locate it among Chapuys's surviving dispatches, despite much assistance from my former student Richard Lundell, the author of an important thesis on him. It may also have been through Chapuys that the news reached Spain, even sooner than Rome. The English ambassador, Sir Thomas Wyatt, included a note in his instructions of around 16 October for Philip Hoby returning to England 'Item, the burning the Saintes [*sic*] bones, Etc.'. (Kenneth Muir, *Life and Letters of Sir Thomas Wyatt* [Liverpool, 1963], p. 81). Much was made of the outrage in Spain, Wyatt complaining on 2 January 1539 that preachers overlooked Henry's laudable actions against sacramentaries, preferring to dilate on 'the burning of the bishoppes [*sic*] bones', ibid., p. 86. Butler (p. 120) probably correctly reads the 'es' on 'Saintes' as possessive singular, although that should have been 'is', as it must be in the case of 'bishoppes'. Wyatt's orthography was notoriously idiosyncratic.

7 See *CRP*, chapt. 3 *passim* and Thomas F. Mayer, *Reginald Pole, Prince and Prophet* (Cambridge, 2000), pp. 36 and 55–7.

8 There are a number of independent reports of the consistory. One of the most detailed and possibly most authoritative comes from Archivio segreto vaticano (hereafter ASV), Archivio concistoriale (hereafter Arch. concist.), Acta vicecancellarii, 5, fo. 92r (copy in ASV, Arch. concist., Acta miscellanea, 8, fo. 157r), with marginal heading 'De impietate regis Angli [*sic*], et de combustione corporis S.ti Thomae cantuarien.', reads 'S. D. N. [the pope] significavit novam saevitiam et Impietatem regis Angli [*sic*], qui corpus Beati Thomae Cantuarien. comburi iusserat, et cineres spargi, et dari vento', adding 'expilata arca, et vasis aureis, et lapidibus preciosis, quorum magnus numerus in ea arca inerat'. One of these is apparently the source behind the abbreviated entry in ASV, Fondo Borghese I, 89, fo. 28r, a diary of extracts from the consistorial acts copied by Gregory XIII after he became pope; this is otherwise full of mistakes, including misdating the consistory to 18 October, calling Pietro Bembo 'Benobi' on the verso of this folio, making William Peto an Augustinian (fo. 36r) and Ireland into 'Albernia' (fo. 34v). Cf. Dominic Conway, 'Guide

only four cardinals, excluding Pole, the best reports include him in the commission, albeit perhaps as an afterthought. The most reliable text of the consistorial acts inserted his name at the very end of the entry, adding him to Lorenzo Campeggi, formerly the cardinal protector of England, Girolamo Ghinucci, Gasparo Contarini and Gian Pietro Carafa.[9] Pole would surely have approved the panel, including even Carafa, to whom he was then close. The investigation resulted in Paul's bull of 17 December 1538 lifting the suspension of Henry's excommunication. The principal pretext was the outrage against Becket, whom, despite his miracle-working bones, Henry 'had called to judgment and condemned as contumacious and declared a traitor, [and] had ordered [the bones] to be exhumed, and burnt, and the ashes scattered in the wind'.[10] The allegation of

to Documents of Irish and British Interests in Fonda Borghese, series I and series II', *Archivium Hibernicum: Irish Historical Records*, 23 and 24 (1960 and 1961), pp. 1–147 and 31–102, 1, p. 21, quoting from National Library of Ireland, Microfilm AV/FB/1-a. Two other authoritative texts are ASV, Arch. concist., Acta camerarii, 2, fo. 98r (formerly 74r), section marked off with square brackets, noting that on 25 Oct 1538 'S. D. N. [the pope] longa oratione significavit Reverendissimis Dominis sevitiam et impietatem Regis Angliae qui corpus beati Thome Cantuarien. comburi fecerit et deinde cineres ventis obiecerit'; and the nearly identical version in Acta camerarii 3, fo. 156r, with a marginal heading 'De impietate Regis Anglie' and manicipium: 25 Oct 1538 'S. D. N. locutus est ad R.mos et significavit eis sevitiam et impietatem Regis anglie qui corpus beati Thome igni comburi fecerit et deinde cineres ventis obiecerit'. An especially poor source lies behind Cesare Baroni, ed. Oderico Rinaldi, *Annales ecclesiastici*, 34 vols (Lucca, 1738–56), XXXII, 1538, ¶XLV, dated 18 October; cf. *L&P*, XIII: 2, no. 684 from a translation of a document from Rome; compare this to Rinaldi, XXXII, p. 494, that is, a different edition of the text just noticed. Finally compare Frederick George Lee, *Reginald Pole Cardinal Archbishop of Canterbury, an Historical Sketch* (London and New York, 1888), p. 27n., from a possibly even less reliable source. The anonymous report referred to another discussion in a consistory in which Ottavio Farnese was made prefect of Rome (30 October, according to ASV, Arch. concist., Acta misc. 8, fo. 158v and Baroni/Rinaldi, 32, p. 495), at which time the pope said he had 'felt greater grief from this [the news about Becket] than from the Christian armada having retreated from the Turk'. The anonymous reporter may therefore have been drawing on a source related to Gregory's diary, since in it the consistory of 30 October follows immediately on the Becket entry.

9   ASV, Arch. concist., Acta camerarii, 3, fo. 156r, inserts Pole's name at the end of the entry; cf. ASV, Arch. consist., Acta camerarii, 2, 98r (formerly 74r), section marked off with square brackets. ASV, Arch. concist., Acta vicecanc. 5, fo. 92r omits Pole. William E. Wilkie, *The Cardinal Protectors of England: Rome and the Tudors before the Reformation* (Cambridge, 1974), p. 235, probably cited Acta camerarii, 2, incorrectly as on fo. 75v, but may have taken his citation from the transcript in TNA, SP 31/10/14, fo. 86; here and in a note Wilkie marshals other evidence for Pole's inclusion. Cf. Ludwig von Pastor, *The History of the Popes from the Close of the Middle Ages*, trans. Ralph Francis Kerr (St Louis, MO, and London, 1914), 11, p. 575. Peter Roberts, 'Politics, Drama and the Cult of Thomas Becket in the Sixteenth Century', in *Pilgrimage: The English Experience from Becket to Bunyan*, ed. Colin Morris and Peter Roberts (Cambridge, 2002), pp. 19–237, p. 228, says four cardinals were named, citing only *L&P*.

10   'Divi enim Thomae Cantuariensis archiepiscopi, cujus ossa, quae in dicto regno Angliae potissimum, ob innumera ab omnipotenti Deo illic perpetrata miracula . . . postquam ipsum divum Thomam . . . in judicium vocari, et tamquam contumacem damnari ac proditorem declarari fecerat, exhumari, et comburi, ac cineres in ventum spargi jussit'. *Magnum bullarium romanum, a beato Leone magno usque ad S. D. N. Benedictum* XIII, ed. Laerzio Cherubini and Angelo Maria Cherubini, 15 in 10 vols (Luxembourg, 1727–58), I, pp. 707–11, quotation at p. 711; reprinted in *Bullarum privilegiorum ac diplomatum romanorum pontificorum amplissima collectio*, ed. Charles Cocquelines, IV (Rome, 1745; reprinted Graz, 1965), pp. 130–2, quotation at p. 131; reprinted in Gilbert Burnet, *The History of the Reformation of the Church of England by Gilbert Burnet*, ed. Nicholas Pocock, 7 vols (Oxford, 1865), IV, pp. 330–4, and less completely and correctly in Baroni/Rinaldi, XXXII, p. 494; *Concilia magnae Britanniae et Hiberniae*, ed. David Wilkins, 4 vols (1737), III, pp. 840–1. Cf. the summary in *L&P*, XIII: 2, no. 1087. ¶4 of the bull of revocation with its medical metaphors sounds especially like Pole in *De unitate*.

exhumation had been added since the charge was originally framed, but the rest of the language is almost identical to that used in October.[11] Already then the news was widespread in Italy, Thomas Theobald reporting to Cromwell on 22 October from Padua that 'they have made here a wondrous matter and report of the shrine and burning of the idols burnt at Canterbury'.[12] He also noted that William Peto, the Observant Franciscan exile and satellite of Pole, had an excellent news service operating through Antwerp: 'they have more news out of England, and with more expedience, than all Englishmen here or in Venice'. As soon as the bull was promulgated, papal diplomacy set to work spreading its language. The cardinal-nephew Alessandro Farnese, for example, wrote the nuncio in Portugal on 27 December using almost the same words as the bull, albeit translated into Italian.[13]

Even though it cannot be demonstrated that Pole contributed to the commission the news of what had happened, he certainly could have. His sources of information about England were numerous and carefully cultivated, in addition to the Franciscan network just noted. The best ones, his two brothers and mother, had unfortunately just been compromised by Sir Geoffrey Pole's arrest at the end of August, triggering the investigation of the so-called Exeter conspiracy.[14] Sir Geoffrey had directed a steady stream of bulletins to his brother on the Continent.[15] During and immediately after writing *De unitate* in 1536 Pole had profited from a flow of reports from 'mine' in England, in addition to official correspondence.[16] During his forced stop in Flanders on his first legation of 1537, he picked up a good deal of information about England, including from Cardinal Campeggi's brother, who had been there for perhaps six months on a private mission of reconciliation.[17] He also took care to forward letters to Pope Paul.[18] It may have been to a conversation with one of the Campeggis that Pole referred in a garbled version of his 'Apology' to Charles V. If the moment is not invented, Pole claimed that his informant had a talk with Cromwell, which Pole used to introduce the celebrated exposure of the Machiavellian Cromwell in the 'Apology' itself.[19] Once back in Italy, Pole continued to receive regular reports from England, including a detailed account of Cromwell's end in 1540.[20]

[11] Butler, p. 120, speculates that 'exhumari' offers a clue that the bones had been buried before being burnt, but the point is of small importance, and probably cannot reflect new evidence gathered since October.
[12] TNA, SP 1/242, fo. 96v (*L&P*, Add., no. 1364); printed in *Original Letters Illustrative of English History*, ed. Henry Ellis, 11 vols in 3 series (1824–1876), Third series, II, pp. 122–9.
[13] '[Henry] ha fatto [outrages] contra l'ossa di santo Thomaso Cantuariense, che ha fatto buttare la sua cenere al venta', *La correspondance des premiers nonces permanents au Portugal 1532–1553*, ed. Charles-Martial de Witte, 2 vols (Lisbon, 1980), II, p. 340.
[14] *Calendar of Letters, Despatches and State Papers Relating to the Negotiations between England and Spain*, ed. Pascual de Gazangos *et al.*, 32 vols (1862–1954), VI (1), p. 31.
[15] *L&P*, XIII: 2, no. 797.2 (TNA, SP 1/138, fos 198r–203r).
[16] *CRP*, nos 92, 98, 100, 113, and 117.
[17] Wilkie, pp. 226–32.
[18] *CRP*, no. 172.
[19] *CRP*, no. 245 and Mayer, *Pole*, pp. 96–9.
[20] *CRP*, nos 237, 257, 307–8.

However much Pole had to do with getting the story to Rome in the first place, his interest in – and devotion to – Becket probably arose under papal stimulus in the immediate aftermath of the events of 1538. Paul III's role is suggested by Becket's absence from Pole's *Pro ecclesiasticae unitatis defensione*, his savage attack on Henry written in 1535–6, despite the obvious opportunity to introduce him during Pole's extended defense of Thomas More, who was very taken with his name saint.[21] Instead at roughly the same time, Paul compared John Fisher to Becket in reporting Fisher's execution to Francis I.[22] Pole is unlikely to have been the pope's inspiration, since he was then still a relative unknown living in Venice and its environs; Paul did not invite him to Rome until a year later.[23] In addition to his probable service on the cardinalatial commission, the best evidence for the intensity of Pole's interest is MS Bodley 493, a life of Becket attributed to Bishop Grandison of Exeter which Pole owned. It bears both the notation 'Reginaldi Poole Liber 1539' on fo. 1v and the probably forged signature 'R. Poole' on fo. 55v at the end. It is possible that Pole commissioned the manuscript, if it was indeed written in the first half of the sixteenth century as one catalogue suggests. Then again, the scribe identified himself as Robertus Plenus Amoris and added what seems to be the date 1489.[24] Pole had been dean of Exeter, so that may be how he acquired the MS, although this possibility must be discounted if the date is authentic. To enter the realm of the truly weird, it is possible that Pole still acquired the manuscript from Devonian sources, through one Gulphinus Abevan or Bevan, a Breton, arrested in the vicinity of Exeter in August 1538 who claimed that he had been Pole's chaplain and that Pole had recently spent large chunks of time in England, an impossibility.[25] However this may be, the book and the date at which Pole acquired it attest the depth and timing of his interest.

Shortly afterwards Pole went on another legation, in 1539. Throughout it Pole constantly drummed on the desecration of Becket's body even though it had not been specifically included in his instructions, almost single-handedly establishing the facts that Henry had tried it and then burnt its bones.[26] Mason and Butler note some of this material (Mason more), but they de-emphasise both its extent and intensity. Pole made Becket, along with Fisher and More, the central figure in his indictment of Henry, first to Charles V and then to Francis I and his ministers. Bishop Burnet could therefore well be correct that it was Pole's defense

21 Roberts, 'Becket', pp. 206–7.
22 Ibid., p. 207.
23 *CRP*, no. 107.
24 The book is described in *Summary Catalogue of Western Manuscripts in the Bodleian Library*, ed. F. Madan, 7 vols (Oxford, 1895), II (1), no. 2097 and a little sloppily in Otto Pächt and J. J. G. Alexander, *Illuminated Manuscripts in the Bodleian Library*, 3 vols (Oxford, 1966–73), III, p. 68. For Pole's ownership, see Alessandro Pastore, 'Due biblioteche umanistiche del Cinquecento (i libri del cardinal Pole e di Marcantonio Flaminio)', *Rinascimento*, ser. 2, 19 (1979), p. 273n. I am grateful to D. R. Woolf, Steven Gunn and especially Nicholas Orme for discussions about this manuscript.
25 *L&P*, XIII: 2, no. 267.2.
26 *CRP*, no. 235. Mason (p. 133) incorrectly claims that Pole did not believe in the trial.

of Becket that irrevocably turned Henry against him.[27] Probably the first attack came around 16 March 1539 in the wake of Pole's highly unsuccessful interview with the emperor in Toledo.[28] As always, Pole embroidered the original words. Having found Becket guilty of treason, 'his bones first having been flung into the fire, then he [Henry] took care so that nothing should be lacking from his hostility for manifesting his rage against the friend of God [and] dispersed the ashes into the wind'.[29] Pole went on for another page, contrasting Henry's behavior to Henry II's in the twelfth century, asking Charles what he would do if a body he venerated had gotten such treatment, and adding that Henry had dealt with the bones of St Augustine, apostle of the English, in the same fashion.[30] The same day Pole wrote Constable Montmorency in very similar terms, generalising the claim about Becket's bones, while making clear that he meant Becket alone with references to his declaration as a traitor and his veneration for three hundred years.[31] Pole really hit his stride in the so-called 'Apology' to Charles V, probably an expanded version of his first expostulation to Charles and written at Carpentras during a lull in his legation. Pole meant the work primarily to defend himself against the accusation that he had appealed in *De unitate* to the English people (whether nobility or lower orders was irrelevant) to depose Henry, a charge that Charles took very seriously. Recently, it has become better known as a major contribution (if it is not virtually the sole source) of Pole's condemnation of the devilish Machiavelli.[32] Right in the middle of Pole's simultaneous attack and auto-defence lay the figure of Becket. At one point, dilating on Henry's monstrous nature, Pole devoted almost six pages to praise of those he had martyred and description of their horrible deaths (93–8). Even worse, Henry had moved on to persecute the dead, a point Pole emphasised with a long insertion on how the devil had treated 'the bodies of the just' (p. 102). These especially included Becket, whose tomb Henry had desecrated and whose bones he had burnt.[33] A contrast between various classical examples and Henry's handling of Becket and his rewriting of history became one of the principal arguments of the 'Apology'. Pole did not fail to note the importance of penance, and drew an extended contrast to Henry II's behavior after Becket's murder which had earned

---

[27] Burnet, ed. Pocock, I, p. 389.

[28] *CRP*, pp. 206–17 for circumstances. The text is no. 245.

[29] *CRP*, no. 245, p. 210, quotation from Biblioteca Apostolica Vaticana (hereafter BAV), Vat. lat. 5970, fo. 306v: 'ossa in ignem primum periicienda curavit deinde ut nihil [306v] ad ostendendum rabiem in amicum dei inimicitia deesset cineres in ventum dispergeret'. Pole's syntax leaves the function of 'inimicitia' up in the air.

[30] 'ossa et cinerem in ventum spargeret'.

[31] 'li santissimi corpi de quali hora sono stati con ogni opprobrio tratti del sepulcro, brusciati, & al vento sparse le cenere con nominarli scelerati & traditori' (*CRP*, no. 246).

[32] Mayer, *Pole*, pp. 96–9.

[33] *Epistolarum Reginaldi Poli . . . [Libri]*, ed. Angelo Maria Querini, 5 vols (Brescia, 1744–1757), I, pp. 101ff.: Becket's 'Mausolaeum tot donariis Regum, Principum, & populorum refertum diriperet, & spoliaret. . . . (p. 103) [H]ominis ossa. . .tot ante eum seculis mortui erueret, igni traderet, in cinerem redacta, per contumeliam postea in ventum spargeret'.

him history's praise (pp. 106–8). Later, Pole turned to his prophetic persona and conjured the charismatically grounded, transcendent protection afforded by Becket's bones (p. 154), not just for himself, but the whole of the English nobility.[34] The 'Apology' was meant as a preface to an edition of *De unitate*. In another such titled 'Qua te tuetur in editione libri ad Henricum viii' and probably dating from about two years later, Pole made even more of Becket.[35]

Once Pole had formulated the precise form of the charge, he passed it on to various dependants and through them to the history of the English Reformation. In their hands, Pole's notion of martyrdom and of its power as a political tool came to maturity. Before turning to them, it would be well to exclude one person from the list, John Legh. Legh apparently really was in Pole's circle in Rome, although he falsely implied that Pole had made him a brother of the English hospice there. He returned to England in early 1540, only to be imprisoned on suspicion of contacts with Pole.[36] From the Tower Legh recalled a lengthy conversation with him about the desecration of Becket's shrine, the martyrdom of More and Fisher, and the danger of Machiavelli's 'poison'. References to reorganisation of the Hospice date the conversation to March 1538, at which time Pole could not have taxed Henry with having pulled Becket out of his shrine (no mention was made of what happened thereafter).[37] Yet there is no doubt of Pole's desire to recruit propagandists who could amplify the power of his already dangerous pen. Already in the late 1520s, Pole's client Thomas Lupset had written a now-lost treatise attacking the making of religious policy during drunken sessions in the royal palace.[38] In 1537, Pole had extended patronage to John Helyar, then studying in Louvain. Helyar, an exile *causa religionis* who had been Pole's mother's domestic chaplain and parish priest, attracted Pole's attention by a long letter proposing both prayer and propaganda as remedies for the state of England.[39] Many of Pole's other clients had the talents required to write more such propaganda.

One of them, Richard Hilliard, formerly a client of Cardinal Beaton of Scotland and a famous preacher, probably joined Pole in 1543. He is especially important in the present context because he wrote a history of the English Reformation, now lost. This makes it more than usually difficult to assess the status of his text, but the effort is worth it, because in it he supposedly reported *in extenso* the proceedings against Becket and their result. Hilliard's history is known from

---

[34] Cf. a draft preface to *De unitate* in BAV, Vat. lat. 5970, fos 326r–27r.

[35] See Thomas F. Mayer, *A Reluctant Author: Cardinal Pole and his Manuscripts* (Philadelphia, PA, 1999), p. 52.

[36] His name does not appear in the records of the College in Anthony Kenny, 'From Hospice to College', *The Venerabile*, 21 (1962), pp. 218–73, nor in the confirmation of Pole's reorganisation, *CRP*, no. 221, which points out other mistakes in Legh's story.

[37] BL, Cleop. E VI, fos 394v–5r (*L&P*, XV, no. 721). This confession is undated, but must be close in time to a report dated 21 May of Legh's imprisonment fifteen days earlier (*L&P*, XV, no. 697).

[38] See my article in *ODNB*.

[39] *CRP*, no. 195a. For Helyar, see my article in *ODNB* and Hazel Pierce, *Margaret Pole, Countess of Salisbury, 1473–1541* (Cardiff, 2003), p. 44.

quotations of it in two other histories, and a few fragments in BL, Arundel MS 152, fos 312r–313r, published by Van Ortroy in his edition of the first life of Fisher.[40] One of these quotations is almost certainly authentic, and occurs in the second edition (but not the first) of Nicholas Sander's *De origine ac progressu schismatis Anglicani* (Rome: Bonfadini, 1586), a collaborative effort of Robert Persons and William Allen.[41] It is set off as 'Richardi Hilliardi de Henrici sacrilegio querela', and is a highly rhetorical sally.[42]

> If you had been with me, reader, and had seen the profanations of temples, the overthrows of altars, the plunderings of gifts or oblations, and the most unworthy violations of and contempts shown (with blasphemies) to venerable reliquaries and images, you would not, I think, temper your tears, grief, sobbing, since you would have seen done by Christian men what is never read in history perpetrated by barbarian tyrants and sworn enemies of Christ. Oh, if Henry VII, the pious father of this impious tyrant, should come back to life, who adorned the church of England with so many and such monuments and should see his son, whom he had taken such care to educate, having overthrown everything, which not only his own father, but indeed all Christian princes of England before him had dedicated to God, he would (I know) curse the hour in which he generated him, and the unfortunate day on which he brought into the light of a most pious family such a monster.[43]

Curiously, Sander's editors did not make much of Becket, even though they introduced him to the volume, merely noting 'causam iterum ad tribunal suum contumeliosissime dicere post tot secula coegit' ('he forced him most rancorously to present a case again at his trial after so many centuries'), and dutifully included the ritual phrase 'exhumari et comburi, cineres in ventum spargi' ('to be exhumed and burnt, and the ashes scattered to the winds').[44] In passing, it might be noted that the Jesuit Persons thus set the precedent for the usual Jesuit

[40] 'Vie du Bienhereux Martyr Jean Fisher', ed. F. van Ortroy, *Analecta Bollandiana*, 12 (1893), pp. 97–287, pp. 270–5.
[41] A complex question, which is under investigation. For interim reports, see Thomas F. Mayer, 'A Sticking-Plaster Saint? Autobiography and Hagiography in the Making of Reginald Pole', in *The Rhetorics of Life-Writing in Early Modern Europe: Forms of Biography from Cassandra Fedele to Louis XIV*, ed. Mayer and D. R. Woolf (Ann Arbor, 1995), pp. 205–22, at p. 213, and my article on Sander in *ODNB*.
[42] Van Ortroy, p. 188. It was quoted and then translated in Girolamo Pollini, *L'historia ecclesiastica della rivoluzion d'Inghilterra* (Rome, 1594), pp. 152–3.
[43] 'Si una mecum lector adfuisses ac vidisses templorum profanationes, altarium eversiones, Donariorum seu oblationum direptiones, venerabilium reliquiarum ac imaginum indignissimos cum blasphemiis contemptus ac violationes; non tibi (credo) temperasses a lachrimis, a luctu, a singultu; cum ea vidisses a Christianis viris fieri, quae a barbaris tyrannis, ac Christi iuratis hostibus nulla in historia perpetrata leguntur; o si in vitam rediisset, huius impii tyranni pius parens Henricus septimus, qui tot & tantis monumentis Ecclesiam Angliae decoravit, vidissetque a filio, quem ille tanta cura educandum curaverat, ea omnia diruta, quae non solum ipse eius pater, verumetiam omnes ante eum Christiani Angliae principes Deo dedicassent; maledixisset (scio) horem, in qua illum geneverat, & diem, quo in lucem prodiit tam infaustum piisimae familiae monstrum.'
[44] Van Ortroy, pp. 189 and 190–3.

treatment of Becket and his bones, detailed by Butler but squarely within the tradition launched by Pole.[45]

The second quotation, of more doubtful authenticity but of direct relevance, comes from *Phoenix reviviscens* by Crisóstomo Enriquez (Henriquez), O. Cist. (1595–1632).[46] Enriquez quoted from Hilliard Becket's sentence and its execution.

> The savage sentence was executed on St Thomas, the tenor of which, as Hilliard reports, was as follows: Henry, by the grace of God king of England, France and Ireland, supreme head of the English church, etc., having seen the case of Thomas, sometime archbishop of Canterbury, and because cited before our supreme council, no one has appeared to act for him within the term established; and because the lawyer given to him alleges nothing in refutation and rejection of the crime laid against him of rebellion, contumacy, lèse majesté and treason against his king in order to avoid his due punishment, and having also seen proof of everything of which he is accused, and because while he was alive he disturbed the kingdom and brought everything to a state in which our predecessors' royal power should be diminished, and because his crimes were the cause of his death and because he did not die for the honor of God and His church, because his high standing [as archbishop] depended on the kings of this realm and not on the bishop of Rome, as he maintained, to the prejudice of our crown; given also that the people take him for a martyr, because he says that those who seek death in defense of that authority are worthy of veneration; in order therefore that such crimes be punished, and the ignorant acknowledge their error and flee abuses introduced to the realm, we judge and decree the said Thomas, once archbishop of Canterbury, from this time must not be taken for a saint nor called a martyr nor listed among the saints, his name and image must be eradicated from churches, nor must he be named in prayers in missals, calendars or litanies; and he has incurred the crime of lèse majesté, treason, perjury, and rebellion. And as such, we order his bones to be exhumed from his grave and publicly burnt in order that from the punishment of the dead the living may learn to revere our laws and not to oppose our authority. The gold and silver indeed, the precious stones and other gifts which simple men because they believed him to be a saint once brought to his tomb we confiscate to our crown as his personal property as the laws and customs of this kingdom dictate, and under the pain of death and loss

---

45 Butler, p. 122.
46 *Phoenix reviviscens: sive, ordinis Cisterciensis scriptorum Angliae & Hispaniae series, libri II* (Brussels, 1626), pp. 203–10. Mason (p. 169) concludes that this passage was certainly not Hilliard's work; his discussion of the relations between Hilliard, Pollini, Sander and Enriquez depends on much assistance from Giovanni Mercati, later cardinal librarian of the BAV (p. viii). While unravelling Wilkins's sources and establishing the status of his text is difficult, Mason and Mercati did not advance the cause much, except for suggesting the likelihood that Wilkins knew Pollini only through Enriquez. Milman, 'Vanished Memorials', p. 228 and Hitchcock (Harpsfield, p. 357) rejects out of hand the story of Becket's trial.

of goods we forbid anyone of our subjects from this day to call him a
saint, or read prayers to him or carry his relics with them or promote his
memory directly or indirectly, for such will be regarded as in the circle of
those who conspire against our royal person or foment conspiracies and
aid them. And in order that no one should pretend ignorance of this our
edict, we order that the same be published in our city of London, Canterbury, and elsewhere in our kingdom. Dated London 11 June 1538. By the
king in his council.[47]

In addition to uncertainty over how Enriquez knew this text, there is one good
internal reason to doubt the accuracy of its content. As the editors of *Letters and
Papers* observed, Henry did not assume the title of 'Rex Hiberniae' until 1541
and 1542 (it was first granted to him by the Irish parliament, but Henry then repudiated the grant and claimed the crown by right of conquest).[48] In defense of
Hilliard/Enriquez, it should be observed that the substance of the charges and
some of the language in their text resemble the proclamation 'unsainting' Becket
issued on 16 November, especially the declaration that 'from henceforth the said
Thomas Becket shall not be esteemed, named, reputed, nor called a saint . . . and
that his images and pictures through the whole realm shall be put down and
avoided out of all churches, chapels, and other places, and that from henceforth
the days used to be festival in his name shall not be observed, nor the service,
office, antiphons, collects, and prayers in his name read, but erased and put out of
all the books', along with the stress on disabusing the 'ignorantes' of their

[47] 'Secuta est saeva in S. Thomam sententia, cujus tenor, ut refert Eliardus, erat, qui sequitur: Henricus,
Dei gratia Angliae, Franciae, et Hiberniae rex, supremum ecclesiae Anglicanae caput, etc. Visa causa
Thomae, quondam archiepiscopi Cantuariensis, et quod coram nostro supremo concilio citatus, nemo, qui
causam ejus ageret, statuto termino comparuerit; et quod causidicus ei datus nihil alleget in refutationem et
rejectionem criminum rebellionis, contumaciae, laesae majestatis, et proditionis contra regem suum, ut
poenam ejus debitam effugeret: visa etiam probatione sufficiente omnium, de quibus accusatur, et quod
vivens regnum turbarit, et totus in hoc fuerit, ut praedecessorum nostrorum regiam potentiam diminueret;
quodque crimina ejus mortis causa fuerint, et quod non ob Dei et ejus ecclesiae honorem occubuerit; quod
ejusdem superioritas pertinet ad hujus regni reges, et non ad episcopum Romanum, ut ille sustinebat, in
coronae nostrae praejudicium: viso [*sic*] etiam quod populus eum habet pro martyre, quod dicat eos, qui pro
ecclesiae Romanae auctoritatis defensione mortem oppetunt, veneratione dignos esse; ut ergo talium
criminum rei puniantur, et ignorantes errorem suum agnoscant, et abusus in regnum introductos fugiant;
judicamus et decernimus dictum Thomam, olim archiepiscopum Cantuariensem, ab hoc tempore non
habendum pro sancto, nec martyrem nominandum, nec inter justos ejus habendam mentionem; nomen et
ejus imagines ex templis eradendas, nec eum in missalibus precationum libris, calendariis, vel litaniis
nominandum; eumque incurrisse crimen laesae majestatis, proditionis, perjurii, et rebellionis. Et quia talis,
mandamus ejus ossa ex sepulchro erui, et publice comburi; ut ex mortui punitione discant viventes leges
nostras revereri, et nostrae se auctoritati non opponere, Aurum vero, argentum, lapillos [*sic*] pretiosos, et
alia dona, quae ad ejus sepulchrum simplices homines, quod eum sanctum crederent, quondam obtulerunt,
tanquam bona ejus propria, coronae nostrae confiscamus, ut regni hujus leges et consuetudo dictitat; et sub
mortis poena, et bonorum amissione vetamus, ne quis subditorum nostrorum eum ab hoc die sanctum
nominet, nec ei preces legat, nec ejus reliquias secum ferat, vel ejus memoriam directe vel indirecte
promoveat; nam tales eorum numero habebuntur, qui contra personam nostram regiam conspirant, vel
conspiratoribus favent, et auxilium ferunt. Et ut nemo hujus edicti nostri ignorantiam praetendat, jubemus,
ut idem in civitate nostra Londoniensi, Cantuariensi, et aliis regni nostri publicetur. Datum Londonii 11. die
Junii M. D. XXXVIII. Per regem in suo concilio.'
[48] *L&P*, XIII: 2, no. 848. Cf. J. J. Scarisbrick, *Henry VIII* (Berkeley, 1968), pp. 424–5.

pernicious belief.[49] It could be that whoever forged the document attributed to Hilliard – if it is a forgery – embellished the printed proclamation in order to give his text a greater ring of authenticity.[50] The fact that the proclamation did not come until November might also seem to raise a difficulty, except that even it was ex post facto.[51]

Much mock has been made of this trial as a flat impossibility and of this text as a bone-headed forgery. A recent theory about how the story of the trial arose combined with the first line of Hilliard's certainly authentic text quoted above may reduce the force of some of the criticism aimed at it and him and consequently increase the value of Enríquez's passage. Peter Roberts hypothesises that the occasion behind the 'trial' could have been either the inquiry into Becket's shrine mounted by Archbishop Cranmer in the summer of 1538 or, building on a suggestion of Richard Rex, a play known to have been performed in Canterbury, possibly by John Bale (if so, it is lost), possibly in Cranmer's house, in tandem with the shrine's destruction.[52] The date of the second was 8 September, the approximate time the shrine was demolished. Could Hilliard have witnessed the play, as he claimed to have witnessed the destruction?[53] Nothing is certainly known of his whereabouts in the summer of 1538, but he was probably still acting as chaplain to Cuthbert Tunstall.[54] It does not appear that Tunstall himself accompanied Henry on the progress that culminated in Canterbury, but could he have sent Hilliard as an observer?[55] If so, could Hilliard have misread the play as a judicial proceeding? Would it have mattered to either him or Pole – for whom there was no line between tragicomedy and history – if he had?[56]

However these questions are answered, one seemingly serious and one comparatively trivial problem in the context Hilliard (or Enriquez) supplied for the text just quoted do raise alarms. Both concern the date on which the royal judgment was executed, 19 August, also identified as St Bernard's day. The minor problem is that I have found no saints' calendar which gives this date. Disagreement about whether it was celebrated on the 20th or the 21st, however, leaves open the possibility that Hilliard/Enriquez was reckoning by some as yet unconsulted calendar.[57] The apparently serious problem is that the shrine was

---

[49] *Tudor Royal Proclamations*, ed. Paul L. Hughes and James Francis Larkin, 3 vols (New Haven, CT, 1964), I, pp. 275–6.

[50] RSTC 7790.

[51] Cf. Roberts, 'Becket', p. 216 and *passim*.

[52] Ibid., pp. 215–16 and 224. Cf. Diarmaid MacCulloch, *Thomas Cranmer. A Life* (New Haven, CT, and London, 1996), p. 227.

[53] Mason, p. 166, over-interprets Persons's 'interfuerat sacreligio' said of Hilliard not as meaning he was present, but merely alive then, ignoring Hilliard's own text.

[54] *The State Papers and Letters of Sir Ralph Sadler*, ed. Arthur Clifford, I (Edinburgh, 1809), p. 12.

[55] For the run-up to the events of mid-September, see Roberts, 'Becket', pp. 214–21, and Butler, pp. 110–14.

[56] Mayer, *Pole*, p. 82.

[57] The editors of *L&P* say 20 August; *Handbook of British Chronology*, ed. E. B. Fryde, D. E. Greenway, S. Porter, and I. Roy (1986), p. 45, give 21 August, on the basis of Christopher Wordsworth, *Ancient*

certainly still intact at the end of August when Madame de Montreuil visited it.[58] Then again, Enriquez as a fellow Cistercian with Bernard would have had an extra incentive to move the date, and by the same token would have been less likely to get St Bernard's day wrong. He nevertheless had a reputation for inaccurate dating.[59]

Despite these difficulties, before leaving this fascinating text it is worth raising another intriguing, if for the moment speculative possibility supporting the authenticity (if not the accuracy) of Enriquez's rendition of Hilliard. Although Enriquez cited as sources for his English biographies Leland, Nicholas Harpsfield, Pitts and Campion plus material from 'Bernardus Britus, Montalbo & aliis' while identifying Hilliard's work only in one place, it still could be that Enriquez saw Hilliard's manuscript in England.[60] The evocative title of one of Enriquez's works, a printed duodecimo book, says that he was in England during the negotiations over the Spanish match proposed for Prince Charles in the early 1620s, reaching their height with the prince's famously frantic dash to Spain in 1623.[61] *Relatio eiusdem ad serenissimos principes Austriacae domus, de servitiis quae in Anglia fecit, tribulationibus, & damnis quae pertulit, periculis in quae incidit, deque libris quos scripsit pro illustratione honoris & defensione iuris dictae domus, & Hispanica corona*, was published in Brussels in 1624 by the same publisher who would issue Enriquez's *Phoenix* two years later, Jean van Meerbeeck.[62] Although this title seems to say that Enriquez had gone in a private

Kalendar of the University of Oxford, Oxford Historical Society, 45 (Oxford, 1904), with a note that 20 August is given in a fourteenth-century source from the University of Paris; cf. pp. 40–1 for discussion of variations in dating. *Breviarium . . . Sarum*, ed. Francis Procter and Christopher Wordsworth, 3 (Cambridge, 1886), 'Index festivitatum', p. xxx, give Bernard on both the 20th and 21st. Stephen J. P. van Dijk, completed by Joan Hazelden Walker, *The Ordinal of the Papal Court from Innocent III to Boniface VIII and Related Documents* (Fribourg, 1975), pp. 49 and 76, two different *ordines*, both giving 20 August, the date of Bernard's death.

[58] *L&P*, XIII: 2, no. 257; cf. Butler, p. 119. The date is likely solid, since Montreuil was in Dover on 5 September. *L&P*, XIII: 2, no. 288.
[59] See the article by Edmond Obrecht in *The Catholic Encyclopedia*, ed. Charles B. Herbermann *et al.*, ed (New York, 1910; 15 vols), VII, pp. 219–20.
[60] Mason snorts that it was 'hardly likely' that Enriquez 'was acquainted with Hilliard at first hand'. He equally categorically and with equally little argument asserts that Hilliard could not have written the document about Becket's trial (pp. 169–70).
[61] For Enriquez's bio-bibliography, see *Phoenix*, pp. 305–32, condensed in Charles de Visch, *Bibliotheca scriptorum sacri ordinis cisterciensis elogiis plurimorum maxime illustrium adornata* (Cologne, 1656), pp. 65–9 and Nicolás Antonio, *Biblioteca hispana nova sive hispanorum scriptorum qui ab anno MD. ad MDCLXXXIV floruere notitia*, 2 vols (Madrid, 1783), second edition reprinted, II, pp. 253–5). For the Spanish match see W. B. Patterson, *King James VI and I and the Reunion of Christendom* (Cambridge, 1997), pp. 314–38, and Glyn Redworth, *The Prince and the Infanta: The Cultural Politics of the Spanish Match* (New Haven, CT, 2003).
[62] *Phoenix*, pp. 324–5; Jean Peeters-Fontainas, *Bibliographie des impressions espagnoles des Pays-bas* (Niewukoop, 1965), second edition, I, p. 199. The unjustly neglected Jean Noël Paquot in his *Mémoires pour servir à l'histoire littéraire des dix-sept provinces des Pays-Bas, de la principauté de Liége, et de quelques contrées voisines*, 18 vols (Louvain, 1763), XI, p. 203, observed 'Je crois que cette Rélation [Enriquez's] étoit en Espagnol', the only student to say this, but it still does not sound as if he had actually seen it. I am grateful to the late Albert Loomie, SJ, for discussion of the *Relatio's* title and to Thomas Amos and Pierre-M. Gason for unsuccessful efforts to locate a copy in Belgium.

capacity, the dedication of *Phoenix* to the conde de Gondomar, Spanish ambassador to England, suggests that he tried to make official contacts there. It was an easy trip from Brussels, where Enriquez had gone from Spain in 1620.[63] He also had relatives in Archduke Albert's service. He had a double motive to be interested in Hilliard's work, since in addition to needing material for the first volume of *Phoenix reviviscens* on English Cistercians, he had also just been appointed historiographer of the Spanish congregation of the Cistercian order, and claimed to have eagerly visited all its houses in Flanders searching for manuscripts. Another work, left unpublished after the marriage failed to materialise, 'Albion-Iberae id est summa historica, politica, geneaologica, motivorum amicitiae, & affinitatis inter Britannos & Hispanos', further supports his interest in British affairs. So does his friendship with Sir James Maxwell of Kirkconnell along with his unpublished translation of a little work of Maxwell's, apparently a geneaology of the royal houses of Spain and Austria.[64] There are a number of men with this name, including one educated at St Andrews in the 1580s said to have written an autobiography and works of Church history, and probably another who became a Jesuit novice in Rome shortly after Enriquez was in England.[65] In addition, Enriquez wrote two books about Ireland, and one biographer theorised that he had spent time there based on his appointment as commissary for the Irish monks professed in the Congregation of St Bernard of Castile.[66] Unfortunately, I have not been able to document Enriquez's presence in England either in English or continental sources.[67] This much is clear. If Enriquez's text is not authentic, it at least resonates closely with the substance of the bull ordering the execution of Henry's excommunication and therefore attests to the existence of a uniform 'Roman' view of Becket's fate, which had been disseminated, if not originated, almost certainly through Pole's agency.[68]

---

[63] *Phoenix*, p. 310.

[64] These manuscripts are likely to be lost, since Antoine Sanderus made no mention of them already in *Bibliotheca belgica manuscripta*, 2 vols in 1 (Lille, 1641–4).

[65] For the first, see William Fraser *The Book of Carlaverock*, 2 vols (Edinburgh, 1873), I, p. 600, and *Early Records of the University of St Andrews: The Graduation Roll 1418–1579 and the Matriculation Roll 1463–1579*, ed. J. M. Anderson, Scottish History Society, 3rd ser., vol. VIII (1926), p. 288. For the second, see *Carlaverock*, 2, p. 67, a letter asking that Maxwell defend his entry to the Jesuits; I am grateful for other information about him to T. M. McCoog, SJ.

[66] *Phoenix*, sig. [3c]r and p. 324. For Ireland, see *Phoenix*, pp. 306–7 and 317, and P. Guerin in *Diccionario de historia eclesiastica de España*, ed. Quintin Aldea Vaquero et al., 4 vols (Madrid, 1972–5), II, p. 1082.

[67] He does not appear in calendars of diplomatic correspondence to and from England, in the correspondence of the English resident in Brussels (1609–25), Sir William Trumbull (TNA, SP 69/77/9–18), in the edition of the letters of the nuncio in Brussels (*Correspondence du nonce Giovanni-Francesco Guidi di Bagno (1621–1627)*, ed. B. de Meester (Brussels and Rome, 1938)), nor in Albert J. Loomie, *Spain and the Jacobean Catholics*, Catholic Record Society, LXIV (1973) and 68 (1978); Loomie kindly tells me he has never run across the name, as does Glyn Redworth. The nuncio did own a copy of one of Enriquez's books (Meester, ed., p. 981). Enriquez may yet turn up in the original records, since none of the printed works I have been able to consult is complete. Then again, the fact that he would almost certainly have come to England under an alias makes tracking him that much more unlikely.

[68] For other criticisms of it as a forgery, see, for example, Mason, p. 170, and J. H. Pollen, 'Henry VIII and St Thomas Becket', *The Month*, 137 (1921), pp. 119–28.

That Becket's bones had been burnt became the dominant view in the sixteenth century, certainly through Pole's doing. There can be very little doubt that the Mantuan ambassador to Philip II, Annibale Litolfi, drew on information from Pole and his circles when drafting in early 1557 his survey of the English reformation. Pole had cooperated closely for years with the regent of Mantua, Cardinal Gonzaga, and had probably sent his long-time secretary Michael Throckmorton to Mantua when Pole returned to England in 1554 partly in order to coordinate policy.[69] Describing Canterbury, Litolfi bluntly wrote 'the body was burned'.[70] At about the same time, Pole's archdeacon of Canterbury, Harpsfield, who by virtue of his office should have been singularly well placed to know the facts even if he may have had help with some of them from Pole (especially the fate of St Augustine's bones, as we have seen), in his life of Thomas More, expostulated against the sacrilege that 'we have of late . . . unshrined him [Becket] and burned his holy bones, and not only unshrined and unsainted him, but have made him also (after so many hundred years) a traitor to the king that honoured him'.[71] Harpsfield repeated this statement in the first edition of his *Dialogi sex* published in 1566 (p. 750) and again in the 1573 revision (pp. 551–2) in the course of defending Pole for having ordered the exhumation and burning of Martin Bucer and Paul Fagius in Oxford.[72] At almost precisely the same time, Pole's former client Mariano Vittori repeated the same charge in a marginal note to his edition of *Sancti Hieronymi Stridonensis Opera omnia*.[73] The only step left was the turn-about of the 1586 edition of Sander, reporting Mary and Pole taking revenge on Henry's bones.[74] Thomas Stapleton tersely reported that Henry had

[69] See my article in *ODNB* for Throckmorton, who in addition had a personal reason for going to Mantua, his marriage.

[70] 'In Contuberi, città a xxv miglia di qua, nel venir da Dovra, nella chiesa maggiore era il corpo di San Thomaso d'Aquino [*sic*], in una sepoltura adornata di tanto oro et gioie, che era stimata centannaia de migliaia de scudi, la quale d'ordine del re fu spogliata et il corpo fu arso'. Archivio di Stato Mantua, Archivio Gonzaga, b. 578, fos 203v–4r; quoted in D. S. Chambers, 'A Mantuan in London in 1557: Further Research on Annibale Litolfi', in *England and the Continental Renaissance: Essays in Honour of J. B. Trapp*, ed. Edward Chaney and Peter Mack (Woodbridge, 1990), p. 107. Chambers (p. 94) theorised that Litolfi got the story from crypto-protestant Italians in London.

[71] Nicholas Harpsfield, *The Life and Death of Sir Thomas Moore*, ed. E. V. Hitchcock, EETS, o.s. 186 (1932), p. 215, which Butler (p. 162) says is not supported by contemporary evidence with citation of Mason, p. 140, although Mason is wrong that no one but Harpsfield reported a trial.

[72] I owe the suggestion to consult the *Dialogi* to T. S. Freeman.

[73] Rome: Manuzio, 1565–1572 according to *Biographical and Bibliographical Dictionary of the Italian Humanists*, ed. Mario Emilio Cosenza, 4 vols (Boston, 1962), IV, p. 3671; the reference to that edition may be II, p. 308 (Angelo Sacchetti, *La vita e gli scritti di Mariano Vittori* (Rieti, 1917), p. 33). I have used the edition of Paris, 1643, where the reference is II, p. 405, col. 1D. Vittori wrote that 'novatores' acted even worse than in Jerome's day, 'verum manus quoque in eos [ossa martyrium] iniecerunt, & in cinerem redegerunt, ut in Tho. [*sic*] Cantuariensis corpus ominum impiisimis Henricus VIII Rex Angliae fecit'.

[74] Nicholas Sander, *De origine ac progressu schismatis anglicani, libri tres . . . aucti per Edouardum Rishtonum* (Rome, 1586), pp. 245–6. This change may well arise from John Foxe's story that Hugh Weston, sometime dean of Windsor, would have 'disclosed the purpose of . . . the cardinal, which was to have taken up King Henry's body at Windsor, and to have burnt it as many thought' had not Weston died (*A&M [1570]*, p. 2301). According to White Kennett, the tale was picked up in the first edition of Holinshed's *Chronicle*, p. 1769 (BL, Lansdowne 980, fo. 239r); cf. Scarisbrick, p. 497 and note, including discussion of the story's reliability. It is perhaps more likely that Sander's editors extrapolated from Pole's

sacreligiously burned the bones as those of 'a heretic or criminal', while Lord Herbert of Cherbury attributed the burning to Henry's pious zeal for the reformation.[75] Whatever 'really' happened to Becket's bones, already by the mid-sixteenth century the overwhelming majority of European opinion, including the influential Protestant historian Johann Sleidan, was convinced that they were no more, in large part by Pole's pen and those of his satellites.[76] Pole's friend, hagiographer and influential historian, Paolo Giovio, joined the chorus by inserting in his *elogium* of Henry the broader claim that 'sanctissimorumque martyrum ossa et cineres sepulchris eruta in Thamesim amnem advehenda in Oceanum proiecit' ('having dug up the bones and ashes of the most holy martyrs he had them carried to the Thames and cast into the ocean').[77]

Pole's polemical deployment of Henry's attempt literally to make Becket's martyrdom disappear is of a piece with his deep-seated faith in the power of the pen. It is no coincidence that the accounts by Harpsfield and Vittori, both close to Pole, were written during his final legation under Mary I. Now Pole, who had always kept an ideologically motivated group of writers around him, had much fuller resources than ever before and put them to maximum use.[78] His efforts naturally funneled into political martyrology. One of the clearest instances came in the attempt to make capital out of Cranmer's end. However badly the Marian authorities may have bungled the original propaganda campaign, Harpsfield a little later made a much better job of it in the form of a manuscript called 'Bishop Cranmer's Recantacyons'.[79] Pole might have been displeased by his first

citation of Sardanapalus's fate as a prophecy of Henry's tomb, added from *De unitate* (fo. CXVIIIr) to the 1586 edition of Sander. Interestingly, when Persons treated Henry's fate in his *Certamen ecclesiae anglicanae*, written in the late 1590s, he still used the 1585 edition of Sander (Robert Persons, *Robert Persons, SJ, Certamen ecclesiae anglicanae* ed. J. S. F. Simons (Assen, 1965)).

[75] Thomas Stapleton, *Tres Thomae* (Cologne, 1612), p. 25: Henry 'sacrilege effodit & effosa publice concremavit'; and p. 58: 'ossa . . . tanquam infamis alicuius vel haeretici vel malefici sacrilege effodit; & flammis publicis (inaudito facinore) concremavit'; Edward, Lord Herbert of Cherbury, *The Life and Reign of King Henry the Eighth* (1683), p. 499. Herbert did not name his sources, except to reject William Thomas's conclusion in *Il pellegrino inglese* that the bones were scattered around the churchyard at Canterbury. The chroniclers Wriothesley and Stow assigned the initiative for the burning to Cromwell (Mason, pp. 145–6).

[76] Johann Sleidan, *De statu religionis et reipublicae Carolo quinto caesare commentarii*, 3 vols (Osnabrück, 1968; reprint of 1785–6 edn), II, p. 125: 'Henricus illum [Becket] exemit hoc anno [1538], reliquiasque corporis incendit.'

[77] 'and the bones and ashes of the most holy martyrs dug up from their graves and thrown into the Thames he [Henry] threw away in the sea'. Paolo Giovio, *Elogia veris clarorum virorum imaginibus apposita* (Venice, 1546), p. 506. I am very grateful to Price Zimmermann for this second reference.

[78] Thomas F. Mayer, 'When Maecenas was Broke: Cardinal Pole's "Spiritual" Patronage', and 'Cardinal Pole's Finances: The Property of a Reformer', both in Thomas F. Mayer, *Cardinal Pole in European Context: A Via Media in the Reformation* (Aldershot, 2000), nos XIV and XV, pp. 9–15.

[79] Paris, Bibliothèque Nationale, MS Lat. 6506, ed. James Gairdner (privately printed, 1877). MacCulloch, *Cranmer*, pp. 596, 606 and 584–5. For its authorship, see the *ODNB* article on Harpsfield (which thinks it likely that Pole commissioned the work) and Mayer, *Reluctant Author*, p. 58. Pole's dependent, George Lily, himself probably a skilled propagandist, had a copy which both confirms Pole's

exposure to Harpsfield's rhetoric, preventing him from finishing a flattering welcoming speech at Canterbury in 1554, but he was perfectly prepared to make full use of Harpsfield's skills in the proper venue.[80] That Harpsfield should later set the seal on Pole's account of Becket fulfilled Pole's hopes for him. Harpsfield's Cranmer was not the only polemical martyr Pole as pope in England helped to create. Perhaps even more important for its role in legitimising the Marian regime on the Continent, Pole almost certainly orchestrated the dissemination in manuscript (and possibly also in print) of the duke of Northumberland's scaffold speech.[81] Speaking *in propria persona* in his until recently neglected St Andrew's day sermon of 1557, Pole publicly took the same line he had in *De unitate* about the importance of Fisher and More as martyrs, at the same time attacking the Protestant pseudo-martyrs.[82] It is more than possible that Pole further underscored More's martyrdom by taking a hand in the 1557 edition of his works.[83] And as William Wizeman points out, the vernacular writer Miles Hogarde took essentially Pole's line, possibly under Pole's patronage.[84]

Although Pole is still much too often read as an exclusively spiritual figure uninterested in politics, there can be no question of the political subtext to his deployment of Becket as a weapon against Henry and of martyrdom in general against the Protestants. Undoubtedly Pole's identification with Becket, Fisher and More indicates a profoundly charismatic religion with very little room for 'secular' notions of authority, especially when directed to Henry's ends. Nonetheless, as I have argued elsewhere, Pole did not use Becket as part of a hieratic defense of papal authority, in no small part because grounding the pope's office in the blood of the martyrs undermined papal monarchy just as much as Henry's.[85] Becket (and Fisher and More) provided Pole with a direct line to God which cut out any human intermediary, the vicar of Christ as well as the supreme head of the Church of England. The pope, whom Pole merely enjoined to imitate Christ including by being crucified, came off better than Henry, who became the Antichrist, in large part because of his treatment of Becket. The enormity of Henry's sacrilege lay in physically breaking the link between Pole and his God. No bones, no divinity. Given the intensity of Pole's belief in the necessity of this physical connection, it is no surprise that he at least countenanced moves to desanctify Protestant martyrs by giving them exactly the treatment Henry had accorded Becket. As legate although acting on the initiative of the University of

interest and the *terminus ante quem* for its composition since Lily died in 1559. BL, Add MS 48029, fos 58r–9v and *ODNB* for Lily.

[80] *Epistolarum Reginaldi Poli . . .*, ed. Angelo Maria Quirini, 5 vols (Brescia, 1744–57), V, p. 307.
[81] Mayer, *Pole*, p. 282. I am working on this point, as is Corinna Streckfuß.
[82] Eamon Duffy, 'Cardinal Pole Preaching: St Andrew's Day 1557', in *The Church of Mary Tudor*, ed. Eamon Duffy and David Loades (Aldershot, 2006), pp. 192–9.
[83] Duffy, 'Pole Preaching', p. 199n.
[84] See William Wizeman's chapter in this volume.
[85] Mayer, *Pole*, pp. 13–40 and 176–80.

Oxford, he ordered exhumed the bones of Bucer, Fagius and Peter Martyr's wife; the first two were burned.[86] That Pole's attitude to heretics was otherwise about as potentially tolerant as possible in the sixteenth century underscores how much he needed his concrete saints.[87] He identified with Becket to the point of literally replacing him in Canterbury cathedral, being buried in Becket's corona where it was thought Becket's head had been interred.[88] In the long run, Pole, who had always insisted that he wished nothing more than martyrdom just as he carefully avoided any circumstances that might have made it possible, thereby manifested his own martyrdom, as his biographers immediately agreed.[89] He and those same satellites simultaneously and in inextricable connection to Pole's martyrdom would put one of the biggest pieces of 'Henry the ogre', Becket's destruction and desecration, securely in place. Thus ironically following the lead of Henry's commissioners who had (re-)politicised Becket's martyrdom, Pole and the pope immediately turned this political act into yet another by making of it a central charge behind Henry's deposition, an ineluctably political act, whatever Innocent III might have said and whatever Pole's own motives. By the time his clients and their successors were done, a politicised martyrdom had become an icon of the entire Henrician reformation.

[86] Ibid., p. 294.

[87] Thomas F. Mayer, ' "Heretics be not in all things heretics": Cardinal Pole and the Potential for Toleration', in *Pole in European Context*, I, pp. 107–24.

[88] Mayer, *Pole*, pp. 348–54.

[89] Both Ludovico Beccadelli and his adapter Andras Dudic concluded their almost contemporary lives by admitting Pole among the martyrs. *Two Early Lives of Reginald Pole*, ed. Thomas F. Mayer (Tempe, AZ, forthcoming).

6

'A saynt in the deuyls name': Heroes and Villains in the Martyrdom of Robert Barnes*

ALEC RYRIE

One of the ugly peculiarities of England's Reformation was the theological calibre of its martyrs. Elsewhere in Europe, leading magisterial Protestants may have been driven into exile, but unlike the Anabaptist theologians, they were rarely executed. Yet almost all of the leaders of the first generation of English Protestantism went to the fire – William Tyndale, John Frith, Thomas Bilney, Hugh Latimer and Thomas Cranmer. Only Miles Coverdale and George Joye died in their beds. For English Protestant theology and biblical scholarship, this holocaust was a disaster. Tyndale's work of translation was cut short, and the career of John Frith, who might have been a theologian of European stature had he lived, barely began. However, the violent deaths of such prominent reformers formed the heart of England's emerging martyrological tradition. The writing of martyrology has always been about doctrine before it is about death. Theologians, therefore, are ideal martyrs, as the orthodoxy of the faith for which they died can be precisely documented. Moreover, in the hands of a skilful martyrologist, their heroic deeds can be used to leaven their doctrine for mass consumption. For this reason, the bulk of John Foxe's *Acts and Monuments* is not formed by descriptions of his martyrs' sufferings, but by expositions of their beliefs.

A similar rationale lies behind a book which should be seen as a companion volume to the *Acts and Monuments*: the 1573 edition of the works of Tyndale, Frith and Robert Barnes, which Foxe edited. This volume's title emphasised the two-fold value which these men held for Foxe, as 'worthy Martyrs, and principall teachers of this Churche of England'. He urged his readers to learn from 'both the valiaunt actes, and the excellent wrytinges of the sayd godly persons'. That

---

* An earlier version of this article was presented to a seminar at the University of Reading in 2002, and I am grateful for comments made on that occasion. I would also like to thank Tom Freeman for numerous comments, suggestions and references, Michael Riordan, whose work on William Palmer and the reputation of Stephen Gardiner have assisted me greatly, and John Craig and Korey Maas, for allowing me to consult their article on Barnes's preaching in advance of publication.

Tyndale and Frith should be thus republished is no surprise, but the inclusion of Barnes is a little unexpected. He is definitely number three of the trio; Foxe's praise of 'Tyndall, Frith and others lyke' reinforces the impression that Barnes was the Cinderella of the volume.[1] He contributed the least volume of material and certainly not his 'whole workes' to the edition. He did meet the basic criteria for inclusion – he was a theologian and preacher of real ability, and he was burned for heresy at Smithfield in 1540. Yet his writings did not shape the English Reformation in the way that Tyndale's and Frith's did. Barnes's strongly Lutheran convictions would have been a poor fit in Elizabethan England. Indeed, it was not principally as a theologian that Elizabethan Protestants remembered him. If Barnes had not been martyred, he would perhaps not have been republished (unlike Tyndale and Frith). This essay will consider the shifting nature of Barnes's reputation during his lifetime and following his death. It will argue that Barnes was remembered principally because he was useful; that aspects of his life and, especially, of his death made significant contributions to how English Protestants, and English Catholics, understood the Reformation through which they were passing.

Robert Barnes was born at Lynn in Norfolk in 1495, became an Augustinian friar and studied at Cambridge. He spent the years 1514–21 at Louvain; during these years he almost certainly learned of the activities of his fellow Augustinian Martin Luther. Soon after his return to Cambridge he became prior of the Augustinian house there, becoming a doctor of divinity around the same time. It appears that during this period he experienced some kind of evangelical conversion, although it is unclear both to what he was converted and by what means. We do know that at Christmas 1525, he preached a sermon in St Edward's church in Cambridge in which he denounced Cardinal Wolsey and the ecclesiastical hierarchy in intemperate terms. Parts of this attack were drawn from a postill of Luther's. Although perhaps not technically heretical, what he had said was enough to warrant his arrest. Moreover, it seems not to have been an isolated incident. Hostile witnesses were present at the sermon, apparently expecting trouble; and if Foxe is to be believed, Barnes's declaration stirred up religious debate across much of the university. Barnes himself was taken before Wolsey, and eventually persuaded to make a formal recantation. However, he was not released, but held under what amounted to house arrest at the Augustinian houses in London and, latterly, Northampton. In 1528 he escaped, having dramatically faked suicide, and travelled to Wittenberg. There he flourished; he became intimate with Luther himself, as well as with Melanchthon and Bugenhagen, and from this point on his theology became thoroughly and unambiguously Lutheran.

He did not, however, forget England. He kept in close touch with the English exiles in Antwerp, including his later bookfellows Tyndale and Frith. He was writing almost constantly through this period, and in 1531 he published his major

---

[1] *The whole workes of W. Tyndall, Iohn Frith and Doct. Barnes*, ed. John Foxe (1573), RSTC 24436, I, sigs. A1r, A2v.

English-language work, a *Supplication* to Henry VIII justifying his beliefs. In the same year, as English religious politics lurched away from Rome, Barnes found himself as an ambassador in London, representing the Lutheran theologians. He visited England again in 1533, and when he came in 1534 it was apparently to stay. In that year he oversaw the printing of a revised version of his *Supplication*, shorn of some of its more provocative and unrealistic passages. The king fulfilled few even of its moderated demands, but Barnes was permitted to remain in England and to preach. His extensive knowledge of Germany made him a valuable diplomat, and Thomas Cromwell used him as such on several occasions during the 1530s. He was not, however, given significant ecclesiastical preferment. His highest office, apparently, was an impoverished prebend in the diocese of St David's, although Archbishop Cranmer tried to secure other livings for him. Yet his preaching was as inflammatory as ever. Perhaps he felt more secure than he was; or perhaps he simply knew no other way. In any case, in the spring of 1540 he engaged in a pulpit war with Stephen Gardiner, the bishop of Winchester, at the wrong moment. He was caught up in the maelstrom of Thomas Cromwell's fall, and burned on 30 July, two days after the minister's own execution.[2]

By the time of his death, Barnes was one of the most notorious men in England. Above all, he had made a name for himself as an outspoken and energetic preacher of evangelical doctrine. Hugh Latimer, no mean preacher himself, judged that Barnes 'is alone in handling a piece of scripture, and in setting forth of Christ he hath no fellow'.[3] Archbishop Cranmer's commissary in Calais, John Butler, a tireless and somewhat tactless promoter of evangelicals in the town, repeatedly begged Cranmer to send him preachers, and repeatedly asked that Barnes should be one of them.[4] Humphrey Monmouth, a London merchant who had supported Tyndale in the 1520s, did not merely name Barnes as an executor of his 1537 will, but left thirty-one marks for thirty-one sermons to be preached by four named preachers, of whom Barnes was one. Another will made a similar request of him two years later.[5] He was equally popular amongst the more radical reformers. Another John Butler, a Warwickshire gentleman who had spent time in Zürich and was a correspondent of Heinrich Bullinger, called Barnes a powerful preacher. Bartholomew Traheron did not merely single Barnes out as an able preacher, but claimed that his attack on Gardiner at Paul's Cross in 1540 was met with 'the most gratifying, and all but universal, applause'.[6]

This last comment was wishful thinking, but it is certainly true that Barnes's

2   The best modern account of Barnes's life is James P. Lusardi, 'The Career of Robert Barnes', in *CWTM*, VIII, pp. 1365–1415. See also Richard Rex, 'The Early Impact of Reformation Theology at Cambridge University, 1521–1547', *Reformation and Renaissance Review*, 2 (1999), pp. 43–9.
3   Hugh Latimer, *Sermons and Remains of Hugh Latimer*, ed. George Elwes Corrie, Parker Society (Cambridge, 1845), p. 389.
4   *L&P*, X, no. 292; XIII: 1, no. 108.
5   John Strype, *Ecclesiastical Memorials, Relating Chiefly to Religion and the Reformation of It* (6 parts in 3 vols, Oxford, 1822), I, ii, pp. 369 and 373; TNA, PCC Prob. 11/27, fos. 232v–233v.
6   *Original Letters Relative to the English Reformation*, ed. Hastings Robinson, Parker Society (Cambridge, 1846) (hereafter *OL*), pp. 317 and 627.

preaching was notorious amongst English religious conservatives. A broadsheet ballad which was printed to celebrate his execution admitted, in a stanza titled 'Of prechynge':

> Many he hath, to the trade brought
> By his teachynge and preachyng, in pulpyt al ofte . . .
> Deceyuyng the people, tyl his workes came to nought
> Suche was the study, of the false fryer.[7]

But Barnes had had a reputation as a preacher of 'abominable sermons' since 1535.[8] He was best known in London, where the conservative John Standish of Whittington College claimed to have heard him preach more than forty times. Another conservative, Rowland Phillips, named him as one of three leading proponents of justification by faith alone in the capital. Two of Standish's colleagues at Whittington also picked Barnes out as a heretic. The city authorities feared that he was preaching in secret to conventicles as well.[9] However, his infamy had spread more widely. In 1535 the curate of Harwich had called Barnes 'false knave and heretic'. When the monks of Coggeshall Abbey in Essex were discussing the spread of heresy in 1536, they bracketed Barnes's name with Luther's. In 1540, a Norwich curate named Bachelor Newman also drew a parallel between Barnes and Luther, alleging that Barnes was the source of all England's heresies.[10] His fame had even reached the northern rebels of 1536; Robert Aske reportedly listed Barnes with Cromwell, Cranmer, Latimer and Lord Chancellor Audley as one who had filled the realm with heresy and would have an evil end.[11]

This may exaggerate his impact, but his sermons were certainly lively. Latimer once described Barnes as preaching 'with great moderation and temperance', but if this was so (and Latimer had not heard the sermon in question himself) it was out of character. While his doctrines were moderate enough, he had a knack for expressing them in provocative terms. A contemporary note of a sermon he preached for the feast of St John the Baptist between 1535 and 1538 has recently been discovered. This note records Barnes's insistence that the saints' role is simply as witnesses to Christ; and while he denied them any intercessory role, he also emphasised their dignity. This much was controversial but not unusual. However, he apparently expressed this opinion by saying that 'John and all

---

[7] *This lytle treatyse declareth the study and frutes of Barnes borned in west smyth felde* (1540), RSTC 1473.5. I am grateful to James Lawson for providing me with access to Shrewsbury School's unique copy of this ballad.

[8] *L&P*, VIII, no. 1000.

[9] John Standish, *A lytle treatise composyd by Iohan Standysshe . . . against the protestacion of Robert Barnes at the tyme of his death* (1540), RSTC 23209, sig. C5v; Thomas Cranmer, *Miscellaneous Writings and Letters of Thomas Cranmer*, Parker Society (Cambridge, 1846), p. 339; *L&P*, XIII: 2, no. 1202, and *A&M [1570]*, p. 1377.

[10] *L&P*, IX, no. 1059; *L&P*, X, no. 774 and Ralph A. Houlbrooke, 'Persecution of Heresy and Protestantism in the Diocese of Norwich under Henry VIII', *Norfolk Archaeology*, 35 (1972), p. 314.

[11] *L&P*, XII: 1, no. 843.

seyntes ar no thyng but voyses', and he also applied the Baptist's violent denunciation of the pharisees to the priests of his own day. Likewise, his reported
comments on the Virgin Mary during a sermon in 1537 – that she was 'no better
than a nother woman' – were doctrinally defensible in Henrician terms, but nevertheless wildly provocative. After one particularly contentious funeral sermon in
1536 Cromwell even had Barnes taken into protective custody. At Paul's Cross in
1540 he threw down his glove, insisting melodramatically that his doctrines
'muste be tryed be bloode'. It did not require malice to read this as a call to insur-
rection. Like his claim in Cambridge in 1525 that 'ye veryte could neuer be
prechid plainly, but persecution dyd follow', this sort of language was bound to
stir up trouble. It was also misleading. Barnes was not a revolutionary, merely a
preacher whose rhetoric was liable to become overheated.[12] It was that which
made him memorable, and it was probably also that which brought about his
destruction.

By contrast, the response to his writings was fairly muted. His only English
work, the *Supplication* of 1531 and 1534, certainly impressed both friends and
opponents. Stephen Vaughan, the evangelical merchant-adventurer who was
Thomas Cromwell's point of contact with the evangelical exiles in the early
1530s, praised the 1531 edition to the skies: 'Look well upon Dr. Barnes's book.
It is such a piece of work as I have not yet seen any like it.' Thomas More's
compliments were more backhanded, but no less sincere. Of the same edition, he
wrote, 'surely of all theyr bookes that yet came abrode in englysshe (of all whych
was neuer one wyse nor good) was neuer none yet so bad, so folysshe, nor so
false'. He then spent a considerable part of the *Confutation of Tyndale's Answer*
replying to Barnes.[13] Yet after Barnes's return to England in 1534, and his book's
republication, it seems to have attracted relatively little attention. Thomas
Swynnerton, an evangelical priest in Cromwell's service, wrote a treatise on rhetoric and scriptural interpretation in the late 1530s, and praised the *Supplication* as
an exceptionally clear exposition of justification by faith alone.[14] The Yorkshire
rebels listed Barnes as one of those whose writings should be suppressed.[15] Yet
by the time of his death, it was clearly as a preacher that he was most respected,
and most hated. It should be no surprise that he apparently preferred preaching to
writing. He was a clearly a preacher of real quality, and moreover, there were
excellent reasons for regarding print as a blunt, indirect and inaccessible medium,

---

[12] John Craig and Korey Maas, 'A Sermon by Robert Barnes, c.1535', *Journal of Ecclesiastical History*,
55 (2004), pp. 542–51 (I am grateful to the authors for allowing me to consult this article before it was
published). Also see Susan Brigden, *London and the Reformation* (Oxford, 1989), pp. 253 and 267;
Standish, *A lytle treatise*, sigs. A5v–6r, and cf. Miles Coverdale, *A confutacion of that treatise, which one
Iohn Standish made agaynst the protestacion of D. Barnes* (Zurich, 1541), RSTC 5888, sigs. C6v–7r.
[13] *L&P*, V, no. 533; Thomas More, *The Confutation of Tyndale's Answer*, CWTM, VIII, p. 10.
[14] Swynnerton had also spent time in Wittenberg and may have known Barnes of old (Thomas
Swynnerton, *A Reformation Rhetoric*, ed. Richard Rex [Cambridge, 1999], pp. 129, 143).
[15] *L&P*, XI, no. 1246.

a clear second best to God's chosen instrument, the preached word.[16] However, of course, his sermons died with him.

Neither Barnes's books nor his sermons vanished from memory immediately. Some six months after his execution, his old friend Miles Coverdale published a defence of his doctrine, which included numerous detailed references to the sermons.[17] The London radical Henry Brinklow mourned the loss of one whose preaching had urged Londoners 'to loke vppon the pore'.[18] In 1547 the evangelical courtier William Palmer recalled Barnes as one of three preachers who, in the mid-1530s, had begun 'to preche the truthe w'out any glose/ whiche causyde many, goddes worde to Imbrace'.[19] The *Supplication* remained on the lists of prohibited books circulated in London in 1542 and 1546. The 1546 list also banned 'a boke in articles touchinge christian religion' attributed to Barnes.[20] The *Supplication* was even reprinted in 1548,[21] and his Latin works continued to be reprinted in Germany and the Netherlands into the seventeenth century. The universities' probate inventories reveal that a copy of Barnes's *Sententiae ex doctoribus collectae* was owned by William Robinson, a fellow of Pembroke College, Cambridge, who died in 1547–8; however, the only one of Barnes's other books to appear in the inventories is his *Vitae Romanorum pontificum*, of which single copies are recorded in Oxford in 1577 and in Cambridge in 1589.[22] Another copy of the same book had made its way into the library of the Scottish bishop Henry Sinclair by 1565.[23] The bibliographer and proto-martyrologist John Bale was particularly warm about Barnes's achievements. He praised 'good Doctor Barnes that right disciple of Christ', 'an energetic professor of the Gospel', and anticipated his protégé Foxe by bracketing Barnes with Frith and Tyndale as a leading English reformer. Elsewhere, Bale made Barnes and Tyndale a twosome, as latter-day Elijahs. Bale specifically praised Barnes's writings, especially his attack on clerical celibacy in the *Sententiae* and the *Supplication*.[24] However, by the late 1540s Bale's attention to Barnes's life and work was

---

[16] Alexandra Walsham, 'Preaching without Speaking: Script, Print and Religious Dissent', in *The Uses of Script and Print 1300–1700*, ed. Julia Crick and Alexandra Walsham (Cambridge 2004), pp. 211–34.

[17] Coverdale, *Confutacion of . . . Iohn Standish*.

[18] Henry Brinklow, *The Lamentacion of a Christian, against the Citie of London* (1542), RSTC 3764, sig. B3v.

[19] Trinity College, Cambridge, MS R3.33, fo. 36r.

[20] Guildhall Library, London, MS 9531/12, fos. 40v, 92r–v; cf. *A&M [1563]*, p. 574. This last item is likely Barnes's *Sententiae ex doctoribus collectae*. I am grateful to Korey Maas for discussions on this point.

[21] Robert Barnes, *The supplication of doctour Barnes vnto the moost gracyous kynge Henrye the eyght* (1548), RSTC 1472.

[22] Elisabeth Leedham-Green, *Books in Cambridge Inventories*, 2 vols (Cambridge, 1986), II, p. 74 and *Private Libraries in Renaissance England*, ed. R. J. Fehrenbach and Elizabeth Leedham-Green, 6 vols (Tempe, AZ, 1992–2004), V, p. 155.

[23] James Kirk, *Patterns of Reform: Continuity and Change in the Reformation Kirk* (Edinburgh, 1989), p. 67.

[24] John Bale, *A mysterye of inyquyte contayned within the heretycall genealogye of P. Pantolabus* (Antwerp,1545), RSTC 1303, fos. 29r, 58r–v; Bale, *The actes of Englysh votaryes, comprehendynge their vnchast practyses and examples by all ages* (Antwerp, 1546), RSTC 1270, fo. 9r; Anne Askew and John

rather unusual in England. Bale's antiquarian leanings, as well as his fellow feeling for another East Anglian-born and Cambridge-educated ex-friar, kept his interest in Barnes alive. By then, however, for most evangelicals, Barnes's sermons were all but forgotten, and his writings, never numerous, already seemed to be addressed to a different age.

Moreover, there was a very specific reason why English Protestants after about 1550 might have been expected to draw a veil over Robert Barnes, while German Lutherans continued to remember him. For all his energy in the evangelical cause, Barnes's theology was unmistakably Lutheran. This meant, of course, that he was opposed to any doctrine of the Eucharist which denied the real, objective presence of Christ in the elements. A well-known letter from Tyndale to Frith when the latter was imprisoned warned him to steer clear of discussing the Eucharistic presence, for if he did, 'Barnes will be whote agaynst you'.[25] It was no exaggeration. In 1538, Barnes was pivotal in bringing John Lambert to trial for denial of the Real Presence, for which he was duly burned. This belief, and the vehemence with which Barnes held to it, seemed embarrassingly outdated by the 1550s. John Foxe was well aware of the problem, and did his best to finesse it. In his account of Lambert's trial, he explained Barnes's opposition to Lambert's sacramental views thus:

> Barnes, although he did otherwise fauor the Gospell, and was an earnest preacher, notwithstanding seemed not greatly to fauour this cause, fearing peraduenture, that it woulde breede some let or hinderaunce among the people, to the preaching of the Gospell, whiche was now in a good forwardnes, if suche sacramentaries should be suffered.[26]

He referred the reader back from this passage to Tyndale's original remark about Barnes, which he had reproduced earlier in the book with a marginal comment: 'Tindall here beareth with tyme'.[27] Foxe's concern here was to emphasise Tyndale's radicalism, but in doing so he left an open target for Catholic polemicists. Robert Persons made particular play of this point, repeatedly describing Barnes as an 'earnest Lutheran' who was so much at odds with other evangelicals that he was ready to see them burn.[28] For all that such criticisms had an element of anachronism to them, they retained considerable polemical bite. This was not the stuff of which heroes of the faith are made. And there was more. Barnes's conduct did not always live up to the precise standards of a confessional age. Persons emphasised his humiliating recantation of 1526, and also drew attention to the deception involved in his escape from Northampton in 1528, 'a notable coseninge

Bale, *The first examinacyon of Anne Askew, latelye martyred in Smythfelde* (Antwerp, 1546), RSTC 848, fo. 3r; John Bale, *Scriptorum illustrium maioris Brytanniae . . .Catalogus* (Basel, 1557), pp. 666–8.
[25] *A&M [1583]*, p. 1081.
[26] Ibid., p. 1121.
[27] Ibid., p. 1081; also in *The whole workes of W. Tyndall*, I, p. 455.
[28] Robert Persons, *A treatise of three conversions of England*, 3 vols (St Omer, 1604), RSTC 19416, I, p. 575, and III, pp. 180–3.

tricke'. Nicholas Harpsfield alleged, plausibly enough, that Barnes would have recanted again in 1540 if it would have saved his life. The English Zwinglian Richard Hilles, although he respected Barnes, commented on his studied silence in the wake of the Act of Six Articles of 1539, and on his willingness to make at least a partial recantation in 1540; Hilles compared him unfavourably to a (then) more steadfast preacher, Edward Crome.[29] Perhaps the very brevity of Persons's treatment of Barnes is the gravest insult, and in this at least, later Protestant historians of the Reformation followed him. Matthew Sutcliffe's rebuttals of Persons made no mention of Barnes. In the 1670s Gilbert Burnet, embarrassed by Barnes's involvement in the Lambert case, dealt with him swiftly and described him chiefly as a diplomat. Perhaps for similar reasons, John Strype scarcely noticed Barnes: he was simply 'Dr. Barnes . . . who was afterwards burnt for his religion', and whose key achievement seems to have been his restoration of classical learning in early 1520s Cambridge.[30] White Kennet, the antiquarian bishop of Peterborough, also made very little of him; he paid scant attention to the books, and his brief account was dominated by the execution.[31] The Parker Society did not produce editions of any of his works; nor are there any other modern editions. Much even of the recent scholarly attention that he has received arises from his controversy with Thomas More rather than his own fame.[32] A more or less worthy footsoldier of the Reformation, then; but not a man whose life and works were especially worthy of memorialisation.

I

The critical ingredient, of course, was martyrdom. As even Kennet's brief notes suggest, it was principally the manner of Barnes's death that secured such posthumous fame as he had. It was predictable that the execution of such a prominent evangelical would immediately be treated as a martyrdom. Martin Luther, who had never shared his English friend's optimism about Henry VIII, was quick to write in commemoration of Barnes and to name him as a martyr. The English

---

[29] Persons, *Three Conversions*, III, p. 181; Nicholas Harpsfield, *Dialogi sex conta Summi Pontificatus, monasticae vitae, sanctorum,sacrarum imaginum oppugnatores, et psuedomartyres* (Antwerp, 1573), pp. 713–14 and *OL*, pp. 210 and 215. Crome himself later acquired a reputation as a serial recanter: Susan Wabuda, 'Equivocation and Recantation during the English Reformation: The "Subtle Shadows" of Dr. Edward Crome', *Journal of Ecclesiastical History*, 44 (1993), pp. 224–42.

[30] Gilbert Burnet, *The History of the Reformation of the Church of England*, ed. Nicholas Pocock, 7 vols (Oxford, 1865), I, pp. 402 and 468–9; Strype, *Ecclesiastical Memorials*, I, ii, pp. 356 and 568 and John Strype, *Annals of the Reformation and Establishment of Religion . . . during Queen Elizabeth's Happy Reign*, 6 parts in 3 vols (Oxford, 1824), I, i, p. 307.

[31] BL, Lansdowne MS 980, fo. 2r–v.

[32] There are, however, detailed studies of Barnes's theology in two modern accounts of early English Protestant thought: William A. Clebsch, *England's Earliest Protestants, 1520–1535* (New Haven, CT, and London, 1964), and (more persuasively) Carl R. Trueman, *Luther's Legacy: Salvation and English Reformers, 1525–1556* (Oxford, 1994).

ballad celebrating his execution mocked the idea that he was a martyr, but in doing so made clear that some in London had already claimed him as such. An English boy named Richard Mekins, who had apparently been an admirer of Barnes, was foolish enough to voice his opinion that the former friar 'died holy'. It was among the heresies which condemned him to burn in 1541.[33]

The simple assertion of martyrdom was fuelled by the events surrounding the execution. Within weeks of Barnes's death – perhaps much sooner – a document purporting to give an account of Barnes's words from the stake came into being. This document is usually known as Barnes's *Protestation*, but we know nothing about its provenance. Our earliest text of the *Protestation* is found in a printed rebuttal of it produced by John Standish, published on 5 October 1540, but we know that other versions existed. At least a month earlier, a Latin text, apparently of the *Protestation*, was printed in Lübeck. An English agent in Danzig acquired a copy and sent it to the Privy Council. Before the end of the year, a German edition was printed in Augsburg, with Luther's imprimatur.[34] In the London conventicles, however, the text originally circulated in manuscript. The conservative Thomas Smith wrote, apparently in August or September 1540, that 'the confessyon of an heretyke, that lately dyd offende / And amonges others, suffred for his deseruyng' was being read in manuscript in evangelical conventicles. Standish himself professed alarm at 'the great numbre of copyes in wrytynge of this his protestacyon . . . which . . . many do secretlye embrace as moste precyous Iewel.'[35] The text we have claims to be a verbatim account of Barnes's words; and while its authorship is unknown, it contains a number of apparently irrelevant circumstantial details, which suggest either an attempt to convey what actually happened on the day, or an unusually subtle forgery.[36] More significantly, perhaps, Standish and other conservatives accepted it as a true account of what was said. As such, this document set the agenda for much of what followed, from both sides.

For Barnes's posthumous reputation was, in the way of things, contested. As Persons would later realise, he was of value to Catholic anti-martyrology as well as to the evangelical cause. Some of the circumstances of his death heightened that value. Although the *Protestation*'s German editor felt that its rhetoric had been toned down to avoid offending English sensibilities,[37] Barnes's reported words gave as many hostages to his conservative opponents as his unguarded preaching ever had. For example, the *Protestation* records how, at the stake, Barnes was

---

33 *L&P*, XVI, no. 106; *This lytle treatyse declareth the study and frutes of Barnes* and Brigden, *London*, p. 334.

34 TNA, SP 1/163, fo. 52r (*L&P*, XVI, no. 105); SP 1/164 fos. 108v–109v (*L&P*, XVI, no. 391) and *OL*, p. 210. Also Martin Luther, *D. Martin Luthers Werke: Kritische Gesamtausgabe* (Weimar, 1914) LI, pp. 445–51.

35 Thomas Smith, *A lytell treatyse agaynst sedicyous persons* (1540), RSTC 22880.4, and Standish, *A lytle treatise*, sig. A2v.

36 For the *Protestation*'s role in the development of English Protestant martyrology, see Alec Ryrie, 'The Unsteady Beginnings of English Protestant Martyrology', in *John Foxe: An Historical Perspective*, ed. David Loades (Aldershot, 1999), pp. 59–60.

37 TNA, SP 1/164, fos. 108v (*L&P*, XVI, no. 391).

pressed for his view on one of his perennial themes, prayer to saints. Doctrinally, his reply was careful enough. He stated that he knew of no scriptural obligation to pray to saints, or of any scriptural evidence that deceased saints pray for the living. However, he added, 'yf Sayntes do praye for you, then I truste within this halfe houre to praye . . . for euery christen ma*n*'.[38] Although perfectly defensible in terms of the evangelical view that all regenerate Christian believers were saints, this piece of gallows humour was characteristically provocative, and conservative commentators were ready to be provoked. The ballad celebrating Barnes's death included a stanza titled 'Of Presumpcion', which vented outrage at

> . . . the pryde, and grea[t] presumpcyon
> Of the false heretyke, that wolde become
> A saynt in the deuyls name.

John Standish seems to have found this claim more genuinely shocking than any other part of Barnes's doctrine.[39] Yet it fitted neatly into the wider conservative claim that evangelicals were consumed with diabolical pride and vainglory. This pride, in conservative eyes, was what led evangelicals to favour their own interpretation of scripture above the collective and inspired wisdom of the Church. But it also, as here, made them pre-empt God himself by presuming on their own salvation. Moreover, it meant that executed evangelicals could be reclassified as suicides, who had deliberately courted martyrdom in order to win applause and worldly glory – a recurrent danger for Christian martyrs, and one of which early evangelicals were painfully aware.[40] In these contexts, Barnes's careless talk was too useful for his conservative enemies to ignore.

A graver charge, which evangelicals were more concerned to rebut, was that of sedition. The *Protestation* has Barnes deny that he had been 'a prea[c]her of sedicion and disobedie*n*ce'. He affirms the necessity of obedience to the secular power, 'not onely for fear of the swerde but also for conscience sake', and denies that resistance to an ungodly tyrant can ever go beyond passive disobedience. But there were persistent rumours that his preaching had not always been so cautious. Standish claimed to have heard Barnes preach that 'mans lawes could not bynde to deadly synne'. Both he and Gardiner also dredged up Barnes's attacks on royal authority in the first edition of his *Supplication*.[41] For John Huntingdon, the author of a popular piece of conservative doggerel published in 1540–2, this was the central charge against Barnes, who had taught

> In wordes playne
> It coude not be founde

---

[38] Standish, *A lytle treatise*, sig. D6r.

[39] *This lytle treatyse declareth the study and frutes of Barnes* and Standish, *A lytle treatise*, sig. D6r.

[40] Alec Ryrie, *The Gospel and Henry VIII: Evangelicals in the Early English Reformation* (Cambridge, 2003), pp. 73 and 190–2.

[41] Standish, *A lytle treatise*, sigs. F1r–2r; TNA, SP 1/158, fo. 50r (*L&P*, XV, no. 354.1), and Susan Brigden, 'Popular Disturbance and the Fall of Thomas Cromwell and the Reformers, 1539–40', *Historical Journal*, 24 (1981), pp. 265, 270.

That we were bounde
To be obedient
To the commanndement
Of the hygh powers
At any howres
On payne of synne.
But what ded he wynne?
He was tyed at a poste
And there ded roste.[42]

Barnes's evangelical defenders, however, were not willing to let this charge stand. Coverdale, of course, rebutted Standish's claims in some detail.[43] Others used the *Protestation* as evidence for the meekness with which Barnes had accepted an unjust death at royal hands. An exiled pamphleteer trying to defend Barnes against various posthumous calumnies in 1540 wrote that he 'mekely departed hence/ Praynge for our kynge. . . . In hys confession, I fynde none other offence.' Bale also emphasised his stillness at his death, noting that even Barnes's 'enemyes' confirmed this – apparently meaning Standish, from whose book Bale learned of the *Protestation*.[44] Foxe likewise emphasised that Barnes and his fellow-sufferers died with 'such pacience as might well testifie the goodnes of their cause and quiet of their conscience'.

The fellow-sufferers themselves were also useful for muddying the water and underlining the injustice of the executions. Barnes was burned together with two other, less prominent evangelical preachers, William Jerome and Thomas Garrett. Alongside them, three conservative opponents of the royal supremacy were hanged, drawn and quartered for treason. This gruesome theatre attracted considerable attention. The French ambassador Marillac – admittedly one of the least reliable observers of English events – believed that the six executions had succeeding in unsettling the whole of London.[45] Bullinger's correspondent Richard Hilles was also driven to dismiss the whole event as a brutal charade of justice, carried out for cynical political reasons. 'It is now no novelty among us', he wrote, 'to see men slain, hung, quartered or beheaded . . . some for one thing, and some for another.'[46] Eighteen years later, Anthony Gilby remembered these executions as the crowning proof of Henry VIII's 'beastlynes' and impiety.[47] Burnet's judgement that the paired deaths were widely condemned as 'an

[42] Bale, *A mysterye of inyquyte*, fos. 59v–60r, 62v–63r. Huntingdon's poem, *The Genealogye of Heresye*, survives only in Bale's lengthy rebuttal of it. However, Bale did record that at least two editions had been printed by 1542.
[43] Coverdale, *Confutacion of . . . Iohn Standish*, sigs. C6v–7r, K3v–4r.
[44] *A brefe apologye or answere to a certen craftye cloynar, or popyshe parasye, called Thomas Smythe* (Antwerp, 1540), RSTC 22880.7, sig. A4r; John Bale, *The Image of bothe churches* (Antwerp, 1548), RSTC 1297, sig. Kk7v.
[45] *L&P*, XV, no. 953.
[46] *OL*, pp. 210–11.
[47] Anthony Gilby, 'An Admonition to England and Scotland, to Call them to Repentance', in *The Works of John Knox*, ed. David Laing, 6 vols (Edinburgh, 1846–64), IV, pp. 563–4.

extravagant affectation of the show of impartial justice' may be too kind; Henry VIII may have intended a blunter message. Yet these executions did allow evangelicals to hurl back, or at least to neutralise, the conservative charge that Barnes and his fellow-sufferers were seditious. Foxe, in the first edition of the *Acts and Monuments*, claimed rather improbably that the three conservatives' deaths were a ploy by Bishop Gardiner 'to couler his owne tirannye'. In subsequent editions, this was replaced by the slightly more plausible claim that the Privy Council was divided between conservatives crying for heretical blood, and evangelicals wishing to execute justice on papists. On this reading, the eventual executions were a grotesque compromise.[48]

More significantly, perhaps, the image of these parallel executions itself proved memorable – as Foxe put it, 'two vpon an hyrdle, one being a Papist, the other a Protestant'. In 1548, an unknown poet produced a brief dialogue between Barnes and the most prominent of the conservatives executed with him, Edward Powell. It gives the conversation between the two men who, dying together, found themselves together at the gates of heaven. Sadly, the author did not make much of this splendid conceit. Barnes is made simply to denounce popish cruelty and sedition, occasionally interrupted by expostulations and insults from Powell. The significance, such as it is, of this ephemeral tract is two-fold. First, it shows that the unusual manner of Barnes's death was still remembered in London nearly a decade later; for the pamphlet provides only the scantiest introduction to Barnes and Powell, assuming that its readers will be familiar with the scenario. Secondly, the Barnes it imagines has already moved some way towards caricature. The violence of his language is realistic enough, but his bitter comment about the Mass – 'to the cake as to our maker / to trust they did vs teache' – runs directly counter to Barnes's own beliefs.[49] Barnes was remembered, it seems, but remembered for the circumstances of his death rather than the content of his life. His usefulness to evangelicals was as an empty category, an Identikit martyr there for the taking.

II

Although Barnes's life was overshadowed by his death, the specifics of his story were not entirely forgotten. However, when they were remembered, they were usually used to illustrate other stories rather to tell Barnes's own. In the torrent of personal narratives that made up the heroic-martyrological view of history, the lesser characters tended to be conscripted to play supporting roles in the dramas of the leading players. As such, their stories would be shaped by narratives which may have been tangential to their own. Justly or unjustly, this was Robert Barnes's fate.

---

[48] Burnet, *History*, I, pp. 471–2; *A&M [1563]*, p. 604, and *A&M [1583]*, p. 1201.
[49] *The metynge of doctor Barons and doctor Powell at Paradise gate* (1548), RSTC 1473, esp. sig. A6v.

Martyrological histories require some core ingredients. They need martyrs – the combination of doctrinal rectitude and suffering, preferably cemented together with heroic virtue. However, they also need villains – who should ideally be paragons of depravity and error as well as persecutors. This allows martyrologists to show their heroes being persecuted specifically because of their true faith and their virtue. The true Church can be known as such most clearly when it is seen in opposition to the false Church. As such, the devil's agents are a necessary part of the drama. Moreover, as Milton knew, they can help to sustain interest in a narrative which might otherwise become weighted down with the repetitiveness of sanctity. For martyrologists dealing with the reign of Henry VIII, however, the martyrological need for a villain was complicated by the political and polemical need to avoid casting the king in that role.[50] Barnes was one of a respectable handful of prominent martyrs from the period. However, his case stood out in the later English Protestant memory in part because his death provided an effective and enduring solution to the problem of finding a politically acceptable and polemically satisfying villain.

Around the time of Barnes's death, evangelical imaginations in England were already beginning to latch on to an appropriate villain: Stephen Gardiner, the bishop of Winchester.[51] Gardiner was the most prominent and energetic opponent of further religious change at court and may already have been winning a half-deserved reputation for underhand dealing. But he remained hopelessly under-qualified for martyrological villainy, because he was no persecutor. He could be linked only to a handful of heresy prosecutions, and worse, he had shown himself to be unwilling to press for executions where they could be avoided. Evangelical polemicists were aware of the problem but could do little other than mutter innuendos.[52] The breakthrough for Gardiner's career as a villain came through his involvement with Robert Barnes.

Gardiner and Barnes had been contemporaries at Cambridge in the 1520s. When Barnes was first arrested, in 1525, Gardiner urged him, as a friend, to recant. Gardiner indeed recalled those days with a measure of cool affection, writing in 1545 that Barnes 'as a good felowe in companye was beloued of many'.[53] When their paths crossed again, Gardiner was less benevolently

---

[50] Ryrie, 'Unsteady Beginnings', pp. 53–5.

[51] For a fuller consideration of Gardiner's role in the evangelical imagination see Michael Riordan and Alec Ryrie, 'Stephen Gardiner and the Making of a Protestant Villain', *Sixteenth Century Journal*, 34 (2003), pp. 1039–63.

[52] James Arthur Muller, *Stephen Gardiner and the Tudor Reaction* (1926), pp. 52–3 and 82; Clayton J. Drees, *Authority and Dissent in the English Church: The Prosecution of Heresy and Religious Non-conformity in the Diocese of Winchester, 1380–1547* (Lewiston, NY, 1997), pp. 111 and 113; G. R. Elton, *Policy and Police: The Enforcement of the Reformation in the Age of Thomas Cromwell* (Cambridge, 1972), pp. 42–4; Henry Brinklow, *The complaynt of Roderyck Mors* (1542?), RSTC 3759.5, sig. C8v, and John Bale, *The Epistle exhortatorye of an Englyshe Christiane* (Antwerp, 1544), RSTC 1291, fo. 13v.

[53] Stephen Gardiner, *A declaration of such true articles as George Ioye hath gone about to confute as false* (1546), RSTC 11588, fo. 2v. The text was completed by November 1545; see Stephen Gardiner, *The Letters of Stephen Gardiner*, ed. James Arthur Muller (Cambridge, 1933), p. 163.

inclined. In August 1538, when Barnes was again sent on a diplomatic mission to Germany, Gardiner could not or would not conceal his opinion that the man was a heretic. For his pains, he was excluded from the Privy Council.[54] Perhaps this rankled with Gardiner, because six months later, on the first Sunday in Lent 1540, Gardiner displaced Barnes from preaching at Paul's Cross, giving him only twenty-four hours' warning.[55] His justification was that it was 'better to dis-apoynte Barnes . . . then some other catholique man'; and his sermon was an attack on justification by faith alone, in which he deplored those who preached such doctrines, who were once called friars and now called themselves brethren. It is conceivable that he had not explicitly intended to goad Barnes, but it is clear that Barnes was goaded. Two weeks later, Barnes took up the challenge in the same pulpit, and described the contest between himself and the bishop as a cock-fight, calling Gardiner (as one listener later recalled) 'a Cocke of the game / whose spurres were blunt and cowlde not pryke'.[56] Barnes, however, had misread the political winds and overestimated the bishop's sense of humour. When Gardiner found that his veiled attack had provoked an open response, he denounced Barnes to the king. By his own account, one reason for this was that he felt his dignity to be offended, 'to here a Bysshop of the realme as I was, so reuiled, and by such one openly'. The king, ominously, took an active interest in the case, and organised for the two men to debate before supposedly impartial judges.

A few hours into the debate, Barnes suddenly crumbled. Perhaps he was begin-ning to understand his peril, or perhaps the quick-witted bishop had actually managed to box him in. (It would not be the first time: Barnes had apparently given way before a similar attack by Thomas More nine years before.[57]) For what-ever reason, Barnes conceded the debate with a speed which apparently startled his opponent, and begged that Gardiner might take him into his household and instruct him in true doctrine. Gardiner agreed, although we can credit his claim that he was a little bewildered by this development. More murkily, he offered Barnes a pension of £40 a year if he would join the episcopal household, which Gardiner's enemies were quick to interpret as a simple bribe.[58] Be that as it may, Barnes duly came to attend 'scoole' with Gardiner on the following Monday morning. However, this somewhat surreal arrangement only lasted two days before Barnes began to demand that he should be treated as an equal rather than a pupil. He may have regained his theological composure, or have felt that he was

---

[54] TNA, SP 1/155, fo. 190r (*L&P*, XIV: 2, no. 750.1); Diarmaid MacCulloch, *Thomas Cranmer: A Life* (New Haven, CT, 1996), p. 257.

[55] For this and most of what follows, see Gardiner's own account of these events in Gardiner, *Declaration of such true articles*, fos. 4v–10v.

[56] Trinity College, Cambridge, MS R3.33, fo. 119r.

[57] More, *The Confutation of Tyndale's Answer*, p. 10.

[58] Even if this were a bribe, it is notable that Gardiner would be willing to pay a substantial sum of money to avoid a burning. As he observed with justified exasperation, he was blamed for cruelty if he was strict, and for corruption if he was lenient.

less exposed after William Jerome (who was soon to join him at the stake) had also preached reforming doctrines at Paul's Cross.[59]

Gardiner refused this demand; and by the bishop's own account, this was the end of his involvement in Barnes's case. Barnes, however, did not forget that it was Gardiner who had first denounced him to the king. He was now arrested, along with Jerome and Thomas Garrett, and agreed to recant. His recantation sermon, however, was an essay in evasion and ambiguity. In one of its most memorable and provocative moments, he pointedly asked Gardiner's forgiveness from the pulpit, and begged the bishop to hold his hand up there and then to indicate that he was indeed willing to forgive his errant pupil. Gardiner was unsurprisingly taken aback by the suddenness and boldness of this request, and complied with a reluctance which was readily interpreted as a symbol of his bloodthirsty mendacity.[60] After the sermon, Barnes was rearrested and, eventually, condemned by attainder. At the stake (according to the *Protestation*) he publicly forgave his accusers, but the only one he mentioned by name was Gardiner. John Standish believed that he did so to 'sturre his fauters and frendes to grudge or mourmure against my Lord'. If so, he succeeded.[61]

For most evangelicals, this became the dominant theme of Barnes's martyrdom. Those who remembered Barnes in the decades after his death seem to have remembered him more as Gardiner's proto-martyr than as a preacher and theologian. The assumption that Gardiner was ultimately to blame for Barnes's death became a commonplace. In 1543, the moderate evangelical Robert Wisdom accused Gardiner of procuring Barnes's death, and alleged that 'a greate many' shared the same opinion.[62] In 1546, George Joye wrote that 'the comon fame can not be stylled' that Gardiner was ultimately responsible.[63] Gardiner was aware of the charge, and sensitive to it – so much so that when Joye first accused Gardiner of Barnes's murder, Gardiner condescended to reply, giving his own, detailed account of the events leading up to the burning. Almost the only point on which he and Joye agreed was that he was widely blamed for Barnes's death.[64] Even the chronicler at the Grey Friars, a normally laconic conservative, noted that Barnes had forgiven Gardiner for procuring his death.[65] In 1547 the courtier William Palmer wrote a comprehensive and at times absurd narrative of Gardiner's villainies; the claim that he had been the prime mover of Barnes's destruction was the centrepiece of the few substantive charges against him.[66] In 1548 the anonymous author of *A caueat for the christians agaynst the archpapist* accused

[59] Muller, *Stephen Gardiner*, p. 88.

[60] *A&M [1563]*, p. 603, and *A&M [1570]*, p. 1372.

[61] Standish, *A lytle treatise*, sigs. E7r–8v.

[62] Emmanuel College, Cambridge, MS 261, fo. 115v.

[63] George Joye, *The refutation of the byshop of Winchesters derke declaration of his false articles* (1546), RSTC 14828.5, fo. 2v.

[64] Gardiner, *Declaration of such true articles*, esp. fos. 4r, 8v.

[65] *Chronicle of the Grey Friars of London*, ed. J. G. Nichols, Camden Society, o.s. 53 (1852), p. 43.

[66] Trinity College, Cambridge, MS R3.33, fos. 117v–126v.

Gardiner of having 'deade mens bones' concealed in his 'whyted sepulchre', but the only victim whom he named was Barnes.[67] Bale blamed the execution squarely on 'Winchester and like tyrants of Antichrist'.[68] William Turner and John Hooper both singled out Barnes, Jerome and Garrett's deaths as a crime for which Gardiner alone was responsible.[69] In 1553, an anonymous *Admonishion* to the restored Catholic bishops made a veiled but unmistakable reference to Barnes's death. It recalled the time 'when menne were burned for the truthes sake', and drew a hollow comfort from the bishops' denials, in their 'writings', that they had procured such executions; this can only refer to Gardiner's published self-exculpation relating to Barnes. However, the 1553 author warned, if a new persecution arose, it would give the lie to such denials. Then

> truely it shalbe manifest to al menne, that ye were gilty of al the blode that
> hath bene shed before time for the word of god. which blod (though it be
> yet vnadueuged [*sic*]) yet it remaineth fresh and new in the syght of God
> ... saying: How longe tariest thou Lorde.[70]

If Barnes as martyr had become an empty category, that emptiness was filled with vitriol towards the bishop of Winchester. Barnes is here reduced to an anonymous archetype, whose significance is less the doctrine he defended in life than the accusation which his blood cries in death.

The fuller narratives of Barnes's death also came, increasingly, to focus on the persecutor rather than the martyr. The *Chronicle* of Edward Hall, published in 1548, told the story at some length. The relevant sections were in fact written by Hall's publisher, the evangelical Richard Grafton, who will almost certainly have known Barnes personally from the late 1530s. Yet Barnes appears throughout chiefly as a foil to Gardiner's villainy. 'Moste menne said', he alleged, that Gardiner 'chiefly procured' Barnes's, Jerome's and Garrett's deaths, and did so because they had preached against his doctrine. Grafton told how Barnes's taunts at Paul's Cross ruffled the bishop; and how, when asked to do so, Gardiner held up his hand in 'but a counterfeat forgeuenes'. He made particular play of the peculiar incident in which Gardiner briefly took Barnes as his pupil. When Gardiner set himself up as Barnes's 'skolemaster', Grafton claimed, 'he prepared the tower for his skole house, and made suche a rod to beate his skoler, that he beate hym as small as ashes, or he left hym'. This allegation was based not only on common rumour, but the report of 'suche, as muche knewe and least cause had to lye'. Garrett and Jerome, he added, were sent to the 'skolehouse' in the Tower merely 'for compaignie sake', as an act of apparently pointless malice. Rather

---

[67] *A caueat for the christians agaynst the archpapist* (1548), RSTC 5195, sig. A5v.

[68] Bale, *Catalogus*, p. 667.

[69] William Turner, *The huntyng of the romyshe vuolfe* (Emden, 1555), RSTC 24356, sigs. B3v, E1r and E4v; John Hooper, *The Later Writings of Bishop Hooper*, ed. Charles Nevinson, Parker Society (Cambridge, 1852), p. 376.

[70] *An Admonishion to the Bishoppes of VVinchester, London and others* (1553), RSTC 11593, sigs. A2v–3r.

than being merely the trigger of events, Gardiner was now the driving force behind them.[71]

John Foxe's account of Barnes's martyrdom was subtler, yet Gardiner remained at the centre. In the first English edition of the 'Book of Martyrs' in 1563, Foxe drew principally on the second edition of Barnes's *Supplication*, which gave an account of his adventures in the 1520s, and on the Hall/Grafton *Chronicle*. The entire section on Barnes was revised for the second, 1570 edition, with the addition of a good deal of fresh material drawn from Gardiner's own account of events in 1540. Thereafter Foxe made no further changes to the text. In both versions, Gardiner's villainy is central to the story. In 1563, Foxe alleged with somewhat shaky chronology (none too rare in that edition) that after Cromwell's death, Gardiner 'hauing gotten free liberties to exercise his cruelties . . . straightaways made hys first assaults upon Robert Barnes, Thomas Gerard, and William Jerome'. The details were tidied up in 1570 but the central allegation of a deliberate plot against the three men remained.[72] In 1563, however, Foxe did not have a great deal of evidence explicitly to tie Gardiner to the case. He observed, rather weakly, that Barnes's troubles began soon after Gardiner's return from a diplomatic mission in France (in reality, some eighteen months later). In a passage excised from later editions, presumably because its insinuations were almost unburdened with fact, Foxe alleged that Gardiner moved against Barnes and his fellows

> so courtly, that he wold seme to do no euel, & yet was the causer of al mischefe, as it folowed after that wolfe in a shepes clothing, suffering these lambes to preach which wold not be his scholers, willed them of a speciall loue to preach iii. notable sermonds at the spitle, which wer baits to minister just occasion of their condempnation.

However, if he was unable to substantiate these particular charges, Foxe had other resources on which he could call. Gardiner had played a small but significant part in Barnes's first troubles, in 1525–6. He and Edward Foxe (later bishop of Hereford) had stood surety for Barnes before Wolsey. They had also persuaded Barnes to make the recantation demanded of him, using, as Foxe put it, 'diuers . . . perswasions that was mighty in the sight of reson and folish flesh'.[73] This did not merely insinuate that it was Gardiner's weasel words that had persuaded Barnes to recant, against his better judgement, so exculpating Barnes and tarring Gardiner with shifty cowardice. By linking Gardiner to Barnes in this way, the bishop's later cruelty was given the bitter edge of personal betrayal. Barnes's earlier adventures could also be used to bolster attacks on some of other villains in the Protestant pantheon, in particular Cardinal Wolsey. In a finely judged piece of

---

[71] Edward Hall, *The vnion of the two noble and illustre families of Lancastre & Yorke*, ed. Richard Grafton (1548), RSTC 12721, fos. 241v and 243r.

[72] *A&M [1563]*, p. 600, and *A&M [1570]*, p. 1363.

[73] *A&M [1563]*, pp. 602–3.

polemical writing, Foxe's account of Barnes's humiliating recantation before Wolsey manages to focus on the cardinal's vainglorious cruelty rather than Barnes's backsliding. Once again, Barnes's usefulness was as a foil for the forces of Antichrist.[74]

In 1570, Foxe's account of Barnes's death became far more detailed and the allegations against Gardiner moved even closer to the centre. Foxe followed Gardiner's account, but took every opportunity which that narrative offered him to cast doubt on the bishop's good faith and impartiality. More significantly, he tried to give Gardiner walk-on parts later in the process, in an attempt to tie him more closely to the executions. At Barnes's recantation sermon, Foxe claims, the lord mayor was seated next to Gardiner, and as it became clear that the supposed 'recantation' was a sham, the mayor asked the bishop if Barnes should be rearrested. Foxe also pointed out, rather weakly and quite gratuitously, that the three preachers were eventually condemned by an act of attainder, and that Gardiner would have participated in the passage of the act through the House of Lords. However, not content with these scraps of circumstantial evidence, Foxe challenged Gardiner directly. He noted the bishop's claim to have had no part in the decision to condemn Barnes and his fellows:

> yet notwithstandyng the sayd Gardiner can not persuade vs to the contrary, but that his priuie complaining to the kyng, and his secret whysperyngs in hys frendes eares, & his other woorkyngs by his factours about the king, was a great sparcle to set their faggottes a fire.[75]

Evidence might fail, but rumour had already convicted the bishop. Later accounts took Gardiner's culpability for granted. Burnet believed that Barnes's death arose from his making 'some unhandsome reflections on Gardiner's person'; suggested that behind the bishop's 'great show of moderation' lurked a deeper malice; and claimed that Gardiner 'was generally looked on as the person that procured their death'.[76]

Such vague assertions did reflect more than malicious prejudice. The course of events leading to Barnes's, Jerome's and Garrett's deaths was and is genuinely opaque. More importantly, contemporaries were vividly aware of this fact, thanks in part to Barnes himself. After their unsatisfactory recantations, the trio were rearrested, but no further proceedings were taken against them. However, they were exempted from the general pardon enacted by parliament that summer, and a hurried act of attainder rushed through in late July condemned them to die as

---

[74] *A&M [1563]*, p. 602; also see John R. Knott, *Discourses of Martyrdom in English Literature, 1563–1694* (Cambridge, 1993), p. 70. Similarly, in 1545, George Joye had cited Barnes less to praise him than to illustrate Sir Thomas More's bloodthirsty treachery: Joye, *The exposicion of Daniel the prophete* (Antwerp, 1545), RSTC 14823, fo. 82r.

[75] *A&M [1570]*, pp. 1370–2.

[76] Burnet, *History*, I, pp. 469–70 and 474. White Kennet also took this approach; his account closely followed that in the Hall/Grafton *Chronicle* (see BL, Lansdowne MS 980, fo. 2r–v).

heretics.[77] This device meant that they could be condemned without evidence and even without charges. The closest that surviving official sources come to defining their crimes is in 1543, when the preacher Robert Wisdom, who had posthumously defended Barnes and his colleagues, was required to admit that they had 'sufferyd moost iustelie for theyre false and vntrwe doctryne'.[78] There were perfectly rational (if cynical) reasons for the regime to adopt this approach. Even in Henrician England, trials were a slow and dangerous business, not wholly susceptible to control, especially when the defendants were as eloquent and well-connected as in this case. As Richard Hilles noted, the three men had taken care to remain within the letter of the law.[79] It seems likely that these preachers, who were perceived to be associates of Cromwell's, were chosen to die with him to underline the regime's rejection of his evangelical programme; and that the three Catholics (who had been attainted separately some weeks previously) were chosen to die alongside them to emphasise that that rejection did not mean that Henry VIII was succumbing to Rome's enticements. It would have been foolhardy to allow the vagaries of the judicial process to endanger such theatre.

Yet the chosen approach could almost have been calculated to foment rumours and conspiracy theories. The appearance of injustice was manifest, and the suggestion that dark forces were at work both tempting and impossible to refute. Questions were widely asked, not least by the condemned men themselves. According to the *Protestation*, when Barnes was at the stake, he asked the sheriff if there were any articles which explained why he must die, and was told that there were not. Barnes then appealed to the crowd for an explanation, and none was forthcoming. He then stated that he himself did not know why he was condemned, although he presumed from the method of execution that it was for heresy. It was then that he pointedly forgave Gardiner for accusing him.[80]

Although transparently disingenuous, Barnes's profession of ignorance as to his crimes was polemically extremely powerful. It was perhaps the element of the *Protestation* which provoked the most comment from others. Robert Wisdom and William Turner both explicitly cited the *Protestation* to establish that Barnes had died without being told why.[81] Richard Hilles, describing the executions to Bullinger in 1541, dwelt on the mystery of their attainder. He had made 'diligent inquiry', he said, but he was nevertheless unable to establish why they had been killed. Reasonably enough, he concluded that all he could know was that their

---

[77] *Statutes of the Realm*, vol. III (1817): 32o Hen. VIII c. 49, c. 60 and *Journal of the House of Lords*, I, pp. 158–60.

[78] Guildhall Library, London, MS 9531/12, fo. 44r.

[79] *OL*, p. 210. The risks of heresy trials were illustrated the following year, when Bishop Bonner's prosecution of Richard Mekins was almost thwarted by an uncooperative jury (*A&M [1583]*, p. 1202).

[80] Standish, *A lytle treatise*, sigs. E4v–5r and E7r–v. Featherstone, Abell and Powell were attainted shortly before Cromwell's own arrest: *Journal of the House of Lords*, I, pp. 140 and 143; *Statutes* III, 32o Henry VIII *c.*59.

[81] Emmanuel College, Cambridge, MS 261, fo. 116v; Turner and *The huntyng of the romyshe vuolfe*, sig. E4v.

deaths were unjust.[82] Grafton's account in Hall's *Chronicle* again mentioned the exchange between Barnes and the sheriff, and added: 'wherefore thei were now thus cruelly executed, I knowe not, although I haue searched to knowe the truth.' Bale's *Catalogus* noted that 'no cause is yet given' for the three deaths. Foxe reprinted the *Protestation* in full, but he emphasised this point with a marginal note: 'No cause shewed why Doct. Barnes dyed.'[83]

Martyrology abhors a vacuum such as this within a story, and the closest plausible suspect is likely to be drawn into the frame. In this case, for all his denials, that suspect was Gardiner. Yet the mysterious attainder did more than ease the process of scapegoating the bishop of Winchester. It also gave the attack on him a bitter twist. If Gardiner had openly sought Barnes's blood, that would have been bad enough. Yet for him to have condemned a man who was once (supposedly) his friend, to have done so by secret means, to have manipulated king and parliament into revenging his wounded pride for him, and to have carefully concealed the evidence that he had done all this – this meant that he was more than a bloodthirsty persecutor. He was a dissembler, an evil genius, a 'secrete worker' relentlessly plotting against the Gospel.[84] As such he could plausibly be accused of almost anything, and subsequently he was. Barnes's death did not merely qualify Gardiner as a villain; it established the bishop's *modus operandi*. His guile and depravity were such that no crime was beyond him. Foxe, and many others, found the explanatory force of Winchester's wiliness irresistible.[85]

Most remarkably, Foxe invoked Gardiner to solve the sticky problem of John Lambert's execution. Lambert's persecutors had included Barnes himself, and other leading evangelicals including Cromwell and Cranmer. Foxe conceded these men's roles, but he minimised them, and he was clear about where the final blame lay:

> throughe the pestiferous & crafty counsaile of this one Bishop of Winchester, Sathan (whiche oftentimes doth raise vp one brother to the destruction of another) did here performe the condemnation of this Lambert by no other ministers, then Gospellers themselues.[86]

This is sheer fiction: Foxe did not have a scrap of evidence to connect Gardiner to the case. But that no longer mattered. Barnes's exoneration for this most inconvenient episode in his career was made possible by the martyrological response to his own death. And yet this episode too attracted the attention it did from later writers not because of Barnes himself, but because of the bigger fish involved in

[82] *OL*, pp. 209–10.
[83] Hall, *The vnion*, fo. 243r; Bale, *Catalogus*, p. 667 and *A&M [1583]*, p. 1199.
[84] So John Dudley called him: *A&M [1563]*, p. 823. For Gardiner's reputation for wiliness, see Riordan and Ryrie, 'Stephen Gardiner', pp. 1049–51.
[85] Indeed, it seems to have been Foxe who coined the memorable tag 'Wily Winchester'; see *A&M [1563]*, p. 1383 and *A&M [1583]*, p. 1135. John Bale had earlier described Gardiner as 'winchester the winker of wyles': Bale, *The image of bothe churches*, sig. k6r.
[86] *A&M [1583]*, p. 1123.

the case. In his account of Lambert's trial, Gilbert Burnet chose to belittle Barnes as one who 'was bred among the Lutherans [and] . . . not only brought over their opinions, but their temper with him'. However, this did not arise from his opinion of Barnes as such, but rather from his attempt to scapegoat Barnes and so to exonerate Burnet's hero Cranmer from responsibility for Lambert's death.[87] Likewise, Harpsfield's contemptuous dismissal of Barnes's claim to martyrdom was made in the context of his attack on Cranmer; Harpsfield used Barnes to demonstrate that the archbishop shared the friar's willingness to recant and to persecute others when it suited him.[88] Harpsfield used Barnes to attack Cranmer, and Burnet used Barnes to defend him; Foxe used Barnes to attack Wolsey, and a vast range of evangelicals used Barnes to attack Gardiner. Barnes remained useful because his story could be used to portray villains and even heroes who were of more importance than himself. Surprisingly soon after his death, the memorialisation of Robert Barnes ceased to be chiefly about Robert Barnes.

III

Barnes's loyal optimism about his king did not blind him to the times. He was well aware that careers such as his tended, in England, to end in fire; and he engaged in a little self-fashioning of his future status as martyr. In the second edition of the *Supplication*, he commented on claims that a price had been set on his head. With that heady mixture of genuine humility and somewhat queasy self-assurance so typical of Protestantism, he asked:

> What can they make of me? I am a sympylie poure wretche and worth noo mans monny in the world (sauyng of theyrs) not the tenth peny y^t they wyll geue for me, and to burne me or to dystroy me can not so greatly profyte them, for whan I am deed the sonne and the mone, the starrys and ye element, water and fier yee & also stonys shall defend thys cause agenst them, soner than the veryte shulde perysh.[89]

Barnes did not court martyrdom – indeed, in 1526 and 1540 he was willing to make uncomfortable compromises to avoid it. He was sure, however, that if it came to it, his blood as a martyr would water the true Church. If we can trust the *Protestation*, he took the same view when martyrdom was an imminent certainty rather than a possibility in the middle distance. From his barbed petitions to the king through to his deft unpicking of his and his colleagues' condemnation, he was at work until the last minute constructing his own martyrdom; even more so if, as seems likely, he took steps to ensure that that last sermon would survive in writing.

---

[87] Burnet, *History*, I, p. 402.
[88] Harpsfield, *Dialogi sex*, pp. 713–14.
[89] Robert Barnes, *A supplicacion vnto the most gracyous prynce H. the .viij.* (1534), RSTC 1471, fo. 34r.

Yet it was not chiefly for his trenchant defence of the cause that he was remembered. This is perhaps surprising, given his ability and his contemporary reputation; but as we have seen, he was left behind by the English Reformation's changes of theological direction, and in any case his surviving writings did not do full justice to the preacher and theologian he had been. His inclusion in Foxe's 1573 compilation of early martyr-theologians' works did not reflect a living memory of Barnes as a theologian. That heavyweight (and massively expensive) volume was a prestige project for the printer and a labour of love for the martyrologist, rather than a serious commercial venture. His real contribution to English Protestant martyrology was rather different from that which he had intended. His death loomed larger than his life. He became simply another of the noble army of martyrs. What distinctiveness he had arose from the ways in which he could be used to illustrate others' stories and wider martyrological themes. In particular, it arose from to the circumstances of his death. Of all the prominent martyrdoms of Henry VIII's reign, Barnes's death could be used most clearly to scapegoat the popish clergy while exonerating the king and the leading court evangelicals. One last twist that Barnes gave to his own martyrdom – that barbed word of forgiveness to Stephen Gardiner – came to dominate his story. Perhaps Barnes's most enduring achievement was giving English Protestantism the villain it needed. Before he died, he spoke of becoming a saint; but if he achieved posthumous sanctity on earth, it was through giving the devil a face and a name.

7

Martyrs and Anti-martyrs and
Mary Tudor's Church*

WILLIAM WIZEMAN, SJ

The Catholic Church in England under Queen Mary Tudor (1553–8) has long been noted, both on scholarly and popular levels, chiefly for the burning alive of nearly three hundred Protestant martyrs. Only recently, through the writings of Eamon Duffy, Christopher Haigh and the late Jennifer Loach, have there been sustained discussions that give a more positive interpretation to the Marian Church's attempt to renew Catholicism in England after the religious revolutions under Henry VIII and Edward VI.[1] An important part of that attempt was the printing of numerous catechetical, devotional, and polemical works to inculcate and explicate Catholic belief and practice, after twenty years of officially sponsored excoriation. Since many of these texts were either written or had the support of members of the Marian regime – including the queen herself – it appears that print was viewed as an important vehicle for reviving Catholicism. Cardinal Reginald Pole said as much when he wrote that 'just as men have been corrupted here even more by books than by the spoken word, so they must be recalled to life by the written word'.[2]

In their resuscitation of Catholic England, Marian authors, editors and theologians met the Protestant challenge to the Church head-on. The sermons and books of controversy, piety and Christian instruction printed by members of the Marian

---

* Material from this essay first appeared in *The Theology and Spirituality of Mary Tudor's Church* (Aldershot, 2006). I am grateful to Ashgate for their permission to reuse it here.

[1] Eamon Duffy, *The Stripping of the Altars: Traditional Religion in England, c.1400–c.1580* (New Haven, CT, 1992), ch. 16; Christopher Haigh, *English Reformations: Religion, Politics and Society under the Tudors* (Oxford, 1993), ch. 12 and 13; Jennifer Loach, 'The Marian Establishment and the Printing Press', *English Historical Review*, 101 (1986), pp. 135–48; 'Mary Tudor and the Re-Catholicisation of England', *History Today*, 44 (1994), pp. 16–22. I wish to thank Dr Thomas Freeman for reading this article and offering insightful suggestions.

[2] Reginald Pole, *Epistolarum Reginaldi Poli S.R.E. cardinalis et aliorum ad ipsum*, ed. A. M. Quirini, 5 vols (Brescia, 1744–1757), V, p. 74, reprint, Farnborough, 1967: 'quemadmodum scriptis magis etiam, quam verbis hic homines corrupti fuerunt, ita scriptis ad sanitatem recovari oportere ...' (my translation).

Church are striking in their common stances on justification through Christ's free gifts of grace and faith, the free and necessary response of Christians to these gifts through good works, the essential role of the Church as the locus of salvation and the seven sacraments – especially the Eucharist – as the chief means of access to grace and salvation.[3] In their emphases and strategies for renewing belief in these doctrines, as well as some of the most controverted issues of the English Reformation – such as papal primacy, the cult of the saints and prayer for the dead – the Marian Church echoed and sometimes prefigured the more militant forms of the Counter-Reformation, and certainly followed the theological stances laid out by John Fisher and Thomas More in their writings of the 1520s and early 1530s.[4] Furthermore, they also defended men like More, Fisher and others who had died for Catholicism during the reign of Mary's father as martyrs. While these authors – many of them were or would become important members of the hierarchy of the Marian Church – produced their texts with pastoral intentions (even the noteworthy polemicist, Miles Hogarde, also wrote devotional works in verse), they were not above denouncing those who refused to recant heretical belief, and believed themselves Christian martyrs when burned alive.[5] This two-sided effort of defending English Catholic martyrs and vilifying Protestant ones was a creation of the Marian Church, and it largely established English Protestant and Catholic historiographies until the Second World War, with their almost exclusive emphases on martyrs. Marian writers saw it as a pastoral duty to ensure that the people, so long engulfed by heresy, understood who were the true martyrs of Christ's Catholic Church, and who merely prefigured their fiery fate in hell at the stakes of Smithfield, lest they be led astray by apparently brave deaths of anti-martyrs: men and women who died for heretical beliefs.

The nascent public cults of the 'true' martyrs of the Catholic Church under Henry VIII commenced in his first daughter's reign. Catholic authors praised them both for the cause for which they died – the unity of Christ's Church – and their virtuous living. Cardinal Pole, archbishop of Canterbury and primate of all England, extolled the cause for which Fisher, More and the martyred monks and friars of London had died, as well as their merits, in an unpublished sermon to the people of London on the third anniversary of England's reconciliation with Rome; in this stance he was in fact reiterating what he had published decades before in his *De unitate*, and so it can be said he initiated the public cult of the Henrician Catholic martyrs.[6] Hogarde, however, possessed a pivotal role in originating and

---

3 For a contrary interpretation to the theological stances of the Marian authors, see Lucy Wooding, *Rethinking Catholicism in Reformation England* (Oxford, 2000).
4 See my Oxford D Phil. thesis, 'Recalled to Life: The Theology and Spirituality of Mary Tudor's Church' (2002).
5 Such authors include Edmund Bonner, Cuthbert Tunstall, Thomas Watson, John Christopherson, James Brooks, John White, John Harpsfield, John Feckenham, Roger Edgeworth, John Standish, Thomas Martin and William Peryn. One might include Stephen Gardiner, whose 1551 *Explication of the blessed Sacrament* received official approbation from Mary's Privy Council in 1553; see Wizeman, 'Recalled to Life', p. 70.
6 John Strype, *Ecclesiastical Memorials of the church of England under Henry VIII, Edward VI, and*

developing the twofold Marian strategy of defending Catholic martyrs and attacking Protestant ones. Regarding the first part of this strategy, he compared John Fisher and Thomas More to the victim of both Henry II and Henry VIII, Thomas Becket; all three had died 'for the zeale [they] had to gods churche'. Fisher was also 'a man of notable learning and innocence of lyfe', and More was a 'second Cicero . . . endewed with heauenlye eloquence'.[7] John White and John Gwynneth also praised the virtues and works of Fisher and More.[8] In his manuscript *Miracles of the Sacrament*, Henry Parker, Lord Morley, extolled Fisher as 'so good a man, and so devine a clerk'.[9] He and more distinguished writers such as Stephen Gardiner, Cuthbert Tunstall, Thomas Watson, Richard Smyth and the late John Redman – whose *Complaint of Grace* had been translated and printed in Mary's reign – were also deeply indebted to Fisher's writings on the Eucharist, justification and the Church.[10] To William Rastell, however, More's son-in-law and the editor of the 1557 edition of his English writings, More was now renowned more for his 'vertue' than for 'his great learnynge'. In his dedicatory epistle to that volume, Rastell told Queen Mary that More was her heavenly intercessor, '(beynge with almightie GOD, and lyuynge in heauen with hym) . . . ceaseth not to praye to God . . . for your hyghnesse, your subiectes, . . . and the catholyke religion of the same'.[11] Brad Gregory has stated that *The workes of More* should be seen in relation to the manuscript hagiographies of the martyred chancellor produced during Mary's reign, by William Roper and Nicholas Harpsfield, and there is possible evidence of their 'fairly wide . . . circulation'.[12] One of the books that appeared first in his collected English works, as well as being printed separately in 1553, was *A Dialogue of Comfort Against Tribulation*, which More had composed in prison prior to his execution; this 'moving defence of the human soul against desolation and despair' had pointedly been given to Cranmer in preparation for his execution. Indeed, the Marian emphases on More and Fisher may be found yet again in the sermon of the provost of Eton, Henry

---

Mary I, vol. III, part ii, pp. 490–7; for references to these martyrs in *De unitate*, see Thomas Mayer, *Reginald Pole, Prince and Prophet* (Cambridge, 2000), pp. 24–8.

[7] Miles Hogarde, *The displaying of the Protestantes, and sondry their practise, with a description of diuers their abuses of late frequented. Newly imprinted agayne, and augmented, with a table on the ende, of all such matter as is specially contained within this volume* (1556), RSTC 13558, fo. 68v.

[8] John White, *Diacosio-Martyrion id est ducentorum virorum testimonium, de veritate corporis, et sanguinis Christi, in eucharistia, ante triennium A.D. uersis Petrum Martyrem, ex profess coscriptum. Sed nunc in lucem aditum* (1553), RSTC 23588, fos. 84r, 87r–v; John Gwynneth, *A Manifest Detection of the notable falshed of that part of Iohn Frithes boke, which he called his foundacion, And bosteth it to be inuincible . . .* (1554), RSTC 12559, fo. 45r.

[9] Richard Rex, 'Morley and the Papacy: Rome, Regime and Religion', in *'Triumphs of English': Henry Parker, Lord Morley, Translator of the Tudor Court. New Essays in Interpretations*, ed. Marie Axton and James P. Carley (2000), p. 94.

[10] Richard Rex, *The Theology of John Fisher* (Cambridge, 1991), pp. 89–90.

[11] Thomas More, *The workes of Sir Thomas More Knyght, sometyme Lorde Chauncellour of England, wrytten by him in the Englysh tonge* (1557), RSTC 18076, sig. C2v.

[12] Brad Gregory, *Salvation at Stake: Christian Martyrdom in Early Modern Europe* (Cambridge, MA, 1999), pp. 270, 477.

Cole, at Cranmer's burning, in which the archbishop's death, along with those of Ridley, Hooper and Ferrar, were described as just retribution for the killing of Fisher, as Northumberland's had been for that of More.[13]

Like Pole, Hogarde played a significant part in the process of venerating the other Henrician martyrs. He also acclaimed the martyred Carthusian priors and monks, as well as the Benedictine abbots of Reading, Colchester and Glastonbury, the friars, Stone and Forest, the priests, Powell, Featherstone and Abell, and the gentleman and bishop's nephew, Germain Gardiner, 'and manye others, to whom death was nothing ferefull for the quarell of God and his church'. They 'and a greate number mo[re] died for the cause of the catholyke fayeth', and their 'memory shall be magnified tyll the ende of the worlde'. Indeed, all of these men were to be associated with Britain's proto-martyr, St Alban.[14] Thus it was the reason for their martyrdoms – 'the quarell of God' – that Marian writers underlined, rather than their power as intercessors, the sanctity of their lives or the horrible manner of their deaths, as had been so common in late-medieval piety. Furthermore, their praise of Fisher, More and the other Henrician martyrs is deafening in comparison to the general silence in much of the rest of the Catholic world in the mid-sixteenth century. This phenomena has been described as the 'crisis of canonisation', the Western Church's 'failure of nerve' to exalt saints in the face of Protestant attacks on the cult of saints. There were no canonisations from 1523 until 1588, twenty-five years after Trent's decree on the veracity of saintly intercession.[15] Thus, by exalting their martyrs, the Marian Church, as in so many other ways, prefigured Tridentine Catholicism.

In contrast to these images of Christian sanctity and fortitude, Marian authors blackened the reputations of their Protestant adversaries. While God's true martyrs had shed their blood for ecclesial unity in the midst of personal displays of heroic virtue, heretics had died raging amidst the flames. As Eamon Duffy has pointed out, with the accession of Mary, Catholics in England had at last found the opportunity and voice to challenge heretical belief. Duffy notes, along with Anne Dillon, that More's theological evaluation and controversial strategies, especially in challenging the notion that heretics could suffer martyrdom, were 'self-consciously' taken upon by Marian polemicists, in particular and closely by Hogarde – who was the chief Marian respondent to Protestant martyrs and their defenders – in his *Displaying of the Protestantes*. Dillon has noted how John Bale replied to Hogarde's writings, and makes the case that Hogarde was responding to

---

13 Thomas More, *A dialogue of comfort against tribulacion, made by Syr Thomas More Knyght, and set foorth by the name of an Hungarien, not before this time imprinted* (1553), and in More, *Workes*, fos. 1139–1269; Diarmaid MacCulloch, *Thomas Cranmer: A Life* (New Haven, CT, 1996), pp. 595, 600–1.

14 Hogarde, *Displaying of the Protestantes*, fos. 68v–69v, 66v–67r.

15 For discussions of late medieval devotion to martyrs, see Gregory, *Salvation at Stake*, ch. 2, and Duffy, *Stripping of the Altars*, pp. 171–9. For hesitancy regarding saints in the mid-sixteenth century, see Peter Burke, 'How to Become a Counter-Reformation Saint', in *The Counter-Reformation*, ed. David Luebke (Oxford, 1999), pp. 131–2, at 139; for an example of the beginning of the recovery from this crisis, see Philip Soergel, *Wondrous in his Saints: Counter-Reformation Propaganda in Bavaria* (Berkeley, CA, 1993), pp. 99–130.

Bale. Furthermore, both she and J. W. Martin offer evidence that in his writing – especially of the second edition of *Displaying of the Protestantes* which appeared in the same year, dedicated to the queen – Hogarde had substantial aid, both in terms of patronage and theological and humanistic acumen, from Bishop Bonner. However, it is possible that Cardinal Pole may also have offered Hogarde support, whether exclusively or in tandem with Bonner. The cardinal's 1557 sermon is certainly among the most protracted, extant attacks on Protestant martyrdom in Mary's reign, making Pole the focal figure of this endeavor. He also supported the publication of Northumberland's scaffold speech and probably 'Cranmer's Recantacyons' by his archdeacon, Nicholas Harpsfield; and, through him, William Rastell's edition of More's English works, which of course included More's writings against heresy and its pseudo-martyrs.[16] These works and their patronage represent one facet of the Catholic rejoinder to the Protestant attempt to glorify their martyrs *as* martyrs.

However, unlike Hogarde's book, most Marian texts were not overtly polemical. At times authors reminded readers of the horrors of heresy from which they had been freed, lest they fall again. They did this to encourage Catholic belief, and to nurture devotion to the Church as the means of participating in the charity Christ shared with his followers; this seems to have been especially necessary in London, where there was not only devout Protestants but also numbers of people who may have had no sympathy for Protestant doctrine but apparently had sympathy with Protestant martyrs as martyrs. In their references to heresy, the strategy of Marian writers contrasted with that of their Parisian contemporary, François le Picart, who spoke of heresy and its effects frequently in his sermons, possibly to reiterate to his charges what they must avoid at all costs.[17] Nevertheless, Marian writers were hardly eirenical, and were just as truculent as later Elizabethan Catholic controversialists.[18] For example, though some of these works, such as Hogarde's *Displaying of the Protestantes* – which helped shape the debate regarding true and false martyrs for centuries to come – and the anonymous *A Treatise concernynge the Masse* defended the policy of persecuting Protestants, other books also attacked heretical belief overtly though not as extensively: Thomas Watson's *Twoo Sermons*, Cuthbert Tunstall's *De veritate*, the two Marian editions of John Fisher's 1521 sermon, and works by John Venaeus, John White, Richard Smyth, John Standish and James Brooks. These were

[16] Eamon Duffy, 'The Conservative Voice in the English Reformation', in *Christianity and Community in the West: Essays for John Bossy*, ed. Simon Ditchfield (Aldershot, 2001), pp. 92–100; Anne Dillon, *The Construction of Martyrdom in the English Catholic Community, 1535–1603* (Aldershot, 2002), 49–52, 43–4; J. W. Martin, 'Miles Hogarde: Artisan and Aspiring Author in Sixteenth-Century England', in *Religious Radicals in Tudor England* (1989), pp. 90–1, 99–100; Thomas Mayer, *Reginald Pole, Prince and Prophet* (Cambridge, 2000), pp. 281–2. I am grateful to Thomas Freeman for pointing out the possibility of Pole's patronage to me.
[17] Larissa Juliet Taylor, *Heresy and Orthodoxy in Sixteenth-Century Paris: François Le Picart and the Beginnings of the Catholic Reformation* (Leiden, 1999), pp. 80–112.
[18] Pace Wooding, *Rethinking Catholicism*, 201.

printed before the burnings commenced in February 1555. It appears that these authors concurred with Fisher when he had stated that the 'blacke cloude of heresie' had brought a 'hideous tempest' against the bright light of Catholic belief, which 'hath been cleare and brighte a good season'.[19] For these polemicists and theologians, Catholic doctrine and the charity which derived from it and Protestant doctrine were antithetical; heretics were deadly enemies with which there could be no truce. From these writings it cannot be said that 'Englishmen in general did not regard heresy as a terrible crime'.[20] Rather, Marian authors produced caricatures of the enemy and its doctrine as both laughable and demonic, to underline Catholicism's salvific value, and to make the case for destroying its would-be destroyers. Unlike writers such as Thomas More, they generally refrained from the use of coarse language, but this was the only compromise they made with their Protestant adversaries.

Marian writers excoriated heretical belief. In *Displaying of the Protestantes*, Hogarde, regarded by his adversaries and modern historians as the leading Marian polemicist, defined heresy simply as 'any false or wrong opinion, which any man choseth to him selfe to defende against the catholike fayth of the vniuersall church'.[21] For Hogarde, his patrons and his fellow authors, the universal belief of the universal Church was salvific, not the multifarious beliefs of Protestants. Nevertheless, heresy spread, according to Roger Edgeworth, Marian chancellor of the diocese of Bath and Wells whose Henrician sermons were reprinted in 1557; the increase in the number of Protestants was due to the fact that while 'many haue faythe, . . . [yet] they be not . . . strong in faythe, . . . therfore they be so[o]ne . . . ouercome. And that is the cause that Heresies . . . peruerteth and turneth the most parte of people'.[22] Still, the stances of Protestants were themselves fragile and could not withstand close scrutiny. Tunstall, one of the more acute Marian theologians, dismissed heretics for regarding themselves greater than St Paul in his ecstasies in their attempts to interpret obscure biblical texts. Ultimately they only believed what they saw, especially regarding the controverted issue of the Eucharist.[23] For Marian authors, heresy had only produced confusion, not salvation.

[19] John Fisher, *A Sermon very notable fruicteful, and Godlie, amde at Paules Crosse in London Anno domini. 1521 . . . by that famous and great Clerke Iohn Fissher Bishop of Rochester, concerning the Heresies of Martine Luther, which he raised vp against the church, wherin it may appeare howe men sithens that tyme haue gone astray . . .* (1554), RSTC 10896, sig. A2v.
[20] Pace David Loades, *The Reign of Mary Tudor: Politics, Government and Religion in England, 1553–58*, 2nd edn (Oxford, 1991), p. 276.
[21] Martin, 'Miles Hogarde', p. 83; see Martin's analysis of *Displaying of the Protestantes*, pp. 90–5. Hogarde, *Displaying of the Protestantes*, fos. 11v–12r.
[22] Roger Edgeworth, *Sermons very fruitfull, godly and learned by Roger Edgeworth: Preaching in the Reformation c.1535–c.1553*, ed. Janet Wilson (Cambridge, 1993), pp. 364, 179.
[23] Cuthbert Tunstall in John Venaeus, *A notable Oration made by Iohn Venaeus a Parisian in the defence of the Sacrament of the aultare . . . Wherevnto is added a Preface, taken out of . . . De ueritate corporis et saguinis Domini in eucharistia, compiled by . . . Cuthbert Tunstall, Bishoppe of Duresme. Translated out of the Latin into Englishe by Iohn Bullingham* (1554), RSTC 24633.5, sigs. A8r–v, D2r–3r.

171

Attacking heretical belief thus accompanied attacking heretics themselves. In the Marian translation of John Redman's *De gratia*, the leaders of the Protestant revolution were expositors of 'a newe Pharisaisme, and delite to appeare in straunge facion with long berdes'.[24] Watson accused Cranmer of being Zwingli's 'disciple', and Smyth had ridiculed him for idolising the opinions of his 'great god, peter martyr'.[25] England's leading heretics were viewed as the minions of continental reformers, and thus, not even original thinkers, but importers of foreign heresy, and not, interestingly, so much the heirs of Lollardy.[26] Their followers were unlearned, even 'huswiues', who were 'desirouse of newe doctrine, and werie of the olde' according to Venaeus' 1536 sermon to the University of Paris, translated and printed by John Bullingham and dedicated to Stephen Gardiner.[27] They 'seke daylye for newe toyes . . . as though the christian religion . . . were not an heuenly ordinaunce'.[28] For the former bishop of Bristol, Paul Bush, himself compromised by clerical marriage, people had fallen into the confusion of heretical belief through pride and lack of learning, and had become as blind as a miller's horse turning the millstone, going round and round while believing they was making progress in the Christian life; the reward for their labor: the 'course branne' of their own novel, damnable opinions.[29] Such was their presumption that, according to Edmund Bonner in his frequently reprinted *Profitable doctryne*,

> of late dayes, in the tyme of oure pestiferous scisme, the new broched brethren, rather would tumble to hel headlonge, then they woulde doo as the catholyke Churche from Chrystes tyme hetherto hath done, concernyng the lawes of God, and the rytes of the sayde catholyke Churche.[30]

[24] John Redman, *A compendious treatise called the complaint of Grace . . . containyng in it muche godly learnyng and veritee of matter, greatly profitable and necessary for all men to loke in . . .* Thomas Smyth, trans. (1556), RSTC 20826, sig.G4v; for the beards of evangelical clergy, see MacCulloch, *Cranmer*, 361.
[25] Thomas Watson, *Twoo notable Sermons made the thirde and fythe Fridays in Lent last past, before the Quenes highnes, concerning the reall presence of Christes body and bloude in the blessed Sacrament: and also the Masse, whiche is the sacrifice of the newe Testament . . .* (1554), RSTC 25115, sig. O5v; Richard Smyth, *A Confutation of a certen booke, called a defence of the true, and Catholike doctrine of the sacrament, etc. sette fourth of late in the name of Thomas Archebysshoppe of Canterburye* (Paris? 1550), RSTC 22819, fos. 50v–1r.
[26] See Richard Smyth, *The seconde parte of the book called a bouclier of the catholyke fayeth, conteyninge seuen chapiters . . .* (1555), RSTC 22817.5, sigs. C8v–E2v; White, *Diacosio-Martyrion*, fos. 68r, 90r–v.
[27] Venaeus, *Notable Oration*, sigs. C5v, A3r–v.
[28] Paul Bush, *A brefe exhortation set fourthe by the vnprofitable seruant of Iesu christ, Paule Bushe, late bishop of Brystowe, to one Margarete Burges wyfe of Jhon Burges, clotheare of kyngewode in the Countie of Wilshere* (1556), RSTC 4184, sig. C2v.
[29] Bush, *Exhortation to Margarete Burges*, sigs. A2v–4v; Leonard Pollard, *Fyue homiles of late . . . dedicated to the ryght reuerende Father in God Rychard . . . byshoppe of Woster . . . Uewed, examined and alowed by . . . Edmonde byshop of London, within whose diocese they are imprinted* (1556), RSTC 20091, sigs I2r–3r.
[30] Edmund Bonner, *A profitable and necessarye doctryne, with certayne homelies adioyned therunto set forth by the reuerende father in God, Edmonde byshop of London, for the instruction and enformation of the people beynge within his Diocese of London, and of his cure and charge* (1555), RSTC 3283.5, fo. F3r;

Going to hell was one of the few things Protestants had in common. Marian Catholics noted the doctrinal divisions among them with horror, fascination and glee. 'The punishementes are not so diuers in hell', Hogarde claimed, 'as are the sondry opinions of these Protestantes.' Here is an example of Hogarde's close following of More, who noted that among hcretics 'there be as many dyuerse myndys almoste as there be men'.[31] In Brooks' 1553 Paul's Cross sermon, there seemed to be as many 'sects' as interpretations of scripture among 'our euangelical brotherhod'.[32] Even in persecution, heretics remained divided, according to Hogarde's account of secret worship during Mary's reign. The leader of this service described three religions in England: 'my lorde Chancellours [Gardiner's or Nicholas Heath's] religion: the other Cranmers, Latymers and Ridleys religion: and the thirde he called goddes religion'. The first was 'nought', the second, 'not good', and the third, 'best'. Once again Hogarde follows More's earlier works in describing a Protestant conventicle, but only in the second edition of *The displaying of the Protestantes*; yet it remains uncertain whether it is actual reportage.[33] Such divisions among underground Protestants were well known to Marian authorities, and some of the beliefs were reckoned as bizarre in the extreme.[34] Some believed 'that Christ is not yet come' and 'that all men's wives ought to be in common'; others that baptism by a priest was invalid, and an underground congregation ordained one of its own members.[35] Such martyrs had not 'demonstrated . . . that English Protestantism had a genuine religious integrity'.[36] Marian authors made no distinctions between the Church's enemies; it seemed nothing was sacred to heretics. To writers like Proctor, facial hair, married clergy and worshipping novelties were the only things upon which Protestants agreed.[37]

The result of seduction by such divided views of Protestants and their martyrs was the loss of not only Christian doctrine, but also of order and charity within the

---

cf. James Brooks, *A Sermon very notable, fruictefull, and Godlie, made at Paules crosse . . .* (1554), RSTC 3839 (augmented version of RSTC 3838 (1553)), fo. B6v.

[31] Hogarde, *Displaying of the Protestantes*, fo. 14r–v. Thomas More, *A Dialogue Concerning Heresies, CWTM*, vol. VI, part 1, ed. Thomas M. C. Lawler, Germain Marc'Hardour and Richard C. Marius (1981), p. 191. I wish to thank Dr Thomas Freeman for alerting me to this passage.

[32] Brooks, *Sermon very notable*, sigs. B6v, D3v.

[33] Hogarde, *Displaying of the Protestantes*, fo. 124v; Martin also notes similarities between this episode and another relating to Robert Barnes in Book VIII of More's *Confutation of Tyndale's Answer*; see Martin, 'Miles Hogarde', pp. 94–5.

[34] See Susan Brigden, *London and the Reformation* (Oxford, 1989), pp. 614–16, and Loades, *Reign of Mary*, p. 274.

[35] Quoted in Brigden, *London and the Reformation*, 615; Thomas Freeman, 'Dissenters from a Dissenting Church: The Challenge of the Freewillers, 1550–1558', in *The Beginnings of English Protestantism*, ed. Peter Marshall and Alec Ryrie (Cambridge, 2002), 138; Brett Usher, ' "In a Time of Persecution": New Light on the Secret Protestant Congregation in Marian London', in *John Foxe and the English Reformation*, ed. David Loades (Aldershot, 1997), pp. 233–51.

[36] Pace Loades, *Reign of Mary*, p. 276.

[37] John Proctor, *The waie home to Christ and truth leadinge from Antichrist and errour, made and set furth in the Latin tongue, by that famous and great clearke, Vincent, Frenche man borne, aboue .xi. hundred years past . . .* (1554), RSTC 24754, sig. B3r–v.

Church. Part of the Edwardine campaign of 'calculated destruction' had been the 'robbing and stealinge . . . ornamentes and goodes of the churche (being more fearse then euer was Iulian th[e] appostata)'.[38] To Watson, Protestants would denigrate the Eucharist and 'leaue vs nothyng, but the bare name of christ'.[39] By 'reasoning against Purgatory' Edgeworth claimed, heretics had 'destroye[d] prayers for the dead, and so consequently put down abbeys, and chauntries whiche were founded for such praiers'.[40] John Pendleton, in the official Marian collection of *Homelies*, also lamented the destruction of abbeys and their charity resulting in 'poore Christ (that is to say,) the h[u]ngry, and nedeful people, famishe, and crye oute therefore'.[41] While Protestants claimed King Josiah as the model for reformation, Marian clergy like Hugh Glasier, canon of Canterbury cathedral, claimed the prophet Jeremiah as the model for grieving for the desecration of churches.[42]

Marian writers also employed the common topos of associating heresy with vice, and attacked the character of martyrs and their supporters.[43] For Hogarde they tripped over sin but vaulted over virtue, under the perceived Antinomian influence of the doctrine of justification by faith alone.[44] The English had foregone Church unity in order to live wantonly, Standish and Watson concurred; there was certainly more sin in England after the break with Rome then before it.[45] In a standard use of providentialism and polemic, Glasier responded to Protestant charges that bad weather was due to the Mass by preaching that it was due to God's displeasure with heresy. The 'exceeding drought and heate' of 1554 and the 'exceeding rayne and moysture' of 1555 were not due to attendance at Mass, as some said 'in corners', but the refusal of some to adore the Eucharist.[46]

Such heretical sins of the flesh paled in comparison to the damnation of souls.

---

[38] Diarmaid MacCulloch, *Tudor Church Militant: Edward VI and the Protestant Reformation* (2000), p. 74; Standish, *A discourse wherin it is debated whether it be expedient that the scripture should be in English for al men to reade that wyll. Here nowe gentle reader in this second edition the authour hath added sundrie thynges not vnworthie to be noted (as he iudgeth) beside many corrections, which lacked in the firste settynge furthe* (1555), RSTC 23208, sigs. L5v–6r.

[39] Watson, *Twoo Sermons*, sig. B5v.

[40] Edgeworth, *Sermons very fruitfull*, p. 126.

[41] Bonner *et al.*, *Homelies sette forth by the right reuerende father in God, Edmunde Byshop of London . . .* (1555), RSTC 3285.7, fos. 41v–42r.

[42] MacCulloch, *Tudor Church Militant*, pp. 57–104; Hugh Glasier, *A notable and very fruictefull sermon made at Paules crosse . . . Perused by the reuerende father in god Edmonde bishop of London, and by him approued . . .* (1555), RSTC 11916.5, sig. D3r–v.

[43] David Bagchi, *Luther's Earliest Opponents: Catholic Controversialists 1518–1525* (Minneapolis, 1989), pp. 178–9.

[44] Hogarde, *Displaying of the Protestantes*, fo. 38v.

[45] John Standish, *The triall of the supremacy wherin is set fourth the vnitie of christes church militant geuen to S. Peter and his successoures by Christe: And that there ought to be one head Bishop in earth Christes Uicar generall ouuer all hys churche militant: wyth answeres to the blasphemous obiections made agaynste the same in the late miserable yeres now paste* (1556), RSTC 23211, sig. B2r; cf. Watson, *Twoo Sermons*, sig. G7v.

[46] Glasier, *Sermon made at Paules crosse*, sig. B8r; similar debates would occur regarding St Paul's cathedral being struck by lightning in 1561, see Alexandra Walsham, *Providence in Early Modern England* (Oxford, 1999), pp. 232–4.

Edgeworth claimed that they led the Christian to 'sinister or false opinion or heresie to kill his soule, vnder the pretence or colour of euangelicall truthe or libertye'.[47] Standish decried Protestants' 'crafty deceite in this matter of the primacy [of the pope] (whiche in these yeares past hath killed a thousande soules)'.[48] In Bonner's *Profitable doctryne*, an official text of belief for the Marian Church, heretics, as soul killers, stood guilty of breaking the Sixth Commandment to the gravest degree possible, for

> the soule, beynge the cheyfe parte of the man, doth incomparablye passe the bodye, . . . [therefore] we are muche more forbydden to kyll or murder our neighbours soule: whiche kynde of murder . . . they do commyt, who by pernitious, hereticall, and vngodlye doctryne, . . . seduce the soule of theyr neighbour, causing it thereby to dye euerlastinglye in hell.

Bonner's remarks, moreover, echoed those made by Brooks in his 1553 Paul's Cross sermon.[49] For Marian authors, as for Cardinal Pole, there was no crime more heinous that advocating heretical doctrine.[50]

The dread of Protestants was such that these authors not only condemned them, they demonised them as well, as Luther's opponents had done in the 1520s.[51] Such murderers of souls were nothing less than a 'Sathanicall secte'.[52] They were 'preachers of Antichrist', Proctor claimed, and too many had been seduced by them to become members of the body of Antichrist.[53] They, like the devil, could not even endure the sign of the cross.[54] Such demonising was not unique. Bartolomé Carranza, whose 1558 *Comentarios sobre el Catechismo Christiano* were written for the Marian Church and would become the basis for the 1566 Catechism of the Council of Trent, divided the world between the churches of Christ and Satan, one guided by the Holy Spirit, the other possessed by many evil spirits.[55] Le Picart equated friendship with heretics to friendship with devils.[56] Labeling religious enemies as Antichrist was nothing new; it had been a common-place of the Edwardine Church, and 'a favourite theme' of Cranmer.[57]

---

[47] Edgeworth, *Sermons, very fruitfull*, p. 229.
[48] Standish, *Triall of the supremacy*, sigs. F4v–5r.
[49] Bonner, *Profitable doctryne*, sig. Qq1r; cf. Brooks, *Sermon very notable*, sigs. E4v–5r.
[50] Strype, *Ecclesiastical Memorials* III, ii, pp. 486–7.
[51] Bagchi, *Luther's Earliest Opponents*, p. 177.
[52] *A plaine and godlye treatise, concernynge the Masse and the blessed Sacrament of the Aulter, for the instruccion of the symple and vnlearned people* (1555?), RSTC 17629, sig. D6v.
[53] Proctor, *The waie home to Christ*, sigs. A6v–7r.
[54] Richard Smyth, *A Bouclier of the catholike fayth of Christes churche conteynyng diuers matiers now of late called into controversy, by the newe gospellers* (1554), RSTC 22816, fo. 56r.
[55] Bartolomé Carranza, *Comentarios sobre el Catechismo Christiano de Bartolomé Carranza*, ed. J. I. Tellechea Idigoras, 2 vols (Madrid, 1972), pp. 389–90; 'La una [church] es de Cristo, y ésta siempre fue y será una, que es la verdadera Iglesia. La segunda es la de Satanás, cuyos miembros son los herejes y los cismáticos. Esta no es una, porque no hay en ella un espíritu ni una cabeza: son muchas espíritus, y contrarios unos de otros . . .' (my translation).
[56] Taylor, *Heresy and Orthodoxy in Paris*, p. 108.
[57] See Haigh, *English Reformations*, p. 205, MacCulloch, *Cranmer*, p. 324, and MacCulloch, *Tudor Church Militant*, pp. 26–30.

Having demonised their adversaries, Marian theologians now literally moved in for the kill. Marian authors used the same arguments for the execution of recalcitrant Protestants as others in early-modern Europe.[58] In an oblique reference to the prayer for deliverance 'from the tyranny of the Bysshop of Rome and al hys detestable enormities' in Cranmer's Litany, Hogarde contended that 'the horrible inormities of the protestantes' and their refusal to return to Catholic belief deserved death; they must suffer execution in order to protect the Christians from their salvation-threatening deceit.[59] Their obstinate denial of Catholicism negated the possibility of their comprehending the word of God. Both Hogarde and the author of *A treatise concernynge the Masse* produced systematic defenses of the executions for heresy.[60] According to the Hogarde, Augustine had written that it was better to dispose of 'the dead flesh' of heretics for the faster healing of the Church; brief pain was preferable to the festering wound of heretics in the community.[61] Bush claimed that St Paul had given the scriptural warrant for a heretic to be 'excluded as one accursed, leaste the dangerous infection of one corrupte shepe, may poison . . . the whole sound flocke of Chryst with his venomous . . . companye'.[62] Marian authors agreed with what Standish had written during Henry's reign: it was the 'very charyte toward Christes flock' to execute heretics who imperiled other Christians by their refusal to recant.[63] Thus, for William Rastell, in the dedicatory epistle of his 1557 edition of the *Workes of Thomas More*, the extirpation of heresy was the 'most godly purpose' of Queen Mary.[64]

Accompanied by such intellectual and emotive underpinnings from Marian Catholic texts, the Marian persecution took place. While the attempt to destroy Protestant belief has been viewed as counter-productive, the leaders of the Marian Church were following what they believed to be the tried-and-true remedy for unrepentant heresy.[65] It was indeed perceived as a 'pastoral duty' on the part of these writers – many of them leaders within the Church and Marian society – and they did not question the burning of heretics in print.[66] And while there was

---

[58] See Gregory, *Salvation at Stake*, pp. 78–90.

[59] *The First and Second Prayer Books of Edward VI* (1999), p. 362; Hogarde, *Displaying of the Protestantes*, fo. 4v; cf. *An Exclamation vpon the erronious and fantasticall sprite of heresy, troubling the vnitie of the Church, deceauing the simple Christians, with her vnperfect, vnprofitable & vayne wordes* (1553?), RSTC 10745.

[60] Hogarde, *Displaying of the Protestantes*, fos. 40r–70v; *Treatise concernynge the Masse*, sigs. F7v–H3v.

[61] Hogarde, *Displaying of the Protestantes*, sig. 59v.

[62] Bush, *Exhortation to Margarete Burges*, sig. C2r.

[63] John Standish, *A Lytle treatyse composed by Iohn Standysshe one of the felowes of Whyttynton Colledge in London, And now by him the fautes of the Prynter in this heretofore newly corrected with certayne addycions to the same againste the protestacion of Robert barnes at the time of his deth* (1540), RSTC 23210, sig. G3r.

[64] More, *Workes*, sig. C2v.

[65] See A. G. Dickens, *The English Reformation*, 2nd edn (University Park, PA, 1989), pp. 293–301, and Loades, *Reign of Mary*, pp. 273–9.

[66] Loades, *Reign of Mary*, p. 275.

questioning of the policy on prudential grounds in Mary's court and the courts of Europe, this was not universal, if Orlandus Lassus's motet, *Te spectant, Reginalde Poli*, is any guide. Possibly written for the cardinal's consecration as archbishop immediately after the burning of Cranmer, the text states that 'England applauds, because you [Cardinal Pole] ignite auspicious fires; and tears, too, you draw forth from [England's] adamantine heart'.[67] Le Picart heartily believed in the burning and torture of heretics, whose activities were tantamount to 'spitting on the cross'.[68] While persecution was one important element of Reformation and Counter-Reformation confessionalisation that Marian churchmen utilised, Robert Bireley wisely cautions against 'exaggerating the element of compulsion in the Catholic Reformation and in the Reformation. This is to overlook the attractiveness of methods of evangelisation, the extent of popular religious devotion, and the widespread desire for a more profound religious life'.[69]

In their attack on heresy, Marian authors found heretical claims to martyrdom to be among the most outrageous of their enemy's beliefs. The sermon of Gloucester's boy bishop stated that Protestants who were burnt lacked the virtue of martyrs like the Holy Innocents – innocence of heresy.[70] However, it was Hogarde and the anonymous author of *A treatise concernynge the Masse* who were the pioneers of anti-martyrology in Marian England. Both made much of Protestants's actions as they underwent martyrdom, and claimed that did not die as true martyrs did. At the stake they acted boldly, but so too had the thief who blasphemed Christ on the cross: was he a martyr? The author of *A treatise concernynge the Masse* further attacked the tales of heretical martyrs being spread by word of mouth or in print. Those

> at the stake and fyre . . . rayle and reuile, they curse and blaspheme vntill the last breath. Such sort of death and maner of dying be it neuer so gorgeously garnished, and paynted with hipocritical pacience, fayned mirth, coloured charitie, canne make them no martirs of god, but declare them to be members of the deuill, sythe the matter wherefore they dye is mooste mischeuous and manyfest heresy.[71]

If heretics were true martyrs, Hogarde asked, why did they not conduct themselves with humility and gentleness at the stake, like true martyrs? They were 'more lyke helhoundes then holy ones: such is their pacience'.[72] Indeed,

> their mad and franticke raylynge at the stake and fyre agaynst the Popes

---

[67] 'Te spectant, Reginaldi Poli, tibi rident, exsultant montes, personat Oceanus, Anglia dum plaudit, quod faustos excutis ignes; elicis et lacrimas ex adamante suo.' I am grateful to Owen Rees for his translation and the complete text.

[68] Taylor, *Heresy and Orthodoxy in Paris*, pp. 109–11.

[69] Robert Bireley, *The Refashioning of Catholicism, 1450–1700* (1999), p. 120.

[70] 'Two Sermons Preached by the Boy-Bishop, one at St Paul's temp. Henry VIII, the other at Gloucester, temp Mary', *Camden Miscellany VII*, Camden new series 14, ed. J. G. Nichols (1875; reprint, 1965), p. 17.

[71] *Treatise concernynge the Masse*, sig. H1r–v.

[72] Hogarde, *Displaying of the Protestantes*, fos. 50v–51r.

holynesse, and agaynst bishops, priests, agaynst al the clergy and other
catholyke people doth declare manifestly what great charitie they haue.
. . . And no meruayle, for when the wolues arse is set on fyre . . . then wil
he woluishly barke and baule agaynst the shepherdes and shepe, and
forgetteth to fayne as he dyd before too blete lyke a shepe.

This is because 'they are no martirs but verye mad and false heretykes'.[73] Other
heretics, not bold enough for the stake, nevertheless acted as 'traytours before
God', encouraging dying Protestants by exclaiming '[t]he Lord comfort the[e],
. . . with other seditious exclamacions or secrete mutteringes'. Thus a heretical
martyr would believe 'he shal lepe out of the fyre into gods bosom: wher in very
dede dying an obstinat heretyke he lepeth like a flounder out of the frying pan of
temporall death in to the perpetuall and vnquenchable fyre of gods iustice'.[74]
Marian accounts contrasted sharply with those of Foxe, who related the stoicism,
not the 'raylynge', of dying Protestants. Both sides were more intent on
producing theological truths than reportage of Smithfield and other burnings.[75]

   Marian writers such as John Gwynneth claimed, even before the burnings
commenced, that reducing heretics to Catholic belief was an almost impossible
task – heretics could not even know they were heretics! Enlightenment given by
grace was the only remedy.[76] Richard Smyth prayed that God would give them
the grace 'to retourne vnto the veritie agayne, . . . that they maye put their fiaunce
and trust in their owne good workes, as Gods giftes'.[77] Tunstall too encouraged
prayer for Protestants, along with prayers for the conversion of Jews and
pagans.[78] They could be shown the way to salvation by such witnesses as young
Joliffe, a precocious sacramentary at Winchester College, who underwent a
deathbed conversion to traditional Eucharistic belief, according to White.[79] To
the same end the Marian *Homelies* presented explicit counter-arguments to
specific elements of heretical teaching throughout the text.[80] And lest people be
'caried with euery waue, and winde of newe learninge', Pendleton offered readers
means 'to discerne and know the trew churche of Christe from the heretycall and
schysmaticall congregations' in his first homily on the Church. He also encouraged all believers in England to beg God's mercy, 'bicause we haue bene oute of
the house of God'; but by remaining faithful to the Church, 'we shall be fedde
wyth lyuelye faythe, oute of whyche wyll sprynge in vs, muche holynesse of lyfe,

[73] *Treatise concernynge the Masse*, sig. G6r–v.
[74] Ibid., sigs. H2v–3r, G1r.
[75] See Gregory, *Salvation at Stake*, pp. 171–6.
[76] John Gwynneth, *A Declaration of the state, wherin all heretikes dooe leade their liues: also of their continuall indeuer, and propre fruictes, which beginneth in the .38. chapiter, and so to thende of the woorke* . . . (1554), RSTC 12558, fos. 2v–4v.
[77] Smyth, *Seconde parte of a Bouclier*, sig. F1v.
[78] Cuthbert Tunstall, *Certaine Godly and Deuout prayers. Made in latin . . . by Cuthbert Tunstall, Bishop of Durham, and translated into English by Thomas Paynell, clerke* (1558), RSTC 24318, sig. B6v.
[79] White, *Diacosio-Martyrion*, fos. 95r–96v.
[80] Bonner *et al.*, *Homelies*, fos. 38r–v, 44r–v, 50r–52r, 58v–61r, 63r–54v (*recte* 73v), 32r–v.

and quietnes of conscience'.[81] It is with such concise apologetics for Catholic belief that Marian theologians laboured to lead people away from heresy and anti-martyrs.

Eamon Duffy writes that 'One of the central concerns of the *Profitable doctryne* was to reaffirm the centrality of the Church in every aspect of Christian life, and . . . this message was hammered home'.[82] This was the case not only with Bonner's book, but with all the religious texts of Mary's reign. In their descriptions of the virtues and power of the Church, the other Marian authors equalled Bonner. It was the locus of salvation both for the next world, through its divinely guaranteed monopoly on right belief; and in this world, through its emphasis on the need for sacred mutuality among the communion of saints on earth and the example and intercession of martyrs like Fisher and More, and through its efforts to exclude all non-believers from Christian charity. Throughout their writings – even in works as idiosyncratic as Hogarde's – Marian authors presented a coherent, if unnuanced, ecclesiology. But they were also consistent with the vision of the Church propounded by More, Fisher, Carranza, the Tridentine Catechism and Catholic apologists in Europe, most especially in reiterating the need for ecclesial unity. This strategy fit their aim of re-educating England in Catholicism, a strategy that also overtly, though usually covertly, but always consistently struck out at heretical belief and its false martyrs. All of these authors, polemicists and theologians invariably defined and described the Catholic Church in contrast to heretical ecclesiology. But they imitated their enemies by equating unity – so vital to Marian Catholics – and universality with uniformity and denouncing the Church's enemies as demonic. Thus the revolution commenced by Luther continued to set the agenda for religious change, but that was true of the entire Counter-Reformation. It is therefore little wonder that in his preface to the *Profitable doctryne* and *Homelies*, Bonner echoed Cranmer's translation of the Sarum collect for Vespers in his wish that these Marian texts would be employed so 'that we may lyue in rest and quietnes, and specyally in the vnitie of Christes catholique churche, and his religion, louynge and seruyng God, with al our hearte in holynes and ryghteousnes, all the days of this our lyfe'.[83]

[81] Bonner *et al.*, *Homelies*, fos. 32r–35v, 42r.
[82] Duffy, *Stripping of the Altars*, p. 535.
[83] Bonner, *Profitable doctryne*, sig. A4r.

8

Robert Persons's Comfortable History of England

VICTOR HOULISTON

John Foxe died in 1587, four years after the publication of the final edition, printed in his lifetime, of the *Acts and Monuments*. By this stage, it has been argued, the work had begun to live up to its name: it became 'monumental' in the sense of glorifying the historical pedigree of the established reformed Church of England. No longer did Foxe's work represent merely the aspirations of a party.[1] The process of appropriation by state propaganda continued after his death, with the first posthumous edition of 1596. Like its predecessors, this was an immense and sturdy volume, admirably designed to be placed prominently, next to the English Bible, in cathedrals, parish churches and houses of senior clergy. In the preliminary 'Protestation . . . [t]o the true and faithfull congregation of Christes vniuersall Church . . . dispersed through the realme of England' one of its purposes was declared: to show that 'God hath euer maintained in [that Church] the truth of his gospell, against heresies and errours of the Church of Rome'. An appeal was made for a moderation of controversy within the Church of England, 'because God hath so placed vs Englishmen here in one commonwealth, also in one Church, as in one shippe together: let vs not mangle or deuide the shippe'.[2] What, one must ask, must the psychological effect of such rhetoric, thus publicised at the centres of the English religious establishment, have been on local English Catholics in 1596? If they were church papists, reluctant attenders of official divine worship, they were uncomfortable fellow-voyagers on a ship that was waving a particularly defiant flag against the tradition they inwardly sought to honour. If they were recusants, paying the high price of absenteeism, Foxe's book simply reinforced their sense of the Church establishment as a centre of hostility. Their community was being poisoned against them.

The most significant Catholic rebuttal to Foxe at the turn of the sixteenth

---

[1] Tom Betteridge, 'From Prophetic to Apocalyptic: John Foxe and the Writing of History', in *John Foxe and the English Reformation*, ed. David Loades (Aldershot, 1997), pp. 210–32, esp. p. 212.
[2] John Foxe, *Actes and Monuments of matters most speciall and memorable, happening in the Church, with an vniuersall history of the same* (1596), RSTC 11226, sig. ¶4v.

century, as Elizabeth's reign came to a close, was Robert Persons's *Treatise of three conuersions of England from paganisme to Christian religion*, published in three volumes at St Omer in 1603–4.[3] The title refers to the argument, in the first volume, that Christianity in England, whether Briton or Saxon in origin, owed its existence and vitality to Rome. Volumes two and three provided a systematic assault on the Foxean martyrs, reaffirming the traditional martyrology of the Roman Catholic Church. Bulky as the work was, running to 2260 quarto pages (excluding the indices), it was of modest proportions in comparison with the massive folio of the 1596 *Acts and Monuments*.[4] That was because it was a kind of interim report, suited to immediate needs, from a much larger project to compile a full-length ecclesiastical history of England to rival Foxe's in every way. Persons had begun to gather materials for a large-scale ecclesiastical history of England from the Roman point of view, concentrating on the period beginning with the reign of Henry VIII. It was, thus, designed to expand the work of Nicholas Sander, the manuscript of whose *De origine ac progressu schismatis Anglicani* (1581/5) Persons had annotated in 1586.[5] Persons began work on the new compilation in 1597, and the fruits of his labours are extant in five thousand pages of manuscript entitled *Certamen Ecclesiae Anglicanae*. As it stands, it is a compendium rather than an original work, containing several relevant histories (by other authors) in their entirety. It would be reasonable to assume that Persons meant to work this material up into a unified ecclesiastical history, given that he was particularly adept at creating impressive and highly readable works out of material he culled from others. Such were the *Christian Directory* (1582), adapted from Luis de Granada, and, if my view of the authorship is correct, the *Conference about the Next Succession* (1595), incorporating the researches of Sir Francis Englefield.[6] Besides the manuscript of the *Certamen* itself, there remain in Rome other working documents, such as a draft history of the reign of Henry

3   RSTC 19416; to be referred to as *Treatise of Three Conversions,* abbreviated *TTC*.

4   Persons's copy is preserved at the Venerable English College, Rome. Grateful thanks to the rector, Mgr Adrian Toffolo, for permission to view this copy. A typed note interleaved between pp. 970 and 971 suggests that the 'heavy binding' (since renewed) may be accounted for by potential exposition in church. For a full discussion of the implementation of Privy Council policy on the *Acts and Monuments* from 1570, see Elizabeth Evenden and Thomas S. Freeman, 'Print, Profit and Propaganda: The Elizabethan Privy Council and the 1570 Edition of Foxe's "Book of Martyrs" ', *English Historical Review*, 119 (2004), 1288–1307.

5   For a summary of the debate on Persons's role in the publication of the two editions of *De origine*, see Thomas F. Mayer, 'A Sticking-Plaster Saint? Autobiography and Hagiography in the Making of Reginald Pole', in *The Rhetorics of Life-Writing in Early Modern Europe: Forms of Biography from Cassandra Fedele to Louis XIV*, ed. Thomas F. Mayer and D. R. Woolf (Ann Arbor, 1995), pp. 205–22, esp. p. 212.

6   *The first booke of the Christian exercise, appertayning to Resolution* (Rouen, 1582), RSTC 19353, enlarged and entitled *A Christian directory guiding men to their saluation* (Rouen, 1585), RSTC 19354.1; on the debt to Granada, see my introduction to *The Christian Directory* (Leiden, 1998), pp. xxxii–xxxix. R. Doleman, pseud., *A Conference about the next succession to the crowne of Ingland* (Antwerp, 1594 scil. 1595), RSTC 19398; on the authorship, see my 'The Hare and the Drum: Robert Persons's Writings on the English Succession, 1593–96', *Renaissance Studies*, 14 (2000): 233–48.

VIII. Persons called on his extensive network of correspondents to send in any relevant material they might have to hand.[7]

What, then, were the urgent considerations prompting the publication of the *Treatise of Three Conversions*? Persons had returned to Rome from Spain in 1597, summoned to help with the troubles at the English College. That conflict reflected the threat to the unity of English Catholicism at large: after the death of William Cardinal Allen in 1594, the tensions within a faith community partly dispersed on the Continent and deprived of regular episcopal authority both at home and abroad were in danger of developing into factionalism. Growing suspicion of the Jesuits (of whom Persons was the English superior) manifested itself at the English College, Rome, the seminary in Douai, amongst English exiles in the Low Countries and France, in the community of priests semi-imprisoned at Wisbech Castle, and among the secular clergy in the field. It came to a head in the so-called appellant controversy over the appointment, in 1598, of the archpriest George Blackwell to govern the secular clergy, a controversial move attributed to Jesuit influence.[8]

One of the chief sources of suspicion was the issue of loyalty to the Elizabethan state, a question on which the debate with Foxe had a significant bearing. In 1598 Sir Francis Hastings published a zealous tract entitled *A Watch-word to all religious, and true-hearted English-men* (RSTC 12927). Drawing heavily on Foxe, he accused English Catholics of complicity in the Antichrist's campaign against the elect nation (to borrow William Haller's much-derided phrase). This was a puritan inflection of the subversion charge that had been spelt out in more explicitly political terms by William Cecil in *The Execution of Iustice in England for maintenance of publique and Christian peace* (RSTC 4902–3, 1583) and the 1591 Proclamation *A declaration of great troubles pretended against the realme by a number of seminarie priests and Iesuists*.[9] Cecil had been concerned to justify the execution of Catholic priests for treason; he argued that adherence to the doctrine of the papal deposing power – that is, the pope's right to invoke force against heretical or tyrannical kings – made a priest a traitor, especially in view of Pius V's excommunication of Queen Elizabeth in 1570. William Allen responded

[7] 'Historia de vita & actis Henrici VIII ab anno 1528 usque ad obitum eiusdem Regis' (archives of the Society of Jesus, Rome. MS Rom. Hist. Coll. Ang. Hib. & Scot.); see also Papers of the Jesuit Fathers, 167–8 (the record of Persons's additions to Sanders) and 170 (a Spanish MS history of the reign of Henry VIII). For a full description of the sources and development of the *Certamen*, see *Robert Persons, Certamen Ecclesiae Anglicanae: A Study of an Unpublished Manuscript*, ed. Jos Simons (Assen, 1965). Henry Garnet sent materials to Persons in 1600: see Philip Caraman, *Henry Garnet 1555–1606 and the Gunpowder Plot* (1964). Letters connected with the project include Richard Hall to Robert Persons, 20 May 1600 (Archives of the British Province of the Society of Jesus, Persons Letters Collection 46/12/5, fos. 1085–6). I am indebted to the Archivist, Fr Thomas M. McCoog, SJ, for permission to consult and quote from this collection, and for valuable assistance and advice.
[8] The standard accounts are in John Bossy, *The English Catholic Community, 1570–1850* (1975), and Arnold Pritchard, *Catholic Loyalism in Elizabethan England* (1979).
[9] See *Tudor Royal Proclamations*, ed. Paul L. Hughes and James F. Larkin, 3 vols (New Haven, 1964–9), III, pp. 86–95.

in his *True, Sincere and Modest Defence of English Catholiques That Suffer for their Faith* (RSTC 373, 1584) to the effect that state action constituted religious persecution and the executed priests were true martyrs.[10]

Allen's case for the Elizabethan Catholic martyrs was complex because it went beyond the relatively straightforward demonstration that there was no hard evidence linking any of the priests to conspiracy against the state. They were convicted of the regular practice of their priestly vocation: saying Mass, hearing confessions, supplying religious objects, etc. Such acts were adjudged treasonable only by recent and unusual royal decree. The injustice of state action was thus exposed in much the same terms as that of the McCarthy witch-hunt in the 1950s where citizens were prosecuted for association with the Communist Party and for holding beliefs on which it could not be shown that they had acted. According to natural law, then as now, treasonable intent is provable only in action. Beliefs could indeed be the subject of a heresy trial, but the priests were executed for treason, not for heresy (and in any case, as Allen pointed out, there were no Protestant heresy laws). On this argument, it could be shown that the treason charge could not stick and that the priests were proceeded against purely for religion, since the acts for which they were convicted were purely religious ones. Technically, then, they were martyrs, since the *cause* makes the martyr.

Allen was not content with this simple position, which he outlined in chapter 1, because the circumstantial evidence linking the religious acts and beliefs with political activism was so strong. There had been a Catholic rebellion in 1569; there were invasion plans involving the duke of Guise in 1582–3; there were to be Spanish Armadas in 1588 and 1596, and plans to ensure a Catholic succession by force. That Allen and Persons and many of the English clergy supported these schemes whole-heartedly and without scruple is beyond question. There was, then, a common perception that the Elizabethan state had good reason to question the loyalty of Catholic priests, so that they were executed – however unjustly – on political grounds, not merely for religion. If the chief concern of persecution was the safety of the state, the status of martyrdom was at least obscured. So Allen had to show that the responsibility for making Catholic religion a danger to the state lay entirely with English political structures and not with the papal right of intervention. He denied the political motive and treated it as a mere cover for religious antagonism: identifying the English authorities with pagan persecutors, he wrote: 'They hated all Catholics and counted them traitors; so do you. They killed them indeed for their belief, but yet pretended other crimes more odious, and specially matters of conspiracy and rebellion against the civil magistrate; so do you' (ch. 2, p. 97).

Such parallels with apostolic and patristic times were rhetorically persuasive, but more was needed to establish political innocence convincingly. Allen did this

---

[10] William Cecil and William Allen, *The Execution of Justice in England, and A True, Sincere, and Modest Defense of English Catholics*, ed. Robert F. Kingdon (Ithaca, NY, 1965); quotations are from this edition, which also has a useful introduction to the debate.

pre-eminently in two ways. First, he elaborated the theme of caesaropapism, that is, the assumption by the monarch of spiritual supremacy in the kingdom: 'calling . . . the Queen's spiritual power, which she challengeth against the pope's supremacy, her "regality"; seeking by all means possible wholly to extinguish the hierarchy and prelacy of Christ's Church, and concluding all in kingly authority' (ch. 7, p. 204). Reviewing the historical contestation between the monarchy and papacy, he argued, by analogy with the warfare between flesh and spirit in each person, that the shifting boundaries were natural and acceptable so long as the pope's spiritual supremacy was not usurped: 'each one seeking after a sort to enlarge his own limits and commodities by some hindrance of the other; which combat and conflict, notwithstanding, is either tolerable or not damnable so long as the inferior, which is the flesh, by over-greedy appetite of her own advance-ment destroyeth not the superior, which is the soul' (ch. 7, p. 207). If, then, the state is guilty of eliminating papal spiritual supremacy, it forces the pope to use necessary temporal measures to restore it.

The second justification of papal intervention consists of an eloquent indict-ment of what is described as the illegal and destructive change of religion at the start of Elizabeth's reign. This is an imaginative re-enactment of the historical moment, portraying the violence done to the people's beliefs and practices, and the fatal conseqences. Allen argues that those who made the alteration must have foreseen the results, including invasion by the Catholic powers, and must take responsibility for them. And now, he asks, what is the pitiful state of this jittery nation?

> So long as our realm was in the unity of the Catholic Church and lived either in just wars or honorable peace with our neighbours, was there any such extreme fears of present invasion? Was there such mustering? Such diligent watch and swearing against the Pope at every port? Such examination of passengers? Such ado generally, and such mistrust of the subjects' fidelity? Such jealousy over all men, as though the whole realm were a camp that feared and expected every hour some secret camisado?[11]

The state could thus be said to have intended the situation, and so the priests, completely exonerated of the political implications of their religious activities, became true martyrs.

Allen's case rested on a time-honoured if by then rather dubious understanding of the unity of Western Christendom. *De iure*, if not *de facto*, he believed, the relations of monarchs and popes had not been changed by the Reformation and its accompanying political upheavals. Priests were practising exactly as they had done for hundreds of years: the meaning of what they did was distorted and obscured by the new context but remained essentially the same. They died, there-fore, as martyrs to the same faith as it had always been. Robert Persons,

[11] Ch. 8, p. 236.

confronted with similar denunciations of Catholic citizenship in 1598, also addressed the question of martyrology – as the structure of the *Treatise of Three Conversions* shows – but by a very different route and with a new emphasis. It was not that his political ideology differed materially from Allen's: in his *Responsio* to the 1591 royal proclamations he had also blamed the state for the conditions that made Jesuits and seminary priests apparently dangerous.[12] In the *Conference about the Next Succession* he had defended the right of the Church to depose tyrants and heretics, and in the debate following the Gunpowder Plot of 1605 he was to deny emphatically that the papal deposing power posed any threat to a legitimate state.[13] In all these works he affirmed that the pope had an interest in the spiritual welfare of Catholics in England, and that this interest bestowed at least an indirect right of intervention. So there was no question in his mind about the status of the Elizabethan martyrs.

Persons's more immediate interest, however, was in the unity and character of the English Catholic community. He responded to Hastings with a *Temperate Ward-word, to the turbulent and seditious Wach-word of Sir Francis Hastinges knight* (RSTC 19415, Antwerp, 1599), defending the record of English Catholics as good citizens and 'true-hearted Englishmen', to appropriate Hastings's phrase. As the 'Watchword' controversy ramified over the next few years, drawing in the noted vainglorious controversialist Matthew Sutcliffe, dean of Exeter, the question of Catholic patriotism remained unresolved.[14] It was obscured by the clamour over post-Reformation events: burning of Protestants as heretics, the legal status of recusants, the actions of recent Popes and princes. In this context, Persons decided to write a history of the English Church that would identify Englishness with Roman Catholicism. To turn to an analysis of the conversions of England in the time of Joseph of Arimathea, then of Pope Eleutherius, and finally of Augustine of Canterbury was thus an astute strategic manoeuvre on his part. Even though his 'examen' of the calendar of Protestant saints prefixed to Foxe's work in 1563 might appear to return the debate to more recent history, in fact the bulk of this 'examen', which proceeds from month to month, was concerned to honour and re-instate all the Catholic saints that Foxe had purposely omitted. Furthermore, in the process of publishing his 'examen', Persons took the opportunity to include two bulky additional treatises connected with the fundamental doctrinal controversies between the Reformers and Rome. Volume two contained a revised version of his account of the public disputation in 1600 between the bishop of Evreux and the Huguenot champion, Philippe du Plessis Mornay.

---

[12] *Elizabethae Angliae Reginae Haeresim Calvinianum Propugnantis, saevissimum in Catholicos sui Regni Edictum . . . Cum responsio . . . Per D. Andream Philopatrum* (Antwerp, 1592); see my 'The Lord Treasurer and the Jesuit: Robert Persons's Satirical *Responsio* to the 1591 Proclamation', *Sixteenth Century Journal*, 32 (2001): 383–401.

[13] *The iudgment of a Catholicke English-man liuing in banishment for his religion . . . Concerning a late booke set forth, and entituled; Triplici nodo, triplex cuneus, or, an apologie for the oath of allegiance* (St Omer, 1608), RSTC 19408.

[14] See Peter Milward, *Religious Controversies of the Elizabethan Age* (1978), pp. 138–45.

Volume three added a review of the main points at issue in the hearings or trials of Foxe's martyrs.[15] These annexures might be seen as opportunistic, but they complement the main treatise by defining and clarifying the faith for which the 'true' saints and martyrs died from earliest times, and which the pseudo-martyrs rejected.

Modern critical reaction to the *Treatise of Three Conversions* has concentrated on Persons's polemical bite, his exposure of inaccuracies and false assumptions in Foxe. Yet, like Allen, he was ultimately more concerned with the continuity of Catholic tradition than with immediate controversial advantage. Just as Allen affirmed the *de iure* reality of an undivided Christendom, temporarily effaced by the history of the Protestant Reformation, so Persons dismissed the claims of the Foxean 'pseudo-martyrs' in order to recover, for his readers, the identity of the contemporaneous Catholic Church with the faith of the English Church down the centuries. He did so, not without some party interest. Anne Dillon, for example, with some justification treats the *Treatise of Three Conversions* as a response to the appellant controversy in which the Jesuits, and Persons in particular, were accused of engineering the appointment of an Archpriest over the English secular clergy. With a small but significant party of secular priests offering to compromise with Richard Bancroft, bishop of London, in an attempt to gain toleration, it was in Persons's interest to encourage English Catholics to hold fast to the recusant position. They would thus be true inheritors of the tradition handed down by the saints and martyrs. Dillon's analysis reflects the current characterisation of Persons as pursuing a vision of the English Catholic Church that would make it a bright shining example of Catholic Reformation piety to the whole world. Yet it should be noted that Persons's record as a martyrologist is not one of rallying heroic resistance: even the *Treatise of Three Conversions* is technically anti-martyrology rather than an emotive proclamation of the sufferings of the English Catholic martyrs.[16]

Persons was, admittedly, a master of polemical demolition. His most memorable 'hit' against Foxe was the claim to have discovered 120 lies in three leaves of the *Acts and Monuments*. His depiction of Foxe as the 'father of lies' thus dominates the brief discussions of the *Treatise of Three Conversions* by Mozley

[15] *A Relation of the triall Made before the King of France, vpon the yeare 1600 betweene the Bishop of Evreux, and the L. Plessis Mornay . . . Newly renewed, and sett forth againe, with a defence therof, against the impugnations both of the L. Plessis in France, & of O.E. in England* (St Omer, 1604), RSTC 19413; *A Review of Ten Publike Disputations Or Conferences held within the compasse of foure yeares, vnder K. Edward & Qu. Mary, concerning some principall points in Religion, especially of the Sacrament & sacrifice of the Altar* (St Omer, 1604), RSTC 19414.
[16] Anne Dillon, *The Construction of Martyrdom in the English Catholic Community, 1535–1603* (Aldershot, 2002), pp. 323–69; cf. Thomas M. McCoog, SJ, 'Construing Martyrdom in the English Catholic Community, 1582–1602', in *Catholics and the 'Protestant nation': Religious Politics and Identity in Early Modern England*, ed. Ethan H. Shagan (Manchester, 2005), pp. 95–127. On Persons's advocacy of recusancy, see Alexandra Walsham, ' "Yielding to the Extremity of the Time": Conformity, Orthodoxy and the Post-Reformation Catholic Community', in *Conformity and Orthodoxy in the English Church, c. 1560–1660*, ed. Peter Lake and Michael Questier (Woodbridge, 2000), pp. 211–36, esp. 233.

and Parry.[17] Mozley finds Persons's elitist or snobbish dismissal of 'unlearned' Protestant martyrs and women distasteful, while Parry, though grudgingly admiring Persons's ability to reduce his opponent's arguments to rubble, deplores the blunt instruments used in this propaganda warfare. Thomas Freeman notes Persons's skill in detecting discrepancies between Foxe's text and his supposed sources.[18] Ceri Sullivan directs our attention to a wider range of rhetorical strategies. Against Parry she insists that the point at issue between Persons and Foxe is not historical accuracy but doctrinal integrity. Still, her emphasis is firmly on the hostilities, castigating Persons for his gracelessness in trying to provoke what she calls a brawl in heaven by invoking Catholic saints to take revenge on Foxe and his pseudo-martyrs for the injuries done to them. But indignation on behalf of the displaced saints was not unique to Persons. Harpsfield, for example, heatedly described the new martyrs dispossessing the old and pushing violently and ambitiously into their places.[19] In singling out Persons Sullivan unconsciously reflects a long-enduring myth about him as the blunt Somersetshire yeoman lacking the social graces of, for example, his former companion Edmund Campion. Campion, the darling of Oxford, favourite of the queen, elegant rhetorician, died an heroic martyr's death at Tyburn. Historians and biographers ever since have found it useful to make a contrast with Robert Persons, the one who got away. This is the picture we get, most famously, in Charles Kingsley's *Westward Ho!* (1855). Persons fought hard, and some would say he fought dirty. He was, as a fellow-Jesuit wrote, the martyr not of a moment but of a lifetime.[20] But there is nothing in his voluminous correspondence to show that he was in any way lacking in diplomacy. The story of his life suggests quite the opposite. This was the man who won the favour of Philip of Spain and the duke of Guise. His enemies almost invariably relented when they actually met him. He settled a long-brewed dispute at the English College, Rome, and had a loyal following among aristocratic Catholic youth.[21] It was said that the coach of the cardinal nephew, Pietro Aldobrandino, was waiting every morning at the gate of the English College, to

---

[17] J. F. Mozley, *John Foxe and His Book* (1940), pp. 176–80; Glyn Parry, 'John Foxe, "Father of Lyes"', and the Papists', in Loades, *John Foxe and the Reformation*, pp. 295–305, referring to *TTC*, 3: 412.

[18] 'John Bale's Book of Martyrs? The Account of King John in *Acts and Monuments*', *Reformation*, 3 (1998), pp. 175–223, esp. pp. 206–207.

[19] 'qui ... antiquis Christi martyribus e possessione sua & sede deturbatis, in eorum locum tam violenter & ambitiose intruduntur': Nicholas Harpsfield, *Dialogi Sex contra Summi Pontificatus, monasticae vitae, sanctorum, sacrarum imaginum oppugnatores, et pseudomartyres* (Antwerp, 1566), p. 820; see also pp. 861–2; Ceri Sullivan, *Dismembered Rhetoric: English Recusant Writing, 1580 to 1603* (Madison/Teaneck, NJ, 1995), esp. pp. 114–15; Ceri Sullivan, ' "Oppressed by the Force of Truth": Robert Persons Edits John Foxe', in *John Foxe: An Historical Perspective*, ed. David Loades (Aldershot, 1999), pp. 154-66.

[20] Pedro de Ribadeneira, *Bibliotheca Scriptorum Societatis Jesu* (Rome, 1676), p. 725: '[n]on semel tantum, sed per totam vitam quodammodo Martyr fieret, multorumque Martyrum pater'.

[21] Contrasting accounts of Persons's personal qualities are given by Francis Edwards, *Robert Persons: The Biography of an Elizabethan* (St Louis, 1995), and A. L. Rowse, *Eminent Elizabethans* (1983), pp. 41–74. See John Bossy, 'The Heart of Robert Persons', in *The Reckoned Expense: Edmund Campion and the Early English Jesuits*, ed. Thomas M. McCoog, SJ (Woodbridge, 1996), pp. 141–58.

take him to the Vatican.[22] The methods of persuasion used in his works of controversy demand closer and more objective scrutiny than Sullivan was able to afford them.[23]

It is true that Persons often appears preoccupied with scoring cheap points off his opponents, or, to put it in a slightly different perspective, often revels in the contest. To count up trivial inaccuracies in Foxe or to dwell on the statistics of du Plessis Mornay's discomfiture in the disputation before Henri IV does not consort well with modern conceptions of moral authority. Persons is as quick as anyone else to retort, when caught out in an error of detail, that this is not 'to the purpose', yet this does not prevent him from swooping impertinently on easy targets in the books he counters. Each inexactitude added to the tally in three leaves of the *Acts and Monuments* is of course multiplied in the calculation of the sum of error in the work as a whole. Similarly, Persons speculates on the radical unreliability of Mornay's writing by extrapolating from the sample that was actually scrutinised in public, arguing shrewdly that since Mornay had been given the choice of details for initial examination, the material in question must have been the most defensible.[24] From this one might imagine how rotten was the entire structure.

A further criticism of Persons's approach is concerned with his social and academic elitism. This was so much a standard polemical ploy at the time – Persons and Allen were themselves dismissed on the grounds of 'base' birth, and bastardy became a common smear on Persons – that Persons should not be singled out on this account. His dismissal of many martyrs of lowly status is based on an expectation that a martyr should be learned enough to understand the doctrine for which he or she is prepared to suffer. Neither the willingness to suffer, nor the intensity of the pain, is sufficient to make a martyr: as it was said, 'Non poena, sed causa, martyrum fecit' ('Not the suffering, but the cause, makes a martyr'). Persons makes the point like this:

> they being ignorant men and women . . . you may immagine with what iudgment, prudence or conformity of learning, or beleefe they did answere, not hauing the vnderstanding to conceaue, what the nature of faith or Sacraments is, & much lesse, what number therof may be proued to haue byn left by Christ, & least of all to determyne about so high and difficult a mistery, as the *reall presence*, the *Sacrifice of the masse*, and other such points of Catholike religion do import[25]

– but sometimes the tone is sneering:

---

[22] Henry Tichbourne to Thomas Derbyshire, 2 February 1597, *CSPD Elizabeth 1595–97*, pp. 356–8, item 28.
[23] See Ronald Corthell, 'Robert Persons and the Writer's Mission', in *Catholicism and Anti-Catholicism in Early-Modern English Texts*, ed. Arthur F. Marotti (Basingstoke, 1999), pp. 35–62, who argues that Persons's 'authority was obtained through the arts of courtship and argumentation' (35).
[24] *Relation of the triall*, pp. 123–4.
[25] *TTC*, 2: 212.

> ... then can it not be, but that the contumacy and stubbornes of Fox his rabblement, both of men, women and children, artificers, sawyers, weauers, shoomakers, spinsters, yea some madd or distracted people, which stood in defiance of their lawfull superiours, pastors and prelates to their faces; and this vpon no other grounds, but only vpon their owne wills, for defence of new opinions, deuised by themselues and others, against the common sense and iudgment of the said generall Church in their dayes, must needs be obstinacy and pertinacity in the highest degree.[26]

Here is the voice of dogmatism, piling up one damning phrase upon another; not for a moment considering the bravery of these people, their right to a voice in theological debate, their heartless treatment, their witty ripostes under interrogation (which seemed divinely inspired). Does Persons not stop to question whether there might perhaps be something in the faith of such common people? Indeed, he does confess to some pity towards them:

> ... truly I will first confesse of my selfe, that in readinge them ouer, I was greatly moued to compassion, not only towards themselues, in respect of their euerlastinge misery, and obstinate madnesse, but also towards their bishopps, pastors, and other Catholicke magistrates, that were forced to punish so great a number of such a base quality for such opinions, as neyther themselues could well vnderstand, nor haue any surer ground therof then their owne foolish apprehensions.[27]

– so that his fiercest words are reserved for those Protestant leaders who encourage obstinacy in the unlearned.[28]

Richard Helgerson argues that Persons resists the development of a new 'social reality' where the availability of the vernacular Bible puts all interpreters on an equal level; the criticism echoes Christopher Hill's notorious animus against all authorities who try to defend a monopoly of dogma against new ideas from 'unqualified' sources.[29] This is to generalise unjustifiably from Persons's position. He is not here primarily concerned with the broader question of theological debate but with adherence to heterodox opinion in the face of official condemnation. It is one thing to question orthodoxy; another to go to the stake for an opinion contrary to the received teaching of the universal Church. For Foxe, the latter is the heroic constancy of which martyrs are made; for Persons, it is sheer obstinacy, especially in those whose lack of formal theological training gives them no sound basis for such assurance that they are right.

If we suspend judgement on Persons's crude number-crunching and intellectual

---

[26] *TTC*, 2: 172.
[27] *TTC*, 3: 391.
[28] *TTC*, 3: 324.
[29] Richard Helgerson, *Forms of Nationhood: The Elizabethan Writing of England* (Chicago, 1992), pp. 265–6; cf. Christopher Hill, *Intellectual Origins of the English Revolution* (Oxford, 1965), *passim*. On Persons's insistence on learning as a prerequisite for martyrdom, see Dillon, *Construction of Martyrdom*, pp. 348–52.

or social snobbishness, we will appreciate that his critique of the 'pseudo-martyrs' is ultimately grounded on a moral analysis of their vaunted constancy, redefining it as stubborn determination to destroy the English Church. The scholastics defined a heretic as one who not only 'chooses' his or her beliefs but obstinately adheres to them.[30] Accordingly, when heretics were led to the stake, the officiating Roman clergyman would intone the Latin for 'yf I should deliuer my body so that I burne, and haue not charity, it doth profitt me nothing' – a use of scripture that chills the modern commentator.[31] The argument, as forcefully developed by Persons, runs: to choose to believe something other than the faith once given to the apostles and preserved and refined by the Roman Church through fifteen centuries and more is to be out of charity with your neighbour. It is to abandon the fellowship of the faithful, discredit the doctors of the Church, and destabilise the steadfastness of others.

Persons goes further: he sees uncharitableness built into the very structure of the *Acts and Monuments*, and reflected in its defiance of genre convention. His contribution to the debate over Foxe is marked by a particular interrogation of the act of writing Church history. Others, such as Harpsfield or Stapleton, could make similar points about inaccuracy and the theology of martyrdom.[32] Persons is interested in the way a writer such as Foxe appropriates the story of the Church to himself. This can be seen most clearly if we compare his treatment of the theme of the disunity of the Protestant 'sects' with that of Stapleton in his *Counterblast*. Both authors draw attention to what they see as the paradox of Protestant latitude and exclusivity. The true Church, scattered and hidden, consists of everyone who believes the pure doctrine: a definition of catholicity that Stapleton satirises as 'lyke to a shooe, that serueth euery fote: or to a Welshmans hose, that serueth euery legge' (fo. 430v). Once the shoe fits, though, the happily qualifying sect is likely to claim exclusive knowledge of the truth – so the result is schism (fos. 432–4). By contrast, Persons's image emphasises the shaping forces, not only of history but of historiography. At first, he claims, Protestantism was a confused heap, a 'rabble of . . . opposite sects' (*TTC*, 1: 512), but then, rather like primeval chaos, they were found to contain four elements. To change the metaphor, these four were in due course licked into shape and 'brought to some fashion of hand-some creatures, such as you know beare whelpes to be' (*TTC*, 1: 571).[33]

---

[30] From *haireisthai*, to choose: *TTC*, 2: 158, citing Thomas Aquinas, *Summa theologiae*, 2.2. q. 11 art. 2.
[31] *TTC*, 2: sig. g6–8; cf. John N. King, 'Fiction and Fact in Foxe's *Book of Martyrs*', in *John Foxe and the Reformation*, ed. Loades, p. 22.
[32] Nicholas Harpsfield, *Dialogi sex* (Antwerp, 1566); Thomas Stapleton, *A counterblast to M. Hornes vayne blast against M. Fekenham . . . touching, the othe of the supremacy* (Louvain, 1567), RSTC 23231; *A fortresse of the faith first planted amonge vs englishmen, and continued hitherto in the vniuersall church of Christ* (Antwerp, 1565), RSTC 23232. Persons frequently echoes specific points made by Harpsfield, Stapleton and Harding (in his famous controversy with John Jewel, 1560–71), but the rhetorical thrust is his own. Harpsfield gives a detailed exposition of the kind of charity that makes a martyr; a pseudo-martyr, on the other hand, puts himself before his neighbour, the whole Church, and God himself ('supra proximum, supra totam Ecclesiam, & supra Deum ipsum diligunt', pp. 760–1).
[33] On the diversity of sects among Protestants, and how they disagreed with each other, see Harpsfield, pp. 800 (*recte* 801) to 812, who emphasises how few Lutherans made it into the Foxe calendar.

At one level, Persons is simply suggesting that behind the apparent order of the Reformation – the four great groupings of Zwinglians, Calvinists, Lutherans and Anabaptists – lies a profound disorder. At another, he is arguing that the Church Foxe constructs in the *Acts and Monuments* is a fictional edifice, and neither Church nor book, as Persons will have it, has coherence or unity. The 'monumental' work disintegrates from within as he deconstructs it.

The question of the generic consistency of the *Acts and Monuments* has exercised numerous commentators. Some stress the degree of authorial direction and control: thus John King draws attention to the way Foxe shaped the original material to his own purposes, 'fictionalising' it to sharpen the anti-papal edge. Thomas Freeman, again, relates the *Acts and Monuments* to a Eusebian model, one that is inherently capable of embracing diversity; but he concedes that the Eusebian influence is more a matter of methodology – using extensive firsthand documentary accounts – than of structure. Others tend to note how the work accommodates many voices and genres, in ways that may remind us of Annabel Patterson's multivocal reading of Holinshed. Patrick Collinson praises the work for the completeness and inclusivity of its documentation. D. R. Woolf treats it as a compendium of genres – hagiography, romance and comedy – each of which, he claims, disturbs the Eusebian pattern of a 'redemptive time scheme'. He turns the work's hybridity into a positive virtue, supposing that it furthered the development of a historiography that combined both the antiquarian and humanist strains, both extensive and thematic.[34]

These modern attempts to find the clue to Foxe's design suggest that he was more or less making up the rules as he went along. There simply was no precedent for the particular blend of narrative and polemic he was writing; and he revised it against an unstable background of politics both at home and abroad. Such generic fluidity afforded Persons the opportunity to make three telling criticisms of the *Acts and Monuments* as a fictional construct. Whatever the intention, Foxe's work appears to present itself as an ecclesiastical history of England with an attendant new calendar of saints. Persons's strategy is to demolish it using criteria drawn from the generic expectations of the kind of work he infers Foxe was imitating. In so doing, he draws on the contemporary distinction between a history and a chronicle.[35] If Foxe were writing a history, humanist practice would prescribe the pursuit of a coherent thesis. What is the thread that joins together all

---

[34] John N. King, 'Fiction and Fact in Foxe's *Book of Martyrs*'; Thomas S. Freeman, ' "Great searching out of bookes and autors": John Foxe as an Ecclesiastical Historian' (Ph.D. diss., Rutgers University, 1995), pp. 44–58; Annabel Patterson, *Reading Holinshed's Chronicles* (Chicago, 1994); Patrick Collinson, 'Truth and Legend: The Veracity of John Foxe's Book of Martyrs' (1985); repr. in *Elizabethan Essays* (1994), pp. 151–78; D. R. Woolf, 'Erudition and the Idea of History in Renaissance England', *Renaissance Quarterly*, 40 (1987): 11–48, and 'The Rhetoric of Martyrdom: Generic Contradiction and Narrative Strategy in John Foxe's *Acts and Monuments*', in *The Rhetorics of Life-Writing in Early Modern Europe*, ed. Thomas Mayer and D. R. Woolf (Ann Arbor, 1995), pp. 243–82. I am indebted to Dr Freeman for detailed advice on this essay, and to Christine Y. Ferdinand (Fellow Librarian) and Sally Speir (Librarian) for permission to consult his dissertation in the Magdalen College Library, Oxford.
[35] See Woolf, 'Erudition and the Idea of History in Renaissance England'.

the martyrs he celebrates? Motifs abound, but there is no grand narrative.[36] Rhetorically speaking, the *Acts and Monuments* is a dispraise of Rome rather than a monument to Canterbury. Persons views Foxe's achievement as entirely destructive:

> . . . these his lyinge Acts and Monuments; a booke composed wholy to deceyue, and by iudgement of many men, hath done more hurt alone to simple soules in our countrey, by infectinge and poysoninge them vnwares, vnder the bayte of pleasant historyes, fayre pictures and painted pageants, then many other the most pestilent bookes together.[37]

Foxe himself conceded that his history did not cohere into a unified doctrinal argument, but claimed the right to entertain his readers with 'the free walke of a story writer'.[38] In the context of contemporary historiographical theory, this could be taken to suggest that the *Actes and Monuments* was really a chronicle. Persons's rejoinder to this is to point to the unevenness of chronological coverage: of the period 800 to 1066, for example, he remarks: 'this is the misery and calamity of this poore fellow and his cause . . . that either he must wryte nothinge at all of these tymes and ages or els he must wryte testimonyes against himself' (*TTC*, 1: 410).

If (on this view) the *Acts and Monuments* qualifies as neither a history nor a chronicle, its calendar also seems to lack credentials. The questions whether or not Foxe approved of the annexure of the mock calendar and what he intended by it are in a sense irrelevant to Persons's strategy. He took it at face value, and demanded to know why it did not conform:

> When Fox setteth downe both men, women, and children in redd or black letters, with this title of martyr or confessor (as the Catholike calendar doth) what is his meaning therin? doth he thinke them to be trulie martyrs and confessors indeede, or no? If he doe, then doth he canonize them for such, so farre forth, as lyeth in him, seeing he placeth them in the canon, rule and ranke of such saints. But if he do not trulie thinke in his mynd and conscience, that they are such indeed, then doth he notably abuse both the reader, and the whole world, in putting them downe for such.[39]

Here Persons exploits Protestant sectarianism: there is no common body of doctrine to which the purported martyrs testify. There is no solid authority for compiling the new calendar. No-one could use this calendar to glorify God in His saints, but only to wonder at the diversity of people's opinions and the supposed cruelty of Rome's handling of heretics. A calendar, Persons implies, is not a polemical weapon but an aid to devotion.[40]

---

[36] William Haller's brilliant argument, *Foxe's Book of Martyrs and the Elect Nation* (1963), is ritually denounced in more recent treatments.
[37] *TTC*, 3: 400.
[38] *A&M [1596]*, fo. 645v, cited in *TTC*, 2: 79.
[39] *TTC*, 2: 80.
[40] On the intentions and authorship of Foxe's calendar, see Damian Nussbaum, 'Reviling the Saints or

According to three established canons of writing, then – history, chronicle and calendar of saints – the *Acts and Monuments* has only a superficial unity. From Persons's point of view, there is a radical contradiction between monumental form and fragmentary content. This tension is shown to best advantage (for Foxe's opponents) by giving undue prominence to the saints' calendar, as Persons does by devoting two volumes of the *Treatise of Three Conversions* to it.[41] It can justifiably be remarked that this strategy is characteristic of anti-Protestant polemic. It gives no credit to the possibility that the adversary may be creating something new. It assumes that Protestant structures – churches, books, beliefs – are false simulacra of the true Roman originals, to be judged by the criteria those originals generate. Just so, the *Acts and Monuments* is to be judged by the standards of the generic models from which it has – perhaps intuitively – departed. What makes Foxe's work so intriguing to modern commentators is exactly what makes it vulnerable to Persons's assault.

Unfair as Persons is, then, we are invited to consider the implications for his own project. The *Treatise of Three Conversions* does not pretend to the status of an ecclesiastical history as such, so Persons does not present it as displaying the unity or monumental quality, the generic stability, that he claims Foxe lacks. The projected *Certamen Ecclesiae Anglicanae* would, he hoped, fulfil that role. His concern in the present work is to show what Church history and martyrology are for. Accordingly, what he offers is not so much a narrative of the three national conversions as a carefully structured argument why Foxe's rejection of the Roman origin and character of true English Christianity is spiritually destructive. The *Treatise* is divided into three unequal parts: the first two, which take up the first volume only, identify the Church militant: how it is indissolubly part of the visible Church of Rome (part one) and how it simply does not exist as an invisible Church as traced by Foxe (part two). The third part, the 'examen' of Foxe's mock-calendar of saints and martyrs, occupies volumes two and three, and purports to deal with the Church triumphant (*TTC*, 2: 29). The Roman saints constitute that heavenly company; Foxe's martyrs have no place in it. The object of setting out the treatise like this is clear: to reassure and comfort the English Catholic faithful that they are one both with the true visible Church of the ages, and also with the blessed Church of eternity. They have their roots in the historical Church, and their destiny in the Church of the world to come. If the recusants are intimidated by the claims of the Protestant Church of England to have emerged triumphant and visible from the invisible Church of the past ages, or disheartened by an army of aggressive and unfamiliar martyrs who have eclipsed

Reforming the Calendar? John Foxe and his "Kalender" of Martyrs', in *Belief and Practice in Reformation England: A Tribute to Patrick Collinson from his Students*, ed. Susan Wabuda and Caroline Litzenberger (Aldershot, 1998), pp. 113–36. Persons deals with the 'Nature' of the calendar at length in *TTC*, 2: 29–57, echoing to some extent points made by Harpsfield, *Dialogi sex*, pp. 861–2.
41 Sullivan analyses Persons's 'editing' of Foxe's calendar in such a way as to highlight 'the embarrassment of a devotional form which was doctrinally inappropriate', in ' "Oppressed by the Force of Truth" ', p. 166.

the old settled calendar of saints, Persons not only seeks to break down the threat-
ening new order but reaffirm the traditional formula of the Church militant and
triumphant.

Parts one and two are designed to repair the breach with Rome: the bold
Protestant claim that true Christianity can exist in England apart from the holy
see. The breach refers not so much to the Henrician secession – Persons treats
Henry VIII as fundamentally a Catholic king – but to the historiographical denial
of the crucial first links. Foxe, following John Bale, argued that the Roman
Church in England had been established only with the conversion of the Saxons
by St Augustine, so that Protestants could claim an inheritance from the primitive
British Church.[42] But for Persons all Christianity in England, whether British or
English (his preferred word for Saxon), was Roman. Hence the importance of
establishing that the conversion of the Britons under King Lucius should be
attributed to the papacy. The point in dispute in this argument is whether Pope
Eleutherius acknowledged the independence of Lucius's Church, and the
Protestant case rests on a letter purported to have been written by the pope.
Eleutherius notes:

> Ye require of vs the Roman lawes and the emperors to be sent ouer vnto
> yow, which yow may practise and put in vre within your realme. The
> Roman lawes and the emperors we may euer reproove: but the law of God
> we may not. Yow haue receyued of late through Gods mercy in the
> realme of Britany the law of Christ, &c.[43]

As presented here in Foxe's translation, the pope appears to give precedence to
the sovereign work of God in the conversion of the English, and to be ready to
give assistance, if appropriate, in setting up a legal infrastructure in the Church
and realm. Such an interpretation would tend to vindicate Canterbury's right of
secession. Persons's strategy is to turn Foxe's argument against him. Does the
letter prove that Lucius was already a Christian before Eleutherius wrote this
letter? Yes indeed. But does it prove that he was converted by some other means
than the pope's? No: Persons supposes, and expects his reader to suppose, that the
letter represents Eleutherius' *second* intervention: first he converts, then he sends
laws: 'what an egregious hypocrite and deceauer [Foxe] was, to argue out of this
letter, that, for so much as it appeareth by the same, that *K. Lucius* was a Christian,
when this letter was written: ergo *K. Lucius was not conuerted by Eleutherius, but
by some other before him*' (*TTC*, 1: 93). Logically, it proves nothing either way,
but the thrust of Persons's rhetoric is to affirm, as powerfully as he can, the act of
Eleutherius in converting the Britons.

It is helpful to dwell on this point because, although it may expose a weakness
in Persons's logic, it illustrates his emphasis on the importance of the formative
role of the papacy in the history of the English Church. Thomas Stapleton, dealing

[42] See Dillon, *Construction of Martyrdom*, pp. 329–37 and (on Henry) pp. 338–9.
[43] *TTC*, 1: 90.

with the same issue and the same letter in his *Counterblast*, refers to Bede, Geoffrey of Monmouth and Polydore Vergil to prove Eleutherius's agency in the conversion, but the question for him is primarily one of ecclesiastical jurisdiction (pp. 395–401). Persons prefers to argue from the internal evidence of the letter itself because it brings his reader closer to the event, vivifying the sense of a spiritual obligation. Here, for example, irony is used to make Foxe his advocate:

> So denieth he the matter, and consider, I pray you, what he attributeth to *Eleutherius* in this conuersion: *Peraduenture* (saith he) *he might help somthing to K. Lucius his conuersion.* And is not this a great matter, especially being qualified (as it is) with the restriction *Peraduenture?* Yf a man should say of Esop's fables, *that peraduenture some of them, in some points might be true:* were it not as much as *Iohn Fox* doth attribute to all this consent of authors for the conuersion vnder *Pope Eleutherius?* . . . Yow may mark the diminutiues vsed by Fox to lessen the benefitt, to witt, *Peraduenture, might somthing, &c.* And thereby consider what a holy stomake he hath to Rome . . .[44]

This is the crux of Persons's critique of Foxe: mean-minded, grudging ingratitude; and, by contrast, he desires to make the recusant faithful alive to their glorious inheritance. A full chronological ecclesiastical history such as he was writing in the *Certamen Ecclesiae Anglicanae* would provide the true monument of the Church to which his Catholic readers belonged, whereas the *Treatise of Three Conversions* applied the lessons of the *Certamen* to the present controversy for the comfort of his flock. '[T]his treatise', he writes in his opening dedicatory epistle, 'doth chiefly and principally belong to yow that are Catholiques, at this day, most woorthy children of so renowned parents, most honorable ofspring of so excellent ancestors, most glorious posterity of so famous antiquity' (*TTC*, 1: sig. ¶3v). They could be equally proud of all their Christian ancestry, British or Saxon.

A significant motif in this simultaneous process of critique and restoration is that of the prodigal son coming home. By asserting the objective historical identification of the Catholic Church in England as representative of Christianity on the island from the earliest times, Persons claims that the recusants are 'at home' while the Protestants are wandering in the wilderness, in exile in the far country. That is, in a sense, the polemical point of the treatise; but the pastoral and formative aims are just as important. Persons wants to bring his reader – vulnerable recusant or thoughtful discreet potential convert – home. He writes:

> Wherfore to avoyd this dangerous and damnable pitt of subuersion and ouerthrow in Christian beleefe, (wherof a man may stand in danger, by so great variety, and contrariety of pretended saincts, as heere yow haue seene represented, in the two former calendars), yf yow would aske my opinion how yt might be done, and how a man might reduce his mynd

---

[44] *TTC*, 1: 87–8.

after so great a tempest of contrary wynds in this behalfe, to a calme and quiett state of deuotion againe, and to the enioying of some sweet peace and tranquillity of conscience, as our forefathers did, and as we were accustomed also to do before we fell into these contentions, my counsell in this case should be, to thinke seriously of the example of the rash and inconsiderate yong man [the prodigal son] . . . not much vnlike to him, who by persuasion of heretiks, or sectaryes, and by their continuall clamors, iests, and scoffs against the Popes calendar and saincts therof hath suffered himselfe to be drawne from the reuerent respect and deuotion, which he had vnto them before, and to thinke of new saincts, and so by little and little, to be drawen on, and to be lead by Iohn Fox into this wyld hogge-field of his husked saincts, wherof yow shall feele the lothsome sauour, and behould their foule behauiour afterward . . . Wherfore to end this direction, I would wish the discreet Christian reader to be deluded no longer with these new fancyes, but to returne rather to the stepps of his forefathers in this behalfe, and to resolue to follow the same for the time to come, and to double his deuotion towards the honour of Christs frends in heauen, for the maledictions, slaunders, and calumni-ations which he hath heard vttered against them by new fangled heretiks.[45]

It is as if Foxe's writings have stirred up the passions – of enmity, false pity and hatred, antagonisms on both sides – thus drawing even the most sober-thinking English Christian away from home, from a restful state of devotion and good works, to a far country where ultimately there is no nutrition for the soul. The term 'wyld hogge-field of . . . husked saincts' is more than abusive; it implies a role for true martyrology that is missing or underplayed in Foxe. The stories of martyrs are not intended to arouse indignation or stir up combat so much as to strengthen the faithful in an orderly structure of virtuous life.

Everything about martyrology as Persons presents it in the *Treatise* can be referred to this pastoral design. He reviews '1600. yeares, wherin this ship of the Cath. Church hath passed thorow no fewer stormes then there are yeares and ouercome them all [as an excellent shipp well tackled and skilfullie guided, breaketh thorow the waues without hurt at all]; wheras many hundred sects and sectaries in the meane space haue byn broken in peeces, perished and consumed' (*TTC*, 1: 232) – perhaps a jab at Foxe's nautical metaphor as cited in my opening paragraph – and repudiates Foxe's offer 'to lay hands on the great illustrious and visible Church of these first 300 yeares' (p. 323). Ultimately the debate is a kind of property dispute over a mansion equally valued (sig. **7r).[46] The ship and the mansion are figures of an admirable organisation, where each Christian has an appointed place. Persons contrasts the self-ordained way Foxe compiled his

---

[45] 'A direction and instruction for vse of the two calendars', *TTC*, 2: 2–3, 20–1.

[46] This image is ultimately derived from St Augustine, 'Ennarratio in Psalmum xxi', 28–30 (*Patrologia Latina*, 36 (1841): 178–80); see Peter Brown, *Augustine of Hippo: A Biography* (Berkeley, 1967), p. 221, and Dillon, *Construction of Martyrdom*, pp. 334–5.

martyrology with the due process of the primitive Church: 'so . . . as to haue speciall care to gather their names, write their actions, note the dayes and places of their sufferings, appoint speciall notaries to attend thervnto, and others to ouersee the same, as deacons and subdeacons ordayned and appointed to that purpose by bishops, as appeareth throughout all antiquitie' (*TTC*, 2: 32).

Where Foxe's martyrs appear adversarial, acting as forerunners or pioneers of reformed Christianity, challenging convention, Persons commends the saints and martyrs for their constructive works of piety. He implies a pattern of Christian exercise, based on freedom from controversy, that entails a constant struggle against the world and the flesh. It is not right belief but right practice that he emphasises in the *Treatise of Three Conversions*: he commends the Fathers for invoking the help of the saints in the struggle (*TTC*, 2: 8) and for venerating those very saints primarily for their 'heroicall actions' (p. 11). He chastises Foxe for failing to mention 'one eminent act' in the lives of his martyrs, 'ether of chasteninge their bodyes, mortifyinge their appetits, contemning the world and pleasures therof'. Nor is this simply a recommendation of an ascetically monkish life, but of a vigorous life of active service, for he goes on to demand, in any true martyr, a 'supernaturall concurrence of God with their actions' (p. 84).

Generally speaking, Persons is more interested, in this work, in the formation of the Catholic Christian than in extraordinary sanctity. Thus, after the examen of the Calendar he gives a lengthy description of 'the Catholike man' (*TTC*, 3: 461–4 *recte* 474). Nevertheless, in criticising Foxe's martyrs he particularly affirms chastity and the subduing of the flesh. The married clergy are denounced as 'men giuen to their sensualityes both of women, and other like their commodityes, after the fashion of ordinary men' (*TTC*, 2: 84). Unmarried women are not virgins but maids; even if he cannot positively prove them unchaste, virginity is not their hallmark: it is not a virtue cultivated especially for the glory of God. Pseudo-martyrs are characterised by human, fleshly passions, as in the case of Savonarola, who, 'being of a hoate & cholericke nature' indulged it rather than subdued it, 'and preached so vehemently against them, that were his aduersaryes, as also scandalously, & with ouer much bitternes' (*TTC*, 2: 454–5). In such a context, constancy is really a passionate stubbornness. Unlike the impassive Catholic martyrs, who went to their deaths unmoved, in imitation of Christ as lambs to the slaughter, these are flesh and blood people who fought and argued and protested. With their cheeky rejoinders they are prone to the human weakness of playing to the gallery. One Robert Smith was called the Controller, 'for commonly he controlled all that was spoken by others', not least Bishop Edmund Bonner:

> *Bonner.* By my troth, *Maister Speaker*, you shall preach at the stake.
> *Smith.* Well sworne, my Lord, yow keep a good watch.
> *Bonner.* Well, *Maister Controller*, I am no Sainct.
> *Smith.* No, my Lord, nor yet good Bishopp . . .[47]

---

47 *TTC*, 3: 114, 116.

Very little of the work is devoted to the true saints and martyrs, although to begin with Persons attempts to make a comparison, at the end of each month, between the Catholic and Protestant calendars. Curiously, there are only a very few scattered references to the importance of miracles. The ascetic looms large in these sections, as in the contrast between St Polycarp and John Hooper:

> *Polycarpe* was a great faster and louer of penance: this man, of good cheere and liberty. *Polycarpe* was a great prayser and obseruer of chastity; this man had his Burgundian sister to keep him dayly company . . . [Hooper confessed] also plainly by his speach afterward, that himselfe had not the gift to lyue chast, no not in those old dayes of his, nor when he was in prison & tribulation, and shortly after like to be burned. Such was the perfection euen of these most principall Foxian Saints and Martyrs.[48]

Appetite, it seems, is given free reign by Protestants. Even in his analogies Persons celebrates virginity:

> [W]hat difference is there betweene our Church, and them in purity of proceedinge? Surely no lesse, then betweene a most honest house or exact monastery of Religious women, that admitt none to their cohabitation, but pure and vnspotted Virgins: and a stewes or brodell house, that imbraceth all broken, stayned, or corrupt people, without difference whatsoeuer.[49]

– even though the primary point is of doctrinal uniformity as opposed to the motley collection of 'Foxian' saints.

Although they might incur the wrath of secular or heretical authorities, the saints in the Roman calendar do not seek martyrdom or even, necessarily, to confront evil structures. Persons himself was sensitive about having taken flight at the time of Campion's arrest and execution, and it is hard to believe that he did not have this in mind when he pointed out how the ancient martyrs, too, often preferred flight: 'much more godly and wisely wrote *Saint Athanasius* to the contrary, in the next age after, in a booke of his owne flight and exile vnder Arrians, shewing by diuerse proofes both of scripture and of practize in the apostles themselues, that it is lawfull to flie in tyme of persecution' (2: 40). Here too one recognises the advocacy – surprising, perhaps, in so vigorous and combative a Jesuit as Persons – of quietness, the ideal of a Church spacious enough for all. There may be a struggle to establish this, a struggle in which there will be heroes, but the final purpose is to establish a space where piety may be practised in peace. The Church militant is always striving to become the Church triumphant.

Persons's confidence in this Roman ideal informs much of the style and manner of the *Treatise*. Buoyed up by the conviction of such a legacy, Persons sets out in conventional fashion both to delight and profit. As the writer of an historical treatise, he promises much matter of 'gratefull variety both of tymes,

---

48 *TTC*, 2: 318, 321.
49 *TTC*, 2: 359.

men, and affaires' (1: sig. **8v), which may appear no different from Foxe's 'free walke of a story writer', except that Persons's confidence in the unity of the Roman Church through the ages means he can draw freely on the full range of historical matter to provide an unforced diversity, 'not indeed so much . . . to delight, as to moove and profit thee'.[50] In contrasting his own historiographical method with Foxe's, he employs a characteristically bourgeois analogy of two London cloth-sellers, one displaying his whole cloth freely at midday, the other craftily offering glimpses of his fragmentary wares in dark corners (1: 629–30).

The most deliberately entertaining aspect of the history is his appropriation of Foxe's notion of an 'invisible' Church to play hide-and-seek with the annals of the early Church, casting about to find traces of Foxe's true but obscure edifice and triumphantly observing everywhere the signs linking the early Church with modern Roman Catholicism. The necessity and scriptural foundation of the Church as a 'knowen multitude' was a staple of Catholic polemic, developed with particular lucidity by Thomas Stapleton in *A fortresse of the faith* (part one, ch. 13–14). Persons lays hold especially on the logical problems associated with the transition, in Protestant historiography, from visible to invisible. He calls it a 'notorious and ridiculous shifte, to say, that the true Church was inuisible to the eye of man, and only seene by God', because it contains a 'fond and ridiculous paradox' (1: 286–7): namely, how can you demonstrate the existence of such a Church without making it visible, and how can you make it visible without applying an entirely subjective criterion – the guidance of the Holy Spirit – which it is impossible to represent historiographically? If only the enlightened can detect the true Church, what kind of historical proof is admissable? The problem is compounded by the Protestant assumption that the true Church only became distinct from the visible Church and hence (paradoxically) lost from view after the first three hundred (some would say six hundred) years. Since the Church is supposedly visible and glorious one moment and invisible and down-trodden the next, how much more difficult it is to find a basis for identification. In short, Foxe's Church is not only invisible, it is 'only imaginary or mathematicall' (1: 484, 643).

The humour of the *Treatise of Three Conversions*, then, is designed to encourage recusants and give them an assured sense of their place in history. The terms of Foxe's history are now inverted: if he traced the development of the true reformed Church from downtrodden obscurity to present establishment, Persons affirms that the persecuted English Catholic Church is even more illustrious now than when it held sway in the land: 'neuer more then in this time, hath the Cath. Church byn perspicuous, honorable and eminent' (1: 269). The Catholic religion has remained 'most substantially rooted', for heresy has entered 'only from the teeth outward' (1: 262). He is concerned, above all, to teach the recusants how to

---

[50] D. R. Woolf argues that Foxe imposes 'figure[s] of sameness' on the diversity of his narrative ('The Rhetoric of Martyrdom', pp. 258ff.).

lay hold on this tradition as part of their spiritual formation. An inner repose, amused by the frivolousness of vain Protestant historiography, is pertinent. So too is a proper reverence for true authority.

The question of authority is crucial to the historical debate. In the preliminaries Persons explains the logical principles on which he will proceed. What is proved beyond dispute by reason alone, he argues, precludes a 'free assent of faith' (1: sig. ***8r), so what he will offer is a combination of revelation, 'credible proofs', and reason, all of it depending on the pure affection of the reader. Here he seems to be influenced by the Aristotelian insistence that rhetorical discourse concerns itself with credible rather than absolute proof, an insistence brilliantly elaborated by John Rainolds in his famous lectures delivered at Oxford during Persons's career there.[51] With this kind of evidence, purely individual judgement is inadequate: as Persons puts it, 'neyther he nor we, as particular men, ought to iudge of these things: but the Catholike Church, which by her bishops and pastors do examine the proofes weight and moment of euery one of these things that fall out' (1: 430). Foxe (he claims) operates on quite the opposite principle, as for example in his treatment of Wyclif and his followers: 'The Parlament saith, that they preached heresies and notorious errors: but Iohn Foxe saith, it was true Christian doctrine' (1: 498). Persons wishes to move his treatise out of the combat zone of mere assertion and counter-assertion, preferring a more leisurely mode where the receptive reader is open to 'suppositional demonstration' (1: sig. ***8v) guaranteed by the consensual wisdom of the Church.

These, then, are the attitudes Persons's rhetoric is designed to inculcate, amply demonstrated by their opposites in Foxe and the Magdeburgians: characterised as the frenetic and the brash. Assured and tractable, the recusants will be, he trusts, receptive to a re-affirmation of the two practices pre-eminently threatened by the *Acts and Monuments*: veneration of saints and the adoration of the Eucharist. The 'examen' of Foxe's 'Calendar' is indirectly – and therefore the more effectively – an exposition of the cult of the saints, and the *Review of Ten Publike Disputations* focuses on questions about the Eucharist.

Eamon Duffy has drawn attention to the way in which Roman Catholic apologists and catechists responded to the Reformers' criticism by clarifying the Christocentric nature of many of the practices that were under attack.[52] Persons certainly exemplifies this process, although he indulges in the occasional playful allusion to what Duffy calls the 'apotropaic' and the Reformers called the 'superstitious' dimension of traditional religion: where a writer such as John Bale taxed St Wilfrid 'for bearing a box of reliques about his necke brought from Rome', these relics would discomfit him as surely as they did 'the diuells and wicked spiritts in England, who cryed and were cast out by the same' (1: 62). If this

[51] Lawrence D. Green, introd., *John Rainolds's Oxford Lectures on Aristotle's 'Rhetoric'* (Newark, 1986), esp. pp. 64–76.
[52] Eamon Duffy, *The Stripping of the Altars: Traditional Religion in England, c. 1400–c.1580* (New Haven, 1992), pp. 535–6.

smacks somewhat of the crudeness Ceri Sullivan attributes to Persons by calling on the saints to fight his battles for him, there is a very different tone in his humble request that they accept this treatise as a 'small oblation', and protect the author with their prayers, so that finally he may join them in everlasting felicity (3: sig. *7v–8r). He seeks *gravitas* by aligning himself with the defence of veneration of saints made by the Fathers against the ancient heretics: 'their defence, our defence, their faith, our faith, their religion, our religion, and their cause, our cause' (3: 76). This is much more than to confirm the identity, for polemical purposes, of primitive and contemporary Catholicism, although it is a superb summation of that argument. It is to emphasise the importance of the communion of saints, a living bond between the recusants and the early Church cemented by the very practice that is in dispute (3: 62–3). So Persons adapts the resolution of the prodigal son for his reader: I will leave the 'hogge-field of [Foxe's] husked saincts . . . rise vp from this folly' and 'returne to my mother the Catholike Churche againe, and will say, I haue synned against God and her, in that I haue left so lightly her house, her company, her iudgment, her obedience, her communion of saincts' (3: 3). He goes on to explain how this practice will draw them all closer to Christ (pp. 4–5).

In comparison with the *Acts and Monuments*, and with his own *Certamen*, Persons's *Treatise of Three Conversions* is of modest proportions. It is, nevertheless, his most substantial printed work. In the context of his commitment to the English Mission it represents his supreme effort to encourage and unify a recusant community that had not only suffered long persecution but considerable internal tension since the death of William Cardinal Allen in 1594. They were divided over the succession, over the question of loyalism, and over the archpriest. When Persons began the *Treatise* in 1602 – the Preface to the first volume is dated Christmas Eve, 1602 – the long wait for the Queen's demise was almost over; by the time he completed it in 1604, James's succession was assured, with dubious hope of relief for Catholics. Never had the English Catholic community been in greater need of comfort. Just how influential the *Treatise* was, it is hard to assess. Anne Dillon judges that it came too late and was too implicated in Persons's polemical agenda about toleration and conformity to counter the anti-Romanist propaganda effectively. The debate about persecution was overtaken by the Gunpowder Plot and its aftermath, and Persons's own interest in English history got diverted into a contestation with Coke over ecclesiastical jurisdiction and the common law. But Persons's opponents did take notice. Matthew Sutcliffe wrote two laborious works in response, referring to the *Treatise of Three Conversions* as a 'confused and worthlesse worke' and a 'Triobular Treatise of Three supposed Conuersions of England to the moderne Romish Religion'. One reader took the time to check Persons's tally of saints in the two calendars and inscribed his findings in a copy of the *Acts and Monuments*. John Strype, the ecclesiastical historian, objected to Persons's claim that Cranmer was the first archbishop to dissent from Rome, and wrote a biography to show that Cranmer's distinction lay in his full defection. Edward Gibbon owned a copy, which suggests that by the eighteenth century it had achieved some measure of notoriety.[53]

It is worth observing, finally, how this treatise complemented Persons's best-known work of spiritual direction, the *Christian Directory*, which he re-published in 1598 and was to revise extensively for publication in 1607.[54] The original version, the so-called *Book of Resolution*, had started from the premise that man is accountable to God, and urged the motives for resolving to serve Him. The much enlarged 1585 revision added two extensive chapters, one to prove that there is a God, the other to show the supremacy of the Christian religion. Curiously, in the Preface to the *Treatise of Three Conversions* Persons referred to these two chapters, observing that the first was based on pure reason but the second, having an historical dimension, involved suppositional demonstration (*TTC*, 1: sig. ***7v–8v). The same form of argument was appropriate to the present treatise, he wrote, and it seems at least probable that he conceived of the *Treatise of Three Conversions* as the next step in the argument, namely, that the Christian religion was truly represented by the Church of Rome.

The intersection between the *Christian Directory* and the *Treatise of Three Conversions* is a reminder of Persons's fundamental commitment to the pastoral aims of the Mission – an Ignatian spiritual apostolate – at the very time when he was working as hard as he could, by promoting the Spanish succession, to ensure the optimal political conditions for that Mission. It could even be said that the peculiar quality of his polemical writing stems from this nervous combination of the political and the pastoral.

---

[53] Dillon, *Construction of Martyrdom*, p. 340; Matthew Sutcliffe, *The Subversion of Robert Parsons His confused and worthlesse worke, entituled, A treatise of three Conversions of England from Paganisme to Christian Religion* (1606), RSTC 23469, and *A Threefold Answer unto the third part of a certaine Triobular Treatise of Three supposed Conversions of England to the moderne Romish Religion* (1606), RSTC 23470; John Strype, *Memorials of the Most Reverend Father in God, Thomas Cranmer* (1694), 'Epistle Dedicatory', sig. B1v. I am indebted to Thomas Freeman for the Strype reference. The contemporary inscription is to be found in a copy of the 1563 edition of the *Actes and Monuments* preserved at the parish church of St Botolph's, Boston (Lincolnshire); the annotation enumerates the (presumably Protestant) martyrs from the reign of Queen Mary. The annotator, writing in a secretary hand probably dating from the early seventeenth century, appears to be responding to, and possibly correcting, the tally of 'Foxian' martyrs calculated by Persons (*TTC*, 2: sig. F7v–8r). See my discussion in 'The Martyr Tallies: Robert Persons and his Anonymous Respondent', in *John Foxe at Home and Abroad*, ed. David Loades (Aldershot, 2004), pp. 47–50.

[54] *A Christian directorie guiding men to their saluation* (Louvain, 1598), RSTC 19354.3; revised again as *The Christian directory guiding men to eternall saluation* (St Omer, 1607), RSTC 19354.5. For a full account of the publishing history and revisions, see the introduction to my edition.

9

'Charles the First, and Christ the Second'*:
The Creation of a Political Martyr

ANDREW LACEY

> I confesse his sufferings make me a royalist that never cared for him.
> W. Sedgwick, *Justice upon the Armie remonstrance*, 1649, p. 31

> If ye suffer for righteousness' sake, happy are ye: and be not afraid of their
> terror, neither be troubled; but sanctify the Lord God in your hearts: and be
> ready always to give an answer to every man that asketh you a reason of the
> hope that is in you with meekness and fear.   1 Peter 3: 14–15

Owen Felltham's designation of Charles I as 'Christ the Second' may be one of
the more extravagant manifestations of the cult surrounding the executed king,
but it is by no means unique. In the 150 years or so following the regicide of 1649
'king Charles's head' occupied an important place in the religious and political
landscape of British society. Whether one revered the memory of the martyr or
despised him as a failed tyrant, one could not ignore him. I have been concerned
for a number of years to research this hitherto neglected cult and in line with the
film industry's penchant for 'prequels' this essay builds upon this work by exam-
ining the prehistory of the cult in the period 1645–9.[1] In other words it examines
the ways in which a political cult of martyrdom was formed around the person of
Charles between his defeat at Naseby in June 1645 and his execution in January
1649.

As part of a volume devoted to aspects of early-modern martyrology the cult of
Charles I is unusual in its overtly political aspects. Many people, both at the time
and subsequently, denied that Charles died for anything other than failed policies
and overweening arrogance. Yet it is precisely because the cult was at the same
time successful and controversial that it is worth studying. Part of its success

---

* 'An epitaph to the eternal memory of Charles the first', printed in the 1661 edition of Felltham's
Resolves, ed. T.-L. Pebworth and C. J. Summers, *The Poems of Owen Felltham, 1604?–1668* (University
Park, PA, 1973), pp. 65–6.

[1] Andrew Lacey, *The Cult of King Charles the Martyr* (Woodbridge, 2003).

derived from the ways in which the cult drew upon and exploited accepted traditions of English martyrology. Another important part of the Charles cult was its literary aspects; in an English Church centred on the Word, here was a cult fashioned almost exclusively around the word. A consideration of the Office for 30 January falls outside the scope of this essay, but I do want to consider the genesis of the *Eikon basilike*, the small book produced as Charles went to his death and which purported to be his very word; his apologia, written during his captivity. The *Eikon* was not just one of the best-selling books of the seventeenth century, it is one of the most popular works of martyrology ever written in English.

At the centre of any consideration of the cult of Charles the martyr stands the paradox of the man Charles Stuart. This man was the focus of a unique, Protestant martyr cult. He is, arguably, one of the greatest political martyrs in English history. Yet, as anyone who has ever taught an adult-education class on the English Civil War will tell you, he remains a deeply controversial and divisive figure. It is also part of this paradox that he should have been so politically inept. By any standards, Charles's political career was a spectacular failure: to paraphrase Oscar Wilde, to lose one kingdom is unfortunate, to lose three suggests incompetence. Yet Charles may be a paradox more apparent to us than the seventeenth century. The failure of his earthly career could be presented in a biblical and martyrological tradition of glorious failure: the martyr loses his life to save it, and the failure of the earthly career is a sign of heavenly victory in the service of truth.[2]

In this respect Charles's trial and execution provided the last act of the drama needed to fashion a martyr, and it is worth spending a moment to consider those events in the light of the martyrology presented in Foxe. Charles Carlton has suggested that Charles read the *Book of Martyrs* whilst a captive at Carisbrooke, and certainly when Charles faced his judges in Westminster Hall it is tempting to think that he had the example of Foxe's martyrs in mind.[3] Like Foxe's victims, Charles refused to acknowledge the authority of the court, referring to it merely as 'a power' without legitimacy to which he refused to doff his hat.[4] Just as Prynne, Burton and Bastwick appealed to the law of God and fidelity to the truth above the sophistry of their judges, so Charles based his defence on the demands of conscience and constancy to principle in just the same way as the victims recorded in Foxe.[5] Commentators noted the fact that Charles spoke throughout

---

[2]   I am reminded of James VII and II's last recorded words to James Edward, 'We can never lose too much for God' (Edward T. Corp, *A Court in Exile: The Stuarts in France, 1689–1718* [Cambridge, 2004], p. 254).
[3]   Charles Carlton, *Charles I: The Personal Monarch* (1983), p. 347. That Foxe was the common property of all English Protestants, whatever their churchmanship, is evidenced by the respect accorded the 'Book of Martyrs' by Nicholas Ferrar at Little Gidding (Patrick Collinson, 'Truth and Legend: The Veracity of John Foxe's Book of Martyrs', in *Elizabethan Essays* [1994], p. 151).
[4]   Ridley and Cranmer made a point at their examinations of doffing their caps to the representatives of royal authority but keeping them on when faced with the representatives of papal authority, *A&M [1563]*, pp. 1357, 1480.
[5]   Suffering for conscience sake and constancy to the truth under pressure is axiomatic for all Foxe's

his trial without his usual stammer and whilst this may reflect the psychological impact of this supreme moment in his life, for contemporaries the fact of his speaking so freely and 'boldly' was highly significant, a sign of God's favour and the reward of a settled conscience.[6] In Foxe's martyrology the verdict of the court is always a foregone conclusion and the prisoner receives the sentence stoically, displaying the classical virtue of apatheia in setting his affairs in order and parting from friends and family. The day of execution is transposed by the victim into a celebration, and Charles remarked to Thomas Herbert on the morning of his execution that 'this is my second marriage day; I would be as trim today as may be, for before tonight I hope to be espoused to my blessed Jesus'.[7] The walk to the scaffold and the drama of death become a central piece of theatre in which the prisoner is required to 'play the man': Charles famously asked for two shirts so that he would not shiver in the cold January air and be thought afraid; the speech to the crowd and the moment of death are faced with calm resolve.[8]

victims, but particular examples which spring to mind include the cases of Adam Wallace before his judges in Edinburgh, *A&M [1570]* pp. 1448–50; Rowland Taylor declaring to his wife just before his execution that he was 'quiet in my conscience', *A&M [1563]*, p. 1076; and John Bradford and Laurence Saunders both declaring before the lord chancellor that they stood by the demands of their conscience, *A&M [1563]*, pp. 1185–8, and *A&M [1563]*, p. 1046. The demands of conscience had been Charles's guiding principle in the years since Naseby and his impressive performance at the trial may stem in part from the confidence which a secure conscience provided. In this respect it is interesting to note that in facing the Star Chamber Burton had stated that he would remain true to 'my cause and my conscience', words which Charles could have used; John R. Knott, *Discourses of Martyrdom in English Literature, 1563–1694* (Cambridge, 1993), p. 139. Appeals to the demands of conscience, the rewards of constancy and the hope of the crown of life were also made by the regicides at their executions: John Cook declared that 'my rejoicing is in a good God, a good cause, a good conscience', again, words which Charles could have used before his own judges; Laura Lunger Knoppers, *Historicizing Milton: Spectacle, Power, and Poetry in Restoration England* (Athens, GA, 1994), p. 49.

[6] The biblical precedents include Christ's charge to the apostles, where he tells them that when they are given up to the authorities 'take no thought how or what ye shall speak, for it shall be given you in that same hour what ye shall speak. For it is not ye that speak, but the spirit of your Father which speaketh in you' (Matthew 10: 19–20), and St Stephen speaking before the Sanhedrin (Acts 7). Foxe follows this tradition in, for example, the account of Walter Mille who, despite age and the effects of imprisonment, 'made the churche to ryng and sounde againe, with so great courage and stoutness, that the Christians which were present, were no less rejoiced, than the adversaries were confounded and ashamed', *A&M [1576]*, p. 1238.

[7] C. V. Wedgwood, *The Trial of Charles I* (1964), p. 180. A Foxean example is that of Nicholas Ridley who rebuked Mrs Irish for her tears on the night before he went to the stake, stating that he was preparing for his 'marriage', *A&M [1563]* p. 1376. The ordeal of Prynne, Burton and Bastwick in 1637 was also likened to 'a glorious wedding day' (David Cressy, *Travesties and Transgressions in Tudor and Stuart England* [Oxford, 2000], p. 225). Mention should also be made of Philippe de Luns, burnt at Paris in 1558, and Le Glee of Tours, executed during the first War of Religion; both described their approaching deaths as a wedding day (David Nicholls, 'The Theatre of Martyrdom in the French Reformation', *Past and Present*, 121 [1998], p. 67).

[8] Just before the end Charles took off his George and handed it to Juxon. It is interesting to speculate whether this moment corresponded to the ritual of degradation by which Charles is un-kinged? Certainly Marvell argued in the *Horatian ode* that Charles's cooperation in the drama of death was a form of abdication which justified Cromwell's rise to power. John Cleveland and Henry Vaughan reflected the ambiguity felt over Charles's escape from Oxford in disguise and the fear that Charles was 'unkinging' himself by hiding his countenance: John Cleveland, 'The kings disguise', in *The Poems of John Cleveland*, ed. Brian Morris and Eleanor Withington (Oxford, 1967), pp. 6–9, Henry Vaughan, 'The king disguised: written about the same time that Mr John Cleveland wrote his', in *Henry Vaughan. The Complete Poems*, ed. Alan Rudrum (1976), pp. 327–8, Robert Wilcher, *The Writing of Royalism 1628–1660* (Cambridge, 2001), pp.

Whether or not Charles consciously modelled his own martyrdom on those found in Foxe is, of course, impossible to prove. But what is striking about Charles's performance at Westminster Hall and on the scaffold is the extent to which it conformed to a tradition of martyrology which reaches back through Foxe to Eusebius and the early Church. Patrick Collinson and Thomas Freeman have demonstrated the extent to which Foxe fashioned his accounts of the Marian martyrs to emphasise this patristic continuity, and David Cressy has shown how the sufferings of Prynne, Burton and Bastwick were placed in a similar context. As Thomas Freeman has remarked in connection with the fate of James Bainham, 'the impact of Bainham's actions lay not only in the conformity of those actions to accepted models of heroic behaviour, but also in the perception of this conformity by others', a comment which gets to the heart of the impact of early-modern martyrology.[9]

Yet these traditions of martyrdom could sometimes be problematic, as is demonstrated by the question of relics. Writing with the benefit of hindsight, Foxe had been assiduous in divorcing his martyrology from the Catholic tradition of saintly miracles associated with relics. Yet writing in the reign of Mary Tudor, the Catholic Miles Hogarde had lampooned the Protestants for relic-hunting in the ashes of their incinerated brethren, describing how they collected up charred bits of bone which they passed amongst each other as healing charms. In recording the case of John Hullier, burnt at Cambridge, Foxe mentions that

> hys flesh being consumed, his bones stoode upright even as if they had bene alive. Of the people some took as they could get of him, as peeces of bones. One had his hart, the which was distributed so farre as it would go: one tooke the scalpe and looked for the tong, but it was consumed except the very roote.[10]

When Charles was executed the crowds pushed forward to dip their handkerchiefs in the royal blood that dripped from the scaffold. Many, no doubt, simply

---

246–7. It is also reflected in Richard II's un-kinging of himself before Bolingbroke in the play which Charles, that great lover of Shakespeare, might have read in captivity. See also Cranmer's degradation, *A&M [1563]*, pp. 1492–6 and that of John Hullier, degraded at Cambridge 'after their popish maner with scrapying crowne & handes' before being burnt, *A&M [1576]*, p. 2196. For the importance of the ceremony of degradation see Nicholls 'The Theatre of Martyrdom', pp. 55–7, and Thomas Freeman's essay in this volume.

9   Patrick Collinson, 'Truth and Legend', pp. 151–78. Thomas S. Freeman, 'The Importance of Dying Earnestly: The Metamorphosis of the Account of James Bainham in Foxe's Book of Martyrs', in *The Church Retrospective*, ed. R. N. Swanson (Woodbridge, 1997), p. 287. David Cressy, 'The Portraiture of Prynne's Pictures: Performance on the Public Stage', in *Travesties and Transgressions*, pp. 213–33. For a discussion of 'edifying protestant biography' and its importance in both commemorating and creating a tradition of Protestant martyrology see: Patrick Collinson ' "A magazine of religious patternes"; An Erasmian Topic Transposed in English Protestantism', in *Godly People: Essays on English Protestantism and Puritanism* (1983), pp. 499–525.

10   M. Hogarde *The displaying of the Protestantes* (1556), RSTC 13557, fo. 54v. Something of the ambiguity surrounding artefacts associated with the martyrs is seen in Foxe's account of John Bradford giving away his velvet nightcap and a handkerchief to a friend in the crowd as he walked to the stake, was this relic or keepsake? *A&M [1563]* p. 1175. See also the references to 'relics' of Prynne, Burton and Bastwick in David Cressy's chapter on Prynne in *Travesties and Transgressions* (Oxford, 2000), pp. 213–33.

wanted a souvenir, but some were eager to obtain the relic of a martyr. Reports were published claiming that this blood had healing properties and was being used to cure sufferers from the King's Evil now that there was no king in England.[11] Whether keepsake, souvenir or holy relic, artefacts associated with Protestant victims of heroic death existed in a grey area of Protestant experience and theology, yet their presence and use reveals a fluidity within the tradition which allowed such disparate figures as Charles, Prynne, Bainham, Hullier and a host of others to partake of the same charisma of martyrdom.

What is particularly striking about the cult surrounding Charles is that from the point of view of imagery and typology, it was already fully formed by the time the axe fell on 30 January 1649. Within a week of that event the king's apologia, the *Eikon basilike*, was on sale in London, and through the course of the year thirty-nine editions were to stream off the presses of Royston, Grismond and Dugard, most containing a version of the famous frontispiece by William Marshall of Charles kneeling before an altar in a chapel bathed in a beam of heavenly light. In his right hand he grasped a crown of thorns, symbol of his 'passion', whilst at his feet was the crown of England, set aside as his gaze was now fixed upon the heavenly crown, the martyr's reward.[12]

Apart from the text of the *Eikon* itself, the edition published in mid-March 1649 included a dedicatory poem and an epitaph, and in the same month Henry King, bishop of Chichester, published *A deepe groan fetch'd at the funeral of that incomparable and glorious monarch, Charles the first*. King's collection of elegies was the first of a series of such commemorations which appeared within six months of the regicide; these included works by John Quarles and further elegies by King, as well as anonymous collections whose authors have variously been identified as John Cleveland, John Ashburnham and Montrose, which further repeated and disseminated an image of Charles as a suffering king and Christian martyr.[13] There were also a number of commemorative sermons preached on the theme of regicide within the first half of 1649, the earliest being delivered on 4 February, only five days after the regicide, by John Warner, bishop of Rochester.[14]

---

[11] *A miracle of miracles: wrought by the blood of King Charles the first, of happy memory, upon a mayd at Detford* (1649), STC [Wing] M2207. *Letter sent into France to the Lord Duke of Buckingham, his Grace: of a great miracle wrought by a piece of a handkerchefe dipped in His Majesties bloud* (1649), STC [Wing] J9. *A second letter to the Lord Duke of Buckingham, his Grace: at the court of France* (1649), STC [Wing] J11. Fragments of Charles's hair were also collected and treasured in lockets etc.

[12] Francis Madan, *A New Bibliography of the Eikon Basilike* (Oxford, 1950), Lacey, *Cult*, pp. 78–80

[13] Andrew Lacey, 'Elegies and Commemorative Verse in Honour of Charles the Martyr, 1649–60', in *The Regicides and the Execution of Charles I*, ed. Jason Peacey (Basingstoke, 2001), pp. 225–47.

[14] R. Brown (attr.), *The subjects sorrow: or, lamentations upon the death of Britaines Josiah, King Charles* (1649), STC [Wing] B5050. John Gauden *[Stratoste liteutikon]. A just invective against those of the army, and their abettors, who murthered King Charles I* (1649/1662), STC [Wing] G372. Henry Leslie, *The martyrdome of King Charles, or his conformity with Christ in his sufferings* (The Hague, 1649), STC [Wing] L1163, Eleasar Lotius, *A speech of Dr. Lotius, to King Charles, the second of that name, King of Great Brittaine etc.* (The Hague, 1649), STC [Wing] L3084. John Warner, *The devilish conspiracy, hellish treason, heathenish condemnation, and damnable murder, committed, and executed by the Jewes, against*

Apart from the speed with which cult material was available after the regicide there is also a high degree of consistency between the *Eikon*, the elegies and the sermons concerning the figure of Charles and the implications of his death. What one encounters throughout the genre is a discussion of the wars and the king which emphasises the parallels between the collective sufferings of the nation and the personal sufferings of the king. This suffering was caused not as a result of Charles's religious and economic policies in the 1630s but by the sins of the nation, which manifested themselves in faction and resistance towards an anointed monarch. In the midst of this turmoil of sin and rebellion stands Charles, secure in the assurance of a sound conscience and innocent of any fault; a king anointed by God, with the power to heal both the individual sufferer and the nation of their distempers. Charles is virtuous, chaste, pious, a good father, husband and master; he is a text we should read for our instruction in holiness and an example of holy living and Christian dying. He is paralleled with kings David and Josiah from the Old Testament and, in his piety, innocence and majesty with Christ himself.[15]

The royalist war effort had always been rooted in a sense of allegiance to the person of the king. This identification was encouraged through the use of the Royal Touch, the presentation of Charles as the embodiment of the 'good old laws' and through the image of suffering kingship associated with the period of confinement after 1646.[16] In particular the image of suffering kingship success-

---

the anointed of the Lord, Christ the king (1649), STC [Wing] W902. Richard Watson *Regicidium Judaicum: or, a discourse about the Jews crucifying Christ, their king* (1649), STC [Wing] W1093.

[15] The Christ–Charles parallel was always one of the more controversial aspects of the cult, summed up in Owen Felltham designation of Charles as 'Christ the second' with which this essay opens. Foxe was always ready to make the link between the experience of his victims and the passion of Christ, remarking that Laurence Saunders was sent by Bishop Bonner to the lord chancellor 'as Annas sente Christe to Caiphas: and lyke favoure founde Saunders, as Christe his mayster dyd before him' (*A&M [1563]*, p. 1039; the reference is to John 18: 24). For Foxe's concern to associate his martyrs with Christ's passion see the essay by Thomas Freeman in this volume.

[16] The political use of the royal touch was of major importance during the Civil Wars, proving that the king was still the Lord's anointed. A tract of 1643 suggested the parallel between the king's power to heal the scrofulous and his power to heal the nation of the 'disease' of rebellion. *The humble petition of divers hundreds of the king's poore subjects, afflicted with that grievous infirmitie, called the King's Evill* (1643), STC [Wing] T1521. John Browne. *Adenochoiradelogia: or, an anatomick-chirugical treatise of gladules and strumaes, or King's-Evil-swelling* (1684), STC [Wing] B5122. Browne's book was published in the wake of the Exclusion Crisis and was intended to support the royal cause. As such he takes the same line as the 1643 tract: the power of the Touch legitimates the ruler. See also R. Crawford, *The King's Evil* (Oxford, 1911), Marc Bloch, *The Royal Touch*, trans. J. E. Anderson (1973), J. Richards, "His Nowe Majestie" and the English Monarchy: The Kingship of Charles I before 1640', *Past and Present*, 113 (1986), pp. 70–96, D. J. Sturdy, 'The Royal Touch in England', in *European Monarchy: Its Evolution and Practice from Roman Antiquity to Modern Times*, ed. H. Duchhardt (Stuttgart, 1992), pp. 171–84, and Lacey, *Cult*, pp. 33–41, 60–6. It is also worth noting the scandal caused by the healings of Valentine Greatrakes in the 1660s, in particular his claim to heal the King's Evil. David Lloyd denounced Greatrakes in 1666, claiming that his presumption in exercising the royal Touch stemmed from the former Cromwellian soldier's desire to pull down Charles II, 'levelling his gift as well as they would his office', Eamon Duffy, 'Valentine Greatrakes, the Irish Stroker: Miracle, Science and Orthodoxy in Restoration England', in *Religion and Humanism*, ed. Keith Robbins, Studies in Church History 17 (Oxford, 1981), p. 264.

fully encouraged all those who hated or feared the victorious parliament and its radical allies to identify their sufferings with those of Charles. Conrad Russell has argued that Charles had always been more successful in sustaining a party than in leading a nation; certainly this insight explains a great deal about the period 1645–9 and the nature of the cult itself.[17] To his followers and sympathisers Charles became an icon and representative of the suffering nation, a Christ-like figure suffering for his people and one able to claim, with some justification, that he was a true 'martyr for his people'. It was an image capable of surviving the negative propaganda of *The king's cabinet opened*, Charles's propensity for dissembling and his engagement with the Scots.[18] But it was an image which also reflected Charles's inability to compromise with or trust those whose loyalty he had come to doubt; consequently he appeared untrustworthy in negotiations because he felt no obligation in conscience to honour his word given under duress to schematics and rebels. Rather, his actions were based upon the absolute demands of sovereign conscience and therefore must, by definition, be correct and command the obedience of duty and conscience from his subjects. Such a view offered only two alternatives: one either submitted to this sovereign conscience or one rebelled, either one recognised the demands of conscience personified in the king, and all that such a recognition entailed, or one rejected it. Charles's own self-perception – the black-and-white world of sovereign conscience – enabled him to create and sustain a royalist party, but it also ensured that the divisions and conflicts within the wider society would be impossible to heal. This 'party' nature of royalism became both the great short-term strength and the fundamental long-term weakness of the cult.

The concept of government Charles defended had been learnt from the manuals of instruction, such as *Basilikon doron* and *A meditation upon the . . . XXVII chapter of Matthew*, written by his father. James taught that the king was the father of his people and that government was an ethical activity centred upon the conscience of the monarch. Charles had always believed that good government was based upon a sound conscience and as his position deteriorated rapidly after Naseby conscience was to become his watchword. In his frequent references to the death of Strafford he readily accused himself of allowing expediency to override conscience, as he put it in the *Eikon*,

> I was persuaded by those that I think wished me well to choose rather what was safe than what seemed just, preferring the outward peace of my kingdoms with me before that inward exactness of conscience before God.[19]

[17] Conrad Russell, *The causes of the English Civil War: The Ford Lectures Delivered in the University of Oxford 1987–88* (Oxford, 1990), pp. 185–211.

[18] For a more detailed discussion of the period 1646–8 see Robert Ashton, *Counter-Revolution: The Second Civil War and its Origins, 1646–48* (1994).

[19] *Eikon Basilike. The Portraiture of His Sacred Majesty in His Solitudes and Sufferings*, ed. P. A. Knachel (Ithaca, NY, 1966), p. 7. The word conscience/s appears around 112 times in the *Eikon*. Such views of conscience were not, however, peculiar to Charles but were a commonplace of devotional

For a man as unsure of himself as Charles, the appeal to sovereign conscience provided a fixed point and guiding principle which could be clung to when all around seemed uncertain and confused. It is not surprising that Charles should have commissioned and even worked upon a translation of Sanderson's book on oaths, *De juramento*, as Sanderson argued eloquently that external peace could not be bought at the price of ignoring one's conscience.[20]

In his responses to the various peace proposals put forward by parliament and the army, Charles consistently refused to abandon what he considered the three most important trusts in his charge, namely his prerogatives, his Church and his friends. To do so would be to repeat the sin of betrayal he committed against Strafford. In 1647, when Charles contemplated allowing the establishment of Presbyterianism in England for a limited period, he first consulted Hammond, Duppa and Bramhall as to the propriety of such a move and whether he could do so in conscience; it was only after gaining their assurances that he was prepared to proceed with the negotiations.

Just as the betrayal of Strafford had been a sin against his conscience, so the experience of Civil War was in part a punishment for that sin. In the same way, the collective sins of the nation had led the country into war and rebellion. In prayers published at the king's command during the first Civil War it was made clear that in his view the wars had nothing to do with the controversies over Charles's civil and religious policies during the 1630s, but everything to do with God's anger at the sins of the people. Thus in prayers appointed to be used on fast days in 1643 the link between national sins and the Civil War was made plain in a collect where the people petitioned that 'in the continued scourge of this wasting rebellion, we may well perceive, that the sinnes we have done have not been barely infirmities, but rebellions against thee'.[21] In the prayer published to coincide with the negotiations over the treaty of Uxbridge in 1644, prayers 'drawn by His Majesties special direction and dictates', Charles was compared to Moses

> Who standeth in the gap beseeching thee to turn thine anger from the
> people; remember what he hath suffer'd, and the heavy things that thou

teaching and casuistry. Ralph Cudworth, in a sermon before the Commons in 1647, was being entirely orthodox when he proclaimed that 'a good conscience within, will be alwayes better to a Christian, than health to his navell, and marrow to his bones; it will be an everlasting cordiall to his heart; it will be softer to him than a bed of doune, and he may sleep securely upon it, in the midst of raging and tempestuous seas, when the winds bluster, and the waves beat round about him. A good conscience, is the best looking-glasse of heaven; in which the soul may see God's thoughts and purposes concerning it, as so many shining starres reflected to it'. Ralph Cudworth, *A sermon preached before the honourable House of Commons at Westminster* (1647), pp. 12–13 (STC [Wing] C7469). Charles, in custody at Holdenby or Newmarket, would have entirely concurred with these sentiments and Cudworth's image of the secure conscience standing firm amidst storm and tempest suggests the emblem of the rock buffeted by the stormy sea found in Marshall's frontispiece to the *Eikon*. It is also worth noting that in Charles's hope that his death would expiate his guilt in allowing the death of Strafford he reflected Cranmer's hope that his death would expiate the guilt of those Protestants persecuted by him in the reign of Henry VIII.

[20] Carlton, *Charles I*, p. 331. See also my forthcoming essay on the *Eikon basilike* and traditions of casuistry.

[21] *A forme of Common-prayer* (Oxford, 1643), p. 37.

hast shewn him; and in the day, when thou makest inquisition for bloud, forget not his desire of peace, the endeavours which he hath used, and the prayers which he hath made to thee for it. Return all this, O Lord, with comfort into his bosome.[22]

This prayer created a pivotal role for the king as advocate, intermediary and, like Moses, the chosen one who was privileged to speak directly with the Lord. It was precisely in the role of intermediary that Charles posited the dictates of sovereign conscience, for all men knew in their hearts that such a role was his and his alone by birth and anointing. Therefore those who fought against him must either be deluded in their conscience or have suppressed what they knew to be true. The fast-day prayers for 1643, which reminded those who used them of the cost of national sins, begged the Lord 'to strike the mindes of the perverse, with a true touch of that conscience, which they goe about to stifle', a phrase repeated in a form of prayer published in the same year to give thanks for royalist victories.[23] Such a view of his enemies allowed Charles to feel assured in his own conscience whilst creating the impression that he pitied his poor deluded subjects in arms against him. This pity allowed him to appear as the concerned father of wayward and stubborn children and, in a Christ-like gesture of forgiveness, to pardon his enemies when he came to the scaffold.

As royalist victories turned to defeats in 1645 royalist writings began to stress the virtues of patient endurance, constancy in a just cause, the bonds of friendship and the pleasures of retirement; they also sought to defend the person of Charles, rather then merely the institution of monarchy, from attack. Thomas Browne's defence of Charles occasioned by the publication of his captured papers in *The king's cabinet opened* is a case in point. Browne and other royalists realised that the *Cabinet* represented a shift in the propaganda war and that from that time on the malignant finger of rebellion would be pointed at Charles himself. Browne argued that rather than condemning Charles, the publication of his papers provided the opportunity for his subjects to see for themselves how fine their king was, and that to read the *Cabinet* was a privileged insight into the king's very thoughts. The same point was made two years later by Edward Symmons, who remarked that Charles's writings constituted his 'gospell', perusal of which would convert the most hardened of adversaries to his cause.[24]

If the *Cabinet* established the power of the king's private word, a power vindicated in the publication of the *Eikon*, so another event of the disastrous year 1645 also presaged future events for the royalists: namely the execution on 10 January of Archbishop Laud after four years in the Tower. Laud's death provided an example of the possible fate awaiting defeated royalists as well as a salutary lesson in how to prepare for and face such an eventuality.

---

[22] *A forme of Common-prayer* (Oxford, 1644), p. 12.
[23] *A forme of Common-prayer* (Oxford, 1643), p. 65.
[24] Wilcher, *Royalism*, p. 241. Edward Symmons, *The king's most gracious messages for peace* (1648), STC [Wing] S6344, sig. a3v.

Laud was, according to Berkenhead, 'the king's and church's martyr', and as Robert Wilcher observed, the presentation of Laud's trial and execution provided 'a model for the royalist management of the more spectacular martyrdom of Charles Stuart in 1649'.[25] Charles's predicament was now presented as representative of the kingdom: as the king suffered, so the kingdom suffered; as the various factions refused to respond to Charles's offers of peace so the nation continued to suffer arbitrary rule and confusion. In a poem of 1647, attributed to Roger L'Estrange, the poet assumed the character of an imprisoned royalist whose personal sufferings were transformed by identification with the sufferings of his king and who gloried in the fact that 'a good conscience is my bail/ And innocence my liberty'.[26] In Nedham's one-act play published in 1646 entitled *The Leveller levell'd*, the narrator asked

> O England, dost thou yet want eyes to see
> How many rogues are digging graves for thee?
> Doth not thy very heart consume with paine,
> When thou considerest thy soveraigne
> Even with chaines unto the earth is held,
> His sufferings being unparalleld?
> Seest thou not his religious constancy,
> His patience, care and zealous piety,
> And canst thou still give credit to these elves,
> Who suck thy bloud for to make fat themselves.[27]

This identification allowed the royalists to insist that only when the king was restored to his rightful place would peace and prosperity return to England, a point John Arnway had neatly summed up the previous year in a pamphlet entitled *No peace 'till the king prosper*.[28] The volume of such writings rose to a

[25] Wilcher, *Royalism*, pp. 232, 233.
[26] Roger L'Estrange, 'The Liberty and Requiem of an Imprisoned Royalist', in *Parnassus biceps or several choice pieces of poetry (1656)*, ed. G. Thorn-Drury (1927), pp. 107–10. The attribution of the poem to L'Estrange and its date of composition is discussed by C. H. Wilkinson in *The Poems of Richard Lovelace* (Oxford, 1930), pp. 276–86, together with its relation to Lovelace's 'To Althea, from prison'. 'The Liberty and Requiem' was reprinted in 1649 in *Vaticinum votivum* (STC [Wing] W3206) a collection of poems and elegies on the regicide. Edward Symmons had made a similar point two years previously when, in *Scripture vindicated*, he reminded his readers that their king was 'under the same burden of persecution with us for our bloudy Domitians scorne to spend their time onely in hurting small flyes, it is the royall eagle who they spight most, as being he who hath most of God upon him, we are but like the disciples of our Saviour, that suffer for our relation and love to him'; Edward Symmons, *Scripture vindicated from the misapprehensions, misinterpretations and misapplications of Mr Stephen Marshall* (Oxford, 1645), STC [Wing] S6348, p. 88.
[27] Marchamont Nedham, *The Levellers levell'd* (1647), STC [Wing] N394, p. 4. The author is already considering the possibility of Charles's death, for the play ends with the prayer 'Let heaven showre upon his head/ The blessings of the day,/ And when his soule is thither fled/ Grant that his sonne may sway', p. 14.
[28] John Arnway, *No peace 'till the king prosper. A letter writ from a true lover of peace, to one that is both, modestly inquiring, and discovering the true and false paths to a present peace* (Oxford, 1645), STC [Wing] A3734. Arnway summed up the general war-weariness of the period and the way this was annexed to the king's cause when he declares that 'He is a block, a stone, not a man, a Christian, that is not weary of warre and greedy of peace' (p. 2).

crescendo during 1647 and 1648 with widespread popular opposition to the army and parliament. The outbreak of the second Civil War encouraged many to hope that the king might again have the military option at his disposal. Royalists such as Paul Knell and Edward Symmons, Presbyterians like William Prynne and 'reformed' Independents like William Sedgwick all denounced the continued imprisonment of the king and, after the army's victories in the autumn of 1648, became increasingly concerned that he might be murdered. Even the army's own *Remonstrance* acknowledged the power of the king's presence, his rising popularity and the threat this posed to their victories.

One such tract produced in 1647 (Thomason records obtaining his copy on 28 June), *His Majesties complaint to his subjects*, purports to be a meditation by Charles on his recent experience of imprisonment by the Scots in Newcastle, by the parliament at Holdenby and, since the beginning of the month, by the army at Newmarket after his abduction by Cornet Joyce. Sidney Gottlieb has suggested that the poem was significant not only for the insight it affords into the construction of the image of the royal martyr, but also for the uses of George Herbert's poetry during the Civil War, for *His Majesties complaint* was based upon Herbert's *Sacrifice.*[29] According to Thomas Herbert, Charles admired George Herbert's poetry, he being one of the authors Charles read in captivity, so it seems appropriate that it was Herbert's poetry which was adapted to present Charles as an innocent and suffering king, unjustly condemned and sacrificed by his rebellious subjects, a king who walked patiently in the footsteps of his Saviour. As such the *Complaint* prefigured the *Eikon* and, as Gottlieb reminds us, was part of the process of composition with which Charles had been engaged since 1642. Both the *Complaint* and the *Eikon* shared a similar chronological pattern; both sought to vindicate the king's motives, both used an epideictic technique to arouse sympathy for the king and both invoked the Christ–Charles parallel. As such the *Complaint* was an important part of the process by which the *Eikon*, like other aspects of the cult, did not appear out of nowhere.

The following year Edward Symmons published two works that are of major importance in the prehistory of the cult. *The king's most gracious messages for peace, and a personal treaty* presented Charles as the protagonist of peace and settlement who was frustrated by the ruthlessness and self-seeking of the rebels. His other work, *A vindication of King Charles: or, a loyal subjects duty*, was a lengthy reply to parliament's *The king's cabinet opened*, and attempted to limit the damage caused by parliament's exposure of Charles's double-dealings. Both these tracts included the familiar recitation of royalist political theology, with substantial sections on the personal qualities of Charles and his identification with the sufferings of his people. Significantly Symmons also detailed the numerous parallels between Charles's predicament and the passion of Christ; indeed this parallel is presented on the title page of the *Vindication*, which advertised

[29] S. Gottlieb, 'A royalist rewriting of George Herbert: His Majesties complaint to his subjects (1647)', *Modern Philology*, 89 (1991), pp. 211–24.

Symmons's intention to add 'a true parallel betwixt the sufferings of our Saviour and our soveraign, in divers particulars'.[30] In *Messages for peace* Symmons addressed the reader directly when he asked

> Have you no feelings of his sufferings? No share in his sorrows? Is it not for your sake that he endures all these hard and heavy things? Can there be named any other reason for them than because he will not yield you up to be slaves and bond men?[31]

This is an early example, already noted in the *Complaint*, of using epideictic rhetoric to focus attention exclusively on the personal qualities of Charles and the pathos of his predicament as a way of arousing sympathy and admiration in the reader or listener. Epideictic techniques were to become central to cult literature as it removed the necessity to consider the constitutional and political issues involved. Charles became the image and type of a Christian hero and martyr and, as such, his motives and actions were beyond reproach.[32]

By late 1648 even the army was aware that the threat of Charles's rising popularity posed a threat to its recent victories. The *Remonstrance* of November detailed the ways in which Charles was increasingly seen by the people as an innocent and suffering victim, whilst from the Presbyterian camp came many shrill condemnations of the radicalism and independency of the army and its civilian allies.[33] In retrospect the death bed repentance of the Scottish Presbyterian Alexander Henderson was of particular use to the royalists, for he confirmed the central argument of royalist propaganda when he said that the disappointments and indignities Charles was obliged to endure as a result of his captivity only served to make ever more apparent 'his undaunted courage and transcendent wisdom', and warned against the growing threat of anarchy which must accompany the continuing failure to reach a settlement with the king.[34]

Most of these themes were summed up in the writings of William Sedgwick in late 1648 and early 1649. If we are to believe Sedgwick, he claimed that he had been both an Independent and a soldier, a man who had shared in the good old

---

[30] Edward Symmons, *A vindication of King Charles* (1648), title page (STC [Wing] S6350).
[31] Edward Symmons, *The king's most gracious messages for peace* (1648), p. 107 (STC [Wing] S6344). As already mentioned, Symmons refers to Charles's various offers of negotiation as 'his majesties gospell to his people', thus equating Charles's word with those of Christ. This was a theme taken up by Paul Knell in three sermons published in London in 1648. Knell takes as his text the parable of the wicked tenants (Luke 20: 12–20), a text usually glossed as foretelling the rejection of Christ by Israel. The parable was included in the Office for 30 January annexed to the *Book of Common Prayer* in 1662.
[32] It may be an early example but not the first; Symmons himself in *Scripture vindicated* had warned that those who remained loyal to Charles could expect martyrdom from the 'Pharisees and Sadducees', the use of such titles in relation to the rebels prefiguring their identification as the rebellious Jews who murdered Christ their king. Symmons, *Scripture vindicated*, p. 89.
[33] *A remonstrance of His Excellency Thomas Lord Fairfax* (1648) (STC [Wing] F229), p. 37. V. Elliot, 'The Quarrel of the Covenant: The London Presbyterians and the Regicide', in *The Regicides*, pp. 202–24.
[34] *Memoirs of the two last years of that unparallell'd prince, of ever blessed memory, King Charles I* (1702), p. 226.

cause 'with as much exactness, faithfulness, power and comfort as any of you'. He now repudiated the army and wrote in favour of the king and settlement; indeed, in a phrase which sums up the argument of this essay and stands at its head, he declared that 'I confesse his sufferings make me a royalist that never cared for him', for

> the people of England desire peace, settled religion, establisht truth, freedome of trade and this with his Majesty, under their king, that he may govern them according to their honest and knowne laws, that they may live in prosperity and honour.

The chief threat to prosperity and honour by 1648 lay with the army, which sought to exploit the continuing confusion to make itself supreme.[35]

The importance of Sedgwick lies in the way he took the royalist commonplace of suffering kingship and developed it into a fully fledged example of Christian martyrdom. Charles's sanctity was revealed in his weakness, which became his true source of strength. As he was stripped of worldly power so the attractiveness of his divine nature was revealed to those with eyes to see. It was the inversion of worldly values present in all Christian sacrifice and in the Catholic belief that God had a special regard for the humble and meek and repudiated the vainglorious and powerful: that in losing one's life, one gained it. In the circumstances of late 1648 Charles had been humbled, 'he is coming downe, you [the grandees] and others are getting up. He is falling, you rising. He is a sufferer, you inflictors of sufferings.' Therefore, the greater Charles's humiliation, the more acceptable he became to God and the more sympathy he evoked from those not blinded by ambition, treason or ideology. As Sedgwick put it in a passage redolent with cult symbolism and typology,

> The more you crush him, the sweeter savour comes from him, and while he suffers the spirit of God and glory rest upon him. There is a sweeter glory sparkling in him by suffering, though you see it not. You do but rend away his corruptions from him, and help to wast his drosse and draw forth that hidden excellency that is in him, and naturally men are ready to pity sufferers ... He that doth and can suffer shall have my heart, you had it whilst you suffered, now you are great and need it not; the poore suffering oppressed king and his party have my compassion.[36]

Sedgwick may not have originated the Christ–Charles parallel, nor the idea of suffering kingship, nevertheless he fashioned the image of Charles as a Christian martyr more fully than any other royalist writer, and published his work whilst the trial was in progress. In such circumstances parallels between Charles before Bradshaw and Christ before Pilate were not far-fetched.

At this point it is necessary to say something more about the *Eikon basilike*, as

---

[35] William Sedgwick, *Justice upon the Armie remonstrance* (1649), STC [Wing] S2384, pp. 12, 31, 9.
[36] Sedgwick, *Justice*, pp. 45, 30–1.

it was undoubtedly this little book, and the frontispiece by William Marshall, which more than anything else confirmed Charles as a saint and martyr in the eyes of many and established the image of the martyr for succeeding generations. The success of the *Eikon* depended on its authority as the word of the king; whilst reading it one could become intimate with Charles's hopes and fears.[37] It also confirmed that with the death of the king the cult became almost exclusively literary and text-based, mediated through elegies, sermons and, of course, the *Eikon* itself. The failure of the healing relics associated with Charles only served to underline this fact, and Charles was consistently presented as a text to be read and an example to be followed rather than as a conduit of intercessary prayer and healing; as Thomas Forde put it, Charles was 'the best of texts'.[38] In this sense the cult conformed to the Foxean model which was patristic but devoid of the Catholic aspects associated with relics and intercession; instead Charles was presented as a shining example of the Protestant doctrine of sanctification.

What was to become the *Eikon basilike* of February 1649 had a long gestation. Charles had indicated as early as 1642 that he wished to write a vindication of himself and his cause, and certainly some early drafts were among the papers of the king captured at Naseby in June 1645. But it was the period of captivity at Holdenby and Hampton Court in 1647 that gave Charles the opportunity to work consistently on his apologia, particularly after the papers captured at Naseby were returned. What transformed the creative process was the defeat of the royalist uprisings in the autumn of 1648, the removal of the king from the Isle of Wight to Hurst Castle in December and the realisation that the army meant to bring him to trial. If the king's writings were to help his cause then they had to be made available as quickly as possible. Now the purpose of the work also changed; until the end of 1648 Charles's writings had been seen as part of the propaganda battle for hearts and minds, but after Pride's Purge these writings became the apologia of a potential martyr. As Robert Wilcher remarked, by January 1649 'those closest to the king had bowed to the inevitable and were already planning a propaganda coup that would transform the execution into a martyrdom'.[39] This may explain why Gauden added the chapter 'Meditations upon death' to the final version, why the suggested title *Suspiria Regalia, or, the royal plea* was changed at the last minute to the *Eikon basilike* and why Marshall's famous frontispiece was inserted. From being a defeated king pleading with his earthly subjects Charles was transformed into a glorious martyr in heaven.[40]

[37] Kevin Sharpe has some interesting things to say about the significance of royal authorship in 'The King's Writ: Royal Authors and Royal Authority in Early Modern England', in *Culture and Politics in Early Stuart England*, ed. Kevin Sharpe and Peter Lake (Basingstoke, 1994), pp. 117–38, and 'Private Conscience and Public Duty in the Writings of Charles I', *Historical Journal*, 40 (1997), pp. 643–65.
[38] Thomas Forde, 'Second anniversary on Charles the first, 1658', in *Virtus deviviva* (1661), STC [Wing] F1549, p. 34.
[39] Robert Wilcher, 'What was the King's Book for?: The Evolution of Eikon Basilike', *Yearbook of English Studies*, 21 (1991), pp. 218–28. See also his *The Writing of Royalism 1628–1660* (Cambridge, 2001), ch. 10.
[40] Francis Madan, *New Bibliography*, pp. 126–63.

William Sancroft, writing to Richard Holdsworth a month after the regicide asking him to acquire six copies of the *Eikon*, remarked on their cost, commenting that 'if they be Royston's, they will be above six shillings'.[41] The cost of Royston's editions reflected the trouble and danger he faced in producing them. His first attempts to publish the manuscript with the printer Grismond were interrupted by the authorities until he moved his presses out of London. It was under these conditions that the first edition of the *Eikon* was produced, coinciding with the king's burial. It was at this point that Royston was arrested for the first time, being summoned to appear before the Council of State and imprisoned for fifteen days. However, this did not deter him: his presses were moved back to Ivy Lane and he continued to print the *Eikon* throughout February and March.

March also witnessed an edition produced by William Dugard, the headmaster of the Merchant Taylors school, who had a press in a house adjacent to his school. Dugard appeared to have received a copy of the manuscript from Edward Symmons via his proofreader Edward Hooker. Dugard's March edition enlarged on that of Royston's by including four prayers of the king used in his confinement, his reasons for refusing the jurisdiction of the High Court of Justice, the letter of the prince of Wales written from The Hague, the *Relations* of the Princess Elizabeth and the duke of Gloucester of their last meeting with their father and the *Epitaph* attributed to James Howell. Hooker also compiled the *Apophthegmata* for this edition, a collection of sayings compiled from the text of the *Eikon*.

The result of all this activity was Dugard's arrest on 16 March and the seizure of most of his stock. But Dugard was not to spend long in prison as the Council of State seemed keen to defuse the situation by releasing him almost immediately. They used, as an excuse, the fact that the four prayers of the king had been licensed by Cranford, the censor, who was made the scapegoat for the affair and dismissed. Dugard's confinement was so short that in early April he was back at Merchant Taylors reprinting the confiscated March edition.

Meanwhile, in the spring of 1649, Royston, undaunted by his brush with the authorities, produced the *Henderson papers*, Charles's debates with Alexander Henderson in 1646 concerning Church government. For this Royston was again summoned before the Council and reprimanded, an experience which seemed to have had some effect as he did not produce another copy of the *Eikon* that year. However, others continued the literary assault on the republic; during the summer Dugard produced a copy of Hooker's *Apophthegmata* for inclusion in John Williams's Latin version of the *Eikon* and Williams continued to produce miniature versions of the *Eikon*, designed for easy concealment, throughout the summer and autumn of 1649.

In September the authorities responded to the growth of royalist printing by passing an ordinance censoring the press and, in the following month, and despite

---

[41] Letter: Sancroft to Holdsworth 27.2.1649, in H. Cary, *Memorials of the Great Civil War in England from 1646–1652*, vol. II (1842), p. 126.

Royston's printing reticence after the *Henderson papers*, he and Grismond were again summoned before the Council. This time Royston's good behaviour was encouraged by the imposition of two sureties of £500. In December John Williams was arrested and imprisoned in the Gatehouse and during February 1650 Dugard was also arrested and imprisoned in Newgate. Whilst Williams's confinement was of a very short duration, Dugard evidently decided that the risks involved in publishing the *Eikon* were too great, for in April he submitted to the Council, who rewarded him by making him their printer, in which capacity he produced Milton's *Pro populo Anglicano defensio*. As well as the *Eikon*, 1650 witnessed the publication in The Hague of *Reliquiae sacrae Carolinae*, the collected works of Charles I, containing letters and speeches by the king bound with the *Eikon*, together with commemorative poems and elegies. This work, produced jointly by Royston and John Williams, went through five English editions between 1650 and 1658 before being reprinted by Royston in a splendid folio edition in 1662.[42]

One of the strengths of the *Eikon* was that it operated on a variety of levels and presented a variety of themes. On one level it was simply a memoir, a retelling, from the king's perspective, of the narrative of the 1640s. This narrative was not presented in chronological order; the account of the Irish rebellion does not appear until chapter twelve and the discussion of the Scottish Covenant is reserved for chapter fourteen. Yet Charles's intention in preparing the book was to achieve more than simply a memoir of the wars. It is often forgotten that Charles never lived to witness the success of his book. With thirty-nine English editions in 1649 alone, of which three were printed in the Netherlands and one in France, as well as twenty foreign language editions including Dutch, Latin, French and German, the *Eikon* was, after the scriptures and the *Book of Common Prayer*, the most successful English book of the century.

Apart from the full editions of the text, numerous sections of the book were printed separately, particularly the prayers and meditations at the end of each chapter and the last two chapters of the book, the 'Letter to the Prince of Wales', and 'Meditations upon death'. Parts of the text were also set to music; in 1653, Thomas Stanley used themes from the *Eikon* as the basis for a series of meditations for three voices and organ called *Psalterium Carolinum*. Taken together with Royston's and Williams's editions of the *Reliquiae* these works achieved what John Kenyon called 'a mixture of pietistic moralising and shrewd historical revisionism' that inspired the fledgling republic to commission Milton to produce a refutation of the *Eikon*.[43] This he did in October 1649 in *Eikonoklastes*, but it has to be said that the response failed to dent the reputation of the martyr.

I have undertaken a detailed analysis of the significance of the *Eikon* elsewhere

---

[42] The Royston edition of 1662 was renamed *Basilika. The Works of Charles I* (STC [Wing] C2075).
[43] John Kenyon, *Stuart England*, 2nd edn (1985), p. 178. It is also worth mentioning other collections of speeches and writings attributed to Charles such as *The princely pelican* (1649), STC [Wing] P3491.

and I do not intend to repeat it here.[44] Suffice it to say that in looking to his Saviour and to traditions of martyrdom for 'a magazine of religious patterns' Charles learnt his part well; hoping that, as the closing words of the *Eikon* has it, 'vota dabunt, quae bella negarunt' ('prayers will give those things which wars have denied'). Like all actors, royal or otherwise, whose art is essentially public, Charles was well aware that the acid test of his constancy and fortitude would occur during the public spectacle of the trial and execution; in the event Charles turned this aspect of his 'passion' into something of a triumph, surprising both his judges and, possibly, himself in the process. The *Eikon* was another such performance on a public stage and, if the number of editions is an indication, a highly successful one. Charles realised, along with Symmons and Sedgwick, that he could save his reputation by losing his life.

Yet the success of the *Eikon* is ironic given that it purported to be the private thoughts and reflections of a very private king. The intimacy of the contents contrasted with their publication in the market place where they were available to all and sundry. Such a tension between the public and the private had always existed in royalist uses of the king, and can be seen in Symmons's suggestion that we can know the king through reading his word, his 'gospell'. Likewise the use of the *Eikon* partakes of this same tension, for the book purchased in the market place is read in the closet. The words of the king are available to us in the privacy of our own room and we indeed feel the privilege of intimacy with the king, an intimacy normally denied to even the most trusted of courtiers.

This ambiguity between the public and the private reflects the ambiguities of Charles's claim to be a true martyr, a claim hotly contested at the time and since. Yet it is significant, as I hope this chapter has demonstrated, that the image of martyrdom was present from the beginnings of the conflict and reflected, on one level, Charles's inability to play the politician. For him government was not the art of the possible but the art of what was right, and what was right was what was compatible with his conscience. Charles could speak of being either a glorious king or a patient martyr because this removed the necessity of playing the political game and taking responsibility for the evasions and compromises such a game demands. Also, images of constancy and martyrdom in the Bible, the Prayer Book and in Foxe, as well as the greatest act of voluntary death, that of Christ on the cross, were always available to Charles and his contemporaries as examples, or patterns, of conduct.

In a society moulded by the imagery of the word it was inevitable that all sides in the conflict should use imagery and language derived from these common sources both to articulate their hopes and fears and to try to make sense of the momentous events happening around them. The difference between Charles and the other martyrs discussed in this book was that he was an anointed king: and in the midst of war, revolution, anxiety and fear, the sight of an innocent and

---

[44] Lacey, *Cult*, and in my forthcoming 'Texts to be Read: Charles I and the *Eikon Basilike*'.

suffering king being judged and led out to die for his people was so reminiscent of Christ's passion that the exaggerated comparisons were probably inevitable. But if there is a political theology underpinning this cult it is more political than theological. A theology of sacred monarchy, radical innocence and losing ones life to save it takes second place to a political conflict over sovereignty, legitimacy and accountability. As such the cult of Charles I is martyrology as politics. Charles himself was fully aware of the political capital to be gained by using his own body as a weapon in the conflict. Whilst all martyrdom partakes of a political aspect, nevertheless, the Foxean tradition was still founded upon a theological and ecclesiastical conflict between Catholics and Protestants, and it was primarily theological heresy which led Foxe's victims to their deaths. But as Milton pointed out, Charles was not condemned because he was a Protestant but because he was a tyrant who had waged war on his people; a political crime rather than a theological heresy.[45]

Whilst it is anachronistic to speculate whether Charles believed himself to be walking in the footsteps of the saints and martyrs, what is not open to question is the power of the traditions of martyrology available to Charles and the royalists. To the likes of Sedgwick, Symmons and Charles himself, his constancy and sufferings had already won him the title of martyr; all the army and its allies did on 30 January 1649 was to remove any doubt as to the application of that title by supplying the corpus of typology, political theology and popular myth with a corpse.

Therefore the origins of the cult lay in the meeting of a political theology of sacred monarchy and suffering kingship centred on the person of Charles with popular needs and sensibilities. In the three and a half years between his military defeat at Naseby and his death, and despite his own propensity for political ineptitude, double-dealing and evasion, the king and increasing numbers of his subjects had the opportunity to identify themselves with this political theology. Therein lies the reason why the corpus of themes and images associated with the cult were identified and made available before Charles went to his death. Therein also lies the reason why the image of the royal martyr, and the political theology that supported it, was to become such a potent symbol in the struggle against the republic and in the Restoration Church. As Gilbert Burnet observed in retrospect, Charles's 'serious and Christian deportment' in death 'made all his former errours be entirely forgot, and raised a compassionate regard to him, that drew a lasting hatred on the actors, and was the true occasion on the great turn of the nation in the year 1660'.[46]

---

[45] John Milton, *Eikonoklastes in answer to a book intitl'ed Eikon Basilike* (1649), STC [Wing] M2112, p. 175.
[46] Gilbert Burnet, *Bishop Burnet's history of his own time*, vol. I (1724), p. 50.

10

The Martyrdom of Sir Henry Vane the Younger: from Apocalyptic Witness to Heroic Whig*

JOHN COFFEY

On 2 June 1662, Sir Henry Vane the younger was brought to trial on a charge of high treason. Vane was not a regicide, but as a brilliant civilian politician with a strong appeal to radical puritans, he was perceived to be a dangerous focus of dissent. With the new Restoration regime committed to eliminating him, Vane was found guilty on 6 June, and five days later sentenced to death. Imprisoned in the Tower of London, he awaited his fate. At midnight on Friday 13th, the sheriff's chaplain came to tell him of the order for his execution the next day. Unperturbed, Vane slept soundly through the night. In the morning, he prayed with his wife, his children and some friends, and prepared himself for the journey to the place of execution on Tower Hill. Having never lost his aristocratic taste for sartorial elegance, he dressed in a black suit and coat, but added a touch of flair. Underneath his suit, but clearly visible, he wore a striking silk waistcoat, scarlet in colour. On his way to the scaffold, bystanders shouted words of encouragement from windows and the tops of houses, crying out 'The Lord go with you, The great God of heaven and earth appear in you and for you'. Vane acknowledged their cries, taking off his hat and bowing. When asked how he was, he answered, 'Never better in all my life'.[1]

On coming to the scaffold, Vane appeared so strangely calm that many assumed he was an onlooker rather than the condemned man. When the sheriff commanded that there be silence, Vane lifted his hands and his eyes to heaven, then rested his hands on the rails, looked out on the great multitude before him and began his speech. He was constantly interrupted by the sheriff and by trumpets, and the guards confiscated notes from onlookers who tried to record his

---

* For helpful comments on this paper I am particularly grateful to Tom Freeman and Gai Ferdon, and to members of the Cambridge Historical Society who responded to a much earlier version. The British Academy provided research funding for the project.

[1] *The Tryal of Sir Henry Vane, Kt* (1662), STC [Wing] T2216, pp. 82–5; [George Sikes], *The Life and Death of Sir Henry Vane* (1662), STC [Wing] S6323C, p. 123.

words. But Vane persevered, relating the story of his life, describing his spiritual conversion and declaring that he was pouring out his blood as a witness and a seal to the good old cause. His speech over, he knelt at the executioner's block, betraying no sign of trembling or shaking. When the axe fell, one observer ('an ancient Traveller') claimed that Vane's severed head – unlike others he had seen – lay perfectly still, suggesting that 'his Death was by the free consent and act of his mind'.[2] Samuel Pepys, who attended the execution, recorded that Vane 'appeared the most resolved man that ever died in that manner'. His performance on the scaffold remained a talking point in the capital for the rest of the month, with Pepys reporting that 'the Courage of Sir H. Vane at his death is talked on everywhere as a miracle'.[3] As Gilbert Burnet later noted, 'it was generally thought the government had lost more than it had gained by his death'.[4]

Vane had performed the role of martyr to perfection. His resolution, courage, calmness and indifference to death contributed greatly to contemporaries' perception of him as a martyr for the Good Old Cause.[5] Contemporary conceptions of martyrdom laid great weight on the Stoic quality of *apatheia*,[6] and on the Christian virtue of patient endurance.[7] Vane, the aristocratic puritan, faced his death as noble Roman and Christian saint.

This chapter will explore the mentality of Sir Henry Vane the martyr. It will suggest that he invested his execution with apocalyptic significance, and that this helps to explain the 'miracle' of his courage. But it will also examine the ways in which Vane was memorialised as a martyr for liberty, arguing that those who celebrated him as a Whig champion effectively secularised him by overlooking his millenarian mindset.

I

By any reckoning, Vane the Younger is one of the most remarkable and shadowy figures in the English Revolution.[8] In contrast to most puritan politicians, he came from an aristocratic family. The decisive event in his early life was his puritan conversion experience in the late 1620s. It turned Vane into a teenage non-

---

[2] *The Tryal of Sir Henry Vane*, pp. 86–96.

[3] *The Diary of Samuel Pepys*, ed. R. Latham and W. Matthews, 11 vols (1970–83), III, pp. 109, 112. Further references to conversations about Vane's death are found on pp. 116, 117, 127.

[4] G. Burnet, *History of His Own Times*, ed. O. Airy, 2 vols (Oxford, 1897), I, p. 286.

[5] On the positive impression made by the regicides at their executions see Laura Lunger Knoppers, *Historicizing Milton: Spectacle, Power and Poetry in Restoration England* (Athens, GA, 1994), pp. 47–8.

[6] See Patrick Collinson, ' "A magazine of religious patterns": An Erasmian Topic Transposed in English Protestantism', in *Godly People* (London, 1983), pp. 511–13; Thomas S. Freeman, 'The Importance of Dying Earnestly: The Metamorphosis of the Account of James Bainham in Foxe's ' "Book of Martyrs" ', in *The Church Retrospective*, ed. R. N. Swanson, Studies in Church History 23 (Woodbridge, 1997), pp. 267–88.

[7] See Brad Gregory, *Salvation at Stake: Christian Martyrdom in Early Modern Europe* (Cambridge, MA, 1999), pp. 50ff.

[8] The best short biographies of Vane are by C. H. Firth (*DNB*) and Ruth E. Mayers (*ODNB*).

conformist, and left him disgusted at the 'popish' trends within the Church of England. By 1635, he could take no more, and set sail for the puritan colony of Massachusetts Bay.

For the next quarter of a century, Vane was at the heart of the puritan movement. Within six months of landing in Boston he was made governor of the colony, at the tender age of twenty-three. Yet in March 1637, he was ousted for supporting the Antinomian prophetess Anne Hutchinson. Returning to England, he played a key role in the trial of Strafford in 1641, masterminded the Solemn League and Covenant in 1643, championed the Independents, helped to set up the New Model Army, worked closely with Cromwell, and became a leading politician in the Rump parliament. When Cromwell expelled the Rump in 1653, Vane protested and Cromwell cried in frustration: 'Sir Henry Vane, Sir Henry Vane, the Lord deliver me from Sir Henry Vane'. In 1656, Vane's criticism of the Protector earned him a short spell in prison, but he re-emerged in 1659–60 as one of the leading figures in the restored commonwealth. At the Restoration, he was placed under arrest, and in 1662 was executed on a charge of high treason. In his life and especially in his death, Vane was revered by a host of distinguished figures on the radical wing of the puritan movement including John Milton, Henry Stubbe, Roger Williams, Edmund Ludlow and Algernon Sidney. By contrast, he was condemned – for various reasons – by Cromwell, James Harrington and Richard Baxter.

For all his centrality, Vane has remained something of a mystery man. His publications have done little to dispel the mists, since most readers have found them almost unreadable. Richard Baxter complained that Vane's doctrines 'were so clowdily formed and expressed, that few could understand them'. The earl of Clarendon confessed that though he had tried to penetrate the clouds of Vane's theology, 'in a crowd of very easy words the sense was too hard to find out'. Gilbert Burnet had also 'taken pains to see if I could find out the meaning in his works', but to no avail; he wondered wryly if Vane had left behind a hidden key to his writings. David Hume declared Vane's works 'absolutely unintelligible'. Even Christopher Hill admitted that he 'shrank from the impenetrable thickets of [Vane's] prose'.[9]

Although Vane has baffled some of the most astute observers of seventeenth-century life and thought, the literature on him is now considerable. Alongside a number of old-fashioned biographies,[10] one can consult several articles on his

[9] Richard Baxter, *Reliquiae Baxterianae* (1696), STC [Wing] B1370, Bk I, Pt I, p. 75; Clarendon, *History of the Rebellion*, ed. W. D. Macray, 6 vols (Oxford, 1888), Bk XVI, section 88; Burnet, *History of His Own Times*, I, p. 285; D. Hume, *The History of England*, 7 vols (1773), VII, p. 384; C. Hill, *The Experience of Defeat: Milton and Some Contemporaries* (1984), p. 18.

[10] C. W. Upham, *The Life of Sir Henry Vane the Younger, Fourth Governor of Massachusetts* (Boston, 1835); J. Forster, *Sir Henry Vane the Younger, 1612–1662* (1838); J. K. Hosmer, *The Life of Young Sir Henry Vane* (Boston, 1888); J. E. Strickland, *Young Sir Henry Vane* (1904); W. W. Ireland, *The Life of Sir Henry the Younger* (1905); M. King, *Sir Henry Vane, Jr.* (Providence, RI, 1909); F. J. C. Hearnshaw, *The Life of Sir Henry Vane the Younger, Puritan Idealist* (1910); J. Willcock, *The Life of Sir Henry Vane the*

career,[11] and a fine monograph by Violet Rowe on his political and administrative activities.[12] A few scholars have even dared to venture where Christopher Hill feared to tread, by plunging into the thickets of Vane's published prose. Margaret Judson has examined his constitutional thought, J. Max Patrick and Paul Harris have discussed his view of liberty, and Ruth Mayers has uncovered the contexts and audiences for his political tract, *A Healing Question*.[13] Most recently, David Parnham has produced a major monograph and several valuable articles on Vane's religious thought.[14]

Yet after reading this literature, one is still left with a sense of dissatisfaction. Some writers (like Rowe) avoid Vane's thought to concentrate on his career; others (like Judson) treat him as a conventional constitutional theorist and simply ignore his apocalypticism. Parnham, who does makes a valiant effort to engage with Vane's religious thought, fails to connect it adequately with his public career, and tends to replicate the opaque style of Vane's religious works.[15] It seems that we are still some way from a convincing portrait of Vane, one that integrates his political career and his religious thought.[16] In what follows, I hope to reconnect Vane's beliefs and his actions, by showing how his apocalyptic mentality shaped his understanding of his own death.

Younger, Statesman and Mystic (1913); J. H. Adamson and H. F. Folland, *Sir Harry Vane: His Life and Times, 1613–1662* (Boston, 1973).

11 C. H. Firth, 'Cromwell and Sir Henry Vane', *English Historical Review*, 26 (1911), pp. 751–4; R. Howell, 'Henry Vane the Younger and the Politics of Religion', *History Today*, 13 (1963), pp. 275–82; T. Eustace, 'Sir Henry Vane the Younger', in *Statesmen and Politicians of the Stuart Age*, ed. Eustace (1985), ch. 6; J. H. F. Hughes, 'The Commonwealthmen Divided: Edmund Ludlowe, Sir Henry Vane and the Good Old Cause, 1653–1659', *Seventeenth Century*, 5 (1990), pp. 55–70.

12 V. Rowe, *Sir Henry Vane the Younger: A Study in Political and Administrative History* (1970).

13 M. Judson, *The Political Thought of Sir Henry Vane the Younger* (Philadelphia, 1969); J. Max Patrick, 'The Idea of Liberty in the Theologian Writings of Sir Henry Vane the Younger', in *The Dissenting Tradition*, ed. C. Robert Cole and M. E. Moody (Athens, GA, 1975), pp. 100–7; P. Harris, 'Young Sir Henry Vane's Arguments for Liberty of Conscience', *Political Science*, 40 (1988), pp. 34–48; R. Mayers, 'Real and Practicable, Not Imaginary and Notional: Sir Henry Vane, *A Healing Question*, and the Problems of the Protectorate', *Albion*, 28 (1996), pp. 37–72. See also the valuable discussion of Vane's biblical politics in Gai Ferdon, 'New modelling English government: biblical hemeneutics, Jewish polity and constitutional forms during the Interregnum, 1649–60' (PhD dissertation, 2004, University of Leicester).

14 D. Parnham, *Sir Henry Vane, Theologian: A Study in Seventeenth-Century Religious and Political Discourse* (Cranbury, NJ, 1997); 'Reconfiguring Mercy and Justice: Sir Henry Vane on Adam, the "Natural Man", and the Politics of Conscience', *Journal of Religion*, 79 (1999), pp. 54–85; 'Politics Spun out of Theology and Prophecy: Sir Henry Vane on the Spiritual Environment of Public Power', *History of Political Thought*, 22 (2001), pp. 53–83; 'The Nurturing of Righteousness: Sir Henry Vane on Freedom and Discipline', *Journal of British Studies*, 42 (2003), pp. 1–34.

15 John Morrill not unfairly complains that Parnham provides 'a study of [Vane's] thought divorced from a study of his life', and decodes Vane's 'concocted intelligibility' only 'to re-encode it into a concocted unintelligibility of his own'. Morrill, review of *Sir Henry Vane, Theologian*, in *Journal of Religious History*, 23 (1999), pp. 133–5. It should be said that Parnham's recent articles go some way to addressing this criticism of his original monograph.

16 However, see M. Winship, *Making Heretics: Militant Protestantism and Free Grace in Massachusetts, 1636–1641* (Princeton, 2002). This superb analysis of 'the free grace controversy' illuminates Vane's role and the impact it had on his future career.

II

To comprehend the apocalyptic mindset of Vane in 1662, we need to step back to examine his writings over the previous decade. During the 1640s, Vane published relatively little, and his speeches are not particularly revealing. But between 1652 and 1662, he wrote extensively on religion and politics, providing ample evidence of his apocalypticism. In what follows, I will argue that Vane's apocalyptic beliefs moulded his political outlook, by fuelling his hostility to persecution, and making him dream of a godly republic.

Vane first expounded his apocalyptic views in an anonymous pamphlet published in 1652, entitled *Zeal Examined*. Ignored by his biographers, it has been firmly attributed to Vane by modern scholars.[17] *Zeal Examined* was published in the midst of a heated national debate about the prosecution of heresy. John Owen had proposed a scheme whereby anyone who denied certain fundamental doctrines would be prosecuted by the state. His proposals angered radical puritans, and two close friends of Vane – Roger Williams and John Milton – orchestrated a campaign against them. As part of the campaign, Vane himself wrote his anonymous fifty-page tract in defence of toleration.

Vane's case against persecution was explicitly apocalyptic. In the first three centuries of the Christian era, the Church had been persecuted rather than persecuting. But with the conversion of Constantine, Antichrist began to subvert the Church. Christendom became the whore of Babylon prophesied in the book of Revelation. The reign of the Beast in Christendom, said Vane, dated from around AD 400. At this time, the Beast of John's Apocalypse transformed its appearance: no longer was it an ugly pagan Dragon, it was now a respectable Christian Leopard, 'zealous against all Idolatrie and Heresie'. Throughout the centuries, the Beast continued to mutate, taking on new forms to disguise its diabolical activities under the cloak of ecclesiastical respectability. At the English Reformation, the Beast assumed the form of Prelacy; in the 1640s it operated under the guise of Presbytery. Now, thanks to conservative Independents, it had adopted another 'most refined form'. Yet all the time it continued its beastly work, destroying the lives of the godly under the pretence that they were heretics.[18]

But the book of Revelation had prophesied that one day the saints would destroy the Beast and the Whore of Babylon. That day, Vane declared, had already dawned. The simple preaching of the truth was already dispelling the false gospel of persecution. Godly tolerationists had put the persecutors on the defensive. If magistrates simply allowed freedom of debate, the light would undoubtedly overcome the darkness. Yet insofar as the Whore employed 'oppression and bloody practices she must be destroyed by the like Bloudy wayes'. In the

---

[17] C. Polizzotto, 'The Campaign against *The Humble Proposals* of 1652', *Journal of Ecclesiastical History*, 38 (1987), pp. 569–81, esp. pp. 578–9; Parnham, 'Reconfiguring Mercy and Justice', p. 57.
[18] *Zeal Examined*, pp. 21–2.

final battle with Antichrist, material force would be met with material force. Persecutors could be 'justly punished by outward punishments'.[19]

In saying this, Vane was reflecting on the English civil wars. In a passage alluding to Cromwell, he praised 'those worthies who have been instrumentall towards the destruction of Babylon in our scene'. The parliamentarians, Vane thought, had been participating in the great end-time war against 'the beastly principle of persecution'.[20] The saints should now build a tolerant godly society, in which heretics and idolaters (including Roman Catholics) were not persecuted for their false doctrine and worship. Instead of hunting for heretics without, Christians should concentrate their fire on the Babylon in their own hearts. Persecution was the defining mark of the Beast. If the godly were serious about ridding England of Antichrist, they must eschew religious coercion.[21]

This conviction was not the only offspring of Vane's apocalyptic imagination. In 1655, during his political exile, he published a major work of theology, entitled *The Retired Man's Meditations*. In the final chapters he laid out his belief in an imminent one-thousand year reign of the saints upon the earth. He taught that the millennium would be ushered in by the Witnesses described in Revelation chapter 11. After proclaiming the coming judgement, and being executed for their boldness, these Witnesses would rise from the dead and see the nations of the earth turn against the Beast. Christ would then return in person to establish his rule.[22]

In *A Healing Question*, published in 1656, Vane concentrated on defending religious freedom and outlining his proposal for a righteous commonwealth governed by the supporters of the good old cause through their elected representatives. But the tract did look forward to Christ's second coming and declared that the ultimate goal of the good old cause was the 'bringing in of Christ, the Desire of all Nations, as the cheife Ruler amongst us'.[23]

Vane elaborated on this vision during 1659 and 1660. With the death of Oliver Cromwell and the collapse of Richard Cromwell's Protectorate, Vane returned from the political wilderness. Exhilarated by this fresh opportunity to establish an ideal commonwealth, his millenarian enthusiasm rose to new heights. In his 1660 pamphlet, *A Needful Corrective or Balance in Popular Government*, Vane replied to James Harrington's suggestion that the English should put their faith in good laws rather than good men. Although he esteemed Harrington as one who had mastered 'human prudence', he chided the author of *Oceana* for ignoring the pattern of magistracy 'shown unto Moses in the Mount'. Vane wanted the English to be 'a holy as well as a free people', and he believed that the godliness of the citizens was the only guarantee of the civil and religious liberty of the state.[24]

---

[19] Ibid., pp. 25, 27.

[20] Ibid., p. 27.

[21] On the practical outworking of Vane's commitment to toleration see Rowe, *Sir Henry Vane the Younger*, pp. 195–201.

[22] Sir Henry Vane, *The Retired Mans Meditations* (1655), STC [Wing] V75, chs. 24–6.

[23] Sir Henry Vane, *A Healing Question* (1656), STC [Wing] V68, p. 21.

[24] Sir Henry Vane, *A Needful Corrective* (1660), STC [Wing] V72, pp. 1–2.

Towards the end of the *Corrective*, Vane suggested that the godly common-wealth might even usher in the millennial rule of Christ. 'Through the mighty and universal pouring out of the Spirit upon all flesh', the commonwealth could 'so grow and increase, as at last to come up unto a perfect day . . . to the setting up of Christ as King throughout the whole earth, and causing nations and Kingdomes of this world to become the Kingdomes of our Lord and of his Christ, in a visible manner here below, for the space of a thousand years.'[25]

III

The collapse of the commonwealth and the restoration of the Stuarts in 1660 threw millenarian dreams into question. Indeed, it has been customary for historians to assume that millenarianism virtually died out after the Restoration. Hugh Trevor-Roper encapsulated the assumption in a characteristically witty index entry: 'Antichrist, due to fall in 1639, 248; or at least thereabouts, 251; perhaps 1655?, 286; evaporates 1660, 293'.[26] But as Warren Johnston has demonstrated, reports of the death of apocalypticism during the Restoration era have been greatly exaggerated.[27] The regular falsification of eschatological speculation led speculators to revise their end-time scenarios, not ditch them. When the new Restoration regime arrested Vane in July 1660, his apocalyptic hopes were not dashed. Instead, he redoubled his study of biblical prophecy, trying desperately to make sense of this sudden twist of fate. In the two years before his execution in June 1662, Vane's thoughts often turned to the apocalypse, as he struggled to discern the connections between the seven trumpets and the seven vials, Daniel's seventy weeks and John's 1260 days, the forty-two months, and the time, times and half a time. Much of this material was published soon after his death, so we possess a remarkable record of his thinking in these final months.[28]

---

[25] *A Needful Corrective*, pp. 9–11.

[26] H. Trevor-Roper, *Religion, the Reformation and Social Change* (1967), 469.

[27] W. Johnston, 'Apocalypticism in Restoration England' (Ph.D. thesis, University of Cambridge, 2001).

[28] Five key sources provide a vivid insight into Vane's mentality in 1660–2: Firstly, Henry Vane, *Two Treatises: viz. I. An Epistle General to the Mystical Body of Christ on Earth, the Church Universal in Babylon. II. The Face of the Times: Wherein is discovered, the Rise, Progresse, and Issue, of the Enmity and Contest, between the Seed of the Woman and the Seed of the Serpent, &c. The Design of it being, To awaken up the present Generation of God's People, to a more diligent and curious Observation of the present Signs of the near Approach of the Day of the Lord* (1662). STC [Wing] V80. Secondly, *A Pilgrimage into the Land of Promise . . . written in the year 1662 by HENRY VANE, Knight, towards the latter end of his prison-state, by himself fully reviewed and perfected, some few dayes before his sufferings, and left as his last Testimony and service to this present generation* (1664) STC [Wing] V73. Thirdly, Forster MS 48.D.41, Victoria and Albert Museum, consists of transcriptions by Vane's daughter Margaret of his sermons and correspondence around 1660, including a significant 'Letter from Mr. H[enry] V[ane] to Mr. H.C.' outlining Vane's apocalyptic beliefs – H.C. may well have been the Fifth Monarchist soldier and politician Hugh Courtney (d. 1666). Fourthly, *The Tryal of Sir Henry Vane* (1662) contains a number of Vane's final speeches before, during and after his trial. Fifthly, Vane's disciple George Sikes wrote a

What this record reveals is that Vane placed his own sufferings in an apocalyptic context. His writings at this time display a fresh conviction that the devout reader of scripture can calculate the precise dating of end-time events. Vane was willing to say that his own calculations might be mistaken, but he believed that he could not be far wrong. He drew on the chronological calculations of three leading millenarians: the Cambridge commentator on Revelation, Joseph Mede; the Independent millenarian John Archer; and the Fifth Monarchists' leading biblical scholar, John Tillinghast.[29] But although he followed the broad outlines of their interpretations, he added some significant details of his own.

Vane divided human history into 'three great Periods and seasons': Creation to Noah's Flood; Flood to Incarnation; and Christ's First Coming to Christ's Second Coming.[30] Like other millenarians, he then proceeded to divide the history of the third age (the Church age) into three distinct periods: 'primitive glory', the 'wilderness state', and the millennial restoration.[31] During its early centuries the Church had been pure and powerful, ministering with spiritual weapons alone. Vane followed Mede in seeing this period as extending for approximately four hundred years.[32] But when Christianity became the religion of the Roman empire, the Church turned to 'the carnall weapons of worldly power', and became a persecuting beast.[33] This ecclesiastical Fall had inaugurated the 'wilderness state', in which true believers, the Witnesses of Revelation chapter 11, would prophesy in sackcloth for 1260 days (i.e. years), 'in a persecuted, wilderness condition'.[34] Vane was convinced that this period was drawing to a close; that God was preparing for a final showdown with the forces of evil. Daniel's fourth monarchy was on its last legs, and 'the time drawing on apace' when the fifth monarchy of God would be established. The testimony of the Witnesses 'is now upon its finishing point'; 'the time of the End . . . is at the very doors'.[35]

The godly, however, had mistaken the nature of this climatic time. Many puritans had assumed that their triumph in the Civil Wars would inaugurate the kingdom, and believed that true religion would prevail over Antichrist by force of

---

substantial political and religious biography explaining Vane's beliefs, *The Life and Death of Sir Henry Vane* (1662).

[29] For Vane's debts to Mede, Archer and Tillinghast, see 'A Letter of Sr. H. V. to Mr. H. C.', fos. 265, 270, 280, 284–6, 290, 306; *Two Treatises*, pp. 75–6, 78.

[30] *Two Treatises*, pp. 63–9.

[31] 'A Letter of Sr. H. V. to Mr. H. C.', fos. 278–86; *Two Treatises*, pp. 70–1; 80. Vane's vision of Church history is very close to that of his friend, Roger Williams. On Williams, see W. C. Gilpin, *The Millenarian Piety of Roger Williams* (Chicago, 1979).

[32] 'A Letter of Sr. H. V. to Mr. H. C.', fo. 280; *Two Treatises*, pp. 44–5. It is not entirely clear whether Vane dated the four hundred years from the *ascension* of Christ, or from his *birth*, a position that fits better with his sense that the final crisis will come in the 1660s (i.e. 400+1260=1660). Either way, the climax was due to occur in the later seventeenth century.

[33] 'A Letter of Sr. H. V. to Mr. H. C.', fos. 280–2.

[34] *The Face of the Times*, p. 69; 'A Letter of Sr. H. V. to Mr. H. C.', fo. 280. Vane had previously devoted an entire chapter to the 'Two Witnesses' in his *Retired Man's Meditations*, ch. 24. On the interpretation of the Two Witnesses in early modern Protestantism, see Rodney L. Petersen, *Preaching in the Last Days: The Theme of 'Two Witnesses' in the Sixteenth and Seventeenth Centuries* (Oxford, 1997).

[35] *Two Treatises*, pp. 43–4, 53.

arms.[36] In 1659–60, Vane himself had thought that the commonwealth might usher in the millennium. The godly had been unprepared for the Beast's final fling. Like the foolish virgins in Christ's parable, they had started to lay aside the sackcloth, thinking that their suffering had come to an end. The renewal of persecution in 1660 had come as a rude awakening. But on reflection, Vane was not surprised. For this was the final persecution of the Witnesses predicted in Revelation 11. According to this passage, the Beast would come up from the Abyss, overpower the Witnesses and kill then, leaving their bodies lying in the streets of the great city, figuratively called Sodom. In Vane's mind, this penultimate victory of evil, this apparent crushing of the saints, had to take place before God's final victory. The Restoration – which had seen the rejection of the Gospel, the persecution of the saints, the shattering of godly hopes, and the exaltation of the ungodly – had been predicted in Revelation 11.[37] Indeed, Vane surely had in mind the fate of the regicides in 1660–1, whose bodies had been disinterred, desecrated, disembowelled, dismembered, and publicly displayed for all to see in the 'great city' of London.[38]

So Vane was convinced that the final destruction of the Witnesses was taking place right before his eyes. He himself was in the eye of the apocalyptic storm that would usher in the rule of Christ. The Gospel, he noted, had been spread to the western lands of Europe, and 'from hence in America, which with these Nations we live in, seem to be the last piece of Ground this Quarrel is to be fought out in. Yea, and probably this is the time as well as the place, wherein the Witnesses are finishing their Testimony, being the last to be slain by the Beast, as the proper accomplishment of that Prophesie, Revel. 11.17'.[39] He was convinced that his own death had eschatological significance. He and the present generation of suffering saints were the final Witnesses to be slaughtered by the Beast.[40]

Vane's millenarian mentality helps us to understand his calm demeanour in the face of death. He went to the scaffold with the words of Revelation 11 ringing in his ears:

> And when they shall have finished their testimony, the beast that ascendeth out of the bottomless pit shall make war against them, and shall overcome them, and kill them. And their dead bodies shall lie in the street

---

[36] See B. Capp, 'The Fifth Monarchists and Popular Millenarianism', in *Radical Religion in the English Revolution*, ed. J. F. McGregor and B. Reay (Oxford, 1984), ch. 7; C. Hill, *The English Bible and the Seventeenth-Century Revolution* (1993), chs. 13–14.

[37] The key source for this paragraph is *A Pilgrimage into the Land of Promise*, pp. 108–9. Remember that *Pilgrimage* was 'written in the year 1662 by HENRY VANE, Knight, towards the latter end of his prison-state' (title page). See also 'A Letter of Sr. H. V. to Mr. H. C.', fos. 301–3.

[38] On the bodily punishment of the regicides in 1660–1, see Knoppers, *Historicizing Milton*, ch. 2.

[39] *Two Treatises*, p. 72.

[40] It is important to stress that Vane understood the number of the Witnesses in collective and figurative terms. He was not so egotistical as to see himself as one half of the Two Witnesses! The Two Witnesses did not represent specific individuals, but 'two sorts of Saints' (those with a single portion of the Spirit, and those with a double portion). See *Two Treatises*, pp. 86, 92–3; 'A Letter of Sr. H. V. to Mr. H. C.', fos. 290–9.

of the great city, which spiritually is called Sodom and Egypt, where also our Lord was crucified. And they of the people and kindreds and tongues and nations shall see their dead bodies three days and an half, and shall not suffer their dead bodies to be put in graves. And they that dwell upon the earth shall rejoice over them, and make merry, and shall send gifts one to another; because these two prophets tormented them that dwelt on the earth.[41]

But that was not the end of the story, for Revelation 11 went on to predict that the slaughtered Witnesses would be miraculously resurrected:

And after three days and an half the spirit of life from God entered into them, and they stood upon their feet; and great fear fell upon them which saw them. And they heard a great voice from heaven saying unto them, Come up hither. And they ascended up to heaven in a cloud; and their enemies beheld them. And the same hour was there a great earthquake, and the tenth part of the city fell, and in the earthquake were slain of men seven thousand, and the remnant were affrighted, and gave glory to the God of heaven.[42]

Vane believed that this 'rising of the Witnesses' was imminent. On the day of his death, he had prayed about the final apocalyptic battle, which 'is in some sort, begun by the Faith of thy poor Servant, that is now going to seal thy Cause with his Blood'.[43] Speaking to his children, he had declared, 'I die in the certain faith and foresight, That this Cause shall have its Resurrection in my Death. My Blood will be the Seed sown, by which this glorious Cause will spring up.'[44] In his gallows speech, he concluded with a prophecy of the coming millennium:

As the present storm we now lie under, and the dark Clouds that yet hang over the Reformed churches of Christ . . . were not unforeseen by me for many years passed (as some Writings of mine declare:) So the coming of Christ in these Clouds in order to a speedy and sudden Revival of his Cause, and spreading of his Kingdom over the face of the whole earth, is most clear to the eye of my Faith, even that Faith in which I dye, whereby the Kingdoms of this world shall become the Kingdom of our Lord, and of his Christ.[45]

Apocalyptic interpreters commonly took the 'three days and an half' of Revelation 11 to signify three and a half years, and Vane himself had noted that both Mede and Archer speculated on the apocalyptic significance of the year 1666. Perhaps this was when the Witnesses would rise, the seventh trumpet would

[41] Revelation 11.7–10 (Authorised Version).
[42] Revelation 11.11–13.
[43] *Tryal of Sir Henry Vane*, p. 82.
[44] Ibid., pp. 79–80.
[45] Ibid., p. 92; *The Substance of what Sr. Henry Vane Intended to have Spoken upon the Scaffold, on Tower-Hill, at the time of his Execution, being the 14th of June 1662* (London, 1662), STC [Wing] V77, pp. 6–7.

sound and the seven vials of God's wrath would be poured out on the earth.[46] In writing to his friend, Vane accepted that eschatological calculations were a tricky business. Either 'yr account or mine' could be correct, he admitted. '[N]or can I dissent from you in the least, in acknowledging & bemoaning my own ignorance & aptness grossly to mistake in ys nice calculation of propheticall numbers, & rightly sorting ym, as they are found in Dan: & ye Revelation, & therfore I lay not wholly ye weight there.'[47] Nevertheless, he was convinced that the end was nigh, and could not resist the intoxicating excitement of end-times speculation. The resurrection of the Witnesses and the destruction of Antichrist were surely imminent, and Vane testified that he did 'desire feelingly & experimentally it may be witnessed in my self & you & other the Dear Saints of the Lord'.[48] As he prepared to die in June 1662, Vane must have wondered: 'If he was one of the last Witnesses, was it not possible that he would be resurrected three and a half years later, in 1666, the very year that Mede and Archer had marked out'?

From Vane's copious writings in 1662, it seems likely that he did entertain a very literal hope of vindication. The Witnesses, Vane had taught, would be resurrected and transfigured like Christ. Onlookers, who had seen their corpses on display in the great city, would be transfixed with terror. Before their eyes, the martyred saints would 'rise out of their graves, stand again upon their feet, and prophecy with power'. But this time, the Witnesses would not follow the non-violent way of the cross, the Lamb and the verbal testimony. Their 'suffering season' was over; their 'ministry of wrath by fire' had begun. The predictions of Revelation 16–20 were about to be fulfilled. Endowed with miraculous powers, the Witnesses would minister the Spirit to the godly and pour out the seven vials of God's judgement on the wicked. Babylon would fall and the Beast would be destroyed. Finally, Christ would return in person and inaugurate his millennial rule.[49] 'Out of the destruction of the present World and frame of things', wrote Vane, 'by this fiery ministry of God's wrath, is the thousand years Reign of Christ to spring up, in that Kingdom of his that shall never end.'[50]

No wonder then, that on the day of his execution, Vane had chosen to wear a scarlet silk waistcoat. As the editor of *The Tryal of Sir Henry Vane* pointed out, scarlet was 'the victorious colour'.[51] Scarlet was also associated, liturgically and iconographically, with martyrdom. Quite self-consciously, it seems, Vane was preparing to die as a victorious martyr. He had stood firm to the end, and was now offering up his life as an apocalyptic Witness.

---

[46] 'A Letter of Sr. H. V. to Mr. H. C.', fos. 285–6.
[47] Ibid., fos. 305–6.
[48] Ibid., fos. 285, 303.
[49] *Two Treatises*, pp. 53, 57, 69, 72–3, 92–3. See also *Pilgrimage*, pp. 106–8; 'A Letter of Sr. H. V. to Mr. H. C.', fos. 272–5; [Sikes], *Life and Death of Sir Henry Vane*, p. 116. It is not altogether clear from Vane's various writings whether the Witnesses's 'ministry of wrath by fire' should be understood literally or metaphorically – would they actually kill people, or simply purge and purify them by their testimony?
[50] *Two Treatises*, p. 73.
[51] *Tryal of Sir Henry Vane*, p. 86.

IV

Vane's execution evoked a powerful response, and the shaping of his posthumous reputation as a martyr began almost immediately. On 22 June, the radical Will Swann told Pepys that 'Sir H. Vane must be gone to heaven, for he died as much a martyr and saint as ever any man died'. On 30 June, Pepys recorded that 'fanatiques of all sorts . . . do much cry up the manner of Sir H. Vanes death, and he deserves it'.[52] In a preface to Vane's *An Epistle General* (1662), one of his followers portrayed him as a Christ-figure, a sacrificial Lamb, who had accepted his death 'willingly and chearfully'.[53] The first biography of Vane was also published in 1662 by his disciple, George Sikes, who clearly inhabited Vane's worldview, and offered a faithful account of his teaching. To Sikes, Vane was 'a Prophet or Seer', 'one of the peculiar Favourites of Heaven', for whose death it would 'be difficult to find a Parallel proceeding for injustice, next that against Christ, in all History, humane or divine'. He and the other martyred Witnesses would be resurrected and vindicated. They would execute 'the flaming angelicall ministry' of judgement on the enemies of God and prepare the way for the parousia and the millennium.[54]

Sikes published for the first time Milton's sonnet on Vane, written back in 1652.[55] Milton had compared Vane to a virtuous Roman Senator:

> Vane, young in years, but in sage counsel old.
> Than whom a better senator ne'er held
> The helm of Rome, when gowns not arms repelled
> The fierce Epirot and the African bold.

In clothing Vane in Roman garb, Milton inaugurated the movement to classicise Vane.[56] Yet in contrast to later Whigs, Milton the puritan also hailed Vane as Religion's 'eldest son'. As ever, the classical and the biblical were inter-twined in Milton's mind. When Milton came to write *Samson Agonistes*, it is likely that he was thinking of Vane once again.[57] Milton seems to recall Vane when he writes of great men 'with gifts and graces eminently adorned/ To some great work', who are cut down in their prime by 'unjust tribunals, under change of times'. But could Milton also be thinking of Vane's apocalyptic visions? Blinded and humiliated, Samson strikes back. His strength restored, he tears down the

---

[52] *The Diary of Samuel Pepys*, III, pp. 117, 127.

[53] *Two Treatises*, A2.

[54] [Sikes], *The Life and Death of Sir Henry Vane*, pp. 3, 96, 113, 115–16.

[55] Ibid., p. 93.

[56] Though it is worth noting that at his trial Vane had compared his own contempt of death to that of heathens like 'Socrates the divine Philosopher', even whilst admitting that he was not well read in history. See *The Tryal of Sir Henry Vane*, pp. 63–4.

[57] Most scholars now see Samson Agonistes as post-Restoration work. For the likely allusions to Vane, see B. Worden, 'Milton, *Samson Agonistes*, and the Restoration', in *Culture and Society in the Stuart Restoration*, ed. Gerald Maclean (Cambridge, 1995), pp. 111–36.

pillars of the temple of Dagon, destroying more Philistines in his death than in his life. Is this meant to be a picture of how the slaughtered Witnesses, resurrected by divine power, would pour out the vials of God's wrath on their persecutors? It is possible, for Milton too was a millenarian, even if his own eschatological reflections were more guarded than those of Vane.[58]

Milton's fellow republicans, Algernon Sidney and Edmund Ludlow, shared his admiration for Vane. Indeed, Blair Worden has suggested that 'If there was a single hero of their time for Ludlow, for Sidney, for Milton, it was Vane'.[59] Both Sidney and Ludlow had worked with Vane during the rule of the Rump, and again in 1659–60, and both went into exile at the Restoration. In August 1660, Sidney wrote that 'Where Vane, Lambert, Haselrig cannot live in safety, I cannot live at all'.[60] In his unpublished *Court Maxims*, written in 1664–5, Sidney fused Christian and classical language to extol Vane as a martyr: 'Ah noble Vane, how ample a testimony hast thou born to his truth, thy condemnation was thy glory, thy death gave thee a famous victory and a never perishing crown.' For Sidney, Vane 'had not another man equal to him in virtue, prudence, courage, industry, reputation and godliness'. In cutting off Vane's head, the king had tried to destroy, 'as in its root, all virtue, wisdom, and godliness, since those, who were eminent in any of those qualities, looked on him as their master, and seemed to have learnt all they knew or practised by his precepts or example'.[61] It is hardly surprising that when Sidney himself was tried for treason in 1683, he drew inspiration from the account of Vane's trial.[62]

Ludlow also looked back on Vane's death with a sense of awe. Ludlow's wife had spoken with Vane on the day before his execution, and found him 'wholy unconcerned' by the prospect of death. He had declared 'as great a confidence in the resurrection of the cause as of his owne body, of which he doubted not', and he assured Mrs Ludlow that God would 'raise up instruments when his time should come'. On the scaffold, says Ludlow, observers were struck by 'The majesty of his presence, the reputation of his person, and the power of his reason'. Ludlow's tribute to Vane combined the Christian language of martyrdom with the Roman language of liberty – Vane was 'This choice martyr of Christ, and eminent champion of this country's liberty'.[63] Like his fellow puritan republicans, Ludlow

---

[58] For further reflections on this point, see J. Coffey, 'Pacifist, Quietist or Patient Militant? John Milton and the Restoration', in *'Paradise Regained' in Context*, ed. A. Labriola and D. Loewenstein (Pittsburgh, 2003), pp. 149–74. Intriguingly, Michael Winship, *Making Heretics*, p. 246, suggests that 'On the scaffold, Vane may have recalled [John] Wheelwright's fast-day exhortation [in 1637]: "Sampson slew more at his death, then in his life, and so we may prevaile more by our deathes, then by our lives".'

[59] B. Worden, *Roundhead Reputations: The English Civil Wars and the Passions of Posterity* (2001), p. 197.

[60] A. Sidney, *Works* (1772), p. 25.

[61] A. Sidney, *Court Maxims*, ed. H. Blom, E. H. Mulier, and R. Janse (Cambridge, 1996), p. 49.

[62] Sidney, *Works*, pp. 5–6, 53.

[63] E. Ludlow, *A Voyce from the Watch Tower, Part Five:1660–1662*, ed. A. B. Worden (1978), pp. 312–13.

identified the cause of true religion with the Good Old Cause of civil and religious liberty – Vane's death was both a political and a religious event. This reflected Vane's own understanding of his death as a 'martyrdom'. Because Milton, Sidney and Ludlow shared Vane's apocalyptic and puritan sensibilities, they were able to lionise Sir Henry without secularising him.

By the 1690s, however, Vane's admirers included men who had little sympathy for hot Protestantism. As Worden has shown, the Deist historian John Toland could do nothing with Vane's writings. Whereas he republished works by Harrington, Milton, Sidney and Ludlow (some heavily expurgated), Toland simply ignored Vane's intensely religious works. It proved too difficult 'to launch a non-Puritan Vane'. Through his intrusive editing of Ludlow's *Memoirs*, however, Toland did continue to allow a significant place for Vane, who was extolled as an incorruptible public servant, a brilliant administrator, and a noble spirit. Vane was no longer Religion's 'favourite son', but he was still the virtuous Roman Senator of Milton's imagination. But with none of his writings in print, Vane's reputation declined in eighteenth-century Britain, where his religious fervour was unappealing to rational men of Enlightenment.[64]

Not that Vane was universally despised and rejected. The republican editor, Thomas Hollis, familiarised his readers with Vane's trial, and reprinted Milton's sonnet.[65] But it was in the nineteenth century that Vane's reputation really revived, under the joint influence of Romanticism and Evangelical Nonconformity. Romantic poets celebrated Vane as a patriot martyr. Flushed with republican ardour, William Wordsworth lauded the heroes of the English commonwealth:

> Great men have been among us; hands that penn'd
> And tongues that uttered wisdom – better none:
> The later Sidney, Marvel, Harrington,
> Young Vane, and others who called Milton friend.
> These moralists could act and comprehend:
> They knew how genuine glory was put on;
> Taught us how rightfully a nation shone
> In splendour: what strength was, that would not bend
> But in magnanimous meekness. France, 'tis strange,
> Hath brought forth no such souls as we had then.[66]

Educated in a Dissenting Academy, John Keats was also enamoured with the English republican past.[67] In his poem, 'Lines Written on 29 May, The Anniversary of the Restoration of Charles the 2nd', Keats bemoaned the English infatuation with royalty and restoration. He reminded his readers of an alternative tradition of noble martyrs, who had died for the commonwealth:

---

[64] Worden, *Roundhead Reputations*, pp. 197–201.
[65] See A. Patterson, *Early Modern Liberalism* (Cambridge, 1997), p. 45.
[66] *The Poetical Works of William Wordsworth*, ed. E. de Selincourt and H. Darbishire (3 vols, Oxford, 1964), III, pp. 116–17.
[67] N. Roe, *John Keats and the Culture of Dissent* (Oxford, 1991), ch. 1.

Infatuate Britons, will you still proclaim
His memory, your direst, foulest shame?
Nor patriots revere?
Ah! When I hear each traitorous lying bell,
'Tis gallant Sidney's, Russell's, Vane's sad knell,
That pains my wounded ear.

One suspects that neither Wordsworth nor Keats knew much about Vane – he was simply a name to conjure with alongside other (more famous) patriots like Milton. But their verse tells us that Vane was now being celebrated simply as a noble moralist and gallant patriot who sacrificed his life for republican liberty. However, the older view of Vane as 'perfect enthusiast' persisted. Samuel Taylor Coleridge – who owned a copy of Vane's *Healing Question* – had a keener sense of history than Wordsworth and Keats, and a more ambivalent opinion of Vane. Referring to anarchist and levelling movements in French politics, he wrote that 'Among these new Fifth Monarchy men are to be found some of crazy talent, the Sir Henry Vanes of France'.[68]

Many Victorians and Edwardians did not share Coleridge's wariness of Vane. He was to appear in John Forster's 'Eminent British Statesmen' series, and was later included among 'Congregational Worthies' and 'British Free Church Heroes'.[69] Unlike their eighteenth-century predecessors, the Victorians found Vane's religious passion a virtue rather than a vice. The most striking evidence is provided by the idealist philosopher T. H. Green, whose lectures on the English Revolution praised Vane as one who from 'his derided theosophy . . . derived certain practical principles, now of recognised value, which no statesman before him had dreamt of'. He credited Vane with discovering the principles of natural right and government by consent, and universal toleration. Green interpreted Vane's death as a martyrdom for liberty – 'his own enthusiasm died that it might rise again. It was sown in the weakness of feeling, that it might be raised in the intellectual comprehension which is power.'[70] This metaphorical/intellectual resurrection was a long way from the literal/physical resurrection Vane himself expected. Like other Victorians, Green could applaud Vane's mysticism but shied away from exploring his apocalyptic hopes, which were so much harder to appropriate.[71]

---

[68] *S. T. Coleridge's Collected Works*, gen. ed. K. Coburn, 16 vols (Princeton, 1969–), III.i, p. 102 (article in *The Morning Post*, 14 Jan 1800). For Coleridge's ownership of *A Healing Question* and other Cromwellian tracts, see *S. T. Coleridge's Collected Works*, XII.ii, p. 111.

[69] J. Forster, *Sir Henry Vane the Younger*, vol. IV of *Lives of Eminent British Statesmen* (1838) and also vol. III of *The Statesmen of the Commonwealth of England* (1840); Hearnshaw, *Life of Sir Henry Vane* (1910), in the Congregational Worthies Series; Strickland, *Young Sir Harry Vane* (1904), in the British Free Church Heroes Series.

[70] T. H. Green, *Lectures on the Principles of Political Obligation and Other Writings*, ed. P. Harris and J. Morrow (Cambridge, 1986), pp. 217, 227.

[71] There are striking parallels here with the post-Enlightenment quest for the historical Jesus, which tended to bowdlerise the Jesus of the Gospels, turning an apocalyptic Jewish prophet into an ethical teacher of timeless, universal truths. See S. Neill and N. T. Wright, *The Interpretation of the New Testament*,

Much the same was true in New England, where Vane was remembered as Massachusetts' youngest governor and champion of liberty. In the eighteenth century, the radical Whig ideas of English Dissenters like Thomas Hollis became mainstream in America. The New Englander John Adams was not alone in naming Vane in his liberal canon alongside the usual suspects like Coke, Milton, Harrington and Marvell.[72] In the nineteenth century, C. W. Upham's biography was republished several times, Vane's *A Healing Question* was available in the *Somer's Tracts*, and Americans were able to read about his fate in the *State Trials*.[73] It is significant that *A Healing Question* was the work least marked by Vane's millenarianism, and most amenable to a Whig interpretation. With its call for a constitutional convention, and its defence of civil and religious liberty, it was seen as foreshadowing the American Revolution. When Bostonians reprinted a series of documents that preceded the American Constitution, Vane's tract appeared as the sixth publication, after the Constitution itself, the articles of confederation, the Declaration of Independence, Washington's Farewell, and Magna Carta.[74] In his *English Traits*, Ralph Waldo Emerson included Vane alongside King Alfred, Isaac Newton and Shakespeare in a list of great Englishmen – Vane was clearly a figure of some renown.[75] Wendell Phillips declared that 'you can find in Vane the pure gold of two hundred and fifty years of American civilisation, with no particle of its dross'.[76] In 1895, the abolitionist James Freeman Clarke prompted the Boston Public Library to commission an imposing statue of Vane by the sculptor Frederick MacMonnies. The statue stands to this day in the entrance vestibule of the library, and its inscription describes Vane as 'An ardent defender of civil liberty and free thought in religion'.[77] Nineteenth-century New Englanders, including Transcendentalists and Unitarians, re-created Vane in their own image, as a freethinker and a libertarian.

In particular, Vane was remembered as a martyr for liberty. When the abolitionist Charles Torrey died in a Baltimore prison in 1846, John Greenleaf Whittier wrote a newspaper column recalling Vane's execution:

1861–1986 (Oxford, 1988); C. Allen, *The Human Christ: The Search for the Historical Jesus* (Oxford, 1998).

[72] Patterson, *Early Modern Liberalism*, p. 279.

[73] C. W. Upham, *The Life of Sir Henry Vane the Younger, Fourth Governor of Massachusetts*, vol. IV of *Library of American Biography* (1835), and also vol. III of *Lives of Eminent Individuals* (1839) and vol. IV of *Library of American Biography* (1851); *Somer's Tracts*, ed. Sir W. Scott, 13 vols (1809–15), vol. VI; *State Trials*, ed. T. B. Howell, 21 vols (1816), VI, pp. 152ff.

[74] *Old South Leaflets Series*, no. 6 (Boston, 1896). *A Healing Question* was also republished in the The Harvard Classics, ed. C. W. Eliot, 51 vols (New York, 1909–14), XLIII.

[75] Emerson, *English Traits*, ed. H. M. Jones (Cambridge, MA, 1966), p. 30.

[76] Wendell Phillips in his Harvard Address on *The Scholar in the Republic*, quoted in Rowe, *Sir Henry Vane the Younger*, p. 260.

[77] Information gleaned on a visit to Boston Public Library on 18 October 2002. Intriguingly, MacMonnies' offer of a nude Bacchante for the Library was turned down after fierce protests from local temperance movements against the statue's 'wanton nudity and drunkenness' – the puritan spirit was alive and well.

'When my blood is shed let it, oh Lord, have a voice afterwards!' was the prayer of Sir Henry Vane, who like, Torrey, died for the cause of freedom. So let it be with our brother. Let his martyrdom have a voice afterward terrible to the oppressor and cheering to the oppressed![78]

In his lecture on 'Beauty', Emerson used Vane's death to illustrate the way that beauty could 'steal in like air, and envelope great actions': 'When Sir Harry Vane was dragged up to the Tower-hill, sitting on a sled, to suffer death as the champion of English laws, one of the multitude cried out to him, "You never sate on so glorious a seat." '[79] Writing in 1899, Eldridge Brooks testified that 'Massachusetts honors and reveres the memory of her boyish governor'. He concluded that 'to Sir Harry Vane Americans and Englishmen owe very much, as the man who, alike in America and England, boldly withstood what he considered tyranny, and gladly died a martyr to the cause of liberty'.[80]

The secular, liberal Vane lives on in twenty-first-century America, a testimony to the American passion for a usable past. A Healing Question can now be accessed on at least three different websites.[81] American libertarians continue to celebrate Vane as a martyr of liberalism. The Acton Institute devotes a page of its website to Vane, who it says 'believed in freedom in the liberal sense, as the right to use oneself as one pleased'.[82] On another website, the libertarian author Sean Gabb writes, 'Along with Locke, Sidney, Pym, Hampden, and a host of others, Vane takes his place behind the Founding Fathers of the American Constitution.'[83]

Of course, one can see why Vane has been assigned a place in the 'liberal tradition' or within 'early classical liberalism' – he was, after all, a passionate advocate of free commonwealths and religious toleration.[84] Next to Oliver Cromwell, Vane arguably did as much as anyone to ensure that the English Revolution was not defined by the conservative mainstream of the puritan movement, which would have made its peace with monarchy and enforced strict religious uniformity. Nevertheless, the concentration of Vane's modern admirers on the 'progressive' aspects of his thought has produced a distorted picture. Vane's

[78] Quoted in *The Letters of John Greenleaf Whittier*, ed. J. B. Pritchard, 3 vols (Cambridge, MA, 1975), II, p. 19.
[79] Emerson, *Nature, Addresses and Lectures*, in *The Complete Works of Ralph Waldo Emerson*, ed. E. W. Emerson, 12 vols (Boston, 1903–4), I, pp. 27–8.
[80] E. Brooks, *Stories of the Old Bay State* (Boston, 1899), p. 68.
[81] *A Healing Question* has been made available online by the Bartleby's 'Great Books Online', the Fordham Modern History Sourcebook, and the libertarian Constitution Society: <www.bartleby.com/43/11.html>; <www.fordham.edu/halsall/mod/1656vane-healing.html>; <http://www.constitution.org/lev/healing.htm>
[82] <www.actoninstitute.org/research/libtrad/vane.html> After reading this, one could be forgiven for thinking that Vane was an early disciple of Robert Nozick!
[83] <www.libertyhaven.com/theoreticalorphilosophicalissues/earlyclassicalliberalism/sirhenry.html>
[84] Edmund Morgan, *Inventing the People: The Rise of Popular Sovereignty in England and America* (New York, 1988), pp. 89–91, reiterates the nineteenth-century view that Vane's proposal for a constitutional convention was 'reinvented in the American Revolution'. For an account of Vane's trial that relates it to the later liberal tradition see A. Patterson, *Early Modern Liberalism*, pp. 117–28, 145–8.

apocalypticism, so central to his tolerationism and even his republicanism, has been lost from view. Vane saw himself as an apocalyptic Witness; his admirers have transformed him into a heroic Whig.

V

As with so many early-modern radical Protestants, Vane's politics were predicated on a projected apocalypse. He was convinced that the last days had arrived, that the climax of history was here. His actions and his words can only be properly understood when we take this into account. Yet later generations were to celebrate Vane as a forerunner of modern liberty. Cutting through the mists of his mystical theology and the rubble of his unfulfilled apocalyptic prophecies, they uncovered a set of radical Whig doctrines – freedom of religion and republican government.

Vane's story tells us something important about the changing definition of martyrdom. Firstly, it reminds us that early-modern martyrdom was a deeply political phenomenon. Politics and religion were so tightly interwoven in the Reformation era that contemporaries invested their spiritual hopes in political movements. This is obviously true of the Wars of Religion fought between Catholics and Protestants, but it was also true of the English Civil Wars, which bore the hallmarks of religious war even if they were fought between Protestants.[85] Although Vane was put to death for treason, not for heresy, he saw himself as a religious martyr. For Vane and other puritan republicans, the fate of true religion was bound up with the fate of the Good Old Cause. Vane's religion was intensely inward, but it was also profoundly political. Godliness involved personal piety *and* public virtue. For him, the Restoration was a religious event, a spiritual catastrophe. This conclusion was reinforced by apocalypticism, for Revelation taught its readers to think in political terms, to identify the Beast and the Whore of Babylon with worldly powers. Apocalypticism was loaded with political implications, and Vane's willingness to set his own death within an apocalyptic context reflects this. In Ludlow's words, he was 'This choice martyr of Christ, and eminent champion of this country's liberty'.[86]

Secondly, the development of Vane's posthumous reputation in the eighteenth and nineteenth centuries highlights what we might call 'the secularisation of martyrdom'. Vane's later admirers still shared his own belief that he had died as a martyr. But in their minds, the political had taken priority over the religious, and politics was no longer set in apocalyptic context. Vane's martyrdom was an essentially political event, not a religious one. Martyrdom had been redefined. A martyr was someone who had died for his or her faith, whether that faith was

[85] See J. Morrill, 'The religious context of the English Civil War', in his *The Nature of the English Revolution* (Harlow, 1993), ch. 3.
[86] Ludlow, *A Voyce from the Watch Tower*, p. 313.

religious or political. Yet even this secular definition of martyrdom carried religious overtones. Like another term that entered the lexicon of modern politics – crusade – martyrdom was a Christian word, with religious connotations. But for many radical Whigs, their political cause was a 'sacred' cause, their battle was a 'crusade', their fallen were 'martyrs'. The language of religion injected spiritual intensity into secular politics. The concept of martyrdom was to have a long afterlife.

INDEX

Boughton, Joan 8 n.33, 54
Bracciolini, Poggio 65
Bradford, John 205 n.5, 206 n.10
Bradshaw, John, Lord Bradshaw 59, 215
Brentford 41
Brewen, Anne 35
Brewen, John 35
Briant, Alexander 42
Brice, Thomas 20, 44
Brigge, William 94, 95
Brinklow, Henry 149
Bristol 50
Brooks, Eldridge 237
Brooks, James 170, 173
Brown, John 66
Brown, William 91
Browne, Thomas 211
Bruni, Leonardo 65
Brussels 123
Brutus, Marcus Junius 66
Bucer, Martin 140, 143
Bugenhagen, Johannes 145
Bull, Henry 20 n.89
Bullinger, Heinrich 15, 146, 154, 162
Bullingham, John 172
Burnet, Gilbert, Bishop of Salisbury 62,
    131–2, 151, 154, 161, 164, 220,
    222–3
Burton, Henry 49, 62, 204, 205 n. 7, 206
Busbridge, Thomas 3
Bush, Paul, Bishop of Bristol 172, 176
Butler, John, commissary 146
Butler, John, gentleman 146
Butler, John 126–8
Bynum, Caroline Walker 83

Caiaphas 59
Caistor, Richard 102
Calais 146
Calamy, Edmund 27, 28, 29, 30
Calvin, Jean 15–17
Cambridge 9–10, 100, 104, 145, 148, 149,
    150, 151, 156, 206
Camille, Michael 86
Campeggi, Lorenzo, Cardinal 129, 130
Campion, Edmund 3, 23–5, 61, 138, 197
    execution 2, 24, 42, 47–8, 50, 198
Canterbury 126, 127, 130, 137, 140, 142,
    143, 174, 194
Capgrave, John 76
Carafa, Gian Pietro, Cardinal 129
Cardmaker, John 98
Carlton, Charles 204
Carranza, Bartolomé 175, 179
Carthusian martyrs, 1535 9, 11, 55 n.102

Carvajal, Luisa de 3
Cato, Marcus Porcius (the elder) 66
Cecil, William 182
Challoner, Richard 31
Chapuys, Eustace 128
Charles I, King of England 31, 61, 138
    cult of 58–9, 68, 204, 207–8, 216
    Eikon basilike 59, 204, 207–9, 211, 213,
        215–19
    execution of 59, 205–7, 219
    imprisonment 204, 213, 216
Charles II, King of England 61, 208 n.16,
    217, 234
Charles V, Holy Roman Emperor 37, 130,
    131, 132
Chaucer, Geoffrey 76, 80, 102
Chauncy, Maurice 9
Chelmsford (Essex) 43–4
Chichele, Henry, Archbishop of Canterbury
    91–2
Child, Lydia 66
church papists 180
Cicero, Marcus Tullius 66, 168
Clarke, James Freeman 236
Clarke, Samuel 27
Clement, of Alexandria 65
Clement, John 91
Cleveland, John 205 n.8, 207
Clitherow, Margaret 2, 39, 50
Coffey, John 31, 34
Coke, Edward 201, 236
Colchester, Abbot of. See Marshall,
    Thomas, Abbot of Colchester
Cole, Henry 168–9
Colet, John 99
Coleridge, Samuel Taylor 235
Coligny, Odet de, Cardinal 127
Colley, Linda 34
Collinson, Patrick 191, 206
Como, David 33
Constantine 42
Constantine, George 10
Contarini, Gasparo, Cardinal 129
Cook, Hugh, of Faringdon, Abbot of
    Reading 169
Cook, John 59, 205 n.5
Copyn, John 94
Cornish, Henry 64
Coverdale, Miles 144, 149
Cranford, James 217
Cranmer, Thomas, Archbishop of Canterbury
    9, 47 n.63, 137, 141–2, 146, 147, 163,
    164, 172, 175, 176, 177, 204 n.4, 206
    n.8
    execution of 38, 169

STUDIES IN MODERN BRITISH RELIGIOUS HISTORY